Best
Danny
O'Bannon.

Xmas. 2000

Dear Mike.

Happy Christmas. Hope you enjoy this book (signed!), especially Page 203 !!!! As well.

Bernard and Lesley

FRINGE BENEFITS

THE GOOD, THE BAD, THE BEAUTIFUL
...AND THE O'BRIENS

FRINGE BENEFITS

THE GOOD, THE BAD, THE BEAUTIFUL
...AND THE O'BRIENS

DONOUGH O'BRIEN

INCLUDING PHOTOGRAPHS BY
PATRICK LICHFIELD & JOHN d. GREEN

FOREWORD BY
JOANNA LUMLEY

WITH SPECIAL THANKS TO
MICHAEL GRIMSDALE AND MY WIFE LIZ

ART DIRECTOR: TONY ECKERSLEY
DESIGNERS: HUGH SYNGE, KATY HOOLE
ASSISTANT EDITORS: EDMOND AND MURROUGH O'BRIEN

BENE FACTUM PUBLISHING

Published in 2000 by

Bene Factum Publishing Ltd
11a Gillingham Street, London SW1V 1HN
Tel.: + (0) 20 7630 8616, Fax: + (0) 20 7630 5202
www.benefactum.co.uk

ISBN 1-903071-02-X

Printed in Italy

CONTENTS FRINGE BENEFITS

FOREWORD

Donough's book is a great mixture of hilarious, cranky humour, obscure information and sobering reflections.

By chance, his background mirrors my own. Grandfather serving on the borders of India, father born there, a post-war rationed middle-class childhood, the social explosion of the Sixties and the struggle to carve out a career.

Full to the brim with characters: politicians and painters; royalty, rascals and racing drivers; dancers and dictators; heroes and horrors; stars, singers and spies.

It's seriously good fun.

Joanna Lumley

ACKNOWLEDGEMENTS

Innumerable people and organisations have helped to make this book possible, to verify the stories and to fill the pages with photographs and illustrations. Let me try to thank you: Patrick Lichfield (with Pedro and Penny) and John d Green for their photographs, Michael Grimsdale for his illustrations. Photographs also came from Regimental Headquarters Irish Guards, the All Arms Drill Wing at Woking, Ballinakella Press, GEC Marconi, Marketing Week, Moët Hennessy, Ogilvy & Mather, Colin Taylor, Magnus Magnusson, Stowe School, Ford Motor Company, Imperial War Museum, Learjet, Raytheon, Lola Cars, Caroline Masterton-Smith, Sportex, PA News, Anthony Montague-Browne, Enterprise IG, Illustrated London News, Conservative Central Office, Jaime Noguera, Dan Litani, Allsport Photographic, Rolf Harris, Cy Laurie, The 100 Club, Flying Pictures, Hulton Getty Picture Collection, Regimental Headquarters Scots Guards and the General Sikorski Museum.

Special thanks must go to my lady taxi driver in Vienna, Anita Mair, who, without me asking, took nine months to track down the O'Brien monument and photograph it.

Many friends helped me to verify my stories: Jonathan Aitken, Brian and Shane Alexander, Giles Allan, Anthony Allfrey, Colin Anderson, Bill Andrewes, Liz Anson, Patricia Barnet, Robin Behar, Tom Bird, Mike Bowling, Michael Boyle, Robin Bullock-Webster, Dermot Butler, the Cowley family, Colin Creswell, Nigel Dempster, Brian Gilbart-Denham, Dr Ian Gordon, Frank Groves, Susan Hill, Roger Horton, Terry Howard, Roddy Ingham-Clark, Peter Lendrum, Rupert Lendrum, Roger Linn, Patrick Lichfield, Ian McMurtry, George Meakin, Christopher Moorsom, Stirling Moss, Sally Neubert, Grania O'Brien, Mick O'Cock, Tony Plummer, Tim Rice, Sam Sampson, David Sheffield, Dave Smylie, Martin Sorrell, Steven Spurrier, Peter Verney, Roland Wells and the Mayor of Vienna.

Please forgive me if I have left anyone out.

PRINCIPAL CHARACTERS

Michael Grimsdale	Artist	1943	51
Gordon Grimsdale	General	1943	51
Osbert Lancaster	Cartoonist	1942	53
Joseph Stalin	Dictator	1945	57
Timothy ffytche	Neighbour, friend, eye surgeon	1945	57
Jorge Potier	Friend, advertising partner	1945	57
Erskine Childers	President of Ireland	1946	58
Natalie O'Brien	Sister. Roger Whittaker's wife	1946	60
Alice Denny	Artist, grandmother	1949	63
Court Denny (Akenhausen)	Businessman, grandfather	1949	63
George Lane	Artist	1949	64
Bryan de Grineau	Motor racing artist	1954	64
The Marquess of Donegall	President, National Jazz Federation	1945	67
Lord Woolton	Chairman, Conservative Party	1948	68
Winston Churchill	Prime Minister	1940	72
General Sikorski	Polish Leader	1940	72
Desmond Morton	Politician	1940	73
Clement Attlee	Lord Privy Seal, Prime Minister	1940	73
Duff Cooper	Minister of Information	1940	73
Frank Pick	Ministry of Information	1940	74
Natalie Bevan	Artist	1966	76
Bobbie Bevan	Chairman, SH Benson	1935	76
Randolph Churchill	MP, writer	1966	76
Geraldine O'Brien	Sister	1947	78
Luis Bolín	Minister, Spain	1948	81
Francisco Franco	Caudillo, Spain	1950	81
Christopher Moorsom	Journalist, Public Relations man	1950	82
Selwyn Lloyd	Foreign Secretary	1960	83
Jonathan Aitken	Future Minister	1961	83
Iain Macleod	Chancellor of the Exchequer	1962	83
José Ensesa	Hotelier, businessman	1962	83
Cecil B de Mille	Film Director	1956	85
Anthony Montague-Browne	Churchill's Private Secretary	1964	85
Anthony Allfrey	PR man, author	1955	86
Sir Robert Renwick	TV businessman	1955	86
Lord Brentford	Guardian	1964	86
Eva Palmer	Cook	1952	87
Leo O'Brien	Stepmother	1952	87
Bernard Braden	Actor/entertainer	1952	88
Barbara Kelly	Actor/entertainer	1952	88
Norman Collins	Writer, TV businessman	1955	89
Lew Grade	Entertainment businessman	1955	89
Lord Donegall	Jazz enthusiast	1955	90
John Boyd-Carpenter	Minister	1955	91
Thomas Boyd-Carpenter	General	1955	91
Brian Alexander	Army friend, manager, Mustique	1958	91
Algy Cluff	Businessman	1954	92
Colin Hart-Leviton	Musician, High Court Recorder	1957	93
Chris Haines	School friend, clarinettist	1957	93
Paddy Pinchbeck	Swimming Master	1956	94

Judy Grinham	Olympic Backstroke Champion	1956	95
Ron Roberts	British swimming champion	1956	95
Bill McElwee	School master and historian	1956	96
Patience McElwee	Novelist	1956	96
Laurence Venn	Godfather, businessman	1958	97
Mike Hawthorn	Racing driver	1957	97
Robert de Vogüé	President, Moët et Chandon	1957	98
Sylviane Baton	Jazz enthusiast	1958	100
Cy Laurie	Jazz clarinettest	1957	101
Humphrey Lyttelton	Grenadier Guards & Trumpet	1957	101
Maureen McDonnell	Dancing partner	1957	102
Ron Wilkins	Coldstream Guards Sergeant	1958	105
Simon Fraser	Master of Lovat	1958	107
Alexander of Tunis	Field Marshal, Governor, artist	1958	108
Bernard Montgomery	Field Marshal	1958	109
Desmond Lynch	Regimental Sergeant Major	1958	110
Laurie Chescoe	Jazz man	1958	112
Brian Alexander	Irish Guards officer	1958	114
Tony Rolt	Racing driver, businessman	1959	115
Giles Allan	Irish Guards Officer	1958	115
George Shannon	Sergeant, Irish Guards	1958	114
Elizabeth	Queen of England	1958	116
Hugh O'Neill	Irish Guards Officer	1959	117
Barry Dinan	Army friend, businessman	1960	117
John McComiskey	Company Sergeant Major	1960	119
Gabriella Licudi	Actress	1960	124
Roland Wells	Copywriter	1960	124
'Docker' Boyle	Irish Guards officer	1960	125
Garry Daintry	Irish Guards officer	1960	128
Sir Roderick Brinkman	Colonel, Grenadier Guards	1960	128
Dave Smylie	Transport Sergeant, Irish Guards	1961	129
Jack Profumo	Army Minister	1962	133
Martin Stevens	MP, businessman	1962	134
Harold Wilson	Prime Minister	1964	139
Bill Andrewes	Businessman	1962	140
Greville Wynne	Spy	1962	141
Jack de Manio	Broadcaster	1962	143
Moise Tshombe	President, Katanga	1962	143
Patrick Lichfield	Earl, Photographer, Businessman	1962	144
Stirling Moss	Racing driver	1962	147
Chris Barber	Trombonist & Racing driver	1960	147
Graham Hill	Racing Driver	1963	148
Jasper Larken	Sailor	1962	150
Sir John Davis	Chairman, Rank Organisation	1965	154
Graham Dowson	Director, Rank Organisation	1965	155
James Robertson Justice	Actor	1965	157
Magnus Magnusson	Columnist, 'Mastermind' host	1965	158
Roger Whittaker	Whistler, singer, brother-in-law	1964	160
Rolf Harris	Entertainer	1964	161
Sibylla Edmondstone	'Sibylla's' namesake	1965	162
Lord Portman	Landowner	1965	165

FRINGE BENEFITS

'Why', said my stepdaughter Katy, looking up from *Friends* and her recently painted fingernails, 'would anyone want to read a book about you?'

I immediately understood her puzzlement.

I had wondered myself. The answer is that by a mixture of luck, good fortune, timing and even birth, I have been on the fringe of so many famous, infamous or just interesting people all my life that I felt that if I didn't record them it would be a pity. Some of what they say is amusing, some touching, some revealing.

This book is dedicated to the memory of my father E. D. (Toby) O'Brien, whose wit and helpfulness is still remembered by many.

However, he never really enjoyed the credit he deserved for the hard work and dedication from which others on his 'fringes' were to benefit, for example, his propaganda against the Germans before and during the war, helping to get the Conservatives back into power, the birth of commercial television and much more.

I like to think that this book will help to redress this.

Toby O'Brien

1

CHAPTER 1 IRISH BEGINNINGS

Brian Boru, High King of Ireland, 1014

(Right) The death of Ireland's white-haired old King Brian Boru at the Battle of Clontarf, 23 April 1014, painted by David Pentland, 1994

By nightfall on Good Friday, 1014, the sea at Clontarf was stained red, with the beach littered with the wreckage of the great battle – helmets, swords, battle-axes and the dead, 10,000 of them, Irish and Norse.

The Irish lost their beloved King, Brian Boru, in his 89th year while his killer, the Danish general Brodar, was captured and suffered a horrifying death.

For Brian, the greatest High King of Ireland, this last victorious battle was the tragic end of years of shifting alliances and struggles against the Danish invader, including marrying one of their beautiful but treacherous princesses, Gormflath. Their son Donough was to start the O'Brien line. For O'Brien means, literally, descendant of Brian.

On my wall is a print of a vast family tree, carefully drawn up in tiny italic writing by a cousin in 1938. Remarkably, Brian Boru appears only a third of the way up the tree. The names march on upwards and back-wards through increasingly primitive-sounding local Irish rulers, (Con of Euclath AD 366, Cas Clan 800BC) to link with Heber Fionn (1289BC), son of King Milesius (King of Spain and Ireland) and Scotia, (daughter of Pharaoh Netanthus), then 22 generations right back through Japhet to Noah.

We owe the fact that we can trace our family so far back *before* Brian to the ancient Celtic law of Tanistry, whereby not necessarily the eldest son became King, but the fittest. You can imagine how much bloodshed and mayhem this led to.

While it is claimed that we are one of the oldest recorded families in Europe, most of our earlier ancestors were probably a lot of cattle thieves and free-booters, as are many great families if you scratch beneath the surface.

Ennobled by grateful Royalty, the English families could be sailors of fortune, even former pirates or robber barons. This was a title soon re-applied to business dynasties in America and especially to the unscrupulous railroad moguls like the Vanderbilts ('The public be damned'), the bootlegging Kennedys and the snobbish Astors whose money came from fur-trading and running New York ghettos. While we and other Irish families may be among the *oldest*, none of us ended up being the *richest* or even rich.

A long love/hate relationship with the English continued when we 'cut a deal' in 1543 with the English King Henry VIII, who persuaded Murrough, 59th King of Thomond (roughly a quarter of Ireland) to give up his 'Title, Captaincy, Superiority and Country' in exchange for the Earldom of Thomond, the Barony of Inchiquin and other titles. Murrough being royal, this deal included the right to dress the family servants in the

After strict investigation and poising the facts fairly in the balance of historical criticism, few of the Continental nobility will be found to be superior in origin, if parallel to the O'Briens, the O'Neills, the McCarthys, the O'Connors, of Ireland, whose progenitors were sovereign princes on the arrival of the English in 1172. No epoch is better attested than the reign of Brian Boroimhe, the conqueror of the Danes. This monarch was coeval with Hugues Capet, which would place his descendants in a co-incident line with the royal houses of Europe of the greatest antiquity – even with the Bourbons, incontestably the oldest of all.

John Burke, "History of the Landed Gentry or Commoners of Great Britain and Ireland", published 1837

*1st Earl of Inchiquin
'Black Murrough
of the Burnings'*

Bunratty Castle, early fortress home

Royal Scarlet, of which more later. From then on, the family tree is scattered with men who distinguished themselves either serving or fighting the English. My father used to claim that the ferocious 1st Earl of Inchiquin, 'Black Murrough of the Burnings', whose name was as vilified as Cromwell's, changed sides four times and his religion twice during the English Civil War.

We O'Briens had our share of the 'Wild Geese,' providing Marshals of France, Generals of Prussia and Captains-General of Spain. One mercenary Colonel O'Brien even gave a phrase to the Portuguese language. On the way to fight the Spanish, his Irish force hung around the coastal town of Peniche eating and drinking for weeks too long. To this day *Um amigo de Peniche* means a friend who has outstayed his welcome. If you visit Vienna, you will see the street 'O'Brien Gasse' and 'O'Brien Denkmal' (above), a monument to Generalmajor Johann Freiherr von O'Brien for outstanding services to Austria, especially at the 1809 battle against Napoleon at Vienna.

You can find another statue in O'Connell Street, in Dublin, which celebrates a truly Irish feat of rebellion against the English. William Smith O'Brien, my great great uncle was, in 1848, the Conservative MP for Limerick when Ireland's third of the total population of the United Kingdom made the Irish vote important.

After the horrors of the Famine in 1845 and 1846, Ireland had lost one quarter of its eight million people. No wonder they call Poland the Ireland of Eastern Europe. Weakened by deprivation and disease, Ireland was in despair. With three colleagues, William Smith O'Brien – in spite of being from a traditional background of Harrow and Cambridge and a Protestant – hatched the ill-fated Young Ireland Revolt, to be fought under the French Revolution-inspired tricolor of green, white and orange, now Ireland's flag.

They were promised 5,000 'fully armed men'. Thoroughly alarmed, that other Irishman, the aged Duke of Wellington, prepared to rush 10,000 troops from England.

In humiliating reality, the rebels mustered only 32 'fully armed men' and another 20 'prepared to throw stones'. On July 29th 1848, this trusty band managed to intercept a troop of mounted constabulary who retreated into a stone cottage near the village of Ballingarry, owned by a widow McCormack. The 'Battle of Widow McCormack's Cabbage Garden' was interrupted by the

4

furious widow returning home to find her house under fire and her children trapped inside. Fiercely she ordered all the combatants to cease fire and go home, and this they did, rather shamefacedly. William Smith O'Brien was arrested by a suspicious guard at Thurles railway station – surely the only time railway staff have arrested a man for High Treason.

He and the other three ringleaders were found guilty and were among the last people to be sentenced to 'hanging, drawing and quartering'. The young Queen Victoria was horrified to find out what this entailed and insisted that the sentence be commuted to transportation to Australia. Smith O'Brien refused this clemency, demanding death or a Royal Pardon. A special Act, the 'Transportation for Treason Act' of 1849, was passed just to be rid of him and his companions.

In the event, the way he handled his exile had a far greater political effect than the original abortive revolt. In Van Diemen's Land (now Tasmania), O'Brien, as an MP and probably the best-connected felon ever to be transported, became the natural focus of the anti-transportation movement. Curiously, this was Australian-led. Previously transported folk, now respectable with families, wanted to prevent the arrival every few weeks of ships carrying disreputable people. These, normally released after a fortnight, often went back to the bad old ways for which they were sentenced in the first place. One notable robber gang used to avoid identification by leaving its victims tied to trees and incoherently drunk!

Smith O'Brien's three companions eventually escaped to America where one, Thomas Meagher, had a distinguished career as a Federal General in the Civil War, leading the Irish Brigade in brutal, sometimes suicidal, battles like Cold Harbor (where he saved the day 'fighting in his shirtsleeves'), Malvern Hill, Antietam and Fredericksburg. Sadly this was often against fellow Irishmen from the South, whose Louisiana Irish Regiment was ironically commanded by a Colonel O'Brien and included the O'Brien Light Infantry.

More poignant still were the losses suffered by Meagher's Young Ireland convict friend, John Mitchel, who had tragically espoused the Confederacy. Of his three sons, Willy died at Pickett's Charge at Gettysburg, and John, who had fired the first shells at Fort Sumter in 1861, was killed in command there by one of the last shells in 1864. Thomas Meagher went on to be Governor of Montana.

After 11 years of exile Smith O'Brien was pardoned and returned to Ireland. He died in 1864, six years before the birth of my grandfather, Aubrey O'Brien, who became one of those O'Briens who served the British loyally.

William Smith O'Brien MP, reluctant Irish revolutionary

Irish military caution (which Brian Boru did not follow!):

'Better a coward for five minutes, than a dead man all yer life.'

'Slattery's Mounted Fut', Percy French

CHAPTER 2 INDIAN SUMMER

Half way round the world towards Britain's experimental prison camp of Australia lay India – the 'Jewel in the Crown' of the British Empire. Looking back, we have to recognise that a comparatively tiny island state such as 'Great' Britain ran its Empire on the cheap. The Empire was a product of privatisation. Many of its highlights and conquests (the slave trade, Suez, Hong Kong) were the result of maverick private enterprise. In contrast to the grandeur or religious overtones of the French or Spanish Empires, it was an extension of the Chamber of Commerce, with monopolistic trade, supported by a navy which really did use little 'gunboats' and a scattering of soldiers and civil servants in a sea of conquered populations. So it was, above all, with India. Leaving this jewel to private enterprise, like the East India Company, and its interests, went tragically and dramatically wrong in the Indian Mutiny of 1857.

My grandfather was a perfect example of a handful of dedicated servants of the Crown. Aubrey O'Brien, who had been in the Lancashire Fusiliers, then transferred to the 110th Maharatta Light Infantry and eventually to a branch of the Indian Civil Service founded by Edwards and Nicholson after the lessons of the Indian Mutiny to cover the frontier districts. This select band – never more than 20 or 30 – had to deal with the whole of the frontier districts between what is now Pakistan and Afghanistan.

They were a remarkable breed. Aubrey's capacity for languages, which has been inherited by several members of the family, caused him to be sent with Sir Louis Dane to Kabul, as Oriental Secretary, for the signature of the Anglo-Afghan Treaty of 1898. There, in the depths of a freezing Afghan Winter, they sat with the Amir exchanging quotations from Firdaussi and Omar. Indeed, the Treaty would not have been signed had it not been for my grandfather's knowledge of classical Persian, the French of Middle Eastern diplomacy, and his familiarity with the Persian poets. After three days of

Colonel Aubrey O'Brien, with the young Prince he was protecting

grinding negotiations, the Treaty was ready for signature.

As the Amir poised his plumed pen to sign, a drop of ink fell on the parchment. This the Amir regarded as a very bad omen and suggested that he should start the negotiations all over again – an appalling prospect. Luckily, His Majesty had a mole on his cheek, which, when translated into classical Persian, is apparently the same as a blot of ink and my grandfather produced an appropriate quotation from Firdaussi, saying something to the effect that 'The mole on thy cheek is as beautiful as the blot on this parchment', whereupon the negotiations, happily for all, were concluded.

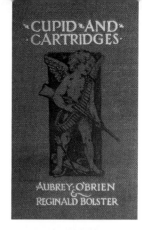

CUPID AND CARTRIDGES

AUBREY O'BRIEN & REGINALD BOLSTER

The first district to which he was assigned at the age of just 25 was about the size of Wales and had only been recently annexed. It was riddled with blood feuds between the Awans, Pathans and Baluchis. My grandfather had become one of the best shots in India. He even wrote a book called 'Cupid and Cartridges'. So he would take the leaders of the tribes out to shoot imperial sandgrouse. This involved being in position on sand dunes below a water hole well before dawn. The Punjab winter is notoriously cold at night. He would place two feuding tribesmen on the same sand dune. The dawn wind would whistle up their skirts and human nature being what it is, sooner or later one would say to the other the equivalent of 'Bloody cold, isn't it?' His companion would not at first reply but a little bit more of the dawn wind would finally produce the reply, 'Yes, isn't it?'

The Watson 12-bore, 250,000 cartridges later

Then the sandgrouse would come over, dip swiftly down to drink and then set off again across the desert. It called for a very quick and very accurate shot. As the tribesmen were very keen sportsmen, when one shot a particularly good bird, the other could not restrain himself from calling out 'Shahbaz!', meaning 'Well done!'. By breakfast time, the blood feud was over.

The Kangra Valley earthquake, which killed thousands including the family of the Deputy Commissioner, required desperately hard relief work, for which he was awarded the CIE (Commander of the Indian Empire). This effort also nearly killed him and he had to go back to England to recover. He returned with a young wife.

Aubrey O'Brien with his CIE

Nowadays, it is difficult to imagine what the wives out in the Districts went through. Except for the Summer period in the cool of the hills, they were without other female companionship. They endured hardships and anxieties of which the cushioned memsahibs of the 'box wallahs' from Surbiton, whose racialism largely lost us India, had, of course, no concept.

When my grandfather first bought his wife out to India they made a tour of his whole district of Dehragrazi Khan. A portable triumphal arch had been created which was packed up on camels overnight and re-erected at the next village. Written on the floral arch was a slogan, which summed up the life she was to lead.

> GOD BLESS CAPTAIN O'BRIEN
> GOD HELP MRS O'BRIEN

THE OTHER HALF

For the first few years of Aubrey's service, the Viceroy of India was the legendary Lord Curzon. In today's egalitarian society it is rare to find quite the degree of unthinking snobbery that you had in the past. As some wag wrote of him at Balliol College:

'My name is George Nathaniel Curzon.
I am a most superior person.'

A Member of Parliament once described his parliamentary manner as 'a divinity addressing black beetles'.

Years later, my father became friends with Harold Nicolson, Curzon's valued Private Secretary, who described driving to an appointment with Curzon. The latter suddenly asked: 'Harold, why am I so unpopular?'

Plucking up courage Nicolson replied: 'Well, Sir, I think you wound people in their little vanities.'

Curzon indignantly denied this, and asked for an example.

'Well, Sir, while I was sitting in your office you made Sir George Clerk stand to attention in front of your desk while you wrote out a number of invitations by hand. I don't think you put matters to right by looking up and saying, "Sorry to keep you waiting, but I'm making out the invitations for a thousand of my close friends to a masked ball. I expect you entertain from time to time, my dear Clerk, *in your own small way.*"'

Lord Curzon, 1913

Curzon was horrified. 'I did not say that!' he exclaimed, 'I can't have said that.' Then he paused and, his shoulders shaking with laughter, he added, 'Oh dear! Perhaps I did say that.'

Mind you he was probably right to put his foot down after attending a wedding as Viceroy. The bride (of a gloomy and pious disposition) chose as the hymn 'Soon shall you and I be lying, each within his narrow bed'. This was too much for both the sense of humour and the sense of propriety of Curzon, who thereafter laid it down that the hymns at any weddings which he was to attend in his official capacity should be submitted to him beforehand for approval.

My grandfather was forced to pretend to exercise our curious historical right, granted by Henry VIII, to use the Royal Livery at a crucial moment at the Delhi Durbar of George V in 1911. He was there in order to receive his C.I.E. for his Kangra Valley earthquake efforts. Louis Dane, now Governor of The Punjab, suddenly realised to his horror that his servants were wearing scarlet and the King was bound to notice as the Royal Family could be very touchy about the 'Royal Scarlet'. Sir Louis could not possibly get new liveries made in time.

Fortunately he was giving a drink to the then Ulster King at Arms who said, 'I understand you have Aubrey, who is an Inchiquin O'Brien, in your camp. Make them over to him.'

The whole investiture was held up for twenty minutes while King George V, who was amused but not hoodwinked, discussed with my grandfather the origin of his bogus servants wearing the royal livery.

ON YOUR OWN

Aubrey's Oriental expertise was of considerable assistance during the First World War. India was stripped of troops (he himself raised two new battalions). Therefore, to guard 450 miles of frontier from the barren mountains to the fertile valley of the Indus, he was left with only 49 armed gendarmerie. The only way he could make appropriate use of his little force was to go over the frontier in disguise, sit in the bazaars and, from the gossip, discover down which valley the next invasion was coming. There, he and his men with their one Lewis machine-gun would be waiting.

It was really very dangerous under-cover work as the slightest error in language or native custom, particularly in such things as eating, would have led to a most unpleasant death.

Once he had been gone for six weeks. My grandmother came out on the veranda at six one morning to discover an old Baluchi faquir with greasy lovelocks sitting in the Buddha position at the end of the veranda. 'I'm sorry, you have to leave the compound,' she ventured.

'Salaam, memshiba, salaam,' said this disconcerting figure, 'All I really want, darling, is a bath.'

GRIMSDALE

He soon acquired a new, unofficial title, 'O'Brien of the Waters', following his enthusiastic work on irrigation in Bahawalpur, a state already fiercely loyal to the British, and made more so by the wealth he then helped to create. By a clever system of weirs and 12 large canals, the surplus waters of three rivers were harnessed and dammed, which transformed millions of acres of dust-driven desert into fertile cultivation, making Aubrey a local hero.

Dromoland Castle, County Clare

ITALIAN GENIUS

While one part of the family was serving in the 'Jewel in the Crown' of the British Empire, back home in Ireland our cousins had moved from their fortress of Bunratty Castle to Dromoland Castle near Ennis in County Clare, a large edifice overlooking a lake, and extremely cold in the Winter. It is now one of Ireland's finest hotels.

My great great aunt Beatrice was strolling in the grounds with her father, the 14th Baron Inchiquin, when she proudly announced a startling fact. 'My new Italian suitor can send messages hundreds of miles.'

'Don't be a fool, girl,' snorted her father. 'Everyone knows you can't shout more than about a hundred yards.'

But her clever Italian boyfriend was Guglielmo Marconi, the inventor of radio (and incidentally the son of Annie Jameson, of the whiskey family), whom she married at one of the most fashionable London weddings of 1905.

Marconi, inventor of radio

My father, Edward Donough O'Brien, was born on 21st November 1909 on the Baluchistan frontier. The nearest other European was my grandfather on his horse 70 miles away, frantically trying to fetch the doctor. But he was delivered perfectly safely by an Indian midwife.

As a child, he recalled the Summer station of Sakesar, 6,000 feet up in the cool of the Himalayas. Sakesar had only two other European families: the Levys and his cousins, the Calverts. Aubrey rode over one morning and was told, 'Aunt Clanis has just given you another little cousin'. This was later to be Brigadier Michael Calvert, the Chindit leader, who fought with Orde Wingate, creator of the guerrilla forces behind the Japanese lines in 1943.

A pampered childhood

Even as young as five, my father remembered the outbreak of World War I, in August 1914, anxiously watching Aubrey on the veranda at Sakesar – with his fat green code book and pages of telegrams. The signals told them that we were at war with Germany and that the Germans would do everything possible, through their agents, to stir up trouble on the frontiers.

One poignant memory of his was of my grandmother suddenly bursting into tears. She knew for certain that her favourite brother had been killed thousands of miles away. Ten days later, the telegram arrived after the second Battle of Ypres. There were about 60,000 such wires.

Visits to church were marred by slight misunderstandings. When he heard, 'Sadly, my cross I'd bear', the little boy, familiar with the rather mangy dancing bears in Indian villages, imagined a cross-eyed bear called 'Sadly'.

An idyllic and pampered childhood was only marred by two of the normal tropical diseases, malaria and amoebic dysentery, so it was probably not before time that he was sent home to England.

Because of disease, it was thought essential that children should be sent home no later than the age of five, but owing to the War he stayed out until he was nearly eight. Sailing with his mother and little sister Moira from Karachi in the SS *City of Paris* took ten weeks, through the stupefying heat of the Red Sea with the poor stokers coming up on deck for a breath of air from the inferno of the engine room. He saw his first aeroplane above the Suez canal and watched the ship pick up, almost daily, people from rafts and lifeboats sunk by U-boats in the Mediterranean.

The saddest sight for the little boy was seeing a fox terrier on a piece of wreckage drifting past him in the opposite direction, barking and barking at the passengers for help. The U-boat threat became so acute that they sheltered in Algiers. (In fact *The City of Paris* was sunk coming back, taking with it some of the crew who had befriended the little children.)

The apprehensive eight-year-old got his first sight of England arriving at Liverpool into the shock of the unexpected, cold dankness of a wartime Winter.

GRIMSDALE

The rude shock of a cold wartime Britain was as nothing compared with the even ruder one awaiting my father at the prep school that his elder brother, Turlough, was already attending. St Cyprian's in Eastbourne was horrible. From the headmaster 'Sammy' Vaughn-Wilkes down to the smallest new boy, everyone was terrified of the tyrant Mrs Wilkes. Certainly my father was. Coming from his pampered life in India, he was so unhappy that he tried to kill himself by sitting in front of a freezing open window. He nearly succeeded by catching double pneumonia.

Years later, because he remembered my father and uncle at St Cyprian's, I was telephoned by David Ogilvy, one of the world's greatest advertising men and my Chairman at the marketing conglomerate, WPP. He invited me to his French chateau at Touffou. There, he confirmed the misery of the school and above all Mrs Wilkes:

> 'My God, I hated that school. Only if your father was a peer, or extraordinarily rich, were you treated half decently by that dreadful woman.'

As most of the boys were from more modest backgrounds, they were very badly treated. I suppose the school was not all bad. There sat the future writer, Cyril Connolly, the photographer, Cecil Beaton, and the golfer, Henry Longhurst.

The O'Brien brothers were now called Toby 1 and Toby 2, names that were to stick and cause endless confusion, especially when they both went in for public relations.

David Ogilvy,
advertising guru

One bizarre school incident involved early exposure to homosexuality. In my father's words:

> 'We had a games master called Major Smart. It became apparent that he had been making passes at about 70 out of 120 little boys. Finally, I went to see Sammy Wilkes but, unfortunately, found his wife in his study. 'I want to see Mr Wilkes, Ma'am.' 'He is out shooting today. What is it?'

> I was in a terrible dilemma because we had no technical phrases (*The News of the World* used such phrases as a 'clergyman accused of a certain offence').

> 'Come on, speak up!'

I was forced to comply. The unexpected problem was that Mrs Wilkes was in love with Major Smart and 'Hell hath no fury like a woman scorned for seventy small boys'.

Her fury created a very alarming sequel. On Saturday afternoon in the Sixth Form we were having our tea. Major Sharp suddenly came in and said 'O'Brien and Cohen, I want to speak to you.'

In the Fifth Form room, he shut the door, and produced from his pocket a '45 Webley service revolver that still looks a pretty huge weapon. For a small boy aged 13, it was like a cannon. He broke it open, loaded it with what appeared to be cannon shells, closed it and waved it first at my nose.

'Do you know what that is? Do you, O'Brien and Cohen?' 'Yeah, Yeah, Yes Sir! It's a revolver!'

'Yes, and I understand certain people have been saying very unpleasant things about me. I want you to know that if this goes any further, I shall shoot myself. But before I do so, I shall shoot you,' he bellowed, waving this enormous barrel at us, 'and those who I consider responsible for telling these stories. Is that clear to you O'Brien and you, Cohen?' 'Yes, Sir' we stuttered meekly.

Luckily at the master's dinner that evening, old Mr Siller the fifth form master extracted the terrifying weapon and Major Smart left the school for good the next morning. As a result of Major Smart's episode, we had a lecture from the school doctor who tried to tell us of the evils of sex, which all the school attended with the greatest enthusiasm.'

Toby really wanted to get a scholarship to Winchester, but was hit by another bout of ill-health and returned from the sick bay to find open scholarships available only at Malvern and at a new school. He blurted to Hugh Ingram, later editor of the *Illustrated London News*. 'I suppose I shall have to go to a dreadful new place called Stowe.' Which he duly and happily did.

A NEW PLACE

Stowe, just North of Buckingham, while new as a school, was housed in one of the most beautiful old buildings in Britain. Built between 1680 and 1805 in the style of a huge Palladian palazzo, it had been the seat of the Dukes of Buckingham and Chandos and a centre of political and financial power in eighteenth century Britain. It was another Duke of Buckingham who sold his rather smaller town house to King George III in 1762; now of course we call it Buckingham Palace.

Stowe's vast, lofty state rooms, by now converted to dormitories and house rooms, were familiar to great figures of the past;

Chatham, the younger Pitt, Pope, Walpole, Peel, Disraeli and even Queen Victoria and her consort.

Indeed, it was the visit in 1845 of Queen Victoria which sealed the financial fate of Stowe as a private house. The second Duke of Buckingham had inherited a colossal sum and had succeeded in frittering it all away, not least by trying to buy all the land on each side of the road from Stowe to Chandos Square in London so that he could refer to the 60 miles as his 'carriage drive'.

The bailiffs were already in residence during the Queen's visit, which was costing £1,000 a day. They refused to move out but they sportingly agreed to wear the Duke's livery and to pretend to be his servants!

As *The Times* wrote acidly: 'He has thrown away his high position for the baubles of a pauper and the tinsels of a fool.' But the Duke's foolishness was to be the school's opportunity. The magnificent home and its hundreds of acres of grounds were purchased in 1921 by the new school's Governors for the comparatively tiny sum of £50,000.

Top, the South Front of Stowe. Lower, the first two miles of the Duke's drive to London; he could not afford the next 58. (Not one of these trees survive, wiped out by Dutch Elm disease.)

The school houses were fittingly named after a roll call of great 18th century Whig families connected by marriage, Grenville, Chandos, Cobham and so on. The first headmaster was the pioneering J. F. Roxburgh, who set the tone of this new and relaxed school. Someone said later, 'Etonians get on a train as if they own it, Stoics appear not to care who does.' During the first two terms when nobody knew who anyone else was, everyone, masters and boys, wore name badges as at a modern convention.

While physically beautiful, the school could be really cold in the Winter. Even with 50 miles of new piping the boilers were incapable of heating the 200,000 square feet of ancient stone and plaster.

The superb marble Assembly Hall

Toby soon spotted an opportunity. In 1923, Stowe had been occupied by the last Duke of Buckingham's daughter, Lady Kinloss, with only two servants for years and the vast grounds were over-run by rabbits. My father and his life-long friend the future actor David Niven decided to turn this to good commercial effect. They stashed dogs, snares, ferrets and even guns out in the woods, and pretty soon their partnership provided both the workmen who were refurbishing the school and the butchers of Buckingham with rabbits. They also became mysteriously rich young schoolboys until the head-master put a stop to it.

In spite of this intervention, J. F. Roxburgh was to be a special mentor for my father and inspired him to become the second Stowe scholar to Oxford in 1928. He only missed heading the scholars' list by the five minutes separating the arrival of the two telegrams, a source of permanent mild irritation.

King George IV, source of Buckingham patronage. In my time at Stowe, naughty boys one night filled the statue with water, drilled a hole and the horse peed for a week.

Instead of idling away the last term at Stowe, he took Roxburgh's advice to go to Leipzig to learn German. An historic decision. Germany was suffering from hyper inflation, with people buying groceries with sacks of money twice a day, and each drink in a café costing hundreds of thousands of Reichsmarks more than the last. Recalling his first sighting of Nazis driving around in an open lorry singing party songs, he wrote what he thought at the time was a very funny article about it. It was of course nothing to laugh about. But, studying twelve hours a day for ten weeks gave him almost perfect German, which was to play a vital role in the years to come.

At Exeter College, Oxford he distinguished himself with the highlight of becoming first the Treasurer, then the Librarian and finally, in 1931, President of the Oxford Union, the legendary debating society. Many of his greatest political friendships in later years were forged in powerful debate with future Tory Ministers like Quintin Hogg (Lord Hailsham) and John Boyd-Carpenter. And with political adversaries too. How strange that in Harold Wilson's Labour Government as late as 1973, no less than 9 members were former Oxford Union Presidents.

Oxford Union Society. Toby, 4th from left standing. John Boyd-Carpenter, sitting far left.

It is now difficult to realise the importance in the thirties of the Oxford Union and how the rest of the country paid attention to the debates and the personalities involved. You would expect University magazines like *Isis* to cover the Union's goings on, even the *Oxford Mail* and *Oxford Times*. But in June 1931 the election of my father to President was covered by *The Times, Observer, Sunday Times, Birmingham Post, The Daily Telegraph, Yorkshire Post, Morning Post, The South Wales Argos* and the *Daily Sketch* – even the *English Churchman* thought it was important enough to record.

One of the most historic debates was organised on the trans-Atlantic telephone between Oxford and Harvard on the subject of 'The cancellation of war debts in the interest of world prosperity'. Toby had received an invitation by cable from the President of the Harvard Debating Society and he had wired back saying they welcomed the idea but wisely stipulating the

OXFORD
VERSUS
HARVARD

WAR DEBTS AND TARIFFS

Tw
ing o
of we
two s
in "
nrst
Des
main
senti
Oxfor
unani
tariff
The
but in
small
Oxfor
Savoy
The
althou
3,000
were
transi
On
Gerra
dor to
York,
A. J.
Engla
that
prospe
celled.

A NOVEL DEBATE

SPEECHES BY WIRELESS TELEPHONE

OXFORD AND HARVARD ON WAR DEBTS

A debate by wireless telephone between the Union Societies of Oxford and Harvard Universities—the first international wireless debate—was successfully conducted between this country and America on Saturday evening. The subject of debate was War debts.

At 11 o'clock the first words were exchanged between the debaters, who were situated in London and New York respectively. The Oxford team—Mr. E. D. O'Brien (Exeter), President of the Oxford Union Society; Mr. A. J. Irvine (Oriel), Librarian and President-elect; and Mr. Brian Davidson (New College), ex-Treasurer of the Union and President of the Oxford University Conservative Club—were assembled in a studio of the British Broadcasting Corporation at Savoy-hill. Harvard University was represented by Mr. Paul C. Reardon, Mr. D. Mark Sullivan, and Mr. P. H. Cohen.

The chairman, Mr. James W. Gerard, formerly United States Ambassador to Germany, speaking from one of the National Broadcasting Company's studios in New York, introduced the first speaker on the motion: "That in the interest of world prosperity War debts (loans and reparations) should be

Oxford Union could not be expected to pay any of the costs.

The papers quoted him as saying that he did not know what the cost of a trans-Atlantic phone call was, but the danger was that it would cost about five shillings for every 'Well, I guess' and any preliminary cough before a speech!

He was right to be cautious because, in the event, the debate cost £8 a minute, the equivalent of £288, and 1,440 times today's cost. Harvard agreed to foot the whole bill. It was listened to by 23 million Americans and only 100 people in Britain because the BBC did not broadcast it. One of the more poignant responses was a letter from a lady in Kansas.

```
                                    Hillsboro, Kansas

                                              Dec 5 1931

Oxford debaters

My dear Sirs:

In the maze of names I address you collectively. For the
splendid debate you should hear from many in the United
States.

I am a country woman, a farmer's wife. Your accent was a
handicap for you in talking convincingly to the people of
the middle west. One of the Harvard men was a bit "back
bay" too.

Matters on the farms have made a steady down grade since
1923. Our government seems pitifully powerless to better
conditions. Tariff begets tariff. Each is higher than the
last. We operate farms at a loss. Sway-backed bank carry
us along. Why? To produce another crop that will not pay
gas and tractor bills. The fine beef cattle went to the
butcher block three years ago. No demand for corn now.
Hogs fed wheat are selling at a few dollars per head.

People are worn and embittered as they were in war days.
Middle class people are at menial tasks and gladly they
work with their hand when work is to be had.

I felt in your English voices a vibrant of deepest con-
cern. It was appreciated. Why did Harvard lack such a
feeling? Can it be that men in eastern U.S. are lacking in
knowledge of our conditions? For a long time this section
has been ignored by our government. Cancellation of war
debts by 1932 - July! This is the answer for our desperate
condition.

Jane Crist Rupp

(Mrs W.E.Rupp)
```

Toby's presidential term appears to have been a success. *Isis* reported:

Passing Hour

Now that Mr O'Brien's term of office is nearly over, we must congratulate him on directing the destiny of the Union with so much ardour and with so much real success. One cannot, of course give Mr O'Brien the full credit for the sudden change we have experienced: the deep interest aroused by the political situation has done much to help him. But this we will say, and the words are not originally our own: 'Toby has been the best President during the recollection of any present undergraduate'. It is a phrase we will heartily endorse. Incidentally, Toby has our congratulations and best wishes on the occasion of his 22nd birthday. God bless him.

The image of the Union later declined, and was dented in 1933 when the motion was passed twice that 'This House will in no circumstances fight for King and Country'. This was despite the last ditch efforts of Winston's son, Randolph Churchill and Frank Pakenham (later Lord Longford).

The view that the Union did not even speak for the rest of Oxford, let alone the nation, prevailed. As one paper put it: 'It is clear that the section of Oxford which attends the Union cares nothing for the smoke of opinion. Obloquy has made its members obdurate and abuse has been fuel to their convictions. Pacifism being a lost cause with the rest of the nation, young Oxford makes it a grand passion. The Union Society should be left to stew in its own predilections.'

However the effects of this debate by some foolish young fellows were to be more significant abroad. An Italian chap called Benito Mussolini revealed to another fellow we are about to meet, Lord Lloyd, that he was 'most struck by the Oxford resolution'. It convinced him that Britain was a flabby old woman and encouraged him to take risks over his plans regarding Abyssinia. And his success convinced another fellow called Hitler that he too could take more risks. You could call the Oxford debate 'a little acorn'. I prefer 'cancer cell'.

For our cousins in Ireland, the twenties had been much more dramatic and dangerous. While the Easter Rising in Dublin had little effect at Dromoland Castle, the War of Independence against the British certainly did. To avoid Dromoland becoming a target, Lucius O'Brien, 15th Baron Inchiquin, sent 'every gun, rifle, revolver, sword, pistol, spear, crossbow, even the old Dublin Castle flintlock muskets to the police barracks at Newmarket-on-Fergus'.

'WE WON'T FIGHT'

Oxford Union Society.

Thursday, 9th February, 1933,

at 8 p.m.

QUESTION FOR DEBATE.

" That this House will in no circumstances fight for its King and Country."

Moved by MR. K. H. DIGBY, St. John's.

Opposed by MR. K. R. F. STEEL-MAITLAND, Balliol.

MR. D. M. GRAHAM, Balliol, Librarian, will speak third.

THE HON. QUINTIN HOGG, Christ Church and All Souls, Ex-President, will speak fourth.

MR. C. E. M. JOAD, Balliol, will speak fifth.

TELLERS.

For the Ayes.	For the Noes.
Mr. M. Beloff, C.C.C.	Mr. R. G. Thomas, Brasenose

Christ Church,   F. M. HARDIE,
4th February, 1933.   *President.*

THE TROUBLES

At the same time, for their own protection, 'all the men had revolvers in their pockets and took their shotguns up to bed'.

Our cousin, Donough O'Brien, had been ADC to Lord Chelmsford, Viceroy of India, and had fallen in love with his daughter Anne. After they married in 1921 and returned to Ireland, they had gone into hiding for a few months lest they be taken as important hostages.

Gradually Ireland settled down after the Civil War between those who had accepted the Treaty to partition Ireland and those who had not – leaving us with the problems we live with today. One solution might have been found through the decision to create the first President of Ireland in 1937. Donough, now the 16th Baron Inchiquin, was approached to see if he would accept. As it included £15,000 in much needed wages he agreed, but sadly for him, Dr Douglas Hyde was eventually chosen.

However, here is an interesting view in the *Cork Examiner*:

> The last runner mentioned for the presidentship is Lord Inchiquin. If heredity counted, he would be first favourite, for he is in the direct line of descent from Brian Boru who, whatever his faults, was the strongest ruler Ireland ever had. If he had survived Clontarf, he might have established the O'Brien dynasty so firmly that the present Earl would be King of all Ireland and there would be no Irish problem to be solved – unless in the meantime the O'Neills had asserted the independence of Ulster, as they probably would try to do; which brings us back to the fact that there was an Ulster problem nine hundred years ago as well as today.

Donough, 16th Baron Inchiquin

In Ireland, whatever the political tensions, quips abound:

> Prime Minister Eamonn de Valera once had the nerve to accuse the Leader of the Opposition, Willie Cosgrave, across the floor of the Dail, of not being Irish enough.

> 'My family,' Cosgrave snapped back, 'have been Irish for centuries, whereas the ancestors of My Honourable Friend were bartering budgerigars in the backstreets of Barcelona.'

Humour intervened, even in the face of unexpected dilemmas:

> With the departure of the British, Oliver St John Gogarty, the Irish politician, writer and wit was co-opted on to a Committee to discuss the subject of contraception. There was a heated debate as to what to call the condom, should it ever be made legal. 'French Letter' or 'Capeau Anglais' were certainly not Irish enough. Gogarty intervened. 'I don't think you could go far wrong with 'Roger Casement'.'

(Sir Roger Casement had been executed by the British for smuggling German arms to Ireland.)

Leaving the rarefied air of Oxford, Toby faced a Britain gripped by the depression. He was fortunate to be offered a journalistic opportunity that really interested him. He became Deputy Editor to Victor Gordon-Lennox of the 'Peterborough' column in *The Daily Telegraph*, and later took over as Editor. Victor remained one of a circle of really good, long-term friends.

The 'Peterborough' column was and still is a mixture of social news, cultural events and general comment, both national and international. It exactly suited my father's training and temperament. Writing there he was to forge connections, friendships and his own reputation in time for serious tasks ahead.

From his personal diary we see the thirties slowly clouded by the threats from Nazi Germany. Meanwhile he had fallen in love with my mother, Sylvia Denny (right), and a relaxed peacetime courtship ensued.

> **Saturday 13th April 1935.** Sylvia and I walked in Kensington Gardens. Met Quintin [Hogg] at the Round Pond. Like ourselves, he was watching the model yachts and marvelling at the oddly variegated types that pad around in gym shoes with rubber-tipped poles in their hands. He is doing much better now. His first year at the bar, he told me he only made 5 guineas! Quintin in very good form, he is probably the most brilliant scholar of his time at Eton and Oxford.

As a history scholar, Hollywood's liberties provoked Toby's amusement:

> **Wednesday 19th June 1935.** Took Sylvia to Leicester Square Theatre for premiere of Joe M. Schenck's (pronounced Skenk) presentation of 'Cardinal Richelieu' (Darryl Zanuck, the producer). Most frightful piffle. His Eminence digs Gustavus Adolphus in the ribs and says 'See here Gustavus, I like you'. Only Mr Schenck's sense of what is due to Royalty stopped him saying 'See here, Gus'. The best wise-crack was a lady next to Sylvia who said, quite seriously, 'I don't seem to remember this part of history.'

In Germany the Nazis had already brutally disposed of their Communist competitors, but in England they were merely a source of mild amusement:

> **Sunday 14th July 1935.** Communists and Green Shirts coming back from demonstration in Trafalgar Square. Green Shirts impressively smart. Communists rag, tag and bob tail. *Daily Worker* says, 'It's due to not having sufficient

King George V

Kremlin-minded bands. We have to hire them. But they only know patriotic tunes like 'Land of Hope and Glory.' (All wrong for Commies!)

With an actual mutiny at the naval base at Invergordon, all was not well in the Royal Navy. Toby's diary offers an interesting insight into the King's personal fury as a former naval officer:

> **Wednesday 14th August 1935.** John Boyd-Carpenter very interesting about the Invergordon Mutiny. King George sent for the acting Commander in Chief (who hopelessly mis-handled the whole thing) and cursed him as only one sailor can curse another. He even followed him to the door in order to curse him all the way down the stairs! John said that the grievances were so bad that the officers would also have mutinied if told to take extreme measures.
>
> The King also sent for Roger Keyes, who was Commander in Chief in the Mediterranean, and he said was too busy playing polo to know what was happening on his ships. He sent for him all the way from Malta and then cursed him and told him to get back to his ship at once, after a 36 hour journey.

An old letter from his tailor illustrates the charm and good manners of a bygone age:

> **October 7th 1935.** Letter from Walters, the tailor in Oxford.
>
> *Dear Mr O'Brien,*
>
> *In view of our former pleasant personal business relations, I would like to acknowledge your kind remittance personally, to insure you that your continued custom is always welcomed on these lines.*
>
> *The balance outstanding still remains a little substantial, but we are never very much concerned about this where moderate payments reach us from time to time, to provide resources for our own claims.*
>
> *I feel that there is an obligation to be helpful to our customers, who in turn, make the fullest use of our services. I trust that you will continue to do so and that the courtesy and attention received at Hanover Street fully carries out the traditions established in Oxford.*
>
> *Yours faithfully ....*

(My father had reduced his £27 bill by £5)

Toby would not be the first fiancé to worry about a film offer:

> **Monday 4th November 1935.** In taxi, Sylvia told me that Charles Laughton had asked her to be Roxanne in Cyrano. Alexander Korda is producing it. Both proud and alarmed, proud because, with her unchained beauty, she would have been considered for such a part, alarmed that she might

well succeed and then her success might come between us. Sylvia looking incredibly beautiful and much happier. Pondering to bed.

Toby need not have worried. Charles Laughton was the most photographed guest of honour at his wedding on 12th February 1936 to a radiant Sylvia. The short-lived acting career evaporated.

Charles Laughton (right) with A.P. Herbert MP

In 1936, Toby and his new wife moved to Germany, where ostensibly he was still working for *The Daily Telegraph*, but he had what is now known as 'a hidden agenda'. The Nazis were aware of this and it became plain that he and his friends were being bugged by the Gestapo because they could always hear a clicking noise on the telephone as the crude wire recorders went into action.

He and his friends countered this by breaking into the nursery rhyme tune 'Who's afraid of the big bad wolf?' but in German,

LIVING WITH THE NAZIS

GRIMSDALE

'Eins, Zwei, Drei. Wer hat Angst vor der Gestapo, Gestapo, Gestapo?' The Germans must have been constantly irritated by this defiant outburst of singing on the telephone, an unusual experience for them.

My father met most of the upper echelons of the Nazi party, including Goering who was as big a gangster as any of them. However, he had the somewhat disarming characteristic of appearing jollier than the rest.

He also appeared to know exactly what my father was trying to achieve in Germany. At an embassy cocktail party one evening he looked up, grinned, and waving his finger in an admonishing way said, 'Ah, Herr O'Brien, Sie ungezoger Junge, Sie ungezoger Junge!' ('You naughty boy').

Using the *Daily Telegraph* as a front, one of my father's roles was to try to identify and encourage a group of civilised and reasonable Germans who might in some way head off Hitler from his disastrous course towards war. He was fairly confident that there were enough of them to have some effect. It was in 1936 that these hopes were shattered. The Nazis had made a huge effort to turn the 1936 Berlin Olympics into a showpiece for Germany. The whole place was smartened up, public persecution of minorities halted and anti-Jewish graffiti was removed. Hitler and Goebbels were also desperate for German athletes to triumph. Hitler had publicly shown his anger at the success of the American, 'non-Aryan', black athletes, especially Jesse Owens.

He was even angrier when, having driven all the way to Baden Baden to witness what promised to be the

final, triumphant holes of the German golfers, he arrived in time to be told that the English pair, Arnold Bentley and Tony Thirsk, had unexpectedly won. The Führer got straight back into his car and drove all the way back to Berlin.

Someone later made a casual joke about this at a dinner party at Toby's Berlin flat. Suddenly one of his best German friends leaped to his feet and screamed at the top of his voice: 'TOBY, YOU HAVE BEEN IN MY HOUSE, I HAVE BEEN IN YOUR HOUSE. YOU HAVE BEEN MY FRIEND AND I HAVE BEEN YOUR FRIEND. BUT ALL THAT IS ENDED NOW. YOU INSULT MY LAND!'

After this chilling outburst he calmed down and stayed until the end of the party. But when all the guests had gone my father sat with his head in his hands, lamenting to my mother: 'If you can't reason with sensible people like that, how on earth can you deal with the rest of the Germans? There will certainly be a war.'

It was quite a good thing that he didn't have to deal with the rest of the Germans too closely. Because of his growing propaganda activities, he was on S.S. leader Walter Schellenberg's *Sonderfahndungsliste-GB*, a death list of 2,000 who were to be shot on identification once Britain was success-fully invaded, with the families automatically sent straight to the new concentration camps which would no doubt have quickly scarred our British countryside.

In March 1937, Toby found himself as the only Western correspondent to cover a significant visit by Mussolini to Libya. His *Daily Telegraph* reports, picked up all over the world, were regarded as a major coup. He accompanied Mussolini's party along a 1,200 mile road but his daily reports and his leader were by no means flattering to the Italian cause.

Waving aloft the two-handed sword of Islam, Mussolini was attempting to hail himself as 'the Protector of Islam' and pledging his friendship for all Islamic states, in so-called 'contrast to the record of the British'. Toby's *Telegraph* leader pointed out that this was both phoney and cynical:

> It is curious that the same Western Power which has so recently disposed of the claims to independence of one State with a large Muslim population – and massacred Moslem and Christians alike after the bomb attack at Addis Ababa – should express so sympathetic an interest in the 'legitimate claims' of Moslem states.

The editorial continued to point out the cleverness and ruthlessness of Italian propaganda:

> But here is an official Italian manifesto pointing a finger of sorrowful scorn at those Arab countries which so far lack

MUSSOLINI, FRIEND OF ISLAM?

Mussolini waves the 'Sword of Islam' (made in Florence)

GRIMSDALE

MUSSOLINI HAILED AS THE PROTECTOR OF ISLAM

PLEDGE OF FRIENDSHIP GIVEN ON LIBYA TOUR

ITALY'S AIM OF CLOSE ACCORD WITH MOSLEM STATES

BRITAIN ACCUSED OF REPRESSION OF ARABS IN PALESTINE

Signor Mussolini is making a triumphal progress through Libya, along the 1,200-mile military road from the Egyptian frontier to Tripoli, which he opened a few hours after landing in the colony on Friday.

. Replying to Moslem leaders who acclaimed him as "Protector of Islam," he said: "Italy will always be the friend and protector of Islam throughout the world."

An official memorandum, issued in Benghazi yesterday, describes Italy's policy to the Moslem States as one of "strong sympathy" and her aim as political and economic collaboration with them.

It contrasts the "religious peace" in Libya with the "cruel repression" of Arabs by Britain in Palestine and the Moslem unrest in Algeria, Morocco, Tunisia, Syria and Irak.

Egypt is assured that Italy has no designs on her and regards her as an independent country.

SIMPLE CEREMONY AT FRONTIER POST

From E. D. O'BRIEN,
"Daily Telegraph" Special Correspondent

the formal 'protection' of the Duce. How much more fortunate, it is implied, is Libya 'pacified' 4 years ago after 20 years of massacres and concentration camps, which have reduced the population of Tripoli from 1.5 million to 600,000 and extirpated village after village.

In spite of the fact that both he and his newspaper had revealed that they had seen through Mussolini's ploy, Toby appeared to enjoy the 10 day trip in Libya and got on rather well with his Italian hosts.

However, back in Rome the *Daily Telegraph* comments were being described as 'poisonous' and 'perfidious insinuations'. *La Tribuna* said 'it has produced the effects of a box on the ears. *The Daily Telegraph*', it went on, 'is insulting and it makes insinuations about the alleged massacre of Moslems by the Italians'.

Suddenly, Toby's relationship with the Italian party was made frosty by an outspoken sermon made by the Dean of Winchester at a service in London attended by Emperor Haile Selassie. 'For all men women and children who were slaughtered in Abyssinia'. By ill luck it was once again the *Telegraph* who reported it:

> There is no Englishman who does not blush with shame when he reflects on the events of the past year, for it was not only Abyssinia's enemies but her friends, not only the brutal invader but those who promised to defend her, who had a part in encompassing her ruin. The law of humanity that Italy has so fearfully violated still stands.

The Archbishop of Canterbury has said the ruler of Italy has seduced his people with the poison of militarism and supposes himself to be a Caesar, but is in reality the untrue ante-type of the Syrian Emperor Antiochus, nicknamed 'Epimanes the Madman'.

No one who knows the Italians will deny they are by nature a kindly, unwarlike people. Their record of savagery in Abyssinia and Libya can only be explained by the view that they have been seized by a spirit of evil of superhuman nature.

Toby scrawled ironically in his press cutting book: 'This made my relations with Musso *so much easier*!'

Emperor Haile Selassie's own fervent protestations about Italian behaviour were spoilt by his English pronounciation problems, 'My enema the douche' being one of the best.

The delicate relationship between the two future allies, Germany and Italy, was also highlighted on this trip by the robust performance of a huge bearded Italian sergeant who, irritated by the pushy behaviour of a German reporter, hit him firmly on the jaw and tumbled him to the bottom of the viewing stand. The German rubbed his jaw and muttered, with a note of new respect, 'Behandeln Sie Ihre Freunde immer so?' ('Do you always treat your friends like this?').

It was a little sign that Germany and Italy would never be comfortable allies, let alone friends. We now know that Mussolini was desperately trying to re-instate Italy's old friendship with Britain and to avoid being forced into a dangerous junior partnership with Germany. Threatening force, he had foiled Hitler's first attempted *Anschluss* with Austria in 1934, had helped to create the 'Stresa Front' to contain the Germans and was on good terms with several leading British politicians including Austen Chamberlain and Winston Churchill, who had once described him as a 'Roman genius'. It was the personal antagonism towards Italy of Anthony Eden that helped to push Italy into Germany's arms and created the climate which hastened the outbreak of the Second World War.

The pleasant myth has grown up that Anthony Eden resigned in February 1938 because of Neville Chamberlain's appeasement. Not true. Eden was perfectly happy to appease Hitler but was locked in a bitter open fight with his Prime Minister about Italy, once even in front of an amazed Count Grandi, the Italian Ambassador.

Temporarily friendly with the Italians

H.C. McClelland, the British Consul in Tripoli told Toby of his own problems, bordering on farce at the same Libyan events:

'We were invited to see a demonstration of Italian military and aerial strength at a desolate point in the desert outside Tripoli. I was given a lift by my French colleague who, to my surprise, turned up in a morning coat and top hat. The French Consul pointed out that we had seats in the 'Tribune of Honour' and it was our duty to appear properly dressed. As France and Great Britain were closely allied against Italian pretensions in North Africa, and as the Frenchman was the senior, I hastily changed into the same garb.

'The Tribune of Honour' turned out to be a trench into which we two diplomats cautiously descended. The sun was infernally hot, the earth shook with the destruction of a native village by the Italian air force, heavy machine guns were fired over our heads, but the climax came when I happened to turn around, and saw a battalion of the camel corps coming straight for us. Diplomatic dignity has its limits. Top hats disappeared into the bottom of the trench as the camels pounded over us.

Worse, when we returned to our car, we found that every drop of petrol had been siphoned out and we had to push the vehicle under a blazing African sun. The humour of it escaped us at the time!'

In January 1938, Toby's role as a voice for Britain became official. The Government were now dissatisfied with just a few Foreign Office handouts as a counter to Dr Goebbel's 'Britain is Decadent' campaign, which portrayed a Britain 'run by plutocrats, peers and Jews'. The British Council, theoretically a cultural organisation, was chosen as the vehicle.

He was interviewed by the Executive Committee, which included Clement Attlee who as always was kind and polite to him, in spite of their opposing political views.

So it was that Lord Lloyd invited him to become the first Press Officer of the invigorated British Council and his formal career as a lonely propagandist against Goebbel's huge machine began. In a spirit of British parsimony, it was seriously suggested at first that he battle the wily Doktor in the mornings and continue with the *Telegraph's* Peterborough column in the afternoons!

The media welcomed his arrival, seeing one of their own helping the country's neglected efforts.

Mr E D O'Brien

Lord Lloyd is not the man to let the grass grow under his feet, and his appointment of Mr E. D. O'Brien to be Press Officer to the British Council proves how seriously he takes his responsibility for this body. 'Toby' O'Brien as he is universally called, is just the man for the post, for he has a quite exceptional charm of manner, a gift for languages, and a thorough knowledge of journalism. Moreover, he is still on the sunny side of thirty, and has the advantage of a wife whose ability and attractiveness equal his own.

The Observer 23rd January 1938

'Toby' O'Brien

Lord Lloyd is bringing all his unusual gifts of imagination to the task of promoting the welfare of the British Council. He has chosen a Press Officer who will shortly travel in Poland and South-East Europe. The Press Officer is Mr E D O'Brien, cousin of Lord Inchiquin. 'Toby' O'Brien is one of the best known of the younger men in London. His abilities were first recognised when he assisted Mr Victor Gordon-Lennox in the compiling of a popular daily column. His father was a great servant of India, whose abilities and candour should have won a more handsome recognition from Edwin Montagu.

Great Britain and the East 21st January 1938

Toby's demanding new boss was a formidable and extraordinary figure. Lord Lloyd of Dolobran was Chairman of the British Council, but also, as Colonial Secretary, administered a large part of the globe.

OXFORD UNIVERSITY
CONSERVATIVE ASSOCIATION

The Right Hon.
LORD LLOYD
P.C., G.C.S.I., G.C.I.E., D.S.O.,

will speak on

"BRITISH INTERESTS IN THE MIDDLE EAST"

AT 8.15 P.M. ON

Friday, November 22nd,

In the UNION DEBATING HALL

Admission will be by ticket only. The Press will not be admitted. Additional tickets may be obtained on application to the Secretaries; or the President, Mr. Patrick Hamilton, Trinity; or the Treasurer, Mr. Boyd-Carpenter, Balliol.

DOROTHY M. MILNES, O.H.S.,
E. D. O'BRIEN, Exeter. } Hon. Secs.

When Toby invited Lloyd to Oxford, could he know that this was his future chief?

Lloyd's father started him on a lifetime of exploration. From the age of 12 onwards he handed his son George a small sum of money every Easter. With this he was to take a holiday at least 400 miles from the English coast. He had to plan his own route, make all his own arrangements, and on his return write his father a thesis on the history, customs, geography and politics of the country he had visited. His first trip – as a good Hellenist – was to Greece, but at the age of 14 the quick and observant Welsh schoolboy was shooting partridges with the then almost unconquered tribesmen of North Africa.

This liking for foreign countries and peoples always remained with him. Long before he was 30 he had travelled in Burma, India, Tibet, Morocco and Asia Minor, including service at the British Embassy in Istanbul.

His wartime service included Egypt, Gallipoli and the Middle East, where he helped T. E. Lawrence to destroy Turkey's power. Lawrence of Arabia claimed that Lloyd was the only British colleague at home on a camel.

Between the wars, Lord Lloyd was Governor of Bombay where in five years he initiated the great barrage scheme at Sind on the Indus which bears his name and where he showed himself a tireless and resourceful administrator at a most complex period – as he did in Egypt.

He seldom worked less than 14 hours a day on the Council's business – for seven days a week. Yet at the same time, he was able to squeeze in a host of other roles, not least becoming a fully qualified fighter-bomber pilot. He became honorary Air-Commodore of No. 600 (City of London Squadron) Auxiliary Air Force, a volunteer squadron partly made up of bankers and stockbrokers.

Lord Lloyd training with his squadron

But honorary status was, for him, not good enough. Somehow he found time to pass all the stringent service tests (including dive bombing) which really entitled him to wear his 'wings'. He was never happier than with his squadron and it is said that in the early days of the war he was frequently over Germany, acting as navigator of one of the squadron's Blenheims – this in his 59th year. 600 Squadron later became the highest scoring

'Fright of the Night'

Allied nightfighter unit, its lethal black Beaufighters earning the Luftwaffe's name 'Fright of the Night'.

While Toby and the British Council team of enthusiastic young men were under no illusions about Lloyd's required speed of action, the Colonial Office was still operating on a sleepy, pre-war timetable, with Civil Servants of the 'abominable no-man' type. On one occasion, one of Lord Lloyd's high-ups came in and said, 'Excuse me, Secretary of State, but what do you mean by the word 'soon'?'

'Quarter of an hour, half an hour, perhaps an hour. If it is very complicated, perhaps twenty-four hours. Why do you ask?'

'Oh well, you see, Lord Lloyd, some of the senior officials were thinking perhaps two or three weeks.'

'Disabuse their minds,' came the reply, 'of that comfortable and lethargic misapprehension.'

Here was both a driven and a driving man, loyal to his team and feared by the incompetent and lazy. When he started with Lord Lloyd, Toby soon realised how impossible and yet how wonderful he was to work for. Lord Camrose, proprietor of *The Daily Telegraph*, had told him his old job was always there, which was reassuring because the first weeks were difficult. He even had his resignation letter written, but his friends used to walk him up and down Ebury Street while he complained bitterly about how unreasonable Lloyd was, saying, 'Don't worry, just hold on and you will find that in the end it will be alright.' This turned out to be true. Once Lloyd had tested you, nothing was too good.

EASTERN APPROACHES

Almost immediately after his appointment, in February 1938, my father set off on a six-week trip, from 21st February to 4th April, covering most of Eastern Europe. His purpose was to find out the lie of the land, both from the embassies and missions and also from newspaper editors to see where Britain's point of view could be put across more successfully against the huge, well-financed and very efficient propaganda efforts of the Germans.

Reading his diary, it is sobering to speculate on the fate of the Eastern Europeans he dealt with. I recently met an elderly Pole whose whole family had been sent to exile for years in Siberia in 1940 along with thousands of others in long trains. Why? Because his father was a doctor and the Russians therefore considered him to be part of the 'intelligentsia'.

How much more horribly certain must have been the fate of

the pro-British editors and friendly government officials Toby met, let alone the Jewish editors and writers when overrun by either the Gestapo or the Russian NKVD.

Some extracts give us an insight into a long-forgotten Eastern Europe. First, the five and a half hour journey to Berlin in a tiny airliner.

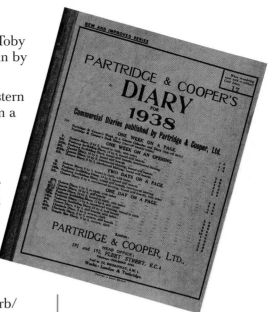

> **Monday 21st February, London.** Rose wearily, bid tearful farewell to Sylvia. To Horseferry House, KLM HQ. 7:40, Croydon in twin-engined Douglas 'hop' for Rotterdam. Berlin Embassy. Ambassador: 'Unless you are prepared to have a war with Italy, you must come to some agreement.' Francois Poncet, very depressed. All his prophecies made to me in 1936 have come true. This time he said, 'One day the time must come when you will **have** to fight'.

Yugoslavia already had all the depressing seeds of the Serb/Croat racial tensions which have re-surfaced so brutally sixty years later.

> **Friday 4th March, Budapest/Belgrade.** Dirty first-class carriage in a dirty, gloomy train. Truly, civilisation seems to end at Budapest! Frontier station of Subotica. Depressing compared with pleasant Strauss Operetta of smart uniforms on Hungarian side. Reminded of Wrzos' remark that 'it was like going into pre-war Russia, similar uniforms, similar searching for bombs under the seat, similar vast, unintelligent soldiers'. Belgrade 9:40. Through dishevelled streets to the Srpski-Kralj, the best hotel. Not bad room but I do not like the dirty looking gaps in the plaster of the walls. One never knows!

Plainly, the fear of listening devices was but one hint of a rather frightening picture of a Balkan region with brutish overtones, already efficiently infiltrated by the Germans.

> **Saturday 5th March, Belgrade.** Legation: Terence Shone, First Secretary, outlined situation, pointed out difference we were up against in propaganda, especially in matching the Germans in the schools.

> **Monday 7th March.** Stopped every few yards by policemen. Visit the fine building in which Sir Ronald Campbell was nearly hit when drunken opposition leader tried to shoot Stoyanidovitch. Sang-froid of Sir R. who confessed he did not know what was happening. Polish Minister complained that when he wanted to duck below the gallery, he found Turkish and Argentine Ministers already lying full length in front of him.

Gun fight at the Belgrade corral

The newspaper clipping reads:

Nos hôtes

M. O'BRIEN,
chef de l'Office de presse du Conseil britannique, à Sofia

Le dix mars, à 16 h. 30, est arrivé, venant d'Angleterre le chef de l'office de presse près le Conseil Britannique, M. O'Brien. Sur le quai de la gare l'h... nent a été salué par l...
de la l...

de presse près la legation de Grande-Bretagne, des journalistes bulgares et des ... s de la presse étrangère.

...hargé d'affaires de la léga-e-Bretagne, M. Coot a of-... de M. O'Brien, un diner

rection de la Ligue Britannique. Vendredi, à 13 h., à l'Union club, un diner a été offert en l'honneur de M. O'Brien. A ce diner assistalent MM. Coot, le président du l'Association des journalistes de Sofia, M. Metchkarov, plusieurs journalistes bulgares

Mister O'Brien İstanbuldan ayrıldı

İstanbul, 21 (Telefonla) — Birkaç gündenberi Ankara ve İstanbulda tedkikler yapan ingiliz enternasyonal fikri iş birliği konseyi basın şefi Mister O'Brien bu akşamki ekspresle Sofyaya hareket etti. Oradan Bükreşe geçecek ve Zagreb'e de uğradıktan sonra Londraya dönecektir.

Mister O'Brien konseyin teşekkül maksadı ve faaliyeti hakkında bana şu izahatı verdi:

— Konsey Sa Majeste Kral Hazretlerinin himayesindedir. 1934 de kurulmuştur. Konseyin teşekkül maksadı "ingiliz milletinin hayat ve tefekkürünü dünyaya tanıtmak,, diye hülâsa edilebilir.

Konsey münhasıran kültür işlerile uğraşır. Siyasi maksadı ve faaliyeti yoktur. Yaptığı ve yapacağı işler, yabancı milletler arasında ingiliz dilinin öğrenilmesi ve etüdünü kolaylaştırmaktır.

Ecnebi talebelerin İngilterede tahsil görmelerine veya tahsillerini bitirmelerine yardım etmek; İngiltere dışında yaşıyan milletlere, ingiliz milletinin yaşayış tarzı, hayat telâkkisi, sanat, ilim ve teknik kabiliyet hakkında malûmat vermek; bütün bunlar için de ecnebi memleketlerdeki ingiliz kültür müesseselerini ve cemiyetleri - ni takviye başta olmak üzere, bu memleketlere profesörler, konferansçılar göndermek; bu memleketlerdeki ing - liz kitabhanelerini ilme, güzel sanatlar ve tekniğe aid kitablar ve mecmualarla takviye etmek, ecnebi memleketler için bibliyografiler, yeni kitablara aid tenk dler neşretmek gibi tamamen kültürel faaliyetlerdir.

B. O'Brien Türkiye ve İngiltere arasındaki ekonomik ve siyasi münasebetlerin inkişafı dolayısile, Türkiyeye de geldiğini ve temaslarından memnun kaldığını ve bu temaslarının yakında güzel neticeler vereceğinden emin...

Sunday 13th March, Sofia. French Legation: Baclen, First Secretary, gloomy: 'We would probably lose the next war because of the effect of aerial bombardment on civilian populations'. German propaganda through the schools excellent. Some journalists bought.

It must have been a relief to reach Turkey, which was to maintain its neutrality in the coming war. Turkey had probably learned its lesson. If it had not foolishly joined Germany in 1914 and had the Ottoman Empire not been dismembered, Turkey would be one of the richest and most powerful countries on earth. In a world powered by oil, control of Saudi Arabia, Iraq, half of Iran, Kuwait and the Gulf would have been spectacular, coupled with a nation formerly rather good at creating empires by force of arms.

Monday 14th March, Istanbul. Under wing of Mr Cook (should have had an 'r' in his name). Offered to 'show me nightlife on my return'. No thank you, Mr Pimp! From Taurus Express, islands are lovely but heavily fortified. Anyone approaching gets fired on. Sir George Clarke's yacht was stopped. He wanted to catch red mullet, being a passionate gourmet and fisherman. Turks could not believe in such things in an Ambassador!

Tale of 'island of dogs'. No water on it. When it was decreed that the stray dogs of Istanbul should go, kind-hearted Turks could not kill them but left them to kill each other and die of thirst on the island!

Tuesday 15th March, Angora. Ambassador, Sir P. Lorraine: 'Turks friendly but absolutely uncultivated. No interest in culture at all.' Turks allow no propaganda from Germans and Italians in the way of pampering students, as in Yugoslavia. Mehmed Essel, Minister at the Turkish Foreign Office. Sent us to Head of *Agence Anatolie*, very helpful Anglophile.

The meticulous care with which the Germans operated came as a shock:

Wednesday 16th March. *Direction de la Presse.* Very helpful, said German press attaché produces stuff of exactly the right length and character for *each page of a newspaper.*

Tuesday 22nd March, Sofia. Woken at 6:00 by frontier officials. Blasted British Council had only got me a visa for one entry into Bulgaria! Officials 'gave' me another but took nearly all my money, so not enough money to pay taxi.

Thursday 24th March. Neat tidy little stations. Station Master and officials standing to attention as we drew out, saluting the guard. Station policemen in spiked helmets like pre-war British infantry of the line.

In Romania, to counter German influence, we read of Toby's plans for a formal state visit to Britain by King Carol and Prince Michael.

Friday 25th March, Bucharest, Romania. Legation: Sir Reginald Hoare, the Minister. Discussed Jewish problem. Girard appeals to personal cupidity of each villager by suggesting a *particular* Jewish house they might be given. Reed, Third Secretary, is very nice but a little pansy. Terrifying driver. Nearly had fearful smash after lunch. Matcescu arrived. He is apparently the local Napoleon and gets a little out of hand. Rare example of Romanian full of energy.

In such difficult times, it is sad to see that opposition to anything as helpful as a Royal state visit came from both Romanian and British directions.

Saturday 26th March. First to Matcescu's stamping ground, the well-appointed premises of the Anglo-Romanian Society. Then to *Curentul*, chief Anglophile paper, where the proprietor was being shaved surrounded by collaborators. Next to *Cuvântul*, Iron Guard newspaper, suppressed for four years. Hopeless! Proprietor pro-German. Reed took me out in his car, after hitting a peasant on the way! Romania is the land of jay-walkers. Reed says King Carol spoke perfect English but gives the impression of not wanting to hear unpleasant things. Would be popular but for Ionescu. Apparently old King George had said, 'And if King Carol wants to come to England, please discourage him from the idea. Some of the younger members of my family do not like the idea of shaking hands with him. Of course, they'd do it if I told them to, but still.'

Monday 28th March. Very pleasant English-speaking reporter of *Cuvântul* came to interview me with a caracaturist, who made me look like Charles Laughton. I have put on

UNE RÉCEPTION A LA «MAISON DES ANGLAIS» EN L'HON-NEUR DE M. O'BRIEN

Sir Reginald Hoare, ministre de Grande Bretagne, M. D. Dimancesco, directeur général de la presse, M. Alfred Hefter, M. Raoul Anasthasiu, M. Alex. Sandulesco et M. Gibson. En haut (à gauche): M. O'Brien du "British Council" et Sir Reginald Hoare

O convorbire cu d. O'Brien

„British Council" pentru propaganda culturală engleză și vizita ziaristului O'Brien în Capitală

D. T. O'Brien și d. Dem. Dimanco Rom

Zilele acestea a sosit în Capitală ziaristul englez D. E. G. O'Brien, colaborator al marelui cotidian londonez, „Daily Telegraph", care împreună cu „Times" și alte câteva ziare de tiraj mare formează aristocrația presei din „Fleet Street".

Ziaristul englez a venit în Capitală în calitate de șef al departamentului presei al institutului en-

M. E. D. O'BRIEN A BUCAREST

M. O'Brien est notre hôte depuis une semaine. Il est très jeune, bien que déjà fort connu dans la presse londonaise. Il fut pendant un certain temps un des principaux collaborateurs du „Daily Telegraph", sous le pseudonyme de „Peterborough".

Actuellement M. O'Brien est chef de la presse au „British Council". Au cours d'une rencontre, nous avons profité d'un trop bref entretien pour faire exposer à M. O'Brien les buts de son voyage. Voici ce que notre distingué hôte a bien voulu nous communiquer pour les lecteurs du „Moment".

— J'ai entrepris ce voyage, comme délégué du British Council, dont je suis le directeur au service de presse. J'ai visité Varsovie, Vienne, Budapest, Belgrade, Sofia, Istamboul, Ankara et me voici à Bucarest.

M. E. D. O'BRIEN

two stone on this trip and I am not a pleasant sight! Popescu's son-in-law very friendly. Will take as much stuff as we can give him. We spoke freely on the German danger. Tipped me off that Romanian General Staff Officer had complained about the waste of money in sending King Carol to London as England was 'finished anyway'. Nice obverse to Labour Party's motion demanding that £5,000 should not be spent by us on the Carol visit!

In Croatia, the incompatible hatreds and tensions with the Serbs were very evident. In the coming war, the Croats eventually joined the Germans– re-fuelling the hatred for generations to come.

Friday 1st April, Zagreb. On leaving *Obzov* newspaper, got caught in a demonstration between Croats and Serbs at the Opera House. Man chased by nasty-looking policeman down street then into doorway. Watched police swinging into him. These police, extra special toughs, use short, nasty bayonets on slightest provocation.

Saturday 2 April. Visited Dr Matchak. Passed guard of hulking peasants into an ante-chamber filled with more. Croats prepared to support France and Britain if Belgrade continued support for Germany (and vice versa). Croats would never go back to Belgrade Parliament. Once bitten, twice shy. Never again! Complete autonomy within boundaries of Yugoslavia is only solution.

Finally, Toby sets off home, but not without a sad reminder that problems existed on our own doorstep.

Sunday 3 April. Orient Express on a glorious gold and green morning. Scenery too lovely to be missed so I ventured to restaurant car. Particularly lovely mountain crowned with a church gleaming white in the morning sun, 3,000 feet above us. I was so impressed that, in want of a better audience, I exclaimed on it to a Belfast businessman, a revolting, smug, lean, Black Protestant type. He eyed it sourly for a moment and growled sullenly, 'I expect it's a Catholic one, though'.

Monday 4 April, Paris/London. Back in Ebury Street and saw my adorable wife looking even more lovely than before.

One striking aspect of this tour was the tremendous media coverage given to a young man who was, after all, 'only' a former fellow journalist and who was not exactly famous. The countries that he visited must have already been urgently searching for friends.

The lessons in Eastern Europe were well learned. Everywhere there was evidence of Germany's propaganda professionalism, backed by a wall of money. In 1940, a US official White Paper on Germany said that the Nazis were spending £50 million each year on Fifth Column and propaganda. The British Council's 1939 budget was £5,000.

Toby came back with an embryo mailing list of foreign editors and with ideas for expansion. Before the end of 1938, he had recruited Tom Lindsay and Colin Mann.

His first venture was a daily *London Letter* in English. The success of this handout illustrates the progress of the British Council's Press Division. The *Letter* then went out as:

Weekly London Letter in English, French and Spanish
Weekly Empire Letter
Weekly Letter for South America in English and Spanish

The daily and weekly letters were further translated into Turkish, Serbo-Croat, Portuguese, German (for Switzerland), Swedish, Arabic, Greek, Iranian, Indian vernaculars, Malay, Chinese and Japanese.

To improve the methods of getting Britain's message to the world's press, he succeeded in getting press attachés appointed in *all* key capitals, instead of just four or five. He also instituted a series of journalists' visits from neutral and other countries, including Denmark, Sweden, Norway, Portugal, Spain, Cyprus, France, and from Turkey twice. According to our Ambassador in Ankara, the first Turkish visit was instrumental in bringing about the Anglo-Turkish Pact and the second helped to keep Turkey undismayed by gathering Axis power.

A typical foreign journalists' group visiting 10 Downing Street. Toby, 3rd from right.

CHAPTER 5 WAR CLOUDS

All through 1938, the visible threat from Germany increased with the unopposed re-occupation of the Rhineland and the *Anschluss* with Austria. Toby's propaganda efforts also increased.

He still had with him Tom Lindsay and Colin Mann, and in addition to the visits from the foreign press and the *Letters*, they strengthened ties with the foreign press. The British Council's Press Division was the first organisation to assist the Foreign Press Association (FPA). It secured special facilities for the FPA for such functions as the launch of the 'Queen Elizabeth' and the visit of President Lebrun – if not without difficulty.

The Press Division encouraged the publication of French and Belgian newspapers. It later brought out, at 36 hours notice, a special 20,000 circulation one-day newspaper, *Le Quatorze Juillet*, for the French National Festival in 1940, and organised celebrations for De Gaulle's forces. Pending the establishment of a regular French paper, the Council issued a daily broadsheet for French camps which reached a 7,000 circulation. The Council's two specials in French and Flemish *La Belgique en Guerre* led to the publication of the Belgian daily *La Belgique Independente*.

Toby's diary continues to give us an insight into an atmosphere growing ever more tense, visited by his Romanian collaborator:

Tuesday 3 May 1938. Matcescu visited me, a more mad megalomaniac glare in his eye than ever. Lunched with Vernon Bartlet who said he thought war was now practically inevitable.

Saturday 7 May 1938. Heard a good story about a publicity agent who went to Berlin with 'publicity' on his passport plus his address as 'Thames House, Millbank'. He lost his camera and luggage. On protesting, he was told that only an Englishman would have the infernal cheek to protest, when he had on his passport the fact that he was in the Secret Service ('publicity'), and gave the address of his HQ. (Thames House actually does contain, on the 5th floor, MI 5).

Sometimes, sadly, the opposition to his efforts did not come from overseas:

Tuesday 10 May 1938. Executive Committee of British Council. Attlee automatically opposed our paying press attachés on the grounds 'we ought to create them and in any case the whole Foreign Office ought to be overhauled'.

Taking part in a military exercise for the benefit of an Icelandic press group

Lord Lloyd rejected this and pointed out the urgency of our problems and by the time the Foreign Office would have been overhauled the 'whole world would be up in smoke'.

The visits of journalists from neutral countries continued as fast as they could be organised:

Tuesday 7 June 1938. Visited Anton Brown, Manager of the Dorchester. Fixed that the Turks could go there for 25 shillings a day. Dinner with Michael Creswell. Very interesting about the Czech crisis. Our ambassador in Berlin, Nevile Henderson very tired, overworked and very disillusioned as a result of Austria. It is always the most ardent Germanophiles who are the most 'untaüscht' (disappointed).

Michael Creswell, one of Toby's greatest friends, was Third Secretary in our Berlin embassy. He became so horrified both by appeasement and how he felt his Ambassador, Nevile Henderson, was being hood-winked by the Nazis, that he was passing evidence of the real and dangerous situation to others – notably Winston Churchill.

Later in Spain, he help to run *Comête*, the Belgium-based escape route for allied airmen, for which he got little help from our Madrid Embassy. This was understandable, as the Ambassador, Sam Hoare, was trying to keep the tricky Franco neutral and he did not need to provoke the Germans and thus to 'compromise the mission.'

Michael's divergence from Foreign Office views seemed to do him no harm in the long run as he ended his career as a distinguished Ambassador.

Toby's job was devoted to heading off the Germans 'at the pass'. But in the case of the Spanish Civil War, Toby's sympathies were with the Nationalists, in spite of their German support, and against the pro-Russian Republic. Luis Bolín in his book *Spain: the vital years* recounts:

'The papers in London reported that the Republicans had released from the Alberche dam a wall of water 20 feet high which had 'swept 20,000 rebels to their doom, submerging 500 tanks and 5,000 lorries' (at a time when on this front we had no tanks and a couple of dozen lorries).

An Irish friend of mine, Toby O'Brien, who in later years helped me to lure countless British tourists to Spain, was walking up St James's Street when he came across Carlos González Gordon, a mutual friend. 'Carlos! The news looks bad!' 'Yes,' answered Carlos, 'and it is even worse than it looks. We are fighting for Church and country, and we had reasonable expectations that Providence would be on our side. Alas, this clearly isn't so. For only God could make water flow uphill!'.'

Sir Nevile Henderson (left) with Goering. Too easily tricked by the Nazis?

Pro-Republican Stephen Spender, who Toby plainly thought should stick to poetry, got a stinging rebuke

TO THE EDITOR OF THE TIMES

Sir, – Your correspondent, Mr. Stephen Spender, in his letter on the Spanish art treasures now in the hands of the Valencian Government, displays a pretty wit.

I liked especially the sentence in which he records with satisfaction for the benefit of art lovers that 'many unknown treasures from private libraries and collections have now been brought to light for the first time.'

It would be interesting to know exactly how these treasures in private hands were 'brought to light'. Also it would be not uninteresting to hear the views of the owners of the treasures – such of the owners, of course, as are still alive to have these views – on these 'discoveries.'

No doubt we shall soon see receivers of stolen property, if not actually the burglars themselves, congratulated in the police courts on their public-spirited action in 'bringing to light' property formerly in private hands.

I am, Sir, yours, &c.,

EDWARD DONOUGH O'BRIEN.

July 21st, 1938

Admiralty Arch

Monday 5 September. At 3:30 pm to Admiralty. Was shown the Wireless Tower, a very exciting room. Aerials on top of the Admiralty are bogus, a sort of memorial to Jackie Fisher. All transmission done by landline to big stations outside London. Incoming calls received direct, coded messages sent down to the War Registry. It's a matter of minutes before an important message is received, decoded, typed and sent to the High Office. Director of Naval Construction has a model office where designs for new ships are produced as models so that the Board can get an idea of what they will look like. Yale lock on the door with a bell to discourage spies!

To most people in Britain, it now looked almost certain that we would soon be at war in 1938:

Cynical post-card at the time of the Munich negotiations

Monday 12 September. Papers said things were looking better. Mentioned it to Lloyd who said, on the contrary, they couldn't be worse. He just had half an hour with Lord Halifax and the Secret Service reports that October 24th was 'der Tag'. Hitler sure that we wouldn't move. Keitel had sent an emissary to Lloyd to try and get him to urge the Government to make the position clear before too late. This General had said again and again, 'Mais alors, Excellence, c'est décidé.'

Tried to listen to German broadcast on the radio but as my set was sold to me by John Stone (alias Jeser Steinberg, British-Polish origin), it refused on ideological grounds to function properly!

The door hasn't slammed quite, the fact that Hitler didn't define his demands is a good sign.

Tuesday 13 September. Things looking very black again today. Rioting in Sudetenland. Bridge asked me whether I was going to join the Territorials or any other unit.

In the event, of course, Chamberlain returned waving his bit of paper and France and Britain sold out the Czechs at Munich, buying a few months respite at the tragic expense of others.

We now know quite how weak Germany was at the

time of Munich and how much brutal bluff played its role. Apart from coal, Germany had no abundance of key metals – oil, rubber or aluminium, little hard currency to buy such materials and complete vulnerability to blockade. During Munich, the Luftwaffe was desperate because it knew that its aviation fuel was at 25% of mobilisation requirements and aviation lubricants at barely 6%. Its engines would have seized!

To try to impress them that Britain was not going to be a walkover, my father took a group of neutral and British Empire journalists to an RAF fighter station. After looking at the Spitfires and Hurricanes, the party was invited back to the Officers' Mess.

The Squadron Leader turned to a huge Nigerian Editor and said: 'Well Mr Umbambo, I don't expect you've ever had British suet pudding before'.

The Editor lifted the plate to his noise, sniffed vigorously and put the plate down, 'Well, it sho' don't smell too entrancin'.

The Nigerian delegation recovering from the suet pudding

THE ROMANIAN CARPET

The culmination of the Romanian royal visit which Toby had been preparing for a year was the investiture of King Carol with the Order of the Garter.

Wednesday 16 November. King Carol learned about being given the Garter from me. Prepare to go to Palace. Sylvia's dress looked perfectly lovely, my knee britches terribly tight at the knee but my calves generally admired!

Left at 10:15 for Palace in a big Daimler plus a footman. Drove into inner courtyard which is huge. Vast portico and red carpet, lashings of flunkies in royal scarlet (which *mine* are entitled to wear!). Difficult to decide whether to wear one's white gloves or not. Compromised by wearing one and carrying the other. Had a few words with Anthony Eden, Harold Nicholson, the Kennedys and old Lady Cory, whom I pleased by christening 'The Belgravia Battler'.

Toby and Sylvia at Buckingham Palace for the King Carol Garter ceremony

The doors were thrown open and we saw Royal Family and King Carol while the band played Romanian national anthem (sounds like a dreary Wesleyan hymn). King and Queen and Queen Mary came down into the room (old Lord Russell being very garrulous to Queen Mum, who took no notice). King Carol and Prince Michael talked to various people. Michael is a tall, handsome boy with a deep voice. He betrays his heredity by quizzing the younger, prettier ladies, over the shoulders of the old trouts who are presented to him. Fell in love with the Duchess of Kent again. Michael was obviously getting off with her.

The whole thing was both glittering and informal and we enjoyed ourselves immensely. Amused by the extremely lower middle-class pleasure of that democrat, Sir Walter Layton, when presented to Carol and by the girlishness of the Queen's voice. Very charming. The whole Family looked as though they were enjoying themselves.

Buckingham Palace is the most overheated house in the land. Happily, about 12:00, when *they* had withdrawn, Ronald Storrs threw up his head like a questing hound and led the way to the Supper Room, the whole company following with lolling tongues!

Sadly, the effort to keep Romania on the side of the Allies was in vain. Nine months later King Carol was deposed by the pro-German Marshal Ion Antonescu who committed his country-men to active German alliance. Told by Hitler of the plans for

---

Decade of deceit

POLAND

'Poland and Germany can look forward to the future with full confidence in the solid basis of their mutual relations.'

Ribbentrop speech, Warsaw
25th January 1939

'During the troubled months of the past year, the friendship between Germany and Poland has been one of the most reassuring factors in the political life of Europe.'

Hitler, Reichstag speech
30th January 1939

'There is therefore no question of sparing Poland, and we are left with the decision to attack Poland at the first suitable opportunity. We cannot expect a repetition of the Czech affair. There will be war. Our task is to isolate Poland. The success of the isolation will be decisive.'

Hitler, military conference,
23rd May 1939

'Now, Poland is in the position in which I wanted her .... I am only afraid that at the last moment some Schweinehund will make a proposal for mediation.'

Hitler, military conference
22nd August 1939

'Barbarossa', the invasion of Russia, he exclaimed with delight, 'Of course, I'll be there from the start. When it's a question of action against the Slavs, you can always count on Romania'.

Such enthusiasm was to cost them dear. Having already lost 98,000 men at the siege of Odessa, it was the two weak, under-equipped Romanian Third and Fourth Armies that the Russians chose to strike and destroy in order to spring the trap on the Germans in Stalingrad.

After his handling of the Royal visit, my father was offered an award by the Romanian Embassy. He could have opted for an important-sounding decoration, complete with sashes and medals to be worn at various functions, but was advised that this would almost certainly get stolen on its way from Bucharest. It would be much better to opt for a traditional peasant carpet! We still have that carpet in the drawing room, somewhat threadbare now, and I often think it is somewhat disrespectful to walk on it as it really represents a obscure but well-earned middle European decoration from a long-destroyed middle European monarchy.

Our Royal Family's reputation for having excellent memories is legendary and not always dependent on briefing. After my father organised the state visit of King Carol of Romania, he met the Royal Family several times. At one of several parties at Buckingham Palace, the Queen sat him down on a sofa with a drink and chatted away. She asked if he was married and whether his wife was at the event, and he very proudly said that she could not attend because 'she had just presented him with a little baby boy'. This is where I come in.

At the height of the war, in the middle of 1943, my mother was by herself at another event and was introduced to the Queen, who amazingly, just from the name, said, 'Ah, the little boy must be about four now, mustn't he?'

I was born on April 23rd 1939, but only just. The doctor arrived hours late, drunk. My father, who had been helping the midwife struggle to extricate me from an umbilical cord wrapped around my neck, took some pleasure in snarling on the doorstep, 'Don't worry, doctor, it's a boy!'

By the middle of 1939, few illusions about Germany's intentions remained as Hitler began to turn his attentions to Poland. In August, the unexpected bombshell of Germany's cynical Non-Aggression Pact with Russia sealed Poland's fate. The German steam-roller was ready to move.

POLAND

ROYAL FAMILY MEMORIES

Queen Elizabeth, during the war

DARKNESS FALLS

On the morning of Friday September 1st, 800 miles to the East, German Panzers and Stukas hurled themselves against a proud but out-gunned Poland.

Saturday 2nd September. The balloon in the square going up – its ears hanging and looking very sad. Out into a strange new world of policemen, their customary helmets discarded, and blue steel helmets and gas mask satchels. Sandbags everywhere. Police look so much less significant in their steel helmets, rather as the Guards bereft of their bearskins and scarlet tunics and clad in service kit look on duty outside the Palace.

The diary of that tense day reveals something which is particularly important to me. My father had always claimed to have written the scurrilous version of Colonel Bogey ('Hitler has only got one ball.') when sitting in the bath chatting to my mother. I never really quite believed him because I thought it was almost too wonderful a propaganda coup. But here is the proof, also written on 2nd September.

To Lawrence's in St. James's Place, drank there with him. His champagne people have broken all his contracts and dropped him flat. Three thousand a year just stopped! To Martinez restaurant, with George Nicholson etc. Shocked everybody by our levity. Sang our excellent song – made up by Sylvia and I last week:

> *Goering has only got one ball,*
> *Hitler's so very small*
> *Himmler's so very similar*
> *And Goebbels has noebbels at all!*

Later, the words, rhyme and scansion were polished, but I am really delighted to verify my father's authorship, which within three weeks the *Daily Mail* further confirmed:

There are now about 40 current war songs with alleged topical appeal.

Miss Gracie Fields has chosen 'Wish Me Luck' as her 'National cheer-up song'. There are two Siegfried Line songs, 'The Old Tin Helmet,' 'With My Gas Mask on My Shoulder', 'Nobody Loves a Lady Like a Soldier', 'The Daughter of a Mademoiselle from Armentières', 'Run, Rabbit, Run', and 'Even Hitler had a Mother' among them.

But the song which is really spreading like wildfire among the troops is a charmingly unprintable version of 'Colonel Bogey', with the most asterisked references to Hitler and his Council of Six.

The new version is attributed to someone not unconnected with our old friend the British Council.

With Britain now officially at war, the well-organised British Council team *tried* to swing smoothly into action:

> **Thursday 7th September.** Ministry of Information had come to me and asked me to order up various photographs for dispatch to our missions and contacts abroad for use the moment war broke out. With super-human efforts, we got photos captioned and several thousand prints in various languages dispatched last Friday morning. Today, the censorship office, which is equally under the Ministry of Information, sent back most of our photographs addressed to Missions, with a pink printed slip saying that 'Picture postcards may no longer be sent abroad!' This, I think, is the all-time height of inefficiency in that incredible Ministry.

Thus the dear old Ministry of Information, which was presumably meant to be a propaganda body, surpassed itself in the early days of the war by failing to allow a single piece of its *own* written material or photographs to get past its own censorship!

In response to a desperate plea from our Embassy in Stockholm for photographs which had all been published, often years before the war, half were blocked by the Ministry. They included a photograph of old H.M.S. *Collingwood* in which King George VI served at the Battle of Jutland – 'Sorry, dear boy, battleship... I'm afraid, battleship'. The censor was still unmoved when Toby pointed out that H.M.S. *Collingwood* was scrapped in 1922.

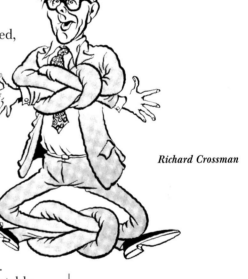

Richard Crossman

One foreign journalist asked for a copy of the millions of leaflets which our aircrews, at great risk, were dropping all over Germany. These leaflets were compiled by Dick Crossman, later MP, and were addressed to a non-existent Socialist opposition which they hoped would cause the walls of the Nazi Jericho to fall flat. The censor was horrified. 'Good God, my dear man' he exclaimed, thumping the table. 'Don't you realise they might get into enemy hands?'

Stories of attempted secrecy must include the admirable War Office directive in the first few weeks of the war, where certain officers received an envelope marked **Confidential**. Inside it was another marked **Secret**. Inside that, was another marked **Very Secret**. And inside this last was a memorandum which read:

> The Royal Automobile Club has extended honorary membership to officers serving in the War Office during the duration of hostilities.

GOING TO THE TOP

Lord Lloyd (centre, right) welcomes a Spanish delegation. Toby, back, left

The Ministry of Information was not the only barrier to the fledgling propaganda efforts.

The Treasury insisted on charging three times the commercial rate for some of the few photographs that Toby *could* get past the censorship. As he noted in his diary in despair: 'If we lose this coming war, on the tombstone of the British Empire should be written:

> Here lies the British Empire, which perished for lack of timely Treasury sanction for its continuation.'

The curious attitude of Ministry of Information and Treasury colleagues was more than matched by the British and French High Command, who did everything in their power to block or delay news from the front. The American media found it much easier to work out of Berlin, where the press corps swelled by 100 correspondents overnight. William Shirer, whose *Berlin Diary* captured the atmosphere so well, witnessed the collapse of his beloved France from travelling with the invading German forces.

Goebbels, himself a journalist by training, even instituted *Propaganda Kompanien* (propaganda companies), staffed with former journalists, photographers and broadcasters who were to perform a valuable service for German combat news-gathering. The PK suffered the same casualties, incidentally, as the units to which they were attached.

After months of intense pressure, Lord Lloyd said, 'I know, Toby, when you first came to work for me you decided, like most other people, that I was a bloody man, but I think now you will agree that I was only trying you out.'

The other and very positive side of the coin continued to be Lloyd's fierce loyalty and his willingness to go to the very top to get his way.

As an example, back in the Spring of 1939 with months to go before the outbreak of war, French President Lebrun was to arrive on a state visit. This was of vast importance as it was, in effect, the re-creation of the 'Entente Cordiale'.

The Department of Works announced that there were no chairs available for the 150-strong Foreign Press Association, a group whom the British Council was desperately trying to nurture. Toby got Lloyd on his side.

Lloyd called an official at the Foreign Office. 'What's the matter? Why can't we have these seats?'

'Well, Barker of the Office of Works says we can't have any more seats.'

'Does he, by God! You know, Charles', said George Lloyd with magnificent effrontery, 'that I am probably the most reasonable man in the British Empire, but I am in danger of losing my temper. Will you tell me please who Mr Barker is, and what the Office of Works is that it should stand between the British Empire and its publicity. Will you tell him, with Lord Lloyd's compliments, that unless I get 150 seats within the hour, I shall get in my car and I shall come down and see Edward Halifax [Foreign Secretary] and Philip Sassoon [Head of the Office of Works] and by the time I have finished speaking to them somebody is going to wish he had never been born – and I rather suspect it is going to be Mr Barker of the Office of Works.'

They received two hundred seats within half an hour.

One of the things he taught Toby is that you must never take anything that officialdom says for granted. Thus:

'We can't do so-and-so.'

'Why not?'

'It's the opinion of the Foreign Office.'

'My dear, how soon will you learn that the opinion of the Foreign Office is far too often only the ill-considered views of a clerk in a garret.'

In the early days of the War, Toby told him that they were unable to do something because it was a 'War Office decision'.

'*Who* at the War Office gave you that message?'

'Brigadier Smith.'

'Put me through to Brigadier Smith at the War Office … 'Brigadier, Lord Lloyd here. What is this damn silly nonsense about our not being able to do so-and-so?'

'I'm sorry Lord Lloyd. That was an Army Council decision.'

'Who on the Army Council conveyed that decision to you?'

'General Jones.'

'Put me through to General Jones … General Jones, what is this damned silly nonsense? Oh, I can't go on arguing with you – put me through to the Secretary of State [who was then Anthony Eden] … Anthony, what the devil is this damn silly nonsense? No wonder we look like losing this war, if that is what your Army Council is like. You must realise, of course, that it is a silly decision. How soon can you let me know that you have rescinded it?'

'Oh, of course George, I will do that at once.'

And rescinded it was!

TURKISH DELIGHT

Lord Lloyd's support was constantly invaluable and never more so over the potential fate of Toby's last Turkish delegation in May 1940. This consisted of the Chiefs of their Army and Naval staffs, plus all the Editors and proprietors of the pro-allied Turkish Press. After success in Britain, Toby was about to deliver them to France.

'For God's sake, don't,' said a colleague in Paris. 'The Germans are winning and we are probably pulling out tonight for Bordeaux.'

It became vital to get this important group back to Turkey, quickly and safely. Toby rang up Transport Command, reached an Air Marshal Peck and asked him to find a flying boat to take the Turks back through the Mediterranean.

He said, 'Absolute nonsense, O'Brien. There is not a hope.'

Toby said, 'Really?' He got in his car and went down to see Lloyd at the Colonial Office, who took the point at once.

'Get me the Secretary of State for Air … Archie, it is too bad. You know how important the Turks are at this stage of the War and yet some bloody fool of an Air Marshal person … what's his name Toby?'

'I think Peck, Sir.'

'Peck says we cannot have a flying boat. Will you let me know how soon and from whence they are to leave?'

'I'll be back to you in half an hour, George.'

Within ten minutes, he rang again, 'Get me Sir Archibald Sinclair … Archie, just too bad. We are still waiting to hear from whence our Turks are going to leave.' The Turks left Poole four hours later in a flying boat and used their influence to keep Turkey out of the war.

This forceful and brilliant man was suddenly lost to the nation in January 1941. He died within a few days 'of a mysterious virus'.

LISBON LAMENT

Toby visited the capital of Britain's oldest ally in the dark days of June and July 1940.

It was considered certain that the victorious Germans would sweep right through Spain to attack Gibraltar and invade Portugal to secure the Atlantic seaboard. The Germans in Lisbon themselves boasted that they would 'take Portugal by telephone'. Indeed, there was nothing to stop them.

In the circumstances, it was perhaps not surprising that the British colony in Lisbon was in a pretty state of jitters. They urged Sir Walford Selby, our Ambassador, that it was his duty to ask for shipping to evacuate. Sir Walford summoned them to the Embassy, where he gave them hell. He pointed out that they had enjoyed the protection of Britain and the hospitality of Portugal for years and it was their duty to remain where they were and accept whatever fate had in store for them. In any case, Britain needed every ton of shipping in her hour of crisis and he had not the slightest intention of asking for even the smallest vessel.

This first-class diatribe did much to strengthen the morale of the British, and through them the Portuguese, at a moment when from outside it looked as if we must be beaten.

There was, above all, a sense of impotent fury and anxiety. The day that France fell, a gigantic Swastika flag flew from the German Embassy, next door to the British. It look as if it had been specially woven for the occasion.

However, life in Lisbon was enlivened by the ineptitude of the German spies, who positively littered the place. At one stage in Lisbon, a German spy of such repeated incompetence prompted Toby to write through diplomatic channels direct to Admiral Canaris, head of the Abwehr saying: 'Surely you can do better than this. Don't you know there's a war on?' Canaris may not have been trying very hard. He was later to die by the Führer's orders, hanging from a meat hook after his role in the attempted 1944 assassination.

Admiral Canaris

Meanwhile, my father's elder brother, my uncle Turlough O'Brien, served as an officer in the Royal Artillery. He started in an anti-aircraft battery where they were equipped with old-fashioned three inch guns which he considered pretty useless. His only military claim to fame was after the Luftwaffe's devastating raid on Coventry in November 1940. His battery had banged away at the unseen raiders all night to no good effect, but in the morning a lone, very high Junkers 88 came over to photograph the Germans' handywork. Turlough said that the only technique left was to try to hit it as you would at a pheasant shoot, 'So, I gave it about a mile lead and hit it right in the beak.'

He then went into the Western desert, where he again regarded the British guns as little short of pathetic, with muzzle velocity and hitting power so feeble that he described his shells as turning lazily end over end!

As we now know, the blitz and the raids on provincial British cities presaged Germany's eventual defeat. The RAF was not to be beaten and Britain could not be invaded. Germany's bluff was at last being called. Years later, my researches as an amateur military historian revealed that in spite of its vigour, efficiency and willpower in other spheres, Germany's attitude to production, especially in aircraft and tanks, was curiously

COVENTRY RIPOSTE

Turlough O'Brien

feeble. Britain was outproducing Germany within weeks of the beginning of the war. For two years, German forces would become relatively weaker. For instance, it attacked France with 2,700 tanks. For the huge scale of the attack on Russia, her Panzer forces could only muster 3,500 tanks. It was partly over-confidence, partly a lack of trained workers and, of course, lack of raw materials. But in 1941 Erhard Milch, desperately trying to sort out the chaos of the Luftwaffe's production, discovered that Messerschmitt were diverting precious engine aluminium to make vineyard ladders!

EVACUATION

I now had a baby sister, Natalie. Like many children during the war, we were evacuated with my mother and grandparents to escape from the bombing and later the 'doodle-bugs', as the V1's were called, first to Edenbridge in Kent and then to Snape in Suffolk. When you are tiny you only remember little impressions. Like seeing London from the train covered in a carpet of barrage balloons. Or the whole place appearing to be full of soldiers. Or the cars in Chelsea with petrol caps hanging out, having had their precious rationed petrol siphoned away by thieves. Or being offered the first banana to be seen in months – and hating it. Or the local bull being killed by a stray V1 rocket. And being told not to move until the resulting jagged window frame from the same explosion was gently removed from round my neck – a narrow escape.

At Snape, my boyish military enthusiasm was also enhanced when waking one morning we found that our well-ordered and charming orchard was entirely full of Sherman tanks. Joy of joys! I spent two days being lifted up on to these apparent monsters, lowered into the turrets, looking through gun-sights, and being thoroughly spoiled by the American crews, who had managed to turn left in the dark through our hedge, rather than right, into their invasion park where they were meant to be.

Much to my disappointment, my grandfather persuaded them to leave and then laboriously, for a whole week, rebuilt the tall hedge between the orchard and the road. After a few days, Heaven! Exactly the

GRIMSDALE

same thing happened and the orchard was full of tanks again, crewed by another troop of our transatlantic allies, who also seemed to have great difficulty navigating.

How they fared in Normandy, who can guess? For what I thought were monster tanks were soon to be dubbed the 'Ronsons' as they burst into flames hit by the dreaded 88's and long 75mm guns of their experienced Panzer opponents.

I must have become a mascot to a lot of troops because in church I used to get bored between the verses of the hymns and sang newly-learned words like, 'She'll be coming round the mountain when she comes'. Thank goodness, it was quite a respectable song compared with some they *might* have taught me!

One of my father's best friends over the years was Mark Chapman-Walker, who followed him into Conservative Central Office and was later Managing Director of the *News of the World.* He was a somewhat raffish character and there are many splendid, often unprintable, stories of his escapades as a young man.

In 1943, Mark was on the staff of Field Marshal 'Jumbo' Wilson in Cairo. One morning his boss informed him that they would be participating in the Ambassador's shoot at the week-end, an event to which King Farouk was traditionally invited. Mark protested that shooting was not high on his list of skills and that he did not even possess any guns. 'Jumbo' brushed his protests aside and so Mark was trapped, knowing full well that he was likely to make a fool of himself.

He found himself out on the mud flats with two Arab boys aged about 12. One was to act as a loader for his two borrowed shotguns (such was the number of birds he was meant to account for), and the other to plunge into the shallows and retrieve the birds, an Egyptian substitute for a spaniel.

All morning, clouds of birds poured over Mark's head. All morning he fired both guns until they were too hot to touch. Not a single bird fell.

This performance became only too public at lunchtime, because in a formal ceremony, the Egyptian boys lined up with notices as to who their masters were and with the birds they had shot. In front of 'Lt. Col. Chapman-Walker', there was no pile of birds, just sand.

The Field Marshal took him aside in a fury and told him to have 'an extremely good lunch'. Perhaps that would relax him enough to shoot straight.

Mark did as he was told. After a liquid lunch, birds poured over his head again, but still he missed. The little Arab retriever

UNEXPECTED HELP

Tom Bird, General 'Jumbo' Wilson and Mark Chapman-Walker, 1943

49

was now hysterically babbling advice in Arabic, and Mark, losing his temper, thrust the gun at him and said, 'If *you're* so bloody clever, *you* do the shooting.' The boy raised the gun with a practised swing and the first two birds splashed into the shallows.

Mark later said, 'I wasn't going to spoil that excellent combination, so I took off my boots, rolled up my trousers and plunged into the water to retrieve the birds while my two Arab boys, like a well-oiled machine, banged bird after bird out of the sky'.

At tea-time 'Jumbo' Wilson looked at the huge pile in front of Mark's well-tipped team and said, 'There, Mark, I told you to have a good lunch'.

ROYAL ACCIDENT

A month later Mark was joined on 'Jumbo's' staff by another ADC, Tom Bird, now a shooting friend of mine. Tom recalls a crash in November 1943 between a British truck and the car of King Farouk, whom the Allies had slowly weaned away from a pro-Axis stance.

Disrespect had set in early. When Farouk staggered into the nearby military hospital and announced himself as King Farouk of Egypt, the Desk Corporal said, 'That's OK, Sir. I'm King George of England. Now please sit down and wait your turn.'

Even though the King was at fault, always driving too fast, the British authorities held a Court of Enquiry in order to satisfy both the Egyptian people and media that they were taking the matter extremely seriously. Trooper Jones was marched in and gave his evidence.

'I was driving along the Canal road when there was a flash of white, and a crash of metal. I stopped the vehicle and ran back down the road and there on its side was a big white Mercedes. Lying in the road were these two wogs.'

Uproar and consternation, not least from the Egyptian press. The President of the Court cleared everyone from the room, ordering that the statement be struck from the record.

'Look, Jones. We are trying to do something called 'a public relations exercise', to demonstrate to the Egyptians that we are friends, that we are not an occupying force. You know perfectly well that the driver of the Mercedes was 'His-Majesty-King-Farouk-of-Egypt'. Have you got that now?'

Jones slowly recited the words. 'Yes, sir. His-Majesty-King-Farouk-of-Egypt. I think I've got that, sir'.

The Court reassembled. Again, Jones gave his version.

'I was travelling along the Canal road when there was a flash of white and a crash of metal. I stopped the vehicle, ran back down the road, and there was a white Mercedes on its side. And lying in the road was 'His-Majesty-King-Farouk-of-Egypt' and another wog.'

By 1944, we noticed more and more Americans arriving. Aged seven, Michael Grimsdale, my artist friend whose drawings we find in this book, was presented by his father, General Gordon Grimsdale, to an American General. Little Michael pointed at his rather over-decorated chest and asked 'Which medal is for being in London?'

A result of the trans-Atlantic influx was the spate of 'how to make a proper dry martini' stories.

Opinions ranged from the appalling English hotel habit of equal measures of gin and vermouth to the extreme American view that you should swill a little vermouth round a mixer, throw it away, and replace it with iced gin without even a squeeze of lemon peel. 'Say, listen, when I want a lemon squash, I'll ask for it.'

One story deals with a group of American officers who had been on a special course to fit them for occasions of extreme difficulty and danger. At the conclusion of the course, the Commanding Officer said that, as they went out, they would each receive a sealed parcel which they were not to open except in moments of utter crisis. One young officer could hardly wait to get back to his quarters to have a look. He found that inside the parcel there was half a bottle of gin and tiny bottle of vermouth and a heavily sealed envelope. When he opened the envelope, he read:

> 'You are in great danger. You are hopelessly lost. There is no one in sight to guide you, advise you or help you.
>
> Mix yourself a dry martini – and within two minutes some sonofabitch will appear from nowhere and tell you how to make it properly.'

During all this time, my father was travelling thousands of miles for his propaganda war against the Germans.

A truly golden moment occurred on one of Toby's trips to Africa. A local King was being shown a squadron of Blenheim light bombers which had been assigned to the country as its airforce. The British High Commissioner asked him if he would like to go up in one of the planes and he duly climbed aboard and they did a couple of circuits of the airfield and landed again.

The Rolls-Royces were lined up and the party was ready to go to lunch when, foolishly, the High Commissioner said to the

DRY MARTINI

AFRICAN SIDESHOW

King as he left the aircraft, 'I expect, your Majesty, you are pleased to have been in a bomber.'

The King stopped in his tracks and a big smile came across his face. 'Been in a bomba,' he intoned, 'Been in a bomba.' The musical resonance of the words triggered some tribal instinct. 'Beeninabomba' he chanted, beginning to dance and hop up and down. '**Beenina, beenina, bomba, bomba, beeninabomba, beeninabomba, bomba, bomba, beeninabomba, beeninabomba.**'

He was still hopping with gusto as the High Commissioner feebly said, 'Your car is ready, Sir. Shall we move on?'

'**Beeninabomba, bomba, bomba**' the King sang all the way down the path until he got into his car and was driven away.

Toby had some lucky escapes, too. In North Africa, he was about to board a plane, when an officious Colonel jumped the queue, pulled rank and ordered him off. The plane crashed in flames on take-off and no-one survived.

Talking of ranks, Lord Lloyd made him unofficially a 'Major General' to impress neutral officials, but I also remember him going off in a truck as a Corporal in the Home Guard!

Corporal in the Home Guard

GERMANY NOT CALLING

Contrast in war-time poster styles

It is fair to say that at the beginning of the war, Germany was winning the propaganda battle, sadly helped by the attitudes and incompetence of some of her enemies. But as the military tide turned, so did the effectiveness of Britain's 'voice' at home and abroad.

However great a master of propaganda Josef Goebbels may have been in Germany and the rest of Europe, he could be beaten. Because the Germans just did not understand foreign mentalities, their propaganda efforts were sometimes clumsy, ineffective and even counter-productive.

For instance, they often translated crowing victory announcements into various languages, making no allowance for the fact that their audiences (often the defeated) would take a rather different view from that of their German listeners. In the recently captured Channel Islands, such radio announcements were made by a strident German woman, who appeared to have learned her English in the backstreets of the Bronx. She quickly became the Islands' main joke.

The worst example of Nazi misunderstanding was Lidice. When Reinhard Heidrich, probably the Nazi's single most dangerous and evil man, was assassinated by British-trained Czechs in Prague, the Germans for revenge picked on a village called Lidice, then shot all the men (and even the dogs in their kennels), shipped all the women and children to concentration camps, dynamited the buildings, bulldozed and removed the rubble and ploughed the place flat. They then seriously thought that it would be a brilliant idea to announce and film what they had done. They were slow to realise that they had made this otherwise totally unknown village the symbol of Nazi atrocities and attempted resistance to them.

In the case of the British, they also never understood how their lack of sense of humour was a disadvantage. Indeed, between the wars, they had tried. The German General Staff set out to study the reasons for their defeat. After close analysis, they came to the conclusion that one strong factor was the sense of humour of the British fighting man which carried him through moments of crisis. They solemnly set out, therefore, to learn a sense of humour. A special study was made of the 'Old Bill' cartoons. In one, a new soldier in the front line looks at the large holes in the remains of a wall and says to Old Bill, 'Who made that 'ole?', to which Old Bill replied 'Mice'.

A solemn German note had been appended: 'This is an example of sense of humour. The holes were not, of course, made by mice but by shell fire'.

The Nazis had succeeded in Germany with their 'repeat the lie' technique. It did not work as well abroad. Telling lies all the time had become a habit. The Germans were for ever claiming to have sunk ships which were still afloat. They also claimed to sink ships which were not ships at all, failing to understand the practice of naming 'HMS' naval establishments on shore. Thus my father had great fun flooding the neutral press with pictures of, for instance, two sailors strolling to the NAAFI canteen with captions such as 'Struggling survivors of 'HMS X', claimed to be sunk by the Luftwaffe, in fact 6 miles inland from Portsmouth.'

I came across a little book of wartime cartoons by Osbert Lancaster which contained on the flap a perfect example of German sense of humour or lack of it.

Osbert had two Germans talking in the street, '… and since the brutal British bombed the power sta-, I mean the children's hospital – we have had no light or water. Heil Hitler!'

So Obvious.

The Young and Talkative One: "Who made that 'ole?"
The Fed-up One: "Mice."

In Goebbels' *Der Angriff*, the Germans responded:

The Hypocrites of Westminster

As a proof of the Conservative sense of humour and at the same time of the absolute lack of original ideas, imagination and really new creative thoughts, on account of which the Englishman has become famous all over the world in the meantime, we now wish to reproduce some stories published in English newspapers. Thus we find, for instance, the following cartoon published by the Daily Express.

The two figures are meant to be Germans. But now please just have a closer look at it, what kind of Germans has this English cartoonist of the year 1941 drawn there? They are two narrow-minded, average specimens of behaviour and clothing of the people living before 1933. The draughtsman has not realised at all that the German type of today does not look like that any more. This type certainly does not drive a tank, conquer the Norwegian mountains, and the Balkans, neither does he so bravely fly the aeroplanes attacking over the Atlantic, the Mediterranean, and the North African deserts. But that is the way England still sees us. She does not visualise us as a young nation with a new idea, with a new conception of Europe in this twentieth century. The cartoonist, on the contrary, considers it far more clever to make one German say to the other: '… and since the brutal British bombed the power station – sorry, I mean the children's hospital – we have had no light or water. Heil Hitler!'

This cartoonist does not realise at all that he is thinking fully from the English standpoint; because, where is the German town in which even only once the supplies of electricity and water have been interrupted, in a way worth mentioning, by English bombs?

Understanding the Germans as he did, Toby recognised that the best way to destroy their propaganda was to continuously knock their habit of repeating lies – often quite stupid lies. Goebbels had been a liar all his life. He had put out several reasons why he had a club foot, none of them true.

Below left is an *Evening News* article by Toby under one of his pseudonyms 'Edward Denny' (Edward his first name, and Denny that of his in-laws).

Mind you, even the greatest 'whopper-knocker' could be caught out in a bit of Irish exaggeration. Toby had a car crash in the blackout. *The Daily Telegraph* and other papers made it quite clear that this was *not* the result of the Luftwaffe's best efforts.

Retroussé or Aquiline?

The British Council suffered a casualty on Monday night. Steel-helmeted wardens and policemen working with a crowbar extricated the Chief of the Council's Press and Reception Division, Mr E D O'Brien, from his smashed car.

He had not been bombed. The accident was of the common or peacetime variety. His passenger, the King's Printer, Mr Douglas Jerrold, was also hurt.

Mr O'Brien spent the night in Charing Cross Hospital. Mr Jerrold, who had been cut on the feet, went home.

One good thing remains out of this minor disaster. So thoroughly was Mr O'Brien's nose broken that his doctors tell him he will be able to remodel it nearer to his heart's desire. Just now he is hesitating between the aquiline and the retroussé.

So what are we to make of this newspaper report from Cyprus a couple of years later? Same joke, rather different slant:

Islander's Diary

By Viator

Mr E D O'Brien, Director of the British Council Press Division, whom we're glad to welcome to our island outpost, expects to cover many thousands of miles by air during his tour of the Middle East

In the Blitz

During the heavy German raids on London two years ago, Mr O'Brien had an amazing escape from death. He was buried beneath the wreckage of his car during a particularly heavy attack and had to be dug out with a crowbar. Like many other blitz victims he suffered considerable facial injuries. Nobody meeting Mr O'Brien today would imagine that his nose is a miracle of "personal plastic surgery". It was so completely broken that he had the rare experience of being able to choose its future shape.

The surgeons having given up the task, he was presented with a mirror and advised to put "his nose straight once an hour". He hesitated, I gather, between the retroussé and the aquiline.

BAULKING IN BUDAPEST

During the 'Siege of Budapest' in the closing months of the war, the Germans were desperately trying to resist the Soviet advance through Hungary and towards Vienna.

A Hungarian Army officer friend of Toby's had been captured while leading a partisan band – luckily by a rather traditional and correct Prussian Regiment.

A hastily convened Court Martial found him guilty and sentenced him to death. 'I am afraid I cannot accept the verdict,' he interrupted.

'Wie, bitte?' exploded the President of the Court, a silver-haired, much decorated Colonel.

'Well, you know your rules. I have to be prosecuted by an officer of equal or senior rank. I am a Major in the Hungarian Army, and you used a Captain.'

Outside, the Russian shells exploded with increasing fury. 'Look Major, we are very busy. You may be right, but *surely* you could consent to be shot?'

'I am sorry Sir. I would like to help out, but I really do feel that military law should be upheld, even in these trying times.'

Of course officers from the SS, like the *Totenkopf* or Deaths Head Division, fighting just a few hundred metres away, would have wasted no more time and shot him at once, but after much conferring the President ordered him to be returned to his cell, with guards which the defenders could ill afford.

The battle intensified outside and after four days the prisoner heard with dread the tramp of many boots marching towards him. Certain it was a firing squad, he started his prayers.

'Abteilung, halt!'

Budapest

He looked up. There was the Colonel. 'The Russians are outside but, I wonder, Major, if *you* would agree to accept the surrender of my garrison?'

The Germans, at this stage of the war in the East, were looking to surrender to *anybody* other than the Russians.

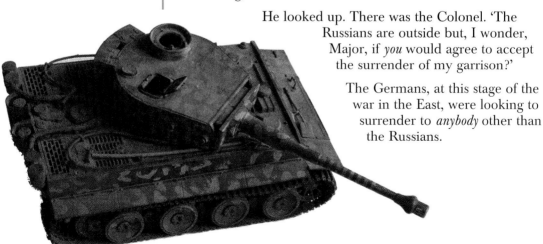

56

Stalin's allies had little idea of his ruthless imperial ambitions and his plans to take control of Eastern Europe, starting with Poland on whose behalf, after all, we had entered the war.

The pro-Russian propaganda which the British authorities poured out in the last few years of the war was fuelled by a sentimental regard for the Russians. It reached such a point that there was a serious suggestion that 'Uncle Joe' might be put up for honorary membership of the Carlton Club. Only two people, stood out against it in public at the time. One was Sir Alan Herbert:

'Let's have no nonsense from the friends of Joe.
We laud, we love him, but the nonsense – no.'

His final acid couplet was considered at the time almost in bad taste:

'In 1940 when we bore the brunt,
We could have done, boys, with a second front.'

Perhaps the last word about Stalin should come from Pope Urban VIII, when he heard of the death of Cardinal Richelieu. 'Well, if there is no God, then he has had a most successful career. If there is one, he is in for a pretty thin time.'

In 1944, we moved into 9 Wellington Square, off the King's Road in Chelsea. To avoid the new menace of the German rockets we were sent off to the country until the Normandy invasion and the rocket sites were overrun and detroyed.

Down in No 1, where he still lives, I found Timothy ffytche, who became my best friend for many years. And it was Tim who introduced me to another life-long friend, Jorge Potier, who lived in the Portuguese Consulate nearby in Sloane Street.

The war ended for me when I was six. I was standing proudly to attention in my bedroom in our new house in Wellington Square with my father's little pistol, listening as they played 'God Save The King' from the Palace on the radio.

CHAPTER 6 PEACE BREAKS OUT

After the war, Britain continued rationing. Actually rationing became worse. It is difficult now to remember the situation then. After all, people assume they can go to the shops to buy anything they fancy and they can afford. They do not have to take their ration books to queue for tiny bits of food, they don't have to pool their clothing coupons to buy a coat or suit, and they do not have to count petrol coupons to check if they can use the car for any particular journey.

It still irritates me that Britain, who had bankrupted herself in the defence of freedom, somehow managed to have rationing until 1954, long after everybody else had abandoned it, including the so-called vanquished.

In 1947, my father took us for a few weeks to Ireland, which had no rationing, to 'fatten us up'. We bumped across the Irish Sea at about 7,000 feet in an unpressurised Aer Lingus Dakota. On arrival we were greeted by Erskine Childers, an old friend of my father and of Donough Inchiquin. He was a Minister and the son of the Irish revolutionary who wrote the classic novel *The Riddle in the Sands* and who was executed during the Civil War in Ireland. Erskine became the fourth President of Ireland in 1973.

Irish Transport System, Spanish Point

We set off from Dublin on a memorable and frightening night drive, which was the first time we had ever heard the word 'pothole'. There were so many potholes on the empty road from Dublin to Limerick that Erskine literally had to swing all over the road to miss them to avoid damage to the precious tyres or suspension.

When we were not visiting Dromoland Castle, we lived for four months in a hamlet in the far West of Ireland called 'Spanish Point'. Three galleons from the Armada of 1588, having managed to sail right round the north of Scotland, had finally foundered there. The Irish, of course, were all for ransoming the surviving noblemen or sailors but it was the English who ordered them to kill all prisoners, because enough Spaniards had come ashore in Catholic Ireland to outnumber the tiny English garrison, 2,000 strong.

We stayed in a little house looking over the Atlantic. The neighbours included a sweet old nun, so garrulous and boring that my mother cut an escape route through a hedge to avoid her. Our main transportation was a trap pulled by a lazy donkey, which only moved at all if tapped by an old cricket bat.

A curious find was hundreds of silver tins of fresh drinking water stacked in the barn. I cannot imagine why. Such measures might have been sensible in a place like London, vulnerable to bombing or gas attack, but in the West of Ireland it was a complete enigma. Another curiosity for an eight year old was a visit to a creamery. This strange yellow stuff came pouring out of the rotating churns and I asked what it was.

'That's butter', said our host.

I stared, 'No, no, butter is something you get in tiny little bits, once a week', I said, conscious of the ration back in England.

There was also a rickety narrow gauge railway line, the West Clare Railway – soon to be shipped, engines, rolling stock, track and all to Nigeria. Only a little preserved steam engine at Ennis Station remains, together with the traces of overgrown cuttings and embankments, if you look for them.

WEST CLARE RAILWAY

Years before, the Irish song-writer Percy French was so angry at the railway's erratic performance that he wrote a ballad for which he was sued by the management. Rightly, he won. Perhaps the judge had tried travelling on the line! Here are some verses:

> You may talk of Columbus's sailing, across the Atlantical Sea,
> But he never tried to go railing, from Ennis as far as Kilkee
> You run for the train in the morning, the excursion train starting at eight
> You're there when the clock gives the warning, but there for an hour you will wait.
> And, as you're waiting in the train, you'll hear the guard sing this refrain:
>> Are you right there, Michael, are you right?

Do you think that we'll be home before the night?

Ah, you've been so long in startin', that you couldn't say for sartin', so you might there, Michael so you might.

They'll find out where the engine's be hiding, and it drags you to sweet Corofin

Says the guard 'Back her down on the sidin', there's a goods from Kilrush coming in'

Perhaps it comes in two hours, perhaps it breaks down on the way.

'If it does', sez the guard' be the powers, we are here for the rest of the day'

And as you sit and curse your luck, the train backs down into a truck:

Are you right there, Michael, are you right?

Have you got the parcel there for Mrs White?

Oh, you haven't, oh Begorrah, Say it's coming down tomorrow, and it might there, Michael, so it might.

At Lahinch, the sea shines like a jewel, with joy you are ready to shout!

When the stoker cries out; 'There's no fuel and the fire is taytotally out'

But hand up that bit of a log there, I'll soon have you out of a fix

There's a fine clump of turf in the bog there, and the rest go a'gatherin' sticks.

And while you're breakin' bits off trees, you hear some wise remarks like these:

Are you right there, Michael, are you right?

Do you think that you can get the fire to light?

Oh, an hour you'll require, for the turf it might be drier, and it might be, Michael, so it might!

Kilkee, oh you never get near it, you're in luck if the train brings you back.

For the permanent way is so queer, it spends most of its time off the track.

Up hill the ol'engine is climbin', while the passengers push with a will

You're in luck when you reach Ennistymon, for all the way home is downhill.

And, as you're wobblin' through the dark, you hear the Guard make this remark:

Are you right there, Michael, are you right?

Do you think that you'll be home before it's light?

Tis all depending whether, the ole engine holds together and it might now, Michael, so it might!

Always a bit demonstrative, my sister Natalie!

Talking of Ireland's railways, a friend of mine, just after the war, was changing trains at Limerick Junction. He nearly missed his train because one of the clocks was showing a time ten minutes earlier than the other. When he remonstrated with the porter as he was flinging himself into the compartment the porter said, 'Well sir, what would be the point of having two clocks showing the same?'

People from Kerry are regarded as less intelligent by other Irishmen. Three Irish priests were captured by cannibals who began to dance around in a frenzy while warming up a huge cooking pot. The huge chief says to the first cleric, 'Where are you from?'

'Dublin.'

'In the pot!' Splash! He turns to the second one and says, 'Where are you from?'

'Tipperary.'

'In the pot!' Splash! He turns to the third, 'Where are you from?'

'County Kerry, your Honour.'

'Stay right there! Don't move. Don't go near the pot.'

The dancing continues. The water is warming up when the priest from Kerry tugs at the sleeve of the chief and demands, 'I'd like to know why I am not being martyred with my two religious colleagues.'

'That's easy. The last man we had from Kerry ate all the potatoes.'

In 1949, I was packed off to a prep school in Kent, called St. Ronan's. One of the things you begin to realise about education is that so much depends on the headmaster, the house master or the tutor. St Ronan's was my first experience of a place which had been built on one man's reputation. Unfortunately, he had just died. When my mother and father were ushered in to his younger and rather less clever brother's study, they were somewhat shaken by his opening words. 'Ripping little codgers, I always say'.

Like so many other little boys suddenly removed from home, I was lonely and homesick and I wasn't terribly good at anything at prep school. I wore leg-irons to help with rickets, quite common in those days of vitamin deficiency. No real problem at the time, indeed attracting sympathy, but long-term it made me clumsy, especially when intercepting any moving ball. This cuts out virtually all the games so revered then at British schools.

With food rationing continuing, we managed to get vegetables from the local Kent farmer. Anyone who is against pesticides should have seen us on a Saturday morning, when we were forced to shell the peas. The fat maggots that came out of the pods were then raced against each other for money or ration stamps. I'm not sure how many modern children would have enjoyed it as much as we did – or how many consumers would relish the side effects of real organic vegetables.

On the way to achieving local air superiority

My lack of an ability on the playing field may have made me over-competitive in my hobby. We built model aerodromes around the edge of the grounds complete with runways, hangars and perimeter tracks. Gradually I built up more and more powerful aerodromes and, indeed, alliances of aerodromes. One day I wrote: 'Dear Mummy, I am buying three more planes from C-Smith, my old enemy who has one plane left and can't fight any more.' Every Saturday we had a 'war'. The next aerodrome had superior ground forces to ours but we dominated the air. Their tanks would come down model roads to be held up by a little anti-tank crew I called 'The Heavenly Twins'. Then my ground attack planes (dropping little bits of mud) devastated their attack. Every Saturday, without fail, I won. The headmaster finally called me in to say that he didn't mind me monotonously beating the other small boys, but taking their meagre sweet rations off them every week was really not on and would I please desist.

In an age of jet fighters and atomic bombs our education did seem somewhat stuck in the past. It was easy to be sympathetic with the young member of the choir school attached to St Paul's who, asked to write a poem about any aspect of his studies, wrote:

> Latin, Latin, Latin
> As dead as dead can be.
> It killed all the old Romans
> And now it's killing me.

It was at St Ronan's that my father first subjected me to a bad habit. If you are a lonely, small boy and you are eating the school food of 1948, you really look forward to seeing your parents and perhaps having a decent meal. My father developed the terrible practice of promising that he was going to come down to take me out to lunch and then not turning up. So I stood on the steps of the school with twenty of my friends and gradually one by one, they were picked up by some Humber or Austin and driven away for lunch. I walked up and down the drive, waited and waited, and he never came. My mother was already getting ill or she would not have allowed this to happen. This selfish habit continued at my public school, and it was now even more depressing because now a hundred boys reduced to just one between 12.30 and 1.00 o'clock, and I went disconsolately back to the normal filthy school lunch. I have never been a minute late visiting a child since.

But most of the time at St Ronan's I enjoyed myself and a specially important influence was the art mistress, a sweet little old lady who lived nearby in a rose-covered cottage. Her kindly and patient help set me on a modest art career which, in the holidays, was then encouraged by my grandmother, Alice Denny. She was a splendid down-to-earth figure from the North of England who had married a blond, raw-boned man that I knew as Court Denny. I did not know then that he was actually an East Prussian called Kurt von Akenhausen.

He had, wisely, adopted his wife's English surname because he served in the trenches as a stretcher-bearer during the first World War on the side of the British. There, a name like von Akenhausen could cause the odd misunderstanding!

'Granny Denny' was a children's artist. She probably illustrated most of the books that the older readers will remember from their childhood. She sat at a big round table in Addison Road with paints all around her and the radio playing. I used to go

Court Denny aka Kurt von Akenhausen, British Army stretcher-bearer

One of Alice Denny's book covers, 1943

GRIMM'S FAIRY TALES

One of my paintings under George Lane's influence. Fifties Grand Prix drivers were seriously at risk from death or injury. Not surprising. 180 mph, sitting in front of 50 gallons of volatile fuel in a T-shirt and cloth helmet!

KOREA

A US Marine, annoyed with media misunderstanding of the successful Chinese *small-scale* battle tactics, asked 'Just how many hordes *are* there in a Chinese platoon?'

Successful advance, unsuccessful education?

YOU ARE NOW CROSSING 38TH PARALLEL BY CURTESY OF THE 0 CAVALRY REGIMENT

there at least every other day on my holidays as it was my idea of second heaven.

She was with the same agent for 60 years, painting professionally from the age of 18 to 78. Her partner, George Lane, was especially good at mechanical subjects and had been a motor-racing artist before the war, although less well known than Gordon Crosby or Brian De Grineau. This was at a time when magazines like the *Autocar* and the *Motor* were full of drawings rather than photographs. It was George Lane who taught me how to draw and paint cars, which I later turned into a modest, semi-professional activity. 'I don't care where the sun is, never put shadow in front of a car, it slows it down visually', advised George.

I met Brian De Grineau because he was Toby's fellow contributor to the *Illustrated London News*. One of the extraordinary features of my father's life before, during and after the war was his prolific writing. In addition to hundreds of articles under his name or that of his chiefs and colleagues, he was still contributing to the *Telegraph's* Peterborough column. He was also 'Edward Denny' – Foreign Correspondent for the *Daily Express*, 'John Gaunt', 'Brian Desmond' of the *Irish Independent* and many others. He had also started *Our Motley Notes* in the Sketch and wrote the weekly book review column in the *Illustrated London News*, for which he received eight guineas.

On the other side of the world, the North Koreans invaded South Korea. Aged eleven, I kept a diary of the Korean War, at least for the first exciting months. I recorded the collapse of the South Koreans, the first retreat or 'bug-out' of the unprepared Americans, the retreat to the Pusan perimeter. After that came entries on MacArthur's brilliant ambitious counter-attack half way up the country at Inchon, his over-confident advance towards the Yalu River and then the catastrophic Chinese intervention.

It was usually Americans who were surprised at this youthful knowledge of a mostly American war. That is because American children were and are incredibly uninterested in things outside the USA – or even inside. Bill Bryson in his excellent *Lost Continent* quotes a recent survey among 18 year old high school seniors. Two-thirds of them did not know when their own Civil War took place or who Churchill and Stalin were. Half of them thought World War 1 had started before 1900, one third thought Roosevelt was President during Vietnam and 42% could not name one Asian country.

In Britain's greatest ally and friend, most people should find that depressing and more than a little frightening.

CHAPTER 7 POLITICS

I n 1945, just at the end of the war, Sir William Rootes asked my father to become Head of Publicity at the Rootes group. Later taken over by Chrysler, it was then one of Britain's leading car and truck makers, building Humber, Hillman, Sunbeam-Talbot, Commer and Karrier, as I used to proudly list.

On some Saturdays I used to watch Toby while he caught up with his Rootes work. He had a splendid office in Devonshire House, Piccadilly, and often took me for a lemonade at the old Berkeley Buttery, his local watering hole. As a small boy I was particularly fascinated by an early recording machine on his desk, worked by a needle cutting into a wax cylinder.

In 1945 Winston Churchill was soundly defeated in the first general election of peacetime and a new Labour government took over, to the dismay of many. Months before, my father's interest in domestic politics had been expressed in a 20,000-word electioneering book he wrote in just 36 hours called *Big 3 or Big 2½? Can we afford a Socialist Foreign Policy?*

In the foreword, he is fairly gentlemanly in his approach, at least by modern standards. After all, Clement Attlee had been a courteous British Council colleague:

> This book deals with politics and was written because I believe the Socialist leaders to be inadequate and their political doctrines wrong. It has been necessary to say some hard things. But that is not to suggest that those leaders, and particularly Mr Attlee himself, are not men of the highest integrity and the best intentions.

> Unfortunately, personal agreeableness, devotion to duty and good intentions are not of themselves enough to deal with the monstrous problems these islands will have to face.

This was written before the new Labour Government actually *gave* the Rolls-Royce Nene jet engine to the Russians. Stalin could not believe they would be so naive and stupid to hand over such an advantage and actually feared a trick.

In the book, Toby makes some interesting points about the Germans (and, please remember, I am one quarter German).

> It is utterly beyond the bounds of some good people's comprehension that a nation – or the vast overwhelming bulk of it – should be afflicted at the same time by the same psychological complaint. It is only when you realise – and it comes as a shock when you do – that there are not good Germans and bad Germans but good Germans and bad Germans in exactly the same man or woman. The German reacts in utterly different ways to two different sets of stimuli.

BIG 3
OR
BIG 2½ ?

Can we afford a Socialist Foreign Policy?

E. D. O'BRIEN

HUTCHINSON

A blistering attack written in 36 hours

That is why the Englishman finds him so hard to understand. He finds it almost impossible to believe that the kindly Christmas-tree-cum-folk-song-loving German, sentimentally devoted to his wife and his golden-haired children, is exactly and precisely the same man who will, without compunction, commit the most appalling atrocities on the wives and children of others – if ordered to do so.

He illustrates this paradox with two stories:

Driving into a Saxon town, two Allied officers were hailed by a German woman – educated, well-dressed and obviously of the class to which the Germans, even under the Weimar Republic, gave the courtesy title 'high well born'. She was very glad to see these Allied officers she said, as one of her Polish slaves – she used the German word 'Sklave' – seemed to think that he was free and had stolen one of her dresses. Would they please have him shot?

The German woman was obviously not merely hurt, but amazed, at the pungent comments of the Allied officers. To her, after twelve years of Nazi propaganda and two generations of German philosophic teaching, the Pole was a slave by nature, and it was in the laws of nature that he should be utterly submissive to her, whatever the regime ruling Germany.

In the second case, an Allied officer, who had formerly been connected with an American firm dealing in optical instruments, arrived in the headquarters of a famous firm of optical instrument makers with which his firm had been linked before the war. They had first explored the camp for slave labour attached to the works. Here 4,000 men had lived in conditions which, while they were not of those of Belsen or Buchenwald, were, nevertheless, appalling slights on human dignity. In the administration buildings, they came upon two directors of the firm cowering in a cellar. The Allied officer, who had known them well before the war, was recognised by the directors, who dashed forward with effusively outstretched hands. They were obviously a little hurt when his greeting took the form of a curt order for them to follow him.

They tumbled over themselves in their eagerness to show him all their records, but apologised for the fact that they were in a certain confusion due to the defection of the foreign 'slaves' (here they used the word 'Sklaven' again). They were, they explained, rather puzzled at the behaviour of these slaves who, in spite of the fact that they had been well treated, apparently wanted to kill them. When the Allied officer asked them what they meant by 'well treated' they replied, a trifle apologetically, that although they were slaves, they were high-class technicians and therefore had to be treated better than normal slave labour, as otherwise it would be impossible to get the best work out of them. The Allied officers could scarcely believe their ears.

The point is that these men were well-educated, travelled technocrats, with plenty of contact with the outside world, and therefore none of the excuses open to the ignorant, lower-middle or working-class Nazi who has been insulated from the outside world by propaganda. If that was *their* attitude, what must be the attitude of the average German between the age of 18 and 35 whose formative years have been spent entirely under the Nazi regime and who has never left the country except as a Government-directed tourist, a spy or a conqueror?

The main thrust of the little booklet created quite a stir in the media. For instance, the *Manchester Dispatch* under the headline 'Right Wing's Devastating Barrage' reported:

Mr O'Brien asks, 'Can a record of consistent wrong-headedness be a recommendation to the electors to place foreign affairs in the hands of these doubtless well-meaning individuals?'

If the Test Match selectors were to pick a team exclusively composed of those who have made consistently low scores in second-class county cricket, you would expect eyebrows to be raised.

Mr O'Brien, in some blistering pages, dismisses the Labour team.

The Recorder was one of many papers to give him good reviews.

It is said that hard writing makes easy reading. Mr. E. D. O'Brien has proved in his book *Big 3 or Big 2½* (Hutchinson, 2/6) that swift writing can make exhilarating reading.

Mr O'Brien was one of Lord Lloyd's chiefs in the days when the British Council was spreading its wings. He and Lord Lloyd were close friends, and O'Brien's mind has much of the directness and vigour of the great proconsul whose passing was such a loss to the nation.

Principally in the realm of foreign policy Mr O'Brien flays the Socialists, but maintains his humour and high spirits. A book to buy and a book to read.

And Lord Donegall, whom we shall hear more about later as a jazz enthusiast, found the book invaluable as his only briefing on foreign policy as he electioneered for a candidate in the Highlands of Scotland.

We had a good meeting of some 700 people in Wick last Wednesday. It was the first time in my life that I have appeared on a political platform. To my dismay our candidate, Gandar Dower, had billed me all over the town to speak on foreign affairs.

Fortunately, I had with me a little book, written in 36 hours by my old friend Toby O'Brien, late of the British Council. It only appeared the day I left, and I calculated that it was unlikely already to have percolated to Wick.

CONSERVATIVE CALLING

The little book proved to be a great help to Toby's career. While at Rootes, he was still determined to become a Member of Parliament. However, in August 1946 on the very day that he had been selected for the constituency of North Hendon, Lord Woolton, Chairman of the Tory Party, asked him to stand aside for Ian Orr-Ewing in order to take over as Director of Information at Conservative Central Office. This not only postponed any parliamentary career, it also involved a major financial sacrifice. It was quite a risk for a man with a young family to balance such an important challenge against a real 50% cut in wages. Against that, it was tacitly assumed that, after his stint, he would be given the compensating rewards of a 'safe seat' and eventually a knighthood.

The move was welcomed by friends in the press. *The Evening Standard* commented:

A Smile for the Tories

To the resources of the Conservative Party is added today a charming Irish smile. It belongs to Mr. E. D. O'Brien, and it is guaranteed to penetrate the crust of the most pachydermatous Blimp.

When Lord Woolton became chairman of the Conservative Central Office, he quickly observed its big deficiency; it lacked an effective voice. Now, after some negotiation, he has persuaded Sir William Rootes to lend his Public Relations expert, Mr. O'Brien, to the Party. His title is Director of Information Services.

I can think of no shrewder choice. 'Toby' O'Brien was under 30 when, in 1938, he helped Lord Lloyd to put the British Council on the world map.

When he arrived at Conservative Central Office, he discovered that the Party's idea of issuing information to the world was to send a press release to *The Times* and one to *The Daily Telegraph*. Not only were no other newspapers on the list but neither was the BBC, whether on radio or the new thing called 'television'.

There was just one typist in the building, 'nearly able' to take shorthand.

He also discovered that he was expected to furnish his office with a war surplus trestle table and two tin chairs. Needing to entertain and having been used to some measure of style, or at least comfort, at Rootes, he protested to the retired Major who was in charge of equipment at Central Office only to be told that 'that's what the rules allowed'. Having got nowhere with further protestations, my father promptly returned to his Rootes office at Devonshire house. Every day for a week, Lord Woolton rang him to plead for his return, finally promising him some furniture that a visitor would not be embarrassed to sit on.

Once he got into his stride at Conservative Central Office, there was really no way that the Labour Party could compete with my father's machinations. After all, he had spent many of the previous years achieving sneaky propaganda successes over that arch-propagandist, Dr Goebbels.

Years later, one of his old friends from the Tory hierarchy told me of his famous 'New Year' ruse. Toby franked all the mail going out from Central Office with the slogan 'A Happy New Year and a New Government soon'. Nothing particularly clever in that, you might think. The clever thing was then to get a friend at the Post Office to have all this mail banned! The result was a wonderful six week furore in the media concerning 'freedom of speech'. The story ran and ran with headlines like:

Innocuous slogan withdrawn

Conservatives see funny side of Slogan Ban

Affair of the envelopes

One bizarre side issue was that the few surviving franked one penny stamps immediately leaped to £2 in value on the stamp-collecting market! It also, as it was partly designed to do, caught out the Labour Party who were sending Fabian propaganda in envelopes marked 'On the official business of the Ministry of Agriculture and Fisheries.'

A useful ally was a spy in the Labour Party's printing works. Thus he obtained a proof of their posters days before they did and was then able to design a poster precisely refuting what Labour's posters were about to say.

Indeed, one night his Labour Party opposite number was discovered slumped crying at his desk with an empty bottle of whisky. Asked by his colleagues what the matter was, he moaned, 'That f...ing Irishman has done it to me again!'

Like George Lloyd, 'Uncle Fred' Woolton proved to be another very supportive leader for the two and a half years that Toby worked with him.

If he trusted you, he gave you an entirely free hand, and only intervened to help or to support you with his authority and influence.

Lord Woolton

He also had a healthily cynical attitude towards his colleagues' real level of support.

Struggling to make up for twenty years of neglect, Toby sometimes showed Woolton his feelings. 'Bloody-minded but unbowed!' as he put it.

'You are not disheartened, are you, my dear Toby?' smiled Uncle Fred. Then he pointed through his window at the Houses of Parliament. 'You are not expecting any thanks from, them are you? Good. Because you see, if, in spite of their shortcomings, you and I succeed in getting them back into power, that feat will be entirely due to their own individual, unguided, unparalleled personal genius.

If, on the other hand, their shortcomings are such that even you and I can do nothing for them, that failure will be due to my declining powers as an organiser and administrator and, I fear, to your lousy propaganda.'

Anthony Eden , Foreign Secretary, then Prime Minister and always Britain's best-dressed man

One of Toby's achievements was to convince the Conservative leaders to talk in a way that ordinary people could understand. Anthony Eden was due to make a speech full of long words and convoluted phrases. Toby intervened by urging, 'Anthony, try to imagine going to Chelsea football ground and saying the same words to your cloth-capped neighbours.' Eden grasped the point.

An almost unbelievable controversy arose from a Conservative candidate accusing the Labour Government's housing programme of making 'snail's progress'. There was a farcical 'political correctness' about the protest from the British Snail-Watching Society that is so bizarre that I reproduce it, with Toby's urbane response, from the *Evening Standard* of 15th January 1947.

To E.D. O'Brien, Esq.,
Conservative and Unionist Central Office,
24, Old Queen Street, S.W.1.

Dear Sir,

In a recent speech at Chorley, Mr. R. S. Hudson is reported to have referred to the Government's housing programme as making 'snail's progress.' The remark was obviously intended to be derogatory to the housing programme, but it was also both derogatory and unfair to the snail. The snail may move slowly, but its unhurried and undeviating persistence brings it efficiently and on time to any destination which it sets. The aim of this Society is 'to promote interest in and appreciation of the snail.' I am therefore directed by my Executive Committee to request that you will discourage Conservative speakers from employing a metaphor which both prejudices the reputation of the snail and fails to convey what the speaker has intended.

      Hoping to hear from you that you will take action in this matter. I remain, Sir, yours faithfully.

PETER HENNIKER HEATON.

Secretary, British Snail-Watching Society, 14 Ladbroke Square, W.11.

To Peter Henniker Heaton,
Secretary,
British Snail-Watching Society,
14, Ladbroke Square, W.11.

Dear Mr. Henniker Heaton,

Many thanks for your letter. I fully appreciate the feeling of any gastropodophile when he reads derogatory remarks made by politicians about the object of his affections and his interests.

I will certainly draw Mr. Hudson's attention to the obvious unfairness of comparing the progress of a lowly creature which has so admirably solved the housing problem with that of another lowly creature which has still so far to go. I am, Sir, Yours faithfully.

E. D. O'BRIEN,
Director of Information Services,
Conservative Central Office

Mr. Hudson and the snail

The following is a record of correspondence that has been exchanged:

To E. D. O'Brien, Esq., Conservative and Unionist Central Office, 24, Old Queen-street, S.W.1.

DEAR Sir, In a recent speech at Chorley Mr. R. S. Hudson is reported to have referred to the Government's housing programme as making "snail's progress." The remark was obviously intended to be derogatory to the housing programme, but it was also both derogatory and unfair to th...

Semper Domi.

★

To Peter Henniker Heaton, Secretary, British Snail-Watching Society, 14, Ladbroke-square, W.11.

DEAR Mr. Henniker Heaton, Many thanks for your letter. I fully appreciate the feeling of any gasteropodophile when he reads derogatory remarks made by politicians about the object of his affections and his interests.

I will certainly draw Mr. Hudson's attention to the obvious unfairness of comparing the progress of a lowly creature which has so admirably solved the housing problem with that of another lowly creature which has still so far to go. I am, Sir, Yours faithfully.

E. D. O'BRIEN, Director of Information Services, Conservative Central Office.

Another source of humour arose from my father working with and for Winston Churchill, culminating at Conservative Central Office.

Although he never completed his memoirs, I have a few of the tapes my father recorded. Even though it is slightly unnerving to hear the voice of your long dead father, I do thank heavens that his secretary did not obey his wishes when you hear him say plaintively, 'Caroline, dear, please wipe the tapes after I've dictated – I get so muddled.' Even when dictating, born raconteur that he was, he could not help dropping into the accents of those he was describing. In the case of Churchill, his imitation was well-nigh perfect. So let me quote just some of his stories just as he dictated them. Please try to imagine that unique, ponderous, Churchillian delivery:

'The signature of perpetual friendship, or whatever it was, which constituted the Anglo-Polish Treaty, signed with the Polish Government already in exile, is something which, of course, we would like to forget. After the signature, the two cabinets went out into the garden of 10 Downing Street and there they were photographed.

After this ceremony, Winston found himself on a bench with Sikorski, then the Generalissimo, and later Prime Minister and head of the Polish armies. Sikorski, who at that time understood English but did not speak much of it, said to Winston, 'Monsieur, le Premier Lord de l'Amirauté, what is your attitude towards Russia?'

This would have stumped anybody but Winston. We knew perfectly well that by that time France was rotten, that we would have difficulty in fighting Germany alone, and that we certainly could not fight Germany with Italy and Japan. But on the other hand, Russia had invaded half the territory of Poland, the country whose integrity we had gone to war to defend. Nobody yet knew of the thousands of Polish officers murdered by the Russians in Katyn Wood.

Winston looked at his boots for a moment and said, 'My dear Generalissimo, the antics of a baboon at large in the darkness of a primeval forest or the barren mountains which are his natural habitat, are of interest only to the

Winston at British Council/Ministry of Information meeting (Toby fourth from right)

traveller and such unfortunate natives as may have the unenviable lot to reside in the vicinity. The antics of that same baboon in zoological gardens are of interest only to the lewd, the idle, the vulgar, and the passers-by. But the antics of that same baboon in bed with your wife, your daughter, or it may be your girlfriend, can only prove, my dear Generalissimo, the source of the most acute pain, annoyance, nay anxiety to yourself.'

Sikorski roared with laughter.

There was a sequel in Russia.

> When Winston went to Kuibischef for his first meeting with Stalin, the first day's talks went extremely badly. As Moscow was under immediate threat, Kuibischef was the temporary capital. The British delegation was put up in one of the few fairly respectable hotels and Sir Alexander Cadogan said to Winston, 'Prime Minister, all these walls will have microphones in them and, therefore, if I might suggest Sir, if you have anything confidential to say I would say it in the centre of the room, and preferably in a whisper'.

> 'OH' said Winston, and then, in a voice which would have carried without any artificial aids to Paris, he boomed, 'I HAVE ALREADY ON A PREVIOUS OCCASION GIVEN IT AS MY CONSIDERED OPINION THAT THE RULERS OF RUSSIA ARE BABOONS. THAT, BELIEVE ME, IS NO COMPLIMENT TO THE MONKEY TRIBE'.

> The next day the talks went perfectly.

Toby was given a bizarre insight into our Government's efforts to counteract German infiltration of the Balkans:

> I was very anxious to hear the outcome of a key meeting, as at the time I was most interested in the Balkans. I therefore invited Desmond Morton to dine with me immediately afterwards, and I went back and tapped out his version of what happened on a typewriter.

> In early 1941, the Germans, in order to soften up the Balkans for their invasion, had been buying up every organ of public opinion, from the proprietor to the office boy.

> The meeting, chaired by Winston, was in the Cabinet room where he sat in his fat armchair with his great rack of note-paper of various sorts in front of him. Present on his right was Clement Attlee, then the Lord Privy Seal, with Desmond Morton on his left and across the way, Duff Cooper, then the Minister of Information, together with

Sikorski and Churchill discuss the antics of baboons

IMMACULATE BUS CONDUCTOR

Frank Pick, who had just become Director General of the Ministry of Information, after being Head of London Transport, where he was a visionary and noted patron of the arts, commissioning posters by great artists.

Winston outlined the situation and enquired whether it was not possible to use some of our wealth 'as the richest country in the world' to suborn the views of a literary weekly in Ljubljana.

Frank Pick suddenly upped and said, 'I think you ought to know Prime Minister, that I belong to a very strict non-conformist sect. I have never committed a sin in my life and I do not propose to start doing so now, and as long as I am in charge of the Ministry of Information', he said with his Minister sitting beside him, 'it will have nothing whatsoever to do with anything so dirty, so underhand, or so un-British as politics'.

Winston was beginning to swell visibly. He growled to Frank Pick, 'Far be it from me to impugn or in any way derogate from the religious beliefs sincerely held of any man, however fantastic, ludicrous, nay lunatic they may appear to a man of ordinary common-sense, but if your Ministry, Sir, is not going to handle politics, in God's name what will it handle? I, Sir, have had the honour, and I do indeed count it as an honour, of having been connected with politics for nearly half a century. Would you describe me, Sir, as dirty, underhand or un-British?'

Pick, foolishly, did not take warning from this and a little while later he again intervened. 'But Prime Minister, you must realise that in politics your right hand cannot do two things at the same time.'

There then ensued a fantastic scene.

Winston suddenly put two fingers in his mouth and scratched his nose with the other two fingers. He said, 'Look, this is my right hand. I have got two fingers in my mouth and two fingers scratching my nose. It is doing two things at the same time. You are a bloody fool!'.

Whereupon Attlee literally fell off his chair with laughter. Winston turned to him and said, 'Get up, get up, my dear Lord Privy Seal, this, believe you me, is no laughing matter'.

At the end of an hour of what had become a very acidulated conversation, Winston turned to Duff Cooper and said, 'My dear Duffy, every man is at liberty to choose his own subordinates and if this person, this immaculate bus conductor, pleases you, keep him by all means. But do me the honour and the privilege of seeing to it that I never have to set eyes on him again.'

Then he turned to Pick, whom I think had realised at last that he had perhaps bitten off a little more than he could chew and said, 'But you Sir, you, from such desultory, sporadic, nay cursory readings of Holy Scriptures as I have been able to indulge in for the last sixty years or more, I had hitherto supposed in my abysmal ignorance that only one being in the whole Christian era had ever laid claim to being without sin. I refer, Sir, for your information, to our Lord Jesus Christ himself.

But, nay, I am delighted to find that in this wicked and perverse generation there is one person with a becoming modesty who is prepared to lay claim to all these divine attributes. I refer, Sir, for your information, to yourself, and when tomorrow I go down to inspect our defences at Dover it may very well be that through the malice of the enemy or from some other cause I am cut off in the midst of my manifold sins and wickednesses, and if that should be the case I do beg of you, Sir, that you will remember that in my last moments I was upheld, uplifted, nay sublimated, by the thought that before I died I had met one Christ-like individual. Good day to you Sir.'

Later Toby worked with Churchill as Party Leader. He noted that:

> After the Conservative defeat in 1946, Lord Woolton bamboozled me into re-creating from scratch the Tory Party's publicity machine and gave up a safe seat to Ian Orr-Ewing for which I was going to be adopted that very evening. He also asked me to accept half the salary I was getting from the Rootes Group. He gave me as a real compensation the entrée to Winston's levée, that is to say that any Tuesday, Wednesday, or Thursday morning at the drop of a telephone call I could go round to see him at his house in Hyde Park Gate between 10.30 a.m. and 1.00 p.m. He would often be in his vast double bed with a big bedside table with a large lectern, which could be raised or lowered in the middle of it and two long rubber pads for his forearms.

> Whatever hour you arrived he would always say, 'Will you have a glass of port wine and a cigar?'

> I always used to have a glass of port, because in my youth various relatives used to have a glass of port or Madeira and a piece of seed cake or canary cake for elevenses. I used to try and dictate what I could remember of these wonderful sessions. At one of the earliest, I told him that I had established at Smith Square this department or that department, but I added, 'I feel at the moment, Sir, they are vestigial.'

WORD GAMES

Hate-love relationship?

I wonder if my father ever discussed with his illustrious boss how Winston's ancestor killed Toby's.

Charles O'Brien, Fifth Viscount Clare, was one of the now impoverished 'Wild Geese' who fled Ireland after the Treaty of Limerick in 1691, leaving behind 57,000 acres of land. As a French General, he fought Churchill's ancestor, the Duke of Marlborough, at Blenheim and two years later at Ramillies in 1706, where he died of his wounds. By a twist of family fate his brother-in-law, the Duke of Berwick, was the son of James II and Arabella Churchill!

The Sixth Viscount fought so well at Dettingen and Fontenoy that he became the famous Maréchal Clare. All these exiled Scots and Irish lived in the Jacobite enclave of the old Chateau at St Germain-en-Laye, given to James II by Louis XIV when he moved to larger premises at Versailles.

'What did you say?'

'Vestigial, Sir.'

'Pray proceed'.

About twenty minutes later, he suddenly interrupted me and said, 'I think you meant skeletal.'

'I beg your pardon, Sir'.

'A little while ago you used the word vestigial. I think you meant skeletal. I accuse you of using words in their wrong meaning. Have you looked it up in a dictionary?'

I laughed, 'No.'

He picked up on of the four telephones by his bedside and said, 'Pray, bring me the Oxford English Dictionary opened at the word vestigial.' So a little mouse of an under-under-secretary appeared with this large volume.

He erected the lectern, put on his bifocals, ran a steady finger down the right hand side of the page and said, 'Hm, vestigial – appertaining to a vestige. Surviving in a degenerate, atrophied or imperfect condition' and then he smiled at me and said, 'And never let those phrases apply to you, my dear.'

RANDOLPH CHURCHILL AND AUNT NATALIE

Robert Bevan

While I sadly never met Winston Churchill in private, I later saw quite a lot (or even quite enough of) Randolph his son. This was not through my father's influence, although they were moderately good friends and occasionally went on holiday together. It was my aunt Natalie who exposed me to Randolph and not always in the most agreeable way.

Natalie, my mother's sister, was a very glamorous figure all her life. She had married the pioneer broadcaster Lance Sieveking and then Bobby Bevan. Bobby was the son of Robert Bevan, a wonderful landscape painter, particularly renowned for his horse paintings. He had known Gauguin in Brittany and, later

in London, with Gore, Sickert and Augustus John he had founded the historic Camden Town Group.

This side of my family and their friends were as gifted in the visual arts as my father was with the written word. Natalie was a painter and sculptor, her mother Alice a children's artist for 60 years, and her daughter Anthea a photographer – the house in Boxted was rich with paintings, drawings and sculptures, a real delight.

When I knew him, Bobby was Chairman of SH Benson the advertising agency, and one of the people who sent David Ogilvy to New York, where he became one of the legends of advertising. Bobby Bevan made his name in 1929, when he went off to pubs to find out why a curious Irish stout called Guinness sold so well. 'Guinness is good for you' was the answer. Guinness, under his guidance, became one of Benson's most prestigious accounts.

Natalie and Bobby's house at Boxted in Essex was not far from Randolph Churchill's home at Stour, East Bergholt. Although I did not realise it at the time, Natalie was having a 10 year affair with Randolph and Bobby Bevan seemed to tolerate this *menage à trois*. This attitude of a *mari complaisant* caused some tensions to say the least.

We had several lunches and dinners at Boxted or at Randolph's house, which sometimes ended with amazing and drunken rows. Even at the beginning of this period when I was only twelve or thirteen years old, it was fairly easy to see that Randolph had too little of the humour, intelligence or greatness of his father, even though he had inherited some of Winston's less agreeable characteristics.

Bobby Bevan's barbecue

Randolph and Natalie

CHAPTER 8 PUBLIC RELATIONS

'Mr Oldcastle' on right and left, railings gone to make tanks.

Natalie, Geraldine, me and Michael and Bran. Michael used to bite the window-cleaner's legs, once he had trapped himself by pulling down the window on his knees.

Britain was drifting. Any lingering euphoria about 'winning the war' had evaporated. Attlee's Labour Government had triumphantly nationalised 'the commanding heights of the economy', steel, coal, railways, just as they had ceased to be commanding. Toby's predictions in his booklet had come true. The Empire was crumbling, with countries rapidly leaving the fold, some like India at horrendous human cost. Britain was still having to fulfil its obligations with a huge, expensive conscripted army, fighting curious but successful jungle wars as in Malaya. And we still clutched our ration books to take to school.

We were now three children. My sisters, Natalie and Geraldine, had been born in 1942 and 1945. We still lived in our large, very tall house in Wellington Square, Chelsea. This was bought pretty cheaply in 1944, when the Luftwaffe's bombing had ceased but the V1 and V2 rockets certainly had not.

It is interesting to see photographs of us playing in the square. All the iron railings had been cut down to make into Spitfires or tanks and there are precisely two cars in the whole square, including our Humber. This had replaced an ancient, pre-war Austin which we called 'Mr Oldcastle', so the Humber had to be named 'Mr Youngturret'.

We used to love driving to my Aunt Moira's eccentric but welcoming Hampstead house (complete with ducks and chickens) reached by a Finchley Road so badly damaged by wartime bombing that we called it 'Broken Down Road'.

Moira's husband Michael Barstow was remarkable. Blinded in the desert war, yet he went to work in the City every day with his bowler hat and white stick. He was so knowledgeable that you had to remind yourself that he had never seen his six children and could not, of course, read a newspaper or watch television. It was particularly uncanny to be told, stroke by stroke, how a particular cricketer had performed. Moira had quietly described it to him.

During this difficult economic period, a Russian trade union delegation visited a factory in the North of England. A Russian delegate asked a worker about the output of his section.

'About forty an hour', said the man.

'That's very low', said the Russian. 'In Magnetogorsk we get a hundred.'

'Maybe you do', said the Englishman. 'But we've got a lot of Communists in this shop!'

Nor was rural Britain untouched by the malaise. As Toby

reported in his column 'Our Motley Notes', a farmer was visited by a representative of the Ministry of Labour, who found him working in the fields, and asked him how many men he employed. The answer was four. The ministry official, consulting his records as to the size of the farm, said, 'I suppose you have to pay them a lot of over-time?'

'Oh, no', replied the farmer, 'They just work their eight hours, and then they go off.'

'How much do you pay them?'

'Oh, about seven pounds a week.'

'And those are the only people who work here?'

'Oh, well', said the farmer, 'There is a half-wit who does all the rest of the work, and works right through weekends as well.'

'What does he get?'

'Oh, between two and three pounds a week.'

'This is very serious', said the Ministry official. It must be looked into. Who is the half-wit?'

'Me!', said the poor farmer.

> In Socialist Britain anything which was not still rationed appeared very expensive. This led to some silly gags:
>
> A kangaroo went into a West End hotel, and ordered a whisky and soda. When the drink was produced, he fumbled in his pouch and produced half-a-crown. Said the barman, 'I am sorry sir, but I am afraid it is five shillings'. After reading the evening paper for a bit, the kangaroo ordered another one, producing a ten shilling note. The barman, as he brought the drink and the change, said conversationally, 'We don't get many kangaroos in this bar'. To which the kangaroo replied acidly, 'I am not surprised, seeing how much you charge for whisky.'

Halfway through Toby's planned stint at Central Office, disaster struck the family. My beloved mother, Sylvia, was diagnosed as suffering from cancer. We children were spared knowledge of this, partly because of her great courage and good humour. Our sad little letters reveal our anxiety that she always seemed to be going to hospital or to doctors. This is when the financial aspect of halving his income to help the Conservatives struck home. My father rapidly began to run out of money to pay for expensive drugs, our education and the family's living expenses. So, he had to make the decision to go into public relations consultancy. His professional publicity efforts on behalf of the Conservative Party had had a major effect on their victory in the 1951 election. However, because he left early, his political ambitions had to be abandoned, and the 'safe seat' and the knighthood eluded him.

He did go before several selection committees, but I am sure that with Sylvia ill he was hardly likely to be at his best and he was not selected. In retrospect, this was probably a good thing. I am not sure he would have made more than an average

CRISIS

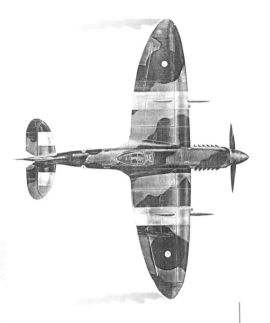

constituency MP, whereas he definitely made it as one of the world's leading public relations consultants.

In April 1950, I was sent off to a riding school in Hampshire owned by cousins of ours. I did not realise it at the time but I was being sent away while my mother was dying, aged 38. I had a strange few weeks looking after horses. One frightening experience was, all on my own, taking four of them several miles down a busy Hampshire road to an air show – quite unpleasant for a twelve year old. Much more fun was breaking away from the riding classes we were giving and being allowed to request over the Tannoy a series of aerobatics by a Spitfire pilot.

I also fell in love for the first time. Janet was tall and blonde and two years older than me. The calf-like moonings of a twelve-year-old were cut short. In September, my father asked me to come back to London and as we both sat in tears he told me my mother was dead. I had had no real idea how serious her illness was. It was a terrible, unexpected shock.

At least I found out in a dignified way. My poor little sister Natalie had also been sent away, to stay with the Railtons, family friends in Wales. Always sensitive to the supernormal, she awoke to see our mother at the end of the bed. The figure disappeared and she ran into the hall calling, 'Mummy, Mummy', to the annoyance and then the anguish of the family who received the telephone call the next morning that Sylvia was dead, but they should not break the news. Two weeks later, Natalie was taken to Chester station, where a strange new nanny turned up. In the train, the little girl danced around exclaiming on 'how she looked forward to seeing her Mummy'. 'Oh, for goodness sake, you stupid child. You know your mother's dead.' The resulting weeks of anguish were not helped by this feeble lack of briefing and communication.

The last time I had seen her alive had been in hospital when she paid a great deal of kind attention to my chatter about model aerodromes and indeed, expressed apparent grave and detailed concern as to whether I had weakened my forces by swapping two particular model planes. Later, I heard that she had been incredibly brave in hospital, characteristically ignoring her own suffering and constantly going to the aid of others. The staff were so moved by this that a plaque of appreciation was erected in St Thomas' above the bed where she died.

The financial pressures caused by my mother's illness having forced Toby to abandon a political career, he set himself up as a public relations consultant. This was a role in which he excelled and which was destined to take him to the top of

GRIMSDALE

the profession. He started out by working from home in Chelsea, and I remember as a boy helping him send out releases by the hundred, working out ingenious ways of sealing up envelopes without licking each one individually, using a complex form of sponging.

One of his first clients was the Spanish Government. Luis Bolín, a very old friend of his from before the war, turned to him for help to promote Spanish tourism in Britain through public relations. Throughout the struggle of the Spanish Civil War, my father, while dedicated to the overthrow of Fascism as far as Germany was concerned, nevertheless believed that in Spain, Communism was even more of a danger and had been broadly a friend of the Franco regime. It was Luis Bolín, London correspondent of the Spanish monarchist newspaper *ABC*, who had organised the secret flight in a British Dragon Rapide which brought Franco from the Canary Islands to North Africa which triggered the Civil War.

Luis Bolín

The Dragon Rapide that flew General Franco (left) to North Africa

In some ways Spain was hardly ready for tourism. Nowadays it is quite difficult to recall the Spain of the 1950's. Unlike the rich, open and democratic country of today, with complete freedom of behaviour and movement, Franco's Spain was closed, regulated and suspicious of potential enemies at home and abroad. Having come through the horrors of the Civil War in which a million Spaniards lost their lives, Spain was only just emerging into the beginnings of normality at the time my father started his public relations efforts for tourism.

At exactly this time, Toby's future partner, Christopher Moorsom, was a young reporter for the Northcliffe Press in Madrid. He spoke perfect Spanish but occasionally forgot the rules.

Returning on the train from Malaga he was suddenly confronted by the secret police asking for his papers. He had left both his passport and identity card in his apartment in Madrid and was promptly marched off the train to the sinister building of 'La Dirección General de Seguridad'. A horrible little Captain of Police started haranguing him with questions. 'Who do you work for, Señor Moorsom?'

'The *Continental Daily Mail* and *Evening News*.'

'Ha! Those damn rags that insult our Caudillo, Generalísimo Franco! Well, that won't help you much. ¡Número treinta y dos!' he shouted at a fellow jailer, revealing that cell thirty-two was to be Christopher's new home. 'Well Señor Moorsom, who can you get to vouch for you in Madrid?' he sneered.

Christopher Moorsom, Madrid 1948

Christopher answered, 'Manolo de Pollero.'

'Ha', he said. 'You mean the drunken anarchist poet?'

He turned to his colleague and said, 'Sesenta y tres, Pedro', indicating that Christopher was now to be assigned ever deeper into the bowels of the jail.

'So, who else?' said the Captain with mounting triumph and contempt.

'Well Fernando Rived, I suppose.'

'You mean that red sculptor fellow? Pedro, cell eighty seven would be more appropriate.'

Christopher continued to recite ever more raffish and left-wing celebrity friends until finally the Captain said, 'Is there anyone else?'

'Well', mused Christopher, 'I suppose Juan Lojendio.'

Suddenly the Captain stopped smiling and an expression of doubt and anxiety crossed his face. 'Not Don Juan?'

Christopher shrugged.

'Not el Ministro?'

Christopher nodded.

'Not nuestro Ministro?', meaning the Minister of the Interior and the Captain's ultimate boss.

'Yes,' said Christopher. Very relaxed he looked at his watch. 'And, do you know, if you keep me here much longer, I am afraid I am going to be rather late for my lunch with him.'

The Captain stared at him bug-eyed and then blurted out. 'Un coñac para Señor Moorsom. Y mi coche, rápido!'

So Christopher ended up being driven at high speed in the Captain's own official car to his (very real) meeting with the Minister. I am not sure I would have had the nerve not to reveal my influential friends rather earlier in the conversation.

PUTTING SPAIN ON THE TOURIST MAP

In addition to what we would now call an 'attitude problem', Spanish tourism faced other difficulties. First, Spain was not on the holiday map. 'The Costa Brava, where is that?', said my father, when told by Bolín about the first place that he wanted to promote. Secondly, in 1950, it must be remembered that Spain had few enough British friends in the first few years after the end of the war. After all, the Labour Party had been in power for 5 years and many of their leaders were pro-Republican. Some of them had even fought in the International Brigades against Franco and the Nationalists in the Spanish Civil War. Toby therefore had to make Spain 'respectable' as well as attractive, starting from the low base of 20,000 British people who visited Spain each year.

SELWYN TAKES A HOLIDAY

Selwyn, with Nora Coleman, the 'merry widow' with whom the papers tried to link him, and my brother Fionn, soon to fall in love with everything Spanish.

José Ensesa, with distinguished guest Selwyn Lloyd

One of the methods he used was to take his own holidays in S'Agaró on the Costa Brava, accompanied by prominent politician friends. The most effective of these was Selwyn Lloyd. Who better to take to Spain to be photographed in S'Agaró than the Foreign Secretary?

Selwyn was a delightful character and became the god-father to my younger brother Fionn. We had many wonderful Summers with him at the Hostal de la Gavina. This hotel, now one of the finest in the world, was the dream of José Ensesa, a citric acid millionaire, built on a rugged bluff between San Feliú and Palamós.

When we first went there it had only 12 rooms, and you had to sleep under mosquito nets because the marshes inland had not yet been drained and sprayed. Ensesa owned much of the headland and was able to ensure that all the new houses built complied to certain architectural styles including height limits. Both of the places I've been most associated with in Spain, S'Agaro and Sotogrande, were able to maintain standards in this way.

Young Jonathan Aitken was also Selwyn's god-son, Selwyn having shared a flat with Jonathan's father. In spite of the

83

fact that he had been a candidate at 22, at S'Agaro he was acting as Selwyn's speech-writer, secretary and gopher. (Although the newspapers captioned him and Toby as Selwyn's body-guards.) Filming *Suddenly Last Summer*, Elizabeth Taylor once begged José Ensesa to use his private pool to avoid the photographers. Jonathan was all for it, as was Ensesa, 'She asked me with those eyes'. But Toby and Selwyn, fearing helicopters and press speculation, persuaded them against it.

One year, Selwyn Lloyd did not come and another of my father's good political friends Iain Macleod arrived. Things did not seem to go quite as well with the Macleods.

Selwyn with secretary, gopher and future Minister, Jonathan Aitken

Iain, normally nice, was suffering from a stiff neck, which seemed to get steadily worse during the holiday. Too late we discovered that he had been taking iron pills by mistake.

Iain Macleod (centre) with daughter Caroline, son Torquil and my sister Natalie (left)

There was one peculiar incident several years later involving Iain. Brian Alexander was staying with us and we were in the annexe 400 yards down the hill. We all went to a cocktail party up in the hills and returned to the restaurant late. The head waiter, somewhat embarrassed because of the status of 'El Ministro', approached us and said that he was very sorry but we would have to wear jackets in the restaurant, which was, after all, one of the finest in Spain. Iain exploded in a fit of pique. Even though his children volunteered to collect his jacket, and in spite of the fact that Brian Alexander and I had a great deal further to go to collect ours from the annexe, he announced that he would have his meal in his room. My father commented that Selwyn would never have done such a thing. Later I wondered if, had Iain lived longer, rising to lead the Conservative Party as many predicted, this flaw in his personality would have shown itself in some more serious way.

Eventually, the number of British tourists visiting Spain topped two million. As a reward, Toby was personally awarded the order of *Isabel La Católica* by General Franco, a great honour which had the theoretical benefits of being able to travel on the Madrid metro at half price, or crossing the borders of Spain with an escort of cavalry, 'providing you pay for them yourself'. Neither perk he ever used.

At about this time, another of Toby's clients brought him back to meet Winston Churchill for the last time.

One of my first memories of actually 'working' with my father was during a holiday from school addressing 200 envelopes to all the Bishops in Britain. This was for a special Bishops' preview of the Paramount film *The Ten Commandments*, the Cecil B. de Mille epic. Earlier, Paramount had sent a disgruntled cable in response to my father's initial proposals:

```
WE DO NOT REGARD THIS AS AN ADEQUATE
PUBLIC RELATIONS PROGRAMME STOP MR DE
MILLE DOES NOT APPEAR TO BE HAVING AN
AUDIENCE WITH THE QUEEN STOP NOR IS THERE
ANY MENTION OF A DECORATION OR ORDER BEING
GIVEN BY QUEEN TO MR DE MILLE STOP WE
UNDERSTAND THAT ORDER OF GARTER WOULD BE
ONE TO GO FOR STOP ADVISE STOP...
```

It took some time for Toby to persuade Paramount that foreign film directors were not automatically given the Order of the Garter, the highest decoration in the land. Nevertheless, he felt he had to make up for the fact that his PR programme appeared so mundane because, as part of De Mille's European tour, the Pope was to grant him an audience, and the French were giving him the 'Légion d'Honneur'. (I doubt if anyone had told the Paramount team of the cynical French phase, 'Two things no man can avoid, death and the Légion d'Honneur.')

Remembering his wartime and Conservative Party experiences with Winston, Toby rang Churchill's Private Secretary, Anthony Montague-Browne, who arranged for De Mille to come down and meet the great man. This honour was partly due to Churchill's memories of working with my father but also, luckily, because he was very keen on the movies. They sent a 16mm print down in advance, which Churchill watched twice.

Winston was sitting in bed wriggling his exposed toes when they were ushered in. First De Mille explained that the film had been inspired by Churchill's own essay on Moses. 'In which of my books was that published, Anthony?' Absently, Anthony replied, '*Great Contemporaries*, I think'. Winston exploded, 'Damn your skin! That's not funny'. But things settled down and there was an hour of animated discussion, with Churchill even contesting the design of the Egyptian chariots. But soon it was time to go. After pumping Churchill's hand vigorously, De Mille enthused, 'I have been given many honours, especially on this trip, but I would like to say, Sir Winston, that *the* greatest honour is to shake you by the hand.'

With a characteristic twinkle in his eye, Churchill responded impishly, 'Well then, pray, shake it again, shake it again'.

CHURCHILL, DE MILLE'S MOVIE FAN

Charlton Heston as Moses in The Ten Commandments

BUT SERIOUSLY

Anthony (right) with his navigator

Anthony Montague-Browne was a good friend of my father's and, as we have seen, was his helpful link to Churchill over the De Mille visit. But among all the lunch and dinner parties that I have had with Anthony, a much more serious conversation stands out as the one by which I will always remember him.

During a walk in the country he told me his feelings about the war, where he flew Beaufighters both in Europe and the Far East. The Beaufighter was a formidable twin-engined fighter bomber. With its massive armament of machine guns, cannons and rockets, it was a terrible killing machine. It was also very quiet, earning the Japanese name 'Whispering Death'.

Anthony told me of two incidents which had sobered and shocked him. The first was in Burma when he was attacking a 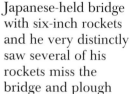 Japanese-held bridge with six-inch rockets and he very distinctly saw several of his rockets miss the bridge and plough into the village beyond. The second was intercepting a number of small vessels, packed with Japanese soldiers. In the space of five minutes in three passes Anthony's plane destroyed the lot, with not a vessel left afloat. He said that the knowledge of having killed many men personally, however much he may have *thought* he hated them, was something that had made him wake in the night sweating many times since the end of the war.

He was luckily saved at the end of the war from killing his own countrymen. He roared over Rangoon which had gone strangely silent. Suddenly he spotted painted on the roof of the jail 'JAPS GONE' and on the other side the urgent exhortation, 'EXTRACT DIGIT'.

Welcome news at Rangoon jail

LAUGHING STOCK OF OXFORD

My father's first partner was a slim, elegant young man called Anthony Allfrey. Anthony got up to all sorts of things at Oxford and even afterwards. His guardian was Lord Brentford, son of the legendary Joynson-Hicks or 'Jix' the Home Secretary of the twenties. Brentford became anxious about the large number of bills for restaurants, bars and night-clubs that Anthony's allowance was spent on. He decided to cut his allowance, explaining this in a series of prissy letters such as:

> *My dear Anthony,*
>
> *I do not think I can sustain your allowance at the present level, bearing in mind the uses for which the money seems to be going.*
>
> *I cannot understand why you cannot live a simpler life. In my old days at Oxford, after a brisk game of footer, and a bracing tub, we would make ourselves a mug of cocoa, lean up against the mantel-piece and mull over things.*

Anthony retaliated in a simple and devastating way by publishing the letters in ISIS, the University Magazine, under the title *A Guardian's Letter to his Ward.* This was soon the talk of London's club-land and, as everyone could plainly identify who the guardian was, Anthony's allowance was quickly restored.

The first day he joined my father, Anthony arrived with an appalling hangover and later revealed, 'I knew if I moved my head too much it would fall off'.

He had to join a very serious meeting and could bring himself to say nothing, but to nod his head very slowly from side to side when in disagreement, or up and down when agreeing. At the break for coffee, one of the elderly and important clients leaned forward and whispered, 'I like your new young partner, Toby. Wise head on young shoulders.'

The establishment of the Joynson-Hicks name was a result of a useful marriage. Joynson married the daughter of Mr Hicks, his largest commercial client. Thus Mr Hicks became Joynson-Hicks, and later founded his own law firm of that name as well as starting on a distinguished political career.

Years later, 'Jix' was addressing the House of Commons, when a backbencher asked, 'What about unearned increment?' David Lloyd George crisply intervened. 'That's easy. It's the hyphen between the Joynson and the Hicks.'

A tower of strength during the period of my mother's illness and death was our cook, Eva Palmer. Eva was immensely fat and very jolly. She became a surrogate mother during these difficult months and we loved her dearly. This is not to say that we were not adverse to teasing her. I remember the only time that I saw her move faster than a slow walk, when I presented her with a dead mouse to whom we were about to give a ceremonial burial together with a volley of shots over the grave with our air guns.

Only about a year after my mother's death, my father introduced us to Leo Railton. Leo was very pretty and had been working with him in his office. Whilst somewhat suspicious of her to start with, we grew to love her dearly. She later confessed that she was nervous of us. Taking on three children when you are under thirty is a daunting task. She was also extremely awed by my father's lifestyle, with his many and varied friends, especially the political figures who often filled the house.

She had been a cypher officer in the war on General Alexander's staff, and at one stage had been called 'Sten Gun Susie' because of her ability with that rather cheap British submachine gun. She had also had quite an eventful time in

*Anthony Allfrey,
'wise head on young shoulders'*

EVA AND STENGUN SUSIE

both the North African and in the Italian campaign. One of her tougher moments was a jeep crash which killed nearly all the other people in the vehicle.

'STEN GUN SUSIE' MARRIES

Miss Leonora (Leo) Railton, who was given the name Sten Gun Susie while serving in Italy during the war, leaves Holy Trinity, Brompton, to-day, after her wedding to Mr. Edward Donough O'Brien. Mr. O'Brien was formerly head of Conservative Party publicity.

Sten Gun Susie

After their wedding, she took over the house in Chelsea and got us organised. Probably much less easy was getting my father organised. I notice in his pre-war diaries constant references to parties and 'having drinks with his friends' and even references to 'hangovers' or 'not feeling well in the morning.' The trouble was, he did not really suffer from hangovers and therefore undoubtedly drank too much. This was made worse a couple of years later when, skiing in Switzerland, he was walking across a bridge and was run over by two skiers, the second of whose skis went right into the small of his back. He suffered from severe back pain for the rest of his life, and I am quite sure he used to drink to make up for it.

One day, for some reason I cannot remember, Leo and Eva quarrelled.

Eva had always been besotted with the television show, *What's My Line?*, presented by Barbara Kelly with Eamonn Andrews, Isobel Barnet, Gilbert Harding and David Nixon. This she watched on her little black and white television in the basement. She announced to Leo that she was going to ring up Barbara Kelly and her husband Bernard Braden and see if they wanted a cook. By an amazing coincidence, their cook had left that day. Our beloved Eva left us just before Christmas, and Leo who had never really cooked in her life was forced to learn in a matter of hours. It was a blessing in disguise, because Leo went on to become a great cook and even made a commercial career later out of providing executive lunches.

COMMERCIAL TELEVISION IS BORN

Between 1953 and 1955 my father was involved in one of the era's most momentous business decisions. This was to help to create commercial television which had plenty of enemies, notably the BBC's then monopoly and at first, the newspapers, who thought that their advertising revenue was to be threatened.

It may not be surprising that Toby was the choice to fight for commercial television. Ian Orr-Ewing, to whom he had handed the Hendon North constituency was, with Jack Profumo, one of the driving forces behind the breaking of the BBC monopoly. Other friends such as Lord Woolton, as Chairman of the Cabinet's Broadcasting Committee, with Selwyn Lloyd marshalling the backbenchers, were powerful forces indeed. Eventually the opposition of Lord Salisbury and the hesitancy of Winston Churchill, then Prime Minister, were to be overcome.

Toby's friend Norman Collins was to be Deputy Chairman of the newly formed Associated Television Ltd (ATV), with Prince Littler as Chairman. Val Parnell and Lew Grade were also on the board (when first told about Lew Grade, later Lord Grade, Toby said 'there *can't* be anybody called Lew Grade!') In the fascinating file on the subject, I find my father objecting about the programme contractors to Sir Robert Fraser, head of the Independent Television Authority, thus:

> 'I must confess however that the ITA's appointment of the programme contractors has tried that stomach very hard. I am not referring of course to your wealthy barrow boys. I am referring to the two newspaper groups who were most violently against competitive television and who have now been allowed such important contracts.'

Attached to this is a return letter saying, 'Dear Toby, we have often agreed but not this time. Ever, Bob.'

There was a critical article in the *Evening Standard* by Randolph Churchill, who ended his piece by saying, 'But the real trouble stems from the fact that the Bill was passed through Parliament in a series of debates in which those who denounced commercial television knew even less about its possibilities that those who were promoting it. Hence today's many headaches and cold feet in the world of commercial television.'

Without Toby's lobbying skills and, of course, his network of friends in the Conservative Party, commercial television might have been long delayed.

So, considering the fortunes which were soon to be made by others, it is salutary to realise how little such a vital professional advisor was paid:

> *Dear Mr O'Brien, I enclose a cheque for £30 being your fee for this week. Would you please acknowledge receipt on the enclosed receipt form.*

Even these paltry fees did not carry on very long because, having achieved success, Norman Collins told my father that the Littler Organisation was going to take over the public relations:

> *My dear Toby, I warned you when we spoke that the present arrangement might have to terminate abruptly, and the object of this letter is to avoid some of the abruptness.*

Years later I asked my father why he did not do the work for nothing and ask instead for shares in ATV. He replied that at the time he desperately needed the ready cash, however little.

It is interesting to scan the headed paper of the Popular Television Committee with people as varied as Alec Bedser the cricketer, Cannon Collins, Rex Harrison, Valerie Hobson, Sir Compton MacKenzie and Somerset Maugham. The old friend who had used Toby's book to campaign in the Highlands, the Marquis of Donegall, also features. Lord Donegall was Chairman of the National Jazz Federation and was responsible for bringing over many of America's most famous jazzmen (I met Louis Armstrong and Mezz Mezzro at two of his dinners.)

My father didn't care for jazz, but regarded Donegall as an amusing drinking companion. He was once invited round to his friend's flat for what he thought was to be a quiet tipple and was appalled to find a whole crowd of jazz enthusiasts listening to a massive hi-fi system.

'Sit down, my dear Toby. I think you will really like Mugsy Spanier's version of Sobbing Blues.'

Toby's horror increased when he noticed everyone was sipping cups of tea. Donegall's explanation was that, 'I'm on the wagon, so nobody else can have a drink.'

This became infuriating because his host kept going to the kitchen to 'fix things' and had plainly stashed a bottle of vodka there, from which he was personally having some secret gulps.

STOIC REPRISE

The Rotunda, Stowe

Meanwhile, like my father before me, I went from being a big boy in a little school to being a small boy in a large and magnificent school, Stowe.

Stowe is probably the most beautiful school, not just in Britain but in the world. It is one of the very finest examples of Palladian architecture, with buildings by Vanbrugh, William Kent, and the Adam Brothers. Moreover, 'Capability' Brown learned his landscape gardening skills at Stowe on his way to his own triumphs at Blenheim.

When the art master, Michael Mounsey, told me to pause from painting war scenes and to study the classical architectural orders like Doric, Ionic or Corinthian, I did not have to go to Greece or Rome – merely to the North Front or the Queen's Temple or whatever. The house is as big as Buckingham Palace and the grounds are laid out in the 'natural' style, with charming temples in glades and valleys. All this had been carved out on the orders of its immensely rich Whig owners, with lakes filled and whole villages moved as the gardens evolved.

You arrived by the Stowe Special train from London, chuffing behind its steam engine after Bletchley along the, now closed, Buckingham Branch Line.

Stowe, North Front

For all its beauty, inside and out, Stowe had a definite menace for a new boy. It was huge and cold, the food was awful and probably illegal. The discipline was probably tougher than that of nearly all modern military units. Bullying existed, but it was not out of hand. Punishments graduated through detention to 'defaulter parades', beating and expulsion.

I must explain defaulter parades. These were awarded for quite minor offences and involved 30 minutes of very tough physical training in some distant and hidden clearing supervised by a Monitor. If you were fit they were not a problem, but I often saw small boys collapse or start vomiting after a few minutes, depending on the carelessness or even sadism of the Monitor. My friend Anthony Provest, who was Second in Command of *HMS Invincible* in the Falklands, years later revealed that Chandos House defaulters were, unknown to us, much tougher than those in the rest of the school. When he first held a school defaulter, he applied the normal Chandos House standards and there was a storm of protest.

One of the first people I met was a 15-year-old called Thomas Boyd-Carpenter. He was the son of Tory Minister John Boyd-Carpenter, a lifelong friend of my father. For years my father monotonously used to intone, 'John's son has got a scholarship, John's boy is doing this, etc.'. So by the time I met Thomas I hated him. He continued to out-perform me academically, but the joke was that when he went into National Service he signed on in the Scots Guards, never went up to Oxford and never continued the shining academic career that had made me so jealous. But he did become a General.

O'BRIEN

Art prize. Battle on the Russian Front, but I had to cover a naked woman with the wagon on the right in case it shocked the parents.

HAVING A BALL

One highlight of my five years at Stowe was, believe it or not, a snowball fight. It had snowed very heavily for two days and all normal games activities were cancelled. Being inside the building of Stowe often felt no warmer than being exposed to the elements.

One day my father turned to me and said, 'By the way, there are two filthy, disgusting words I never want to hear you utter in my presence.' My imagination raced to the many new, disgusting words I was beginning to learn at school.

'What are they, Daddy?' I ventured.

'Civil Servant,' said my father with great emphasis.

Out on the South Front, one or two boys started throwing snowballs and gradually more and more joined in. With nothing else to do all afternoon, the word spread that something was going on, and gradually the majority of the six hundred and forty Stoics gathered on the South Front. The corner flags for the rugger fields were pulled out of the ground and made into makeshift battle standards, and gradually the snowball fight became organised on House lines with four Houses fighting four Houses with occasional changing alliances. Without any formal reorganisation, gradually boys like me who could only throw short distances formed themselves into the infantry while those with better throwing ability, like the cricketers, stood back and like artillery, hurled their snowballs over our heads. I know it sounds very silly but forty years later I can safely state that that two hour maelstrom of snow was one of the best times of my life!

Another big influence was just three miles away. Silverstone Circuit was an old airfield and is now the home of British

The brave but ill-fated BRM

motor racing. It was during a boring maths lesson that we first heard the scream of the BRM practising. Even the Master stopped writing on the blackboard as the shattering noise from those tiny 16 super-charged cylinders filled the classroom.

Most Summer Saturdays we slogged across the fields to Stowe Corner and sneaked into the Circuit. Favourite memories must include Fangio's streamlined Mercedes smashing marker barrels into the air in his attempts to catch Gonzalez's out-dated Ferrari. It was one of the first events I decided to paint.

ALGY, MAN OF MANY PARTS

I had many friends from the North of England, like John Utley and 'Jeg' Naylor. Most of them came from a prep school called Mostyn House in Cheshire.

One of the rather more enigmatic and sensitive boys from that school became a good friend; John Cluff, the son of a wealthy Cheshire businessman. Despite his somewhat foppish demeanour, which earned him his nickname 'Algy', John had a steely determination and grit that totally belied his appearance.

He probably surprised his parents and, indeed, his peers when he eventually volunteered for the SAS and fought in Borneo in the successful jungle war against the Communists with all the bravery and extreme discomfort such fighting entailed. This was the surprising contrast to the other 'Algy', the tall, urbane and extremely well-dressed individual we all knew, who had first gone into the Grenadier Guards, where he met Patrick Lichfield after which we all shared a flat. Algy continued to surprise us. After a brief foray into politics, he went on to own the *Spectator* and to become a highly successful businessman with oil in the North Sea, and later a huge investor in gold mines in Zimbabwe where he was extremely important to the economy and luckily sold out before the political turmoil there.

VOTE
CLUFF
CONSERVATIVE

It was at Stowe that I first began to listen to jazz, not only with friends but with Brian Stephan, my Housemaster. At his memorial service in 1998, the school jazz band played in the chapel. This was an amazing sign of change because our 1955 jazz band, The Rhythm Ramblers, was actually closed down by the music department as 'an evil influence on the school's music', and its leader, Colin Hart-Leviton, severely reprimanded.

Years later another jazz-loving pal, Chris Haines, told me his wonderful revenge story. The School's Director of Music, Dr Hilaire Kelynack, had gone so far as to threaten him, as his star *classical* clarinettist, with expulsion if he 'ever played another note of Dixieland during term' (almost certainly against the law). Chris was so furious that, on the day of the classical school concert, he carefully slashed his finger tips with a razor blade, wrapped ten little bandages round them and walked into the Director's study saying, 'Sorry Sir, I have had this *very* curious accident. I'm afraid cannot play tonight.'

NO JAZZ ON A SUMMER'S DAY

Chris Haines

In 1956, two conflicts suddenly and simultaneously filled our newspapers, Suez and the Hungarian uprising. It is curious to recall how much more interested we were in the events in Budapest than those in Egypt. I remember vividly the images of early success: the Hungarian Army joining the people; the toppling of statues of Stalin; the happiness of the crowds and the despair after Russia's treachery; the fighting in the streets; the murder of General Pal Maleter and later Imre Nagy; and the flight and defection to escape Communist retaliation. Nearly all the Hungarian athletes at the Melbourne Olympics defected. My British Olympic swimming team friends described with awe the ferocity of the blood-soaked water polo final between Russia and Hungary – not a good time to be in the Russian team.

Of Suez, I recall almost nothing, perhaps because it dragged on for so long. It took Britain five months to get the Suez invasion force ready, while in 1982 it took Margaret Thatcher 72 hours to have her task force sailing for the Falklands.

SUEZ AND HUNGARY – DOUBLE CATASTROPHE

RECONNAISSANCE

'Time spent on reconnaissance is seldom wasted.' A military maxim equally applicable to other aspects of life.

At Stowe, our big rugby rival was Oundle. We were told the story of a visiting Bishop who went to preach in Oundle's school chapel, and chose as his theme an epitaph in a West country churchyard: 'Born a man, died a grocer'. His lordship enlarged on the sadness of such materialism, with great eloquence. The Bishop was not a little puzzled at the scarcely suppressed amusement of the boys and the black faces of the members of the governing body.

It was only later that he discovered that Oundle was endowed by the Grocers' Company, prominent members of which comprise the Governors.

IN THE SWIM

In those days, being good at sport at school was felt to be just as important as academic performance. On this physical side, my inability to intercept a moving ball continued and I was really rather a pathetic specimen, painfully thin, sometimes relegated to the feeblest level of physical activity, 'Medical Walks' – wandering off for an hour into the countryside.

My only stardom was in the Art School, where the Art Master, Michael Mounsey, encouraged me to steadily improve.

I showed no leadership abilities and seemed to be on the way to a thoroughly undistinguished school career. Fate intervened in the holidays. Years before, when we first arrived in Wellington Square, I had made friends with another little boy in the street, Timothy ffytche. Two years older than me, he was small and wiry but a natural athlete. When I was 15, he was already Captain of Lancing's swimming team and went training in the Victoria baths every day. If I wanted to be with him, I had to go swimming too. So I went and inevitably copied him. I discovered that the one stroke a thin person can excel at is backstroke. I began to plough up and down with him and, after some months, began to realise at last I was potentially quite good at something.

So back at Stowe I went down to the cold windswept lake into which the wooden swimming pool was built and presented myself to 'Paddy' Pinchbeck, the master in charge of swimming. Pinchbeck was huge and burly with menacing eyes and a moustache. He had also been a Commonwealth Games free-style trialist and was not much fun to play water polo against.

He stared incredulously at my weedy frame and told me to get changed. When my thin white cold body appeared, everybody laughed. I looked like a prototype Mr Bean.

But the fact was that I was already very fast at backstroke and was immediately allowed to swim for the junior team. That immediately transformed my life. I threw all my energies into

'Paddy' Pinchbeck

the sport, training thousands of yards a day, especially in the holidays. I signed on with a coach, Fred Laxton and I trained with his other young swimmers, the star being Judy Grinham, soon to win the Melbourne 1956 Olympic backstroke gold medal.

I put on two stone, became Secretary and then Captain of Swimming, submitting my team-mates to the kind of brutal regime of training (with weights and length after length in the 60° F lake) that I had learned to love. Often I helped to transform boys who had been failures like myself. (A good lesson: an interest, however obscure, can change a personality.)

Just before the Melbourne Olympics, I switched coach to a former Danish champion called Tove Brownsey. She had several members of our British team under training, including Ron Roberts, a policeman, who reached the 100 metres final. When he returned from Australia, Ron used to regale us with outrageous stories as we all sat in the hot tub in the old Nine Elms baths in Battersea. At wild parties after the Games, Gary Chapman (the Australian freestyler) broke his months of strict, abstemious training by making love to a different air hostess every hour until an ambulance took him away. Ron also saved Takashi Ishimoto from death by stopping him repeatedly from diving into a 6-inch-deep ornamental pond while muttering drunkenly, 'I'm going to break my world 200 metres butterfly record.'

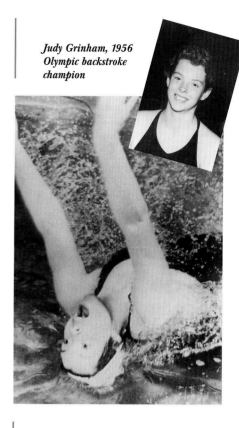

Judy Grinham, 1956 Olympic backstroke champion

RELIGIOUS HOLIDAY

One Summer, Timothy ffytche came up with a novel and, as it turned out, rather peculiar suggestion. Why didn't Jorge Potier, Tim and I go off for a couple of weeks during the Summer holiday to a kind of public schoolboys' camp in Dorset? What he had neglected to tell us was that this was a religious holiday camp, with a full programme of church services and religious discussion groups. This was not to our liking at all, least of all to Jorge, who took it upon himself to shock our rather prissy companions.

On coach expeditions, Jorge would insist on singing dirty songs:

> *And when I woke next morning,*
> *my p.... was very sore.*
> *It felt as though I pushed it*
> *through the key hole in the door.*

We made the best of this fortnight however. Tim, by going to Lulworth Cove to find the unique butterfly, the Lulworth Skipper, and I by going to the Tank Museum at Bovington, which impressed me a great deal, not least because the guns of the German tanks seemed to come over to our side of the hall, so long and powerful were they.

The highlight of this rather bizarre holiday was a game called 'Fighters and Bombers'. All the boys where divided into two groups and the 'bombers' had numbers strapped to their backs. The objective was for the 'bombers' to run from one side of a football pitch to the other and plant handkerchiefs on the touch-line to indicate that they had landed their bombs. The 'fighters' were to run up behind them, and if they could correctly read out the numbers strapped to the back of the bomber they had duly shot it down.

Jorge set off in his rather slow and Portuguese way and fighter after fighter locked on to his back shouting out '412' and banking away. Jorge proceeded straight and level, ignoring all these theoretical hits and duly planted his bombs. So religious and honourable were the other participants that they just assumed they had got the number wrong. They simply could not conceive of anyone ignoring their correct identification and cheating successfully.

SCHOLARSHIP STOPPED

Bill McElwee

My enthusiasm for competitive swimming suddenly created a real and unfair sacrifice. My tutor, Bill McElwee burst into the art school one afternoon. I now assume he must have been drunk. 'I hear you have been elected Captain of Swimming', he literally shouted. 'If you accept, you are out of my Side!'

It should be explained that Bill McElwee was a brilliant historian, whose 'Side', or form, had the best scholarship record from Stowe to Oxford and Cambridge. He held court in his house, Vancouver Lodge, in Dadford, where his wife, the novelist Patience McElwee, served tea to the adoring acolytes. Something of a hero to me, he now seemed grossly offended that the son of Stowe's first History Scholar should wish to devote himself to a boorish sport.

I calmly responded, 'Sir, I think, on balance, my swimming responsibilities are actually doing me as much good as history'.

He stared, stormed off and duly fired me from his Side. Quite illegal, of course. Result: no history scholarship, and no Oxford, but I'm still glad it happened.

This did nothing, of course, to help my relationship with my father. Not only did he start talking in public about his son becoming 'a baths attendant', he also surpassed himself in his habit of failing to turn up at school. The final occasion was the Swimming Sports Day – my carefully planned moment of triumph, when I collected cup after cup for my House.

When I say carefully planned, I mean it. Because a year earlier my friend John Utley, the Head of House, and I had laid our plans to win every trophy we could compete for, including discoloured little cups lurking on shelves for sports events everyone else had forgotten about.

'**Abroad is bloody and all foreigners are buggers.**' This was the reaction at the turn of the nineteenth century of one young English aristocrat to the Grand Tour from which he had just returned. The Grand Tour of cultural cities throughout Europe was meant to broaden the mind of the cloistered Englishman to finish off his education. My (not very) Grand Tour started, at least, with champagne!

In 1957, Epernay was a sleepy little town based entirely on champagne and surrounded by those wonderful villages with names evocative of drunkenness, like Bouzy, Rilly and Dizy! After leaving Stowe, there was an enforced 'gap year' before my call-up date for National Service. So my godfather, Lawrence Venn, had suggested Epernay.

Lawrence was a splendid character, elegant and urbane. During the depression, a company of which he was a director was going to be destroyed by the votes of their shareholders from the North. Lawrence rented the smallest hall in the City and some weeks before had hired a hundred out-of-work actors and given them shares, fitted them out in City clothes, morning coats and spats. He packed the hall. When the men from the North arrived, they could not get past the masses of people voting enthusiastically for the management, and the day was saved.

Later, as Chairman of Moët et Chandon UK, Lawrence instituted a system of recruiting young guides, 'stagiaires', for the Summer to guide visitors around 'les caves', the miles of deep, cool cellars under Epernay. I was the second to go there, following Patrick Forbes, later Moët's Managing Director in London. I had a wonderful Summer. I arrived at their Chateau, Saran, the day after the Rheims 12-hour sports car race and

Laurence Venn

met, as they were leaving, my greatest heroes, the full Ferrari team: Mike Hawthorn, Peter Collins, Luigi Musso and Eugenio Castelotti. All of them were dead from accidents within months, three of them in racing Ferraris, but Mike Hawthorn, foolishly 'dicing', on the Guildford by-pass.

Every day I had to guide about 6 groups of English-speaking tourists through

Mike Hawthorn, World Formula One Champion, 1957

97

'les caves', of which Moët alone had about 17 miles, ending with final production and with a glass or two of champagne with each group. (After several groups and glasses of champagne, I once got hopelessly lost, but was rescued by a workman passing on a fork-lift truck.)

In the evenings we entertained VIPs at Saran, where I was expected to put on my dinner jacket and join in. Sir Timothy Eden, Anthony Eden's brother, was the first guest that I met.

Chateau de Saran

Comte Robert-Jean de Vogüé

The Chateau, under the accomplished direction of Moyra Campbell, boasted the finest food and wine. From the same local champagne grapes we would have a pre-dinner drink, probably of 1910 champagne (champagne survives much longer if the sediment is kept in the bottle, only possible near the cellars), a still white wine, a red wine, a sweet liqueur wine, and even an eau de vie called Marc.

The host at Saran was Comte Robert-Jean de Vogüé, who was head of Moët et Chandon, and one of the great figures in the champagne country. Bob was a hero of the French Resistance and during the eighteen months after he was arrested, he spent some time in 'all the best concentration camps', including Belsen and Buchenwald. His wife had no idea that he was alive until a British intelligence officer, who found him in Belsen, broke Army regulations and sent a message to her. (Incidentally, can you imagine anything more silly than a security regulation which does not permit you to tell a wife of the survival of her hero husband?)

In my spare time, I became backstroke champion of the Marne. Not very difficult, but curiously we swam in the river. With the current, two lengths were incredibly fast and the other two very slow.

More useful, I learned all about champagne and, months later when, as potential officers at the War Office Selection Board, potential officers were asked to do a 5-minute 'lecturette', I used a version of my well-practised tour of Moët's underground empire and it took me straight to the top.

After Epernay, Moët delivered me to Paris in Bob de Vogué's huge American car, which turned out to be General Eisenhower's former staff Cadillac, no less. I moved into some friends' magnificent apartment on the Avenue Victor Hugo but into a room entirely devoid of any furniture and curtains, so that I had to remember to turn off all the lights before getting dressed or undressed.

I suppose that for every new visitor, Paris is a wonder. In 1957 it was full of students who seemed to be striking about something all the time, and I remember once that the doors of the Sorbonne were picketed by the Paris University rugby team supporting some strike about student grants. When they realised I was a foreigner, they immediately offered to let me through to my class, but I would have none of it, insisting on proper student solidarity, mainly so that I could go off and sit in cafés and perhaps talk to girls, who were becoming a serious influence.

This new interest taught me the dangers of 'blind dates'. At the university, I fell under the influence of a rogue of a Russian-born older student called Sasha. For reasons that became obvious, he was known among his friends as 'Dirty Sasha'. At a time when I had scarcely spoken to a girl, Sasha's success with girls excited admiration and envy combined. I was forever going home alone, leaving him in a café with ever-more beautiful and adoring females of many nationalities.

You can imagine my gratitude and pleasure when he asked me if I would like to attend a very exciting Champs Elysées party with the 'beautiful flatmate' of his current girlfriend, who herself seemed to me to be a pinnacle of desirability. This was to be my very first blind date. It was to be my last.

As we waited by the metro station in the Boulevard St. Michel, I eagerly probed about my date's charms.

'But what does she look like? How old is she? What colour hair does she have?'

The normally over-confident Sasha became uneasy, almost shifty. The description of my date dropped from 'extremely beautiful', to 'attractive' and down to 'interesting'.

Just at that moment, I looked down the Boulevard towards the exit from the Metro. Coming towards us was his beautiful girlfriend and her friend, who was walking with a pronounced limp. As she approached, all I could say out of the corner of my mouth before breaking into a smile of welcome, were the words, 'You bastard, Sasha'.

My intended date was (to my eighteen year old eyes) apparently about forty-five, ordinary-looking to the point of ugliness and actually had cross-eyes. This was in addition to the limp. She also spoke not one word of English, and my French was improving only slowly beyond the schoolboy stage.

What compounded the disaster was that the party in the Champs Elysées was full, actually overcrowded with beautiful, available girls. A couple of years later, I suppose, I would have chatted away, been nice, danced with her a couple of times, and then sneaked off into another room and made a pass at somebody else. As it was, I chatted away, was nice, danced a bit and then feigned an appalling headache, and walked miserably home to my lonely room in the Avenue Victor Hugo. It taught me that one should never accept gifts of blind dates from Russians.

MUNICH MUDDLE

Sylviane

Paris passed all too quickly. My father decided it was time for me to learn German. In 1928 and at the same age, he had learned German in ten weeks, or so he claimed. In fact, having spoken to many Germans about him, I think this claim was one of those which holds water. I was very dubious, having never touched German and with far less of a gift for languages than my father.

I duly arrived in a little guesthouse in Gauting, on the railway line from Munich to the ski resorts of Starnberg and Garmisch. One of the queasy things about the area was that only four miles up the road was the village of Dachau, which was, of course, the site of the very first Nazi concentration camp. I confess I never went there. I used to go and wait in the railway station café for my train, where there was a group of middle-aged men who used to play chess. It was easy to muse that statistically some of those men were probably camp guards only a few years before. How nice and innocent and homely they now looked.

I went off on the train to Munich for my first day of German classes. I noticed a very pretty girl walking down the road and into the same building. She showed up at the same class and I sat next to her. Sylviane Baton was French and, as it turned out, shared my love of jazz, having  been the fifties equivalent of a 'groupie', dating many of the jazz musicians in Paris and almost living in the Caveau de la Huchette. We fell in love right there. My German proceeded nowhere and my French continued to improve a treat.

Only a few weeks later, my swimming career ended forever. I had joined the local club, Wasserfreunde München, and was swimming regularly with future members of Germany's 1960

Rome Olympic squad. One day, our coach walked up to us and pointed to a newspaper cutting which stated that Jon and Ilsa Konrads, a Latvian brother and sister now living in Australia, had broken twelve world records in one day in training. The truly amazing thing was that Jon Konrads had broken four world records in one swim. The officials had stopped the watches at 800 metres, 880 yards and 1500 metres on the way to the mile! (That's exactly like Roger Bannister breaking the four minute mile on the way to a two mile race.) Moreover, Jon was just fourteen and Ilsa was twelve. At 19, I suddenly realised I was an old man in swimming terms and the book in which I wrote up my training schedules shows a blank thereafter. My swimming stopped and my knowledge of French further improved.

Indeed, the only German I can really speak with any fluency now is an excellent imitation of the tram driver's announcements on the streets of Munich, and a word-perfect rendition of the loudspeaker announcements for the final of the 100 metres freestyle in the German indoor championships of that year: '*Wettkampf nummer neun. Entscheidung einhundert Meter Kraul. Auf Bahn eins startet Wolfgang Baumann, Bremen '85*' ('Event number 9. Final. 100 metres freestyle. In lane one starts Wolfgang Baumann, Bremen '85'). No wonder my father was irritated on my return.

While a love of New Orleans jazz was a major shared interest with Sylviane, it had played a major role in my life starting before Munich. I had first became interested in it at Stowe listening to Fats Waller and other American records.

In the Britain of the fifties there was little enough choice if you wanted to go out and dance. There were real nightclubs like The 400 and The Blue Angel for sophisticated rich people in dinner jackets, more mundane places such as The Hammersmith Palais and The Orchid Ballroom at Purley and nothing much in between – except jazz clubs. Because my friends were older than me, they took me along to clubs and to the jazz dances at St Martin's School of Art and Chelsea College of Art.

The main jazz clubs we frequented were Cy Laurie's, in Windmill Street, Soho, and Humphrey Lyttelton's in Oxford Street, still surviving as The 100 Club all these years later.

Jazz clubs then were for dancing. There were virtually no seats and everyone danced. You can still see films of the swirling skirts as couples jived, a curious stylised dance brought over by American servicemen.

Many of the dancers were very good indeed, and I resolved that jiving was one of the things that I was going to be good at. You had to start at the bottom. No girl was going to dance with

The Konrads Kids, holders of 37 World Records between them.

Not many people realise that Rolf Harris (page 161) was a top flight swimmer. Following his hit song *Tie Me Kangaroo Down, Sport*, he wrote special verses for his friends in the 1960 Australian Olympic Team:

*Swim a lap underneath, Keith
Swim a lap underneath
Tell 'em you've lost your false teeth, Keith
Swim a lap underneath.
All together now ...*

ALL THAT JAZZ

Cy Laurie in his club near Piccadilly

30 years on. 'Mad Maureen', George Melly and me. Would the Old Stoic Society approve?

a total stranger in fast traditional jazz dancing because you could literally break arms if people were clumsy. Gradually, I worked up to being able to dance with the four best dancers at Cy Laurie's. Two tiny girls called Maggie and Vera, a tall willowy girl – later a girlfriend – called Barbara, and Maureen. Maureen, who will feature later as 'Mad Maureen', was the 'heavy metal' of the really good dancers and used to dance regularly with a tall, bearded blond man who was so like so many paintings and sculptures of the crucifixion that everyone called him 'Jesus'. We later discovered that he was called 'Abraham', which still seemed fairly appropriate.

There was no alcohol served, so there was a quick rush to the pub in the intervals. Jazz clubs were very scruffy places with low fashion standards. Jazz clubs also taught most of us about the new invention of the deodorant. In fact, I remember the classic occasion when at the Lyttelton Club I asked a girl to dance and she said, 'Do you mind dancin' with my friend? I'm sweatin'.'

On Sunday afternoons, what the papers called the 'Chelsea Smart Set' (Suna Portman and company) descended on Cy Laurie's, and for two or three hours what was basically a working-class form of amusement was graced by the highest in the land.

There were many London jazz clubs at that time, but only The 100 Club survives. It looks exactly the same as it did all those years ago except that only a few of us middle-aged ones still dance, stared at by the bewildered Japanese, American and Germans who sit listening religiously to the music. Cy Laurie, 'Humph' and fellow Old Stoic George Melly still come to play.

In the Spring of 1958, it was time to leave Munich to return to this London scene, to plan to meet Sylviane in England, to cut my hair and prepare for a very different new home called Caterham.

CHAPTER 10 SERVING THE NATION

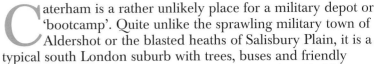

aterham is a rather unlikely place for a military depot or 'bootcamp'. Quite unlike the sprawling military town of Aldershot or the blasted heaths of Salisbury Plain, it is a typical south London suburb with trees, buses and friendly family homes with dogs and cats. In April 1958, I began the long climb up the hill from the railway station, lugging a heavy suitcase. Having spent in Paris and Munich an enforced 'gap year', I was one of the last to be called up for National Service. I am also among those who claim that they 'would not have missed it for the world.' But then, I was lucky, destined for an elite part of the Army, the Brigade of Guards, with standards of professional excellence, courage and style that were immediately apparent, whatever the initial discomfort.

Reporting to the legendary Guards Depot in Caterham proved a shattering experience. Blessed with what I thought was a short new haircut and, already tired and hot, having toiled up from the station, I slowly entered those great, sinister gates. Standing in the entrance was a huge man. He stared down at me from under the peak of his cap. 'WHAT'S YOUR NAME?' he roared.

'O'Brien, Sergeant', I stuttered. Even at that stage I knew what three stripes meant.

He ticked my name off on a list. He then screamed over his shoulder the enigmatic word 'RUNNER'. A young Guardsman clattered out of the Guardroom and crashed to a halt facing away from us.

'RUNNER, QUICK MARCH' the Sergeant bellowed at him, and off into the distance, somewhat mysteriously I thought, marched the Guardsman at an enormous speed. The Sergeant watched him go fifty yards and then turned to me and screamed three inches from my ear, 'CATCH HIM UP'.

Recovering from the shock, I picked up my heavy suitcase and pursued the distant Guardsman who was maintaining a furious pace. As we emerged from the shadow of the Guardroom, a vast parade ground appeared on my left with dozens of squads marching and counter-marching, supervised by bawling drill instructors. Every one of them took great pleasure in pausing from his duty, staring after me and screaming something about 'THE HORRIBLE, IDLE, DOZY ONE WITH THE SUITCASE, GET A MOVE ON YOURSELF'.

After half a mile of following the pounding Guardsman, I was trembling with fear, heat exhaustion and fatigue. I entered an induction room littered with ashen-faced young men who had just gone through a similar experience. We were 'The Brigade

Squad' and were due to become officers, providing we made it through Caterham and passed the War Office Selection Board. We had to pass through Caterham in twelve weeks, whereas a normal Guardsman went through in sixteen, so it was going to be much tougher than the normal recruit period.

We were all just starting to recover and introduce ourselves when suddenly the door flew open and in stalked an immaculate Sergeant with the white cap band of the Coldstream Guards, accompanied by a Welsh Guardsman. We scrambled to our feet.

He stared at us coldly and said, 'My name is Sergeant Wilkins, Coldstream Guards. This is Trained Soldier Gibson, Welsh Guards. If I 'ave any trouble from any of you, YOU WILL 'AVE TROUBLE WITH A CAPITAL 'T' THE HEIGHT OF THIS CEILING!'

Wilkins was just warming to his theme when the door opened and in lounged a tall, relaxed young man who we later discovered was Simon Fraser, the Master of Lovat, son of Lord Lovat of D-Day fame. 'Good evening' he drawled. The incredibly languid appearance of Simon stopped even Wilkins in mid-track, but not for long.

(Simon became a special target for Wilkins in the weeks ahead. He seemed curiously incensed that people should enjoy themselves and regarded it as an especially successful insult to sneer, 'Fraser, I expect you have been laughin' and jokin' with your friends again'.)

We were almost immediately marched to the barbers where we were given a 'proper' haircut, which took off any remaining hair. We then collected battledress, boots, belts, and caps, all of which would need endless work to make them half-respectable.

During National Service there were nearly 2,000 recruits at Caterham, all at different stages. On our first parade we were shambling about still dressed in civilian clothes. By contrast, some of the squads were 16-week squads who had just 'passed out' and were immaculate in their drill.

I am really very sorry no one ever filmed the instructors going on parade. When the fearsome Regimental Sergeant Major, RSM 'Jolly' Rodger, shouted 'MARKERS, GET ON PARADE' a block of men ten deep by ten wide crashed to attention, and marched on at an incredible pace. At that time they were probably the hundred best men at drill in the world, and to see them halt and then spread out on the huge parade ground was a magnificent sight that you had to admire, however frightened you might have been.

Our second morning at Caterham gave me the useful legacy of never again having any trouble getting up early. Our hut was half a mile from the main barracks and it was quite difficult to

Sergeant Wilkins,
Coldstream Guards

RSM Rodger, Scots Guards

LICHFIELD

hear the bugle blowing Reveille. We all slumbered on, exhausted. Suddenly the door slammed open and Wilkins started shouting, 'GET OUT OF BED, GODDAMN AND BLAST YOUR EYES!' Such was the shock that I have woken with a start at about six ever since!

The day at the Depot was divided into six periods, two of drill, two of weapon training, and two of physical training. The idea of Caterham was to break you down from a shambling civilian into a drill automaton.

While it was tough, it was not really that much of a shock, especially as we had all come from hard disciplined schools, with high standards of physical education. What is more, the food had improved! At Caterham we had marvellous fresh bread, not the mouldy stuff that our school had allowed to get stale to save money.

Only occasionally did life get really unpleasant, usually after public criticism. 'The Brigade Squad looks idle, Sergeant Wilkins.' That's when we were 'rifted', drilled until some of us started to collapse, littering the parade ground with inert figures. As someone once said, 'When your Sergeant stops in front of you with eyes bulging, face purple and froth around the lips, pay attention! These are some of the little signs that tell the keen observer that all is not well.'

I noticed something early on. As potential officers we were from all five Foot Guards Regiments – Grenadier, Coldstream, Scots, Irish, Welsh. So, when walking around the barracks, our mixed cap badges gave us away and the Sergeants picked on us as future officers while they could.

This I solved by never walking with my friends but running everywhere with a piece of paper in my hand. It looked as if I was on an urgent errand. Nobody ever bothered me.

THE GENTLE HOMILIES OF SERGEANT WILKINS

In the evening we sat astride our beds and polished everything. A century-old tradition, the 'shining parade' was two hours of silence, broken only by Wilkins and Gibson quizzing us about the history and traditions of our regiments. The first night we suddenly heard the measured click of thirty men going past with their heels hitting the ground at exactly the same time. Wilkins looked up and with a glint in his eye said reverently, 'That, gentlemen, is a Sixteen-Week Squad'.

Wilkins was capable of extreme humour and, because of this, we all grew fond of him. I remember him halting us and growling, 'You remember the click of that sixteen week squad. That is what I want to hear from you. I AM, AT THE MOMENT, ONLY HEARING THE RATTLING NOISE OF TWO SKELETONS HAVING A RUB OUT ON A TIN ROOF!'

During one morning parade, a tiny child from the married quarters went past on a tricycle. Wilkins stared balefully after it and screamed 'HOLD YOUR HEAD UP AND GET THOSE KNEES MOVING IN DOUBLE TIME'. The child nearly fell off and we just had to giggle. He growled, 'I see nothing funny in an idle child'.

He was capable of so many crisp remarks that I used to telephone them to my father every night, knowing how much he would appreciate them. I think the most appalling words Wilkins ever uttered were when we were becoming more friendly with him towards the end of our course. 'I volunteers' he revealed with relish, 'to be Picquet Sergeant on the night of the Depot dance. I enjoys creepin' round the drill sheds hopin' to find some of the recruits with their young ladies'. His eyes then became manic with satisfaction. 'And just as they are gettin' to the short strokes, I PULLS THEM OFF!'

The thought of youthful love-making being curtailed by a screaming Sergeant Wilkins in the dark made our flesh creep.

The Commander of our Brigade Squad was Captain Trevor Dawson, later to emerge rather incongruously as a shareholder in 'Sibylla's', the discotheque. Trevor's really memorable moment was the Depot Sports Day. He strolled up to the discus throwing competition, removed his hat but did not bother to take off his Sam Brown belt, picked up the discus and threw it further than everyone, including all the Physical Training Sergeants. He did not spin round or anything – he just picked it up, threw it, collected his trophy and walked away!

THE MASTER OF LOVAT AND THE COAL HOLE

Simon Fraser revealed an eccentric side when we were detailed to do 'fatigues' – painting the hut, cleaning the latrines and so on. Simon inexplicably volunteered, with me, to shift a huge pile of coal to the boiler house. Resentfully, I began to laboriously carry the coal in shovel loads from the heap in which it had been dumped round to the side of the little coal hut. Simon just loaded his shovel and shot the whole lot 20 feet straight through the tiny window in the side of the hut, continuing with untiring accuracy.

Amazed, I asked him how on earth he did it, and he revealed that he had run out of money in Australia and the only way he could get back to England in time to sign on in the Army was to become a stoker on a steamer.

After several weeks of sweating in the tropics, shooting coal accurately through the fire door of the boiler, he got his dinner jacket out of his suitcase, went up to the first class saloon and started playing poker. He made enough money in one evening to buy himself out of his gruelling service below decks and

came back to England in some style. But he had not forgotten his new-found skill with a shovel.

Sadly, Simon and his brother Andrew died within weeks of each other in 1997, followed shortly afterwards by their father, almost of a broken heart.

One of the things we had to learn fairly quickly in the army was the meaning of bugle calls. Most civilians will be familiar with the mnemonics that explain the beginning of a parade: 'FALL IN A, FALL IN B, FALL IN EVERY COMPAN-Y' or meal times: 'COME TO THE COOKHOUSE DOOR BOYS, COME TO THE COOKHOUSE DOOR'.

However, I doubt if many civilians are familiar with the official mnemonic we learned for the 'Quarter for the Parade', i.e. the bugle call quarter of an hour before any parade that goes: 'YOU'VE GOT A FACE LIKE A CHICKEN'S ARSE!'

FIELD MARSHAL 'ALEX'

*Field Marshal Earl
Alexander of Tunis*

It was during my period as a recruit at Caterham that I first met Field Marshal Alexander. As Colonel of the Irish Guards, he paid the Depot an annual visit and I was marched in front of him. The great man looked at my details and then glanced up and said with a smile 'Sie sprechen Deutsch, nicht wahr?' I could not help myself and responded in best Wermacht tradition, 'Jawohl, mein Generalfeldmarshall!'

He grinned again and I was dismissed. I was to meet him very often in the next few years because his younger son Brian became one of my best friends.

London's clubs certainly have their own sense of hierarchy. Just at the end of the war, a big staff car slid to a halt in front of White's and out stepped the immaculate figure of 'Alex', now Field Marshal Earl Alexander of Tunis, recent victor of the Italian campaign and acknowledged war hero.

Up and down St James's, officers saluted and men took off their hats. He strode up the steps of White's Club and disappeared.

An American bystander managed to buttonhole the doorman before he went back into the Club and enquired who the prominent man had been. Puzzled, the doorman replied 'Oh. That's Lord Caledon's younger brother.'

Field Marshal Alexander was a man of impeccable manners and it took a lot to

GRIMSDALE

make him irritated. He accompanied the Queen on an official visit to Italy and found himself seated next to a haughty Roman matron.

Showing considerable lack of both knowledge and tact, the lady turned to him and said 'Field Marshal. Have you ever been to Rome before?'

'Madam, I liberated Rome,' blandly retorted Alexander.

There are many who knew, or served with Alexander, who felt strongly that he was overshadowed in the media by his egotistic, publicity-seeking deputy, Montgomery. This is probably because of his legendary modesty and gentleman's charm. King George VI once visited Alexander and Monty in their desert headquarters. After an hour of declaiming how exactly he was going to use 'his' troops, Monty was briefly called away. Alex quietly apologised to his Monarch that neither had been able to get a word in, commenting ruefully, 'I'm afraid he may be after my job'. 'Thank God for that,' replied his Majesty, 'I thought he was after mine.'

After the war, Monty visited my father-in-law, General Sir John Cowley who had served on Monty's staff and was now Chairman of Bowmaker, the hire purchase company. John recalls:

> He used to come to lunch with the directors of Bowmaker. Clearly he had no knowledge whatever of the business world. At his first lunch with us, he asked: 'John, does your company borrow money?' The Financial Director replied 'Yes, that is our job. We borrow money at a certain rate and lend it to our clients at a higher rate and a greater risk.'
>
> 'You are absolutely wrong to borrow money. Absolutely wrong,' announced Monty. 'Ever since I was a subaltern I have never borrowed a penny from anybody. I keep my money in Lloyds Bank at Alton.'
>
> After a pause the chief accountant asked: 'Do you think your money is *kept* in the Alton bank?' 'Yes, certainly it is,' replied Monty. 'They have kept it there for over fifty years.'

King George VI and 'Alex' at 1950 Irish Guards New Colours Ceremony

'Monty', a brilliant man of the army, but not a man of the world

HALF WAY HOUSE

Before we passed out from Caterham, we attended WOSB, the War Office Selection Board at Barton Stacey camp in Hampshire. As we ran through dozens of written exams, practical tests and interviews, all the potential officers wore denims, with no identification, not even names, just numbers. Thus the selecting officers could not be biased for or against a candidate's regiment.

Most of our Brigade Squad passed and went on to the Officer Cadet School at Mons, a sprawling complex in Aldershot named after the first delaying battle of 1914. The routine was

RSM Desmond Lynch

much more complicated than the six regimented periods that we had left at Caterham. Having been broken down to almost unthinking discipline, we had to be built up to command – both morally and technically.

My principal memories are those of panic. Panic that I would be in the wrong place at the wrong time and with the wrong equipment ('What rifle parade?').

The Regimental Sergeant Major was six foot three and called Lynch, who happened to be an Irish Guardsman but for many reasons I did not feel any particular regimental affinity with him. Believe it or not, his two Drill Sergeants were called Leech and Blood. Discovering that the three men most in charge of my destiny were called Lynch, Leech and Blood was not likely to calm my almost permanent panic.

A SHOT IN THE DARK

But, it was Desmond Lynch who was to help me over a very difficult incident. We had been out on a night exercise during which we had been using blank rounds in our rifles. We were paraded at the end of the exercise in almost pitch dark and ordered to 'clear our weapons'. The procedure with our bolt-action Lee-Enfield rifles was to work the bolt back and forth at least 15 times (we had room for ten rounds in a magazine), close the bolt, pull the trigger with the rifle facing upwards and then put it on 'safe'.

We were half way through this procedure, when with a sudden 'BANG', the scene was lit up by my rifle going off.

'**Who did that?**' bellowed our Company Sergeant Major from the darkness.

'O'Brien, Sir,' I owned up.

'You silly, silly wally, Sir,' muttered my Platoon Sergeant in my ear. '**Got him**, Sir.'

The result was that I was marched in to the Commandant the next day for 'dangerously discharging a weapon', a crime that might have endangered my stay at Mons and therefore my Commission.

The Commandant asked me what I had to say.

'I thank you, Sir, for leave to speak. However, I would have to point out that the whole point of this rifle procedure is to try to clear any round in the rifle, especially in the dark. If there was one jammed in the breech by firing it upwards as part of a drill movement, it would be at least safe.'

'What do you think, Sergeant Major?'

'I actually think he has a point, Sorr,' Regimental Sergeant Major Lynch growled from the corner.

Thus, I was let off with a caution and I have to thank that huge and frightening Irishman for intervening on my behalf.

Another good lesson was provided, near the end of the course, by an exercise called Marathon. We began by marching to a piece of scrubby hillside and digging a major defensive position. Having to prepare for the fall out from atomic attack, the main part of the nine-foot deep trenches had to be covered in another three feet of protective earth. Within hours we were exhausted just from the effort of digging.

There then followed three days of fighting, patrolling and just staying up freezing all night. Luckily, the Scots Guards in a 'machine gun nest' led by Simon Fraser had managed to smuggle in some alcohol, so I felt it was important to go and have 'liaison meetings' about fields of fire and such things with them from time to time.

At night, we were meant to have two sentries for each trench awake for each two-hour stint. I said to my partner that this was silly and 'Why didn't one of us snatch half an hour's sleep and then hand over to the other?' The trouble was we kept shortening the periods. Suddenly, we realised that we had done about ten 'sentry goes' already, only half-way through the stint!

The end of Marathon taught me a lesson never forgotten. Exhausted, at the end of the exercise, in darkness and pouring rain, we had to fill in the trenches and to march off to where the trucks were supposed to be. We trudged down a lane and there at a crossroads was a motorcycle dispatch rider. We asked him which way the trucks were. He told us to turn left. After another mile of sloshing through the dark loaded with our equipment, our Company Commander roared up in his Land Rover, halted us and explained, 'You've just learned a very valuable military lesson. The dispatch rider did not know where the trucks were. Please remember this in future: **never, never trust the word of a private soldier**. ABOUT TURN. QUICK MARCH.'

He could of course have brought the trucks with him, but he did not, and so for two miserable miles every step pounded that lesson into our brains. He was being neither class nor rank conscious, he was merely pointing out the obvious truth that you should not act on advice from somebody who is not qualified to give it without checking. When you think of it, it applies well to the civilian environment.

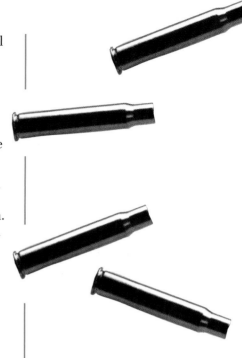

FRENCH DIS-CONNECTION

I did suffer one loss at Mons, my girlfriend Sylviane 'Yanou'. She had, as promised, come to England to be with me but inconveniently had ended up as an au pair near the end of the Central Line at Wanstead. Several times, for the sake of one more doorstep kiss, I had missed the last train to Aldershot and spent the night at Waterloo Station.

One night, calling her from a cold and evil-smelling phone box, she announced that she had fallen for Laurie Chescoe. 'He sells, you know, zee brassieres and zee knickers.' 'A bloody lingerie salesman!' I spluttered, humiliated that my up-coming 'Officer and Gentlemen' status was to be turned down for this. 'And a good jazz drummer', she continued. 'Oh, that's OK, then.' I conceded. They are still happily married and Yanou looks as good and dances as well as she did 40 years ago.

My rival, Laurie Chescoe, and Yano

QUEEN VICTORIA'S IRISH LEGACY

Panic overcome, eventually all went well at Mons and I passed out from Officer Cadet School commissioned as a Second Lieutenant in the Irish Guards.

The Irish Guards were formed in 1900. The ageing Queen Victoria had remarked that one of the few bright spots in the somewhat disastrous battles of the Boer War was the gallantry of her Irish Regiments. So, before her death she decreed that:

'Her Majesty the Queen, having deemed it desirable to commemorate the bravery shown by the Irish Regiments in recent operations in South Africa, has been graciously pleased to command that an Irish Regiment of Foot Guards be formed.'

The poet Rudyard Kipling, who after his son's death in action with the Regiment, volunteered to write the Regiment's Great War history, was to say:

**'We're not so old in the Army List,
But we're not so young at our trade.'**

The regiment was to fulfil all the old Queen's expectations with constant bravery in both World Wars coupled with Irish humour. In their first battle in 1914, Colonel Morris sought to reassure his men about the shell fire: 'D'you hear that? They're doing that to frighten you.'

Some wag replied: 'If that's what they're after, Sorr, they might as well stop. They succeeded with *me* hours ago!'

When you read Peter Verney's excellent book, *The Micks* it is hard not to be moved by the sacrifices. At Festubert in 1915, of

38 officers from the 1st Battalion who went into action at the beginning of the day, only two were untouched by evening and 400 men were casualties out of 1,110. At Loos, their comrades in the 2nd Battalion lost eight officers and 300 men in their first battle.

In the second war the losses were equally devastating. In North Africa in April 1943, at the murderous but successful Battle of the Bou, four companies were reduced to one, and many of the officers and NCO's were killed or wounded. One hero, Lance Corporal Kenneally not just once, *but also again the next day*, single-handedly charged and broke up whole German companies forming up to attack. During the second charge he was wounded but continued to hop around the battlefield supported by a Guardsman and firing his Bren–gun, which he refused to give up 'as he was the only one who understood it'. He was awarded the Victoria Cross.

The future Field Marshal 'Alex' as a Captain in the trenches, 1915

In the final days of the war, our last Victoria Cross winner, Guardsman Charlton, almost exactly duplicated the Medal of Honor exploit of America's Audie Murphy. He leapt back on to his burning tank, dismounted its Browning machine gun and walked firing towards a German counterattack. Then, when hit in the arm, he propped the gun on a gatepost and continued firing until he was mortally wounded. His posthumous VC was endorsed by a German officer who came up to the wire in his prison cage and asked to speak to an officer 'about the bravery of an Irish soldier'.

This, then, in 1958 was the wonderful regiment *The Micks* which returned from Cyprus, to Victoria Barracks, Windsor. We four new officers joined them and with typical Irish levity we were called 'Eeny, Meeny, Miny, Mo.' Mine was the only name that stuck, which is why friends from that time still call me 'Mo O'Brien'.

Joining the Irish Guards was not nearly as traumatic for a new officer as the stories you hear about other regiments, where nobody spoke to you in the Officers' Mess for weeks. For instance, my future friend Patrick Lichfield, then Patrick Anson, described the Officer's Mess in the Grenadiers. He foolishly tried to break the ice at his first breakfast by saying, 'Lovely morning, glorious day.' A pompous Major lowered his newspaper, rose to his feet, banged his spoon on the table and coldly announced, 'Gentlemen, Lord Anson wishes to address the Mess on the subject of the weather.' The Irish Guards from all ranks tend to be more relaxed and jokey than that.

The Guardsmen arrived sun-burned and fit from Cyprus and

AN IRISH HERO!

I IRISHMAN DEFEATS 10 GERMANS.

SERGEANT

MICHAEL O'LEARY, V.C.

• IRISH GUARDS •

HAVE YOU NO WISH TO EMULATE THE SPLENDID BRAVERY OF YOUR FELLOW COUNTRYMAN

JOIN AN IRISH REGIMENT TO·DAY

Recruiting poster, 1915

immediately clashed with the local 'Teddy Boys', young toughs so labelled because of their Edwardian style of attire. Two or three of these in a pub had picked on one Guardsman drinking by himself, failing to notice the large number of short-haired, tall, sun-burned young men surrounding them. There was a very brief fight, and the police merely picked up the Teddy Boys as they bounced from the pavement and quietly took them away. (You could tell many of the friendly Windsor police were former Guardsmen by the way they had slashed the peaks of their caps!) From then on the Teddy Boys of Windsor never dared wear their distinctive clothes and used to go off to Staines and Slough and hang about there as it was less risky.

By 1958, the Irish Guards consisted of one Battalion (it had three during World War II). Its 800 men were divided into five Companies: Headquarters Company (command, supply, signals, transport, medical, etc), Support Company (heavy weapons – machine guns, mortars, anti-tank), and 3 Rifle Companies. These each had a Company Commander (a Major), Second in Command (Captain) and three Platoons of about 32 men, each with 3 sections of about 8 men armed with rifles and one light machine gun.

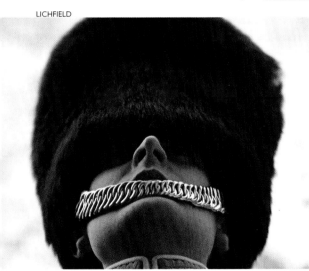

LICHFIELD

I took over command of number 3 Platoon in No.1 Company with the tallest men in the Battalion, with the help of a Platoon Sergeant (George Shannon), a Lance Sergeant and 3 Corporals who commanded my Sections.

My first Irish Guards parade did not start well. The officers all 'patrolled' up and down in front of the parade. We were wearing for the first time our bearskins, perhaps not yet with assurance.

The Adjutant, Major John Head, stopped in his tracks and exclaimed drily, 'Mr O'Brien, you look like a funny man,' and resumed his patrol.

A few weeks after arriving in Windsor, Field Marshal Alex's son, Brian, arrived in the regiment and we became firm friends. Brian was charming and with good looks reminiscent of Jack Kennedy.

LICHFIELD

I had another stroke of luck. My Company Commander was Major Giles Allan, brother-in-law of Tony Rolt who, with Duncan Hamilton, had won the Le Mans twenty-four hour race in a C-Type Jaguar a few years before.

Tony Rolt was Managing Director of Ferguson Projects, a division of Massey-Ferguson Tractors, which was trying to perfect four-wheel drive for cars.

Giles Allan not only commissioned from me six oil paintings for his drawing room, but he introduced me to Tony Rolt and I started doing paintings for him. This resulted in a burgeoning professional painting career, delivering motor racing paintings for individuals or companies, which was to last for about five years.

I soon got to know and depend on my Platoon Sergeant, George Shannon. Like my father, he had a passion for paper-back Westerns and I began to lend him novels by the dozen. It took me some time to realise that my nickname in the Sergeants' Mess had become 'Hopalong Cassidy' (although I would imagine there are worse names for a young officer to be called).

Many of the officers just senior to me when I joined the Irish Guards were the sons of those killed in one of the most tragic incidents in the Regiment's history. In 1940, the Irish Guards were part of the task force trying to stop the Germans in Norway. As they were transferring from one Norwegian port to another, their ship, the *Chobry*, was caught by Heinkel bombers. One bomb went down the funnel and killed the Commanding Officer, the Second-in-Command, three Company Commanders and the Adjutant and wounded the other two Company Commanders, nearly every single person of command importance in the Battalion, yet hardly touching any of the more junior ranks. A freak disaster which is unique in the history of the British Army.

At the time of Norway and the *Chobry* sinking, Goebbel's curious and secret propaganda jazz band, 'Charlie and his Orchestra', had Churchill singing:

'Don't know why,
I can't blockade the sky.
Stormy weather.

Since my ships and the German planes got together,
I'm beaten every time.

Life is bare, bloomin' misery everywhere. Stormy weather.

Just can't keep my ships together, they're sinking all the time.

Oh blimey, they're sinking all the time.'

(Actually, the Germans lost enough ships in Norway to spoil any chance of invading Britain.)

Later the Captain of H.M.S. *Wolverine* who took the Irish Guards off the *Chobry* said:

'I never before realised what the discipline of the Guards was. Their conduct in the most trying circumstances, in the absence of senior officers, on a burning and sinking ship, was as fine or finer than the conduct of the soldiers on the *Birkenhead*. 694 men were got on board in sixteen minutes.'

Peter Verney pointed out something extra in his book:

'The loss of their officers created an overwhelming sense of desolation because the rapport between officers and men is perhaps closer in an Irish regiment than elsewhere. Their loss was of personal friends more than of superiors.'

SPECIAL OCCASION

At Windsor Castle it was our job to provide the Guard, in the same way that Buckingham Palace is guarded. The Queen used to invite the Officer of the Guard up to dinner, but there had been rather a long gap in this practice, caused by a young officer in another Regiment. The Queen asked him if it was not the practice to wear a stiff shirt with his Mess Dress and he replied 'Oh no, Ma'am, that's only for special occasions'. She plainly thought that dining with one's Monarch *might* be a special occasion and had a sense of humour failure. This was redressed by the style and wit of several of my brother officers, one of whom fell off the sofa in a fit of giggles.

DEBS' DELIGHTS

The young officers of 'the Micks' were universally popular during National Service and tended to be invited en masse to debutante parties, whereas their fellows in the rest of the Brigade were chosen more selectively.

At that time, the rather bizarre debutante system was still thriving. It was a procedure designed to bring sheltered society daughters into contact with potential suitors. A girl having left school or finishing school, then 'came out' (a term whose future meaning would have appalled the society hostesses of the time). She was launched into society by being presented to the Queen at Buckingham Palace. For the rest of the Season there was an endless series of cocktail parties, balls and house parties. Apart from the 500 debutantes, this system needed a list of an equal number of single, supposedly respectable, eligible young men. The Brigade of Guards was an obvious source of such 'Debs' Delights'.

Many of my friends, civilian or military, lived on this system for years by necessity. At a time when you were only paid £6 a week ($9), lots of champagne and, more important, plenty of food was a paltry price to pay for the nightly company of the same pretty (and not available) girls and even the less pretty ones (who tended to be more available!).

Chatting up

I heard a nice story about the Queen Mother's sense of humour at this time. She was at a dance and sent her Equerry over to a young officer saying that she would like to have the next dance with him.

The Equerry returned somewhat embarrassed and said that the young officer was 'very sorry but that he had promised the next dance to the Queen'.

Later on the dance floor the Queen Mother came alongside the young man dancing and hissed to him with a grin, 'Snob!' and danced away.

Officers in the Brigade of Guards were theoretically as regimented in their spare time as they were in barracks. In London you were expected to wear a dark suit, a stiff detachable collar and a bowler hat and carry a tightly rolled umbrella. You were not allowed to travel on a bus and, for some reason, you were not allowed to carry a parcel, smoke in the street or hold hands with a girl. All this presumably to preserve the dignity of the position.

At night, you were supposed to wear a dinner jacket or even a white tie and tails, which was fine for nightclubs like the Blue Angel or the Four Hundred and for debs' balls but I don't think would have gone down too well in my jazz clubs. In fact I was breaking all sorts of rules going to such clubs at all. I suppose the perceived danger was of meeting some of my Guardsmen while I was appearing less than dignified.

Indeed, at the very beginning of his jazz career, Humphrey Lyttelton used to be very anxious when he sneaked off to play trumpet in the front line of a jazz band. He was still serving as an officer in the Grenadiers and was worried lest his senior officers might come in for a 'slumming night out'.

One of my more unnerving tasks was to pick up the two young sons of the Duke of Gloucester from Eton and show them some of the battle drills that our Regiment was practising. Hugh O'Neill, now Lord Rathcavan, was particularly frightening, bearing in mind I was in charge of two possible heirs to the throne. Roaring through through Windsor Park with his Machine Gun Platoon, sliding the unstable Champs sideways, left my heart in my mouth.

Sudden panic was a feeling that could be repeated quite often. One morning I was strolling across the central green of Victoria Barracks, Windsor with my friend Barry Dinan. We watched the Windsor Castle Guard forming up.

OFFICERS' CODES

LICHFIELD

Making the umbrella ever tighter

ROYAL RISKS

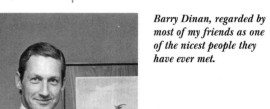

Barry Dinan, regarded by most of my friends as one of the nicest people they have ever met.

Picquet Officer and Picquet Sergeant, thankless 24-hour tasks, which risked more trouble

'Good heavens,' we said, 'It's amazing the slack type of officer we are getting nowadays. Look, there's no Officer of the Guard ready to march off.'

After a few more seconds of this banter, I suddenly stopped in my tracks and blurted out 'It isn't Thursday, is it?' You have never seen someone change from khaki shirtsleeve order into a bearskin and tunic so fast. But not fast enough!

Three minutes later, the inevitable words 'I'll see you in my office the day after tomorrow' came from the Adjutant. Sitting in Windsor Castle I reflected that I had not panicked quite as much as usual, and needed some money to buy a car, so why not sign on for two more years? The Adjutant was most surprised, having handed me seven days as Picquet Officer (a normal punishment), by my request to sign on, apparently for more punishment.

Some time later I learned another lesson from the same Adjutant. Apparently I had called one of my Guardsmen 'a silly bastard'.

The problem was that this Guardsman was a *bastard* in the true sense that he was illegitimate. He thought I knew this and actually put in a formal complaint. I was ordered to apologise to him face to face.

EQUAL OPPORTUNITY

One attractive feature of the Irish Guards is worth mentioning. There was no discrimination whatsoever. Guardsmen were recruited from The Republic of Ireland, Northern Ireland and Liverpool. We were roughly half and half, Catholic and Protestant, including the officers. Except at Church Parade, our origins or religion were never identified – or mentioned.

Only years later, after the Freedom Marches and the rebirth of the IRA, did I become aware of the discrimination that had remained and increased in Northern Ireland, while British Governments looked on. 3,000 people dead and thousands injured in Northern Ireland was the result, but at no time did I get a hint of the problems in our genuinely 'equal opportunity' Regiment, whose motto *Quis Separabit?* (Who will separate us?) is the very antithesis of the sectarian divide.

SERGEANT SKILLS

The British Army has always relied on the calibre and strength of its Non-Commissioned Officers. A somewhat limp-wristed padre was having great difficulty making his choir turn to the altar at the correct moment during the Creed. His Regimental

118

Sergeant Major happened to be watching this shambling, unmilitary performance.

After a few minutes, he could bear it no longer and stepped forward to ask if he could help, whereupon the padre asked him to 'Carry on'. The Sergeant Major fixed his eyes on the cassocked figures with considerable distaste and then helpfully bellowed at them.

WHEN YOU HEAR THE WORDS, 'I BELIEVE IN GOD THE FATHER'. I DON'T WANT TO SEE A FLICKER OF MOVEMENT FROM ANY OF YOU. THEM'S WORDS OF COMMAND ARE ONLY CAUTIONARY.

BUT, WHEN YOU HEAR THE PADRE SAY, 'AND JESUS CHRIST', ROUND YOU GO WITH A CLICK OF THE HEELS!

'I think that should do it, Sir,' he said, handing back to the padre.

Mention of the deity reminds me of the Sergeant giving evidence against some Guardsmen, who had left the lights on after 'lights out':

'As I was passing 'B' hutment I saw a light and shouted 'Put that light out at once'. From out of 'B' hutment came the words 'hush, it is the Lord Jesus Christ himself'. On entering 'B' hutment, I found this not to be the case.'

LICHFIELD

MAKING UP THE NUMBERS

My Company Sergeant Major, John McComiskey, was a very effective Warrant Officer and one you would have to describe as a bit of a character.

For instance, the annual tug-of-war tended to be won by big men, either a platoon from the tallest rifle company, our No 1 Company, or other specialists who had to heave large chunks of equipment around like the Anti-tank Platoon. I once caught McComiskey sorting rather too publicly our teams into one of huge men and another of much smaller men, thus ensuring we were creating the winning team. I didn't stop him but I did suggest that it would be a good idea to do it out of sight.

Soon after the Second World War, the Irish Guards had taken over from another Regiment in Tunisia and had got themselves into real trouble in the handover of the transport. It must be appreciated that, probably unique to the British Army, officers are financially responsible for the equipment. If you were £10 out at the end of pay parade, you made up the difference. If you lost or damaged a piece of equipment by negligence, you paid for it out of your own pocket (although I still do not believe the story of a young officer in a very rich cavalry regiment who lost a Centurion tank in a bog and had the cost added to his monthly mess bill).

The Commanding Officer called into his office a young Captain by the name of Brian Barnes and revealed that they had been thoroughly shafted in the takeover of the previous battalion's transport, including all the trucks and equipment.

Inspection had revealed that most of the tools were ex-Wehrmacht, the tyres were wrong and whole vehicles were missing. The Commanding Officer himself would become financially responsible for a huge sum. They had now one year to make up the shortfall before they handed over in their turn.

Brian was ordered to solve the problem and was then asked who he needed as Transport Sergeant to assist him. Without hesitation he requested that McComiskey join him in what was to be an unholy partnership of 'acquisition'.

Thus, for a whole year it was a very bad idea indeed for any neighbouring battalion to have too much to do with the Irish Guards. Even after a friendly evening of carousel at the end of an exercise, shaken men would wake to find their trucks up on bricks with all the tyres gone.

The Irish Guards were more than up to the mark, with workshops bulging with spare parts and tyres up to the ceiling. The only thing they were missing was a motorcycle, which McComiskey instructed one of his Lance Sergeants to rectify. He wasn't quite as bright as McComiskey and came proudly back a few hours later with a lovely motorbike. Unfortunately, it had 'MP' written on the back of it. Having given the Military Police back their bike, McComiskey had only days to find a replacement. He finally resorted to building a motorcycle from parts, some of which were literally carved from wood by the Pioneer Platoon.

At the end of the long, arduous business, the innocent Welsh Guards Transport Sergeant, already pleased by the massive amounts of surplus equipment being handed over, was even more delighted (after a heavy liquid lunch) to be shown 'my very own personal motorcycle' which McComiskey pretended he had loved and cared for himself through the months.

The poor Welshman did not try to start it up for a couple of weeks. The whole thing collapsed in a pile of wood and metal bits.

By then the Irish Guards were safely long gone back to England.

RECRUITING IN LIVERPOOL

After about a year, my trusty Platoon Sergeant George Shannon announced that, sadly, he had to leave me. He was being promoted to Colour Sergeant and was taking over the important job of recruiting in Liverpool.

He then revealed how he had been recruited into the Irish Guards three years into the war. Young George Shannon was walking down the main street to enrol in the Royal Artillery, where his brothers were serving. He passed the Irish Guards recruiting office, and foolishly paused for a moment. The immaculate Sergeant standing in the doorway said, 'Off to join the Gunners, I suppose, lad? Well, they've got room, of course.'

This remark puzzled the lad and he questioned the Sergeant, who claimed that, even at this stage in the war, an elite regiment like the Irish Guards still had a waiting list.

'You mean, if I really wanted to join, you couldn't get me in?'

'Well, me boy. If you really want to join, I might be able to have a personal word with the Regimental Lieutenant Colonel and ask a real favour. Tell you what. You be back here this time tomorrow, ready to go, and I'll see what I can do.'

Thoroughly intrigued, young George was back the next afternoon. The Sergeant proudly announced that his urgent lobbying in high places had paid off and Shannon had just squeezed into the Regiment, 'absolutely the last to do so for several months'.

Conveniently, he also had his railway warrant and first week's pay all fixed up. So scarcely an hour later, Shannon found himself in a crowded train full of young men steaming South.

Standing in the corridor, he started talking to a tall fellow, who revealed he was on his way to the Guards Depot in Caterham.

'Grenadiers? Coldstream?' asked Shannon.

'No, Irish.'

'But, I thought I was the very last man to get into the Irish Guards.'

'Of course ya did. So did every other focker on the train!'

LICHFIELD

PUBLIC DUTIES

The 'routine' part of Public Duties was providing the ceremonial armed Guards at Buckingham Palace, St James's Palace, Windsor Castle, The Tower of London and the Bank of England. The Officer of the Guard was allowed a male dinner guest at the Bank and at Windsor Castle and female guests (at restricted times) at the Tower and St James's Palace. In charge of Buckingham Palace, the Subaltern of the Guard would walk down The Mall to join

121

the Captain and Ensign at St James's Palace for lunch and later for cocktails and dinner. Otherwise, the Subaltern's day and night consisted of inspecting his men at their posts or watching television.

Once my day was enlivened by my Sergeant catching a Guardsman filling jam jars with gravel from the Buckingham Palace forecourt. I let him off with a caution, figuring that selling 'Royal Pebbles' to tourists was better than some activities they got up to.

WOLFHOUND WORRY

With the next three years committed to Public Duties, it was decided that the Irish Guards should have once again its traditional mascot, an Irish Wolfhound. Shaun duly arrived in the winter of 1960.

Irish Wolfhounds are huge grey hairy dogs the size of a small pony. They also appear to be incredibly gentle, so I am not quite sure how they were used to kill wolves.

Shaun had only been with us three or four days when one night an extremely drunken guardsman arrived back from leave. At the guardroom he managed with a supreme effort to stand straight and pronounce his name for long enough for the Sergeant to let him through as 'clean, shaven, sober and properly dressed'. As he left the lighted area in front of the guardroom, he fell down and began slowly crawling towards his barrack block, humming to himself. The wolfhound happened to be out for a walk and seeing something approximately its own size on all fours crossing the green he lollopped up it to have a play.

The guardsman looked up with horror. He did not know the wolfhound had even arrived and in the moonlight it must have looked like a grey, hairy Tyrannosaurus Rex. He wailed 'Oh, no,' stumbled to his feet and weaved off moaning into the barrack block while Shaun, puzzled, stood wagging his tail forlornly.

JIGS' JAZZ

In 1961, the Irish Guards' share of Public Duties became extremely heavy and was really quite a strain, especially for the Officers. This was because we had recruited an enormous number of guardsmen but we were short of officers. We were allocated, based on the *total* strength of the battalion, a heavier than usual schedule of Public Duties, including, for instance, finding three out of the eight Guards at the Queen's Birthday Parade and literally hundreds of men for street lining. In May and June there was often a daily battle between me and the Adjutant to stop my drivers getting into the clutches of the Sergeant Major who was desperately trying to make up the numbers. My view prevailed that without my drivers to drive them, none of his men would make it to London anyway.

Because we had so few officers, we seemed to be constantly on Guard, coming off from the Palace, going on to Bank Picquet, coming off that, going down to Windsor Castle, sometimes three or four in a week. However, taking away a lot of the tedium was the Director of Music. Major 'Jigs' Jaeger was a kindly character, always an excellent advisor on betting on any horse race and, luckily, a jazz enthusiast. Many of our bandsmen played in night clubs and jazz bands in the evening.

LICHFIELD

Marching out of the Palace after Guard Mounting, one speculated as to what special arrangement Jigs had decided on next, as the band swung into speeded up versions of 'St Louis Blues', or slowed down ones of 'Bugle Boy March' or 'Panama Rag' or 'South Rampart Street Parade'. The spirit of New Orleans definitely gave the 'Micks' an extra swing to their step.

While I was serving in London, Toby devised an extra stunt to publicise one of his favourite PR accounts, the Royal Tournament – a popular international military tattoo held every year at Earls Court until axed by the Blair Government in 1997.

He created a special march of the hundreds of participants round Hyde Park. This disrupted the traffic in central London so much that the following year it was switched to Battersea Park.

I ended up hating this decision as I was sent to act as a marker for the march. By ill luck, I drew the Central Band of the Royal Air Force and for 5 miles had to endure a tuba playing right into my left ear – note the tension in my face as we, at last, reached the saluting stand!

WRONG CHOICE OF CAR

Looking back, my choice of first car must have also marked me as an eccentric officer. Colin Chapman's tiny Lotus 7 was a kit car weighing 700 lbs and the Adjutant referred to it as 'not an officer's car'. This did not stop me deliberately driving my father wearing a bowler hat into Wellington Barracks where the Sergeant of the Guard, just to be safe, ordered a 'Present Arms' as we entered.

My enthusiasm for cars sometimes got me in hot water in the Army. Apart from our routine of Public Duties (guarding Buckingham Palace, Windsor Castle and the Bank of England), we had parades to mark state visits. One such visit, of the Queen of the Netherlands, meant a major presence of the Household Brigade. All the officers from the

several Regiments involved were given their final briefing.

'Remember,' said the Parade Adjutant, 'when you see a gold crown on a black background, it's Royal Household, you order the Salute. When you see a gold crown on a red background, that is Royal Family and you order Present Arms.'

In what I thought was *sotto voce*, I muttered from the back, 'And if you see a black horse on a yellow background, you know they've bought some decent cars for once.'

The cold words, 'I will see you in my office in the morning, Mr O'Brien', indicated that my *voce* had not been nearly *sotto* enough.

REAR WINDOW

It was after this briefing that a Scots Guards friend said to me, 'As it's a Monday, you had better come and see something.' It transpired that one of the more diverting things to see at Wellington Barracks happened every Monday morning.

At exactly the same time as the coffee break between drill parades, a businessman across the road in Buckingham Gate would invite his secretary into his office and make passionate love to her on the top of his desk. This routine, only too visible from the window of the coffee room in the Officers' Mess, only ever seemed to happen on a Monday. So one has to assume that the gentleman was working off some kind of serious marital frustration after the weekend.

NOT AN 'OFFICER'S GIRL'

At about the same time that I acquired a 'not an officer's car', I had also acquired a girlfriend, who was not quite 'an officer's girlfriend'. The normal source of girls in 1960, the debutante scene, was inhabited, with some great exceptions, by girls still running to puppy fat, with very conventional backgrounds and limited conversation to match – mostly last night's ball and their horses.

Gabriella Licudi, by contrast, was a lively and gorgeous blonde, half-Greek, half Spanish, a superb dancer, highly intelligent and fluent in four languages. To ensure she really stood out from the crowd, she was an actress! We met, typically, at a jazz pub in Chelsea and she introduced me to three fellows who became firm friends – Roland Wells, Terry Howard and Dermot Butler.

Gabriella and I were soon hopelessly in love. I used to pick her up in my little Lotus from her mother's flat in Earls Court at 5.00 am and deliver her to Pinewood or Beaconsfield Studios before driving right back through London to Caterham to be on parade by 8.00. (This was only possible with only 4 million cars on the roads, compared with today's 20 million.) It went on every morning for weeks while she filmed *The Roman Spring of Mrs Stone* with Vivien Leigh and a youthful Warren Beatty.

Gabriella was a real hit with my colleagues, especially the Guardsmen. She still remembers the night I told her to 'hop into the cupboard', when we were interrupted at the Tower of London. I was serious enough to give her an engagement ring and to ask Colonel Mick O'Cock, my Commanding Officer, for permission to marry 'in the next few months'. He smiled indulgently and advised 'a little wait', as did her mother.

They were right, of course. Not only was Gabriella two years younger than she had let on (only sixteen when I first met her), but acting can run uneasily with more conventional careers.

Curiously, filming was not the problem – at least it fitted in with my own working hours. The theatre, however, is even more intense and introspective and the hours are unsocial. Her day might not start until noon but could carry on long into the small hours. So when she later started in a play called *Two Stars for Company* with Trevor Howard, the writing was on the wall – not least because of a handsome young actor called Anthony Valentine for whom she soon traded me. Gabriella later graduated to Hollywood. Then, ever unconventional, she went to Africa to run safaris.

Gabriella Licudi

THE LADIES' DIRECTORY

It is hard to imagine it now, but the whole of the West End used to be very visibly full of the 'ladies of the night'. In 1961 the Street Offences Act drove these 'ladies' from London's streets. In a spirit of great enterprise, with commendable speed, they produced their own magazine, *The Ladies' Directory*, to advertise their continuing availability. It was full of such delightful claims as 'the girl you can trust is the one with the bust'. My father was talking about this in White's Club when a fellow member, the Major General commanding London District, overheard him and demanded to be shown a copy. Foolishly (it *was* after lunch) my father said, 'I have lent it to my son, but you can ask him for it, because you are inspecting him next week'.

Indeed this was the case, as it was our turn for the annual Major General's inspection and the whole Battalion waited in some trepidation. I would have waited in even more trepidation had I known what was going to occur. I was standing rigid in scarlet tunic and bearskin, when the Major General's party, flanked by my own Commanding Officer and Adjutant, approached. There was a sudden silence as the band paused. I reported my men ready for inspection. The Major General asked in a voice clearly heard by all thousand men on parade, 'Never mind that, WHERE'S THE TARTS' BOOK?'

'DOCKER'

A better relationship with the same General was that of Captain Michael Boyle, whom Giles Allan nicknamed 'Docker' as he had just bought a Daimler. (Lady Norah Docker, the Daimler Chairman's wife, was a legendary Fifties spendthrift.)

'Docker' Boyle at Toby's 1961 No Strings Party

While Docker appeared richer then most of us, actually our regiment did not appear to have particularly wealthy officers. Not like Sam Vestey with a huge allowance, or the Scots Guards, who at one stage only allowed Rolls-Royces to be parked in front of their Officers' Mess.

Docker was a splendidly colourful character with a smart moustache and a habit of spending his money on lovely yachts. One night on Queen's Guard, Kevin Cooper asked a lot of girls in after dinner. Instead of chucking them out, Docker – who was Captain of the Guard – joined the party in the ante-room. When they went home with their friends, a lot of revving of engines took place in Ambassador's Court, waking up Lord Tryon, who rang up the Major General the next morning. Docker was 'marched in' in front of the Major General and had his leave stopped for months. The Regimental Lieutenant Colonel (Will Berridge), after a lengthy interview, went round and discussed the matter with the Major General and persuaded him to let him off for Cowes Week at least.

Queen's Guard, St James's Palace

The sentence was alleviated by the Major General with words to the effect that 'he did not care much for Docker's feelings on the subject, but that he did feel sorry for his friends who had given up a week of their annual leave to sail with him during Cowes Week'.

CHANGING GUARD WITH MYSELF

A genuinely unique event occurred whilst I was entrusted with guarding the Queen. One Sunday morning I was Subaltern of the Guard, sitting in the guardroom at Buckingham Palace waiting for my Guard to be relieved after 24 hours guarding Her Majesty. The telephone rang. It was Major Dick Hume, the Adjutant. 'We're in trouble. We are five minutes late marching off from Wellington Barracks to relieve you, because something has gone wrong, and there is no Subaltern for the new Guard. I am dressed in a frock coat, so I can't pretend to be him.'

I scrambled to my feet and said, 'I think I get your drift. I'm on my way.'

Leaving the Old Guard in charge of the able Sergeant Corcoran, I marched quickly out of the Palace, through the gates, past the policeman (who was more than surprised to see me leave), through the gates of Wellington Barracks. I drew my sword, saluted the Adjutant, saluted the Colour and fell in front of my New Guard. The band struck up and off we marched.

Luckily, on a Sunday, the whole Guard (both that of St James's Palace and Buckingham Palace) does not form up on the forecourt of the Palace, but splits in two, so that it was only my detachment that paraded in a slightly less public position at Buckingham Palace on that Sunday morning.

In the Palace forecourt, I marched my New Guard straight up to the puzzled members of my Old Guard. I heard someone mutter, 'What the Jasus is Hopalong doing with *them*?'.

I halted, shouted '**Old Guard** (then whispered – 'that's you lot') **Present Arms**!'

'**New Guard**, (that's us now) **Present Arms**!' and so on, through the ceremony, acting both parts.

I then entered the Guardroom and formally and legally took over from *myself*, signed for the food, furniture and ammunition, and finally marched out again at the head of my Old Guard past the puzzled policeman for the third time.

I dismissed my Old Guard at Wellington Barracks, marched back alone for the fourth time through the Palace gates (the policeman now quite thunderstruck), and resumed my duties with the New Guard until someone came to relieve me.

Buckingham Palace

It is a fairly amusing example of Army resourcefulness. Provided you confidently keep shouting and stamping your feet, nobody will notice that anything has gone wrong. But, it is also true to say that for two unique periods of about five minutes Her Majesty was not properly guarded.

As far as I know, this is the first and only time in 350 years that the officer in charge of Buckingham Palace has changed guard with himself.

Sometimes a screw-up on parade cannot be disguised. One Major General, who really hated riding, tried to sheath his sword in the middle of the Mall and succeeded in driving two inches of blade into his horse. Even the quietest and best-trained steed won't put up with that and after galloping the length of the Mall, threw him in front of the Palace.

Another ceremonial occasion with problems was the state visit of President de Gaulle. The President needed all the help he could get. After 13 years of self-imposed isolation, he had returned to become head of state at the most difficult time, the height of the war in Algeria. The pieds noirs settlers had just staged the 'War of the Barricades' in Algiers and the French army was plainly not completely loyal. To enhance his prestige, our Prime Minister, Harold Macmillan, decided on the most

DE GAULLE – YES AND NO

*'Starving soldiery',
Garry Daintry (left)
and John Lockwood.*

MEMORABLE
MEMORANDA

lavish and spectacular State Visit which included a Royal Review, a major military parade on Horse Guards, probably grander than the Trooping of the Colour.

Brian Alexander had been chosen to be Ensign of the Colour, no doubt with the symbolism of the wartime Field Marshal's son paying this honour to his father's French companion in arms. I was standing in line with Brian during the rehearsal when he suddenly said out of the corner of his mouth, 'Donough, please come and take the Colour, *now*'. I sheathed my sword, marched up to him and took over the Colour. Brian, about to faint due to a rare circulation problem, had to leave the parade.

The Commanding Officer judged that no risks could be taken and sadly Brian was not allowed to carry the Colour during the actual event (neither was I, by the way).

But we saw De Gaulle extremely close up, standing as usual ramrod straight next to Prince Philip as he toured the ranks. What was more unusual was that De Gaulle was plainly overcome with emotion, with tears in his eyes. This did not stop him blocking our entry into the Common Market a few weeks later!

The 'starving soldiery' as Toby called them, came to lunch at Wellington Square on Sundays, including Garry Daintry, who Toby called the 'offhand guzzler', having watched him for 20 minutes continuously kissing Talitha Pol in a slowly moving taxi.

Two years before as a recruit Garry had done so well, escaping all punishment at the Guards Depot that Captain Trevor Dawson and the Regimental Sergeant Major thought he was missing vital experience. At next morning's parade, RSM Rodger bellowed 'Sarnt James, Daintry's being idle. LOCK HIM UP.' Sergeant James replied, 'Daintry's not on parade, Sir. He's sick.' 'Doesn't matter, LOCK HIM UP ANYWAY.'

At one stage I had a beautiful girlfriend called Theodora Brinckman who had the largest china-blue eyes I have ever seen. Her father was Colonel Sir Roderick Napoleon Brinckman. He took Theodora and me to a party at the Hurlingham Club where I had great difficulty maintaining a straight face because I knew the story about him when he commanded a Grenadier Company in Egypt:

One morning, 'Naps' Brinckman was conducting his Company Commander's Memoranda, a procedure which includes the punishment parade. This involved a great deal of shouting and stamping as accused and witnesses are marched in, crash to a halt in front of the Company Commander's desk, turn to face him and evidence is then read out.

A Sergeant crashed forward to report that he had found two Guardsmen in the same bed. Naps raised his eyes to the offending Guardsman and said, 'Well, Smith. What have you got to say for yourself?'

Smith crashed one pace forward, 'I thank you, sir, for leave to speak, but I'm a homosexual'.

Naps Brinkman misheard him. Thinking he had said 'home-sick', he said understandingly, 'Well, we all are out here, from time to time'. The ensuing chaos can be imagined.

My Commanding Officer decided that I would suit being Transport Officer, so I went on a course at the Motor Transport School at Bordon, in Hampshire. Once a week I had dinner with Caroline Graham, a pretty debutante, and her parents. Caroline got bored with me but her father did not.

Major Graham told me an agonising story of once being Orderly Officer during a dull, long weekend at the Royal Engineers Depot at Woolwich. He was so bored he devised a game with his batman whereby they each stood at opposite ends of the immense parade ground and sent his little car, empty and with the hand throttle set ever faster, back and forth towards each other. After several runs and now at about 12 miles per hour, it needed skill to leap on to the running board, turn the car round and reset the throttle for its next run back.

'Mr Graham, come here, please.' came the unexpected voice of his Commanding Officer. 'But, Sir...' 'Don't argue, Mr Graham, come here.'

The young man was forced to stand to attention until his car ran full tilt into the Guardroom wall, totally demolishing itself. He then had to explain why nobody was driving it.

While I was on my course, the battalion had moved from Windsor to Caterham, from which the old Depot had moved. I reported to my Transport Office and a friendly and veteran Transport Sergeant greeted me with a curious salute. I was about to start our relationship rather badly by reprimanding Sergeant Smylie for not saluting with all his fingers, when I realised he did not *have* all his fingers.

Having been blown up by a landmine in Palestine, Dave Smylie then lost his fingers to German machine-gun fire in the last-ditch defence of Boulogne harbour. Captured and in hospital, a sympathetic and immaculate Oberstleutnant enquired in perfect English which Regiment Smylie was in. 'Irish Guards, Sir.'

'I might have known it would be the bloody 'Micks' who held us up so long!'

WOOLWICH WOES

TWO FINGERS

After Palestine, Boulogne, a near fatal road accident in Germany, and his recruiting office blown up by the IRA, Smylie's children reckon he got his British Empire Medal 'for being persistently shot and blown up and not complaining.'

129

Our company commander now was Major James Chichester-Clark. A nice, straightforward man who later found himself in the almost impossible job of Prime Minister of Northern Ireland (as had Terence O'Neill, another former 'Mick').

CALMING INFLUENCE

One night at Caterham I was, as Piquet Officer, in charge of the barracks and was relieving the boredom by listening to jazz records on the hi-fi system of my friend the Medical Officer. Suddenly we got a call from the Guard Room. The Sergeant of the Guard said that one of the prisoners, who was plainly a bit loopy and due to be discharged, had gone berserk and 'could we please come and deal with it'.

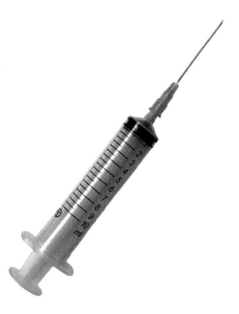

We arrived to find that the Guardsman was breaking up his cell, and my friend the Medical Officer was going to have to give him a shot to sedate him. This was quite dangerous as the prisoner was a huge man and we all entered the cell with clubs behind our backs issuing soothing words, trying to persuade him to take an injection. We had half achieved this when he leapt up and broke away. The trouble was that whatever medication we had half injected him with would either put him to sleep or make him twice as violent.

We went back to listen to jazz. After half an hour, we got the inevitable second call.

Now with the strength of ten men, he was again breaking up his cell and threatening life and limb. This time my friend loaded the syringe with a massive shot. We all charged into the cell, pinned the fellow to the ground and the injection was duly completed.

Our difficult prisoner slept so soundly and for so long that, when he woke up, he had been a civilian for 3 days!

GERMANY CALLING

In 1961, we left Caterham to join the British Army of the Rhine at a former Flak regiments' barracks in Hübbelrath, near Düsseldorf where we took over from the Grenadier Guards. I was part of the Advance Party because, as Transport Officer, it was vital to get the maximum number of drivers qualified under the stringent German road regulations.

I was frantically busy training enough Guardsmen to drive the 3 ton trucks that we needed to transport the Battalion's men and equipment in from the airport. Finally, the rest of the Battalion began flying in, and day and night we drove them from Düsseldorf Airport to the barracks.

I could not have done it at all without the support of my new Transport Sergeant, Ted Keating, who one night had to walk me round and round at Düsseldorf Airport to stop me collapsing. Nor could I have done without my driver Corporal Paddy Thunder, later sadly killed in Aden.

I remember driving behind a truck full of our Guardsmen who were staring in awe at the immaculate figure of a German conductor in the doorway of his tram, who plainly looked to them like every figure of a German officer they had ever seen in a war film. I took some pleasure in leaning round the windscreen and saying 'And that's only a tram conductor'.

During the takeover, one of Algy Cluff's brother officers in the Grenadiers told me a splendid story about Algy's resourcefulness when the Grenadiers had been based at Wellington Barracks in London.

One Winter's night they were driving down Constitution Hill when they were struck from the rear by a large battered car. Algy pulled over to swap insurance details with the occupants, and when he got out several West Indians poured out of the other car.

When Algy politely opened the conversation, the first of them struck him on the jaw, bowling him over under the trees. Algy got up, and thinking very quickly, drawled, 'I am prepared to fight you one by one. How about it? I know a little alley where we can take the cars and we can fight there.' They muttered together, agreed and poured back into their car, which also seemed to be full of women and children.

Algy then led them in convoy round the statue in front of Buckingham Palace and straight into Wellington Barracks, which in the dark may well have looked like the 'alley'. As soon as they had entered the gates, Algy reversed to lock bumpers with them and then shouted at the startled sentry, **'Turn out the guard.'**

'Right, Mr Cluff, Sir, TURN OUT THE GUARD.'

Fifteen guardsmen, in greatcoats and bearskins clattered out of the Guardroom with rifles and fixed bayonets, and then filled the small number of cells with screaming West Indians.

Algy found the Adjutant who then called the police. Apparently there was a problem because Algy's assailants were now on War Department property and could not technically be arrested. The police Inspector made the unusual request that the Grenadier Guards should let the West Indians go, park their car in Birdcage Walk, and then 'perhaps Mr Cluff could appear again, so that they would attack him again'.

Algy very reluctantly agreed to this novel demand, and that is exactly what happened. As soon as the West Indians saw him again, they screamed, 'There's the bastard. Let's get him!' And out of the shadows, just in time, pounced the police to take them out of Algy's life forever.

ALGY'S UNEXPECTED SUPPORT

The statue on the way to 'the alley'

Algy in the Grenadier Officers' Mess

LICHFIELD

THE BOILERMAN

In our sprawling barracks at Hübbelrath, there was an old German who managed the massive heating system and the Guardsmen, many of whom had never been abroad, turned to him for advice.

Either because he spoke no English or pretended not to (our theory was that he was a Russian spy), he used to reply 'Nicht verstehen' ('I don't understand'). Our Irishmen thought he was telling them his name and would say 'Bejasus, we'd better ask Nick Vestane, the boilerman, what to do about that'.

Once they had discovered their mistake, it became a great joke throughout the Battalion, but it did have the effect of teaching them their first two real words of German.

Just a couple of weeks later, there was a major fight in a beer cellar in Düsseldorf involving Irish Guardsmen and German soldiers.

The proprietor sensibly sent for the Military Police who entered the mostly destroyed room and gradually began to disentangle the entwined figures on the floor. Right at the bottom of the heap in somewhat shredded civilian clothes was a charming boy from Belfast. The M.P. Sergeant curtly told him to pick himself up and get in the truck, whereupon, with what he hoped was a disarming smile, the boy said 'Nick Vestane, Sergeant, Ah'm a chermaan'. For some strange reason, he was not believed.

DRIVING INSTRUCTOR

After we had settled into Hübbelrath, my first job was to hand the dozens of new armoured vehicles I had signed for over to the Rifle Companies and their Company Commanders. I urged them to be very careful about this, because of officers' personal financial responsibility. At least one said indulgently, 'Don't be silly Mo, we know what we are doing'.

Sure enough, three weeks later the German winter really set in. The temperature dropped to about –15°C and the engine blocks of two trucks burst because they only had enough anti-freeze to suit the UK. Result: two Majors with an extra £70 added to their Mess bills.

The next job was to train about 150 extra Guardsmen to drive, with the added strain of the German road rules. This was, frankly, a frightening experience, partly because my pupils had never touched a vehicle before, let alone in a foreign country.

It was also because the British Claims Commission was very generous towards Germans who suffered any damage to buildings, crops and, of course, vehicles. So it was not unusual for enterprising Germans to deliberately aim their battered Volkswagens and Mercedes, kamikaze-like, at our vehicles so as to collect the write-off money. I gave up training in Land

Rovers or Champs, preferring the reassurance of the Humber Armoured Personnel Carrier.

During my last months in Germany, I became increasingly disturbed by what appeared to be critical shortages and stupid weaknesses in the equipment of the British Army of the Rhine. Apart from all sorts of bizarre problems with my vehicle fleet, we did not even have enough rifles for our fully up-to-strength Battalion (the Irish Guards were legendary for good recruiting).

I mentioned all this to my father who said that because I was leaving, I could put it in writing to his friend, the Secretary of State for War, Jack Profumo. I wrote a long and detailed report on the subject and received back a friendly, polite but quite idiotic letter. I particularly remember that he pointed out to me that 'not everyone in an Infantry Battalion carries a rifle. Some carry a sub-machine gun', a fact of which I was probably aware after four years of service!

Irritated, I remember saying, 'I don't know about your friend Profumo, but it strikes me he has something else important on his mind'. Only a few weeks later this proved only too true, as the Christine Keeler story erupted.

Indeed, a worried MP friend had phoned my father and asked, 'Who among our House of Common friends would you call the most keen on the girls?'

'Jack, of course.'

'And among our friends in the Upper House?'

'Bill Astor, I suppose.'

'A right and left, Toby. There's going to be a terrible stink.'

Sure enough, some very naughty things had been going on at Lord Astor's magnificent Buckinghamshire house, Cliveden.

Christine Keeler

Jack Profumo visited the Irish Guards' legendary recruiter in Belfast, Sergeant John Kenny. 'Could you persuade *me* to join up, Sergeant Kenny?'

'Well, I don't know, sir. You see, you've got the O at the wrong end of your name.'

FAREWELL TO ARMS

(Only recently did I discover that it had been an O'Brien house in 1750. I wonder what the 4th Earl of Inchiquin, who stares down from my wall, would have thought of the antics in his garden!). The Profumo scandal with its overtones of Tory sleaze was to help let in a new Labour government.

Jack Profumo

Jack Profumo became a friend of mine later and I liked him very much. He was one of the funniest and most agreeable people around, and I remember that it was whilst I was chatting to him out shooting that the lady of the house came stumbling across the ploughed field to tell me of my father's first heart attack.

Some weeks before I was due to leave the Army, my Commanding Officer, Colonel Mick O'Cock told me that there was a young man he knew in The Rank Organisation who insisted on only employing former officers and specifically from the Brigade of Guards.

So, I flew to London and found myself being interviewed in the comfortable if rather intimidating surroundings of the Carlton Club, then at the heart of the Conservative Party. Martin Stevens was a plump, charming, highly intelligent man of 33 and hired me for what he later described as my 'manic enthusiasm'. It was the beginning of a 20-year relationship and Martin was the greatest mentor in my life. I know he also was to others, most of whom became a little club of firm friends (every five years, on the anniversary of his sadly premature death, we all meet for a dinner in his honour).

It was sad leaving 'the Micks', which was and is a wonderful Regiment, with the spirit of a very large, friendly family. What are my lasting memories? First of Irish wit and comradeship. Then curious but powerful details, like the shattering noise produced by a MOBAT anti-tank gun or the frightening precision of a mortar team capable of plastering an enemy before he even realised he was under fire. And drill. Surprisingly, when drill is going well, it is a real pleasure – like ballet or a hit musical.

But the most lasting memory would be the bugle playing the sad and evocative notes of 'The Last Post', as my files of Guardsmen stood rigid in bearskins and long, grey coats in the dark and swirling mist – a scene straight out of the Crimea.

So, after four years my time was up and I left the Battalion behind in Germany. This was not, I may say, without some serious drinking farewells with both officers and non-commissioned officers, not least with my namesake, Regimental Sergeant Major Maurice O'Brien.

Next day, I set off with headache and heart ache in the second-hand Mercedes I had bought for delivery to Gabriella's mother. The car not only nearly expired in Belgium – it actually caught fire in Chelsea! An omen?

Within a few months of leaving the Army, my new flat-mate Patrick Lichfield and I realized that we were in a unique position to produce an international feature on the Brigade of Guards. Being former officers, Patrick as the photographer and I as the writer, we could be trusted to present the Brigade in a realistic, sympathetic and accurate light – as both supreme fighting units and the best-known ceremonial troops anywhere. Here are some of the photographs that went into magazines and newspapers all over the world.

POSTSCRIPT
PORTFOLIO

LICHFIELD

Drum Major's staff gets its shine

Brushing a bearskin

Adjutant inspects Queen's Guard

Regimental informality: Lt James Tedder, with on of his Guardsmen

We were allowed a laugh – from time to time

Rain again!

136

The Regimental Sergeant Major grips his parade.

Ensign dressing for ceremonial duties

Contrast in clothing: the officers go on Guard, while fatigues are completed in denims.

Grenadier Regimental Sergeant Major

The Colonel's watchful eye

LICHFIELD

137

CHAPTER 11 SEA CHANGE

There was still some time to go in 1962 before the first American magazine almost jealously reported on 'Swinging London', but in Britain a fundamental sea change in attitudes was emerging. Old heroes like Eisenhower and Macmillan were fading and new ones like Jack Kennedy and the Beatles came bursting on to the scene.

In class-ridden Britain, above all, symbols and icons would change fast. Elegant upper-class actors like David Niven would soon give way to Michael Caine and David Hemmings. Tom Hustler would be supplanted by working class photographers such as David Bailey and Terry Donovan. Jill Kennington and Sandra Paul gave way to Jean Shrimpton and Twiggy, the models every girl wanted to emulate. The Old Etonians in advertising were replaced by working-class copywriters or ones who suddenly pretended to be working class. Indeed, in the media an upper-class accent became something of an embarrassment – rather than an asset. Some people no doubt could not cope with such changes, others of us revelled in it. Being on the 'Fringe' became more interesting.

Martin Stevens, later the popular Member of Parliament for Fulham

As for me, I arrived in The Rank Organisation, famous for films and film stars, little realising that one day I would myself produce a film about its history (*The Golden Gong*, page 157).

11 Hill Street near Berkeley Square in Mayfair was home to Rank Screen Services, to which I was Public Relations Officer. We were the contractor for all advertising in the Rank chain of Odeon and Gaumont cinemas, numbering in those days no less than 1,200.

Thus I started working for Martin Stevens, undoubtedly one of the great influences on my life and on many others. He lived in a lovely house in Montpelier Square with Peter Lendrum, who had been a major in the Household Cavalry, and Julian Gibbs, who was an insurance broker. Martin always claimed that these houses were built by a Mr Gerry as a speculative development on the assumption that the French under Napoleon would successfully invade England and these houses would suit his officers. He also claimed that the word 'gerrybuilt' derived from that smart opportunist.

Martin played a major role in my business development. He taught me many things, not least the necessity of listening very carefully in a meeting and writing down everything (not some things) on the basis that the information might be crucially important at some time in the future. As PRO for the Screen Advertising Association, I helped to organise the awards each year of the world's finest film and television commercials, showing them at two cinemas in Leicester Square. This involved collaborating closely with people like Ernie Pearl and Jack Dean of Pearl and Dean who contracted the advertising for the other half of the cinema industry.

HAROLD WILSON AND HIS FRIENDS

One person whom Rank regarded as the devil incarnate was Harold Wilson, soon to become Prime Minister. This was

because he had personally nearly wrecked the British film industry some years before, when he was President of the Board of Trade. He had restricted American films, encouraged Rank to expand production ('the Rank quickies'), and then reneged letting American firms back in, leaving Rank with millions in unwanted films.

My father shared these views of Wilson for other reasons.

Left, Harold Wilson as Prime Minister, from a roll of film I found in the gutter outside my house in London. He is apparently setting fire to his thumb.

While no longer officially connected to Tory publicity, Toby was still working unofficially for the party. He had correctly identified Harold Wilson as the real Socialist danger with some really worrying colleagues and supporters, even before Hugh Gaitskell's untimely death. Using top satirical writers, he produced a series of witty and hard hitting booklets like 'The World of Harold Wilson', 'Autumn Madness', 'Breach of Promise', and 'Harold Wilson and his Friends'. (Typical of Toby, years later he and Wilson lunched together and became guardedly friendly.)

ONE SALESMAN, THREE JOBS

Martin was often asked why he always chose army officers to work for him, which seemed at first to be snobbish and old-fashioned. His response was that, providing they were intelligent, the Government had probably also ensured that they would be resourceful, efficient, absolutely honest, never lie and never 'shop' their friends. David Ogilvy had a similar hiring policy of 'gentlemen with brains'.

Eventually Martin was told by his boss that he had to hire somebody a bit different because the next job was that of a salesman to sell screen time. Martin was soon to be vindicated in his recruiting methods. Having gone right through The Rank Organisation's recruiting procedures at their new administrative centre at Whiteleafe, the salesman arrived and went off on the road. A few weeks later he was arrested for taking on three such jobs. I think the actual criminal offence was fiddling his National Insurance.

Ten years later Martin had a reunion lunch with the new boss of Rank Screen Services who told him a bizarre reprise to this story. Once again they needed a salesman and they turned, once again, to their now computerised recruiting system. A salesman had turned up and had duly gone out on the road. After six weeks the projectionist, Reg, who was about to retire, suddenly spotted this man in reception and said, 'Hang on. Isn't that the crook who got put in the slammer ten years ago?' Sure enough, the same man had come for the same job at the same organisation, had landed it and was carrying on the same fiddle and was duly, no doubt, sent to the same jail!

QUICK THINKING

When I took over from Bill Andrewes, another of Martin's ex-officer recruits, he explained these salesmen's methods.

'Our salesmen for local ads are all working class and Jewish, and have wonderful patter and sales skills, guys like Sidney Gaunt, Harry Hoffman and Laurie Lawrence.

When I joined I was told to shadow Laurie Lawrence on a sales trip to Dudley. We visited a draper, Sidney Perk, who complained, 'I will not be renewing my contract, Mr Lawrence. I went to the Odeon Dudley last Wednesday. There weren't more than two other people there.'

'Everybody knows you don't go to the cinema in Dudley on Wednesday', responded Laurie, 'The *rest of the week* it's full. National cinema attendance is going up but you can still get a bargain at the old price'. Mr Perk agreed to renew his contract. I was quite shocked and said, outside, 'Laurie you know the attendance figures have been plummeting'.

'Ah, yes, well that may be a *national* trend, Bill, but not what the Odeon Dudley's doing. In fact, *nobody* knows what the Odeon Dudley's doing and I'm not asking.'

That afternoon we visited a jeweller who also said he was dissatisfied and was not going to renew his contract. After some fruitless minutes, Laurie and I left the shop and after a few yards we noticed a sign, SMITH THE JEWELLERS, COMING SOON.

Laurie spins on his heel and goes in and says, 'I'm really sorry to bother you but I can't find the letter I got yesterday from a Mr Smith. Of course, we don't allow competing firms of jewellers but since you decided not to renew, I really must visit Mr Smith and sign him up'. The jeweller quickly said 'I've been thinking while you were out and perhaps I'd like to renew my contract'. As they walked down the street, I said 'It was a jolly good thing you had that letter from Mr Smith'. Laurie just stared at me pityingly.

SPY IN THE COLD

One of my first assignments after joining Rank was to go with Martin to a workshop in White City to visit an urbane businessman called Greville Wynne. He was building two huge caravans as mobile exhibition centres designed to travel round Eastern Europe to drum up trade for Britain. He was inviting Rank to participate.

In the event, we turned this offer down, which was probably a very good thing. A few weeks later in Budapest, Greville Wynne was abducted by KGB agents, who flew to him Moscow and put him on trial for spying, together with his Russian co-conspirator Colonel Oleg Penkovsky (who had apparently decided to spy against Russia because he was so impressed by Marks and Spencer and 'that ordinary people could buy such things').

The Soviets found them both guilty, shot Penkovsky and sentenced Greville Wynne to eight years in jail. In fact he was exchanged after 17 months for Gordon Lonsdale who had been

Greville Wynne

spying for the Russians against Britain, such exchanges being a regular feature of the Cold War. As far as I know, Greville Wynne was the only real spy I have ever met.

My duties at Rank Advertising's films division included liaison with the various trade media. A space salesman called Turner from *Television Mail* used to tell me his exploits in the Fleet Air Arm during the war.

His most expensive claim to fame was that of accidentaly sinking a Sunderland flying boat all on his own. This was quite simple really. All you had to do was to leave a porthole open. After a night of stormy weather and choppy seas the crew came out to fly their Sunderland. They found instead an empty berth with five or six buoys straining downwards, rather as they did when attached to the shark in the film *Jaws*.

He also explained to me the rigours of flying in a Catalina. A slow American flying boat with the extraordinary ability to remain aloft for about 14 hours, it played a major role in over-turning the Atlantic U-boat threat.

Catalina

There was an observer's position in the open air up at the nose of a Catalina which, in Winter, was a truly horrible duty.

Not only did the observer have to crawl back over the nose and wipe the ice off the pilot's windscreen but, for a one hour stint, he had to stand up at 80 mph, theoretically adding his eyes to those looking for enemy submarines. This could freeze anyone to death. But Turner was having a fling with a girl in the WAAF's who suggested to him that he should wear, for warmth, the silk underwear that the girls were issued with.

The underwear worked a treat until their Catalina hit some driftwood in Gibraltar harbour. The plane sank and the crew were ejected into the freezing water of the Straits. The Air Sea Rescue boat was quickly on the scene and Turner was hauled aboard and filled with rum to revive him, dulling his sense of danger. He was therefore unable to stop the medical staff cutting open his uniform to see if he had broken anything.

Gibraltar, even in the middle of the war, was a very small place and the story of Turner's women's underclothes spread like wildfire. It was many miserable months before the whistling in the streets stopped.

For the first few months back in London, I lived at our home in Wellington Square. One evening I returned home to find my father propped up in bed with flu. He told me that all day he had been interrupted by a stream of telephone calls which indicated that, mysteriously, our telephone had become connected to the switchboard system of the War Office.

After about fifteen calls, irritation set in and with his love of the practical joke, he proceeded to fool about. The next caller he greeted at once with, 'Is that you, John? We're really worried about the latest from Rhodesia. I suppose you'll be at the FO meeting about it?'

He heard the puzzled officer at the other end calling to his secretary to see if there was a meeting scheduled at the Foreign Office before he rang off.

The next call was from an already stroppy General. 'Let me speak to Colonel Holland.'

'Sorry, sir' said my father. 'It's his assistant here.'

'Where is Colonel Holland?'

'He's playing golf.'

'GOLF?'

'Yes, sir, and judging by the load he had on him at the Brazilian Embassy last night, I shouldn't think he is playing that too well.'

The furious General shouted, 'You tell Holland to call me back at once!'

The calls continued, with my father warming to his subject. One startled girl asked, 'Is that Department 326?' 'Yes, but didn't you hear, they all just defected to the East.'

A few days later he recounted his experiences to Jack de Manio, host of the early morning *Today* programme on BBC radio. Jack begged him to come and tell the story on the radio, which he (foolishly) did. This had the effect of at last alerting the War Office to their potentially disastrous security breach, whereupon it became impossible to call Sloane 7022 for two whole years without laboriously revealing who you were and to whom you wanted to speak.

With a leaky military telephone system like that, of course, the Russians didn't really need Kim Philby, Gordon Lonsdale or their other spies at all.

'Voilà O'Brien le mauvais, voici mon ami O'Brien le bon.'

TSHOMBE

These were the words of Moise Tshombe, leader of Katanga, the breakaway province of the Belgian Congo. He was first referring to his enemy, Conor Cruise O'Brien, the UN Secretary-General's representative, and then Toby, who for months ran a Katanga lobby to get recognition on behalf of Belgian mining interests by the Foreign Office.

In spite of his efforts and those of prominent politicians such as Lord Home, Katanga was forced back into the disorganised rest of Zaire, and Tshombe was kidnapped in the air in Spain and taken to Algeria where he died.

Tshombe's answer to O'Brien— another O'Brien!

FROM OUR LONDON STAFF

MUCH play has been made in London these last few days about the two O'Briens—Dr. Conor Cruise O'Brien who, on behalf of the United Nations, opposed Tshombe's policies, and Mr. Edward Donough ('Toby') O'Brien, who is endeavouring to present Tshombe and his province of Katanga in a more favourable light.

Toby O'Brien, a genial figure widely known in London's Clubland, first met Tshombe last July during a visit to Elisabethville for the World Fair. He was then greatly impressed by what he saw of the order and the good relations existing between white and black.

The decline in the situation since finds him a supporter of Tshombe and his regime.

This support takes the form of issuing a fortnightly digest of Katanga news and views, which goes out to about 300 people, mainly holding responsible positions.

Born in India

A member of an ancient Irish line, Toby O'Brien is a kinsman of the proud

LICHFIELD
LEARNS TO SNAP

At Brian Alexander's invitation, I went to live in Wilton Place, a real stroke of luck. It was an old apartment block, purchased for demolition to make way for the Savoy Group's new Berkeley Hotel. The only reason we had been given it was because Patrick Lichfield had gone out with Jenny Wontner, the daughter of the Chairman of the Savoy. Our weekly rent was the princely sum of £5, cheap even for those days.

Patrick Lichfield and Brian Alexander, were the core residents. Algy Cluff, my pal from Stowe and future oilman was moving out and Nick Villiers and Andrew Parker-Bowles had just left.

The Swinging Sixties were beginning to swing and the flat did not really have enough respectable private bedrooms to entertain the ladies. We agreed a complicated system of leaving milk bottles out for flatmates, indicating where people had to sleep.

Patrick had been a regular officer and had only just left the Grenadier Guards. Through the Bowes-Lyon family (the Queen Mother's) he was a cousin of the Queen; slim, good-looking and talented. But he had suffered both a personal tragedy and a financial misfortune when both his father and grandfather died within two years. With the crippling death duties of that time, this meant that as the new and fifth Earl of Lichfield, he no longer owned the magnificent house of Shugborough near Stafford, which was taken over by the National Trust, although he was left a lovely section which he had re-designed by David Mlinaric. He had strict guardians and was on a tight financial reign. This was probably a good thing because he threw himself into making his hobby of photography into a paying profession.

Two floors below us was the studio of Dmitri Kasterine and Michael Wallis. Dmitri was an excellent all-round photographer and Michael Wallis was a superb still-life technician. From them Patrick learned a tremendous amount.

LICHFIELD

Shugborough is often the background for Burberry advertising. Here Patrick himself models with Lady Annunziata Asquith.

LICHFIELD

I played a useful role in starting his professional career, because I introduced him to Robin Esser of the *Daily Express*, who then offered Patrick the role of photographer to William Hickey, providing he created the stories himself. This started a process of grabbing all the society girls he could persuade, thinking up some spurious story to make them interesting, and photographing them, sometimes working with Nigel Dempster. For each, Patrick received the princely sum of £15. It was good money for the effort.

I was given a tiny, scruffy but entirely private room at the end of the passage. A couple of times, ready for seduction, I would switch on the light to find Patrick (perhaps jealous) had pinned a huge photographic blow-up of myself with a distorted nose (through a wide-angle lens) and scrawled 'I'm not really ugly'.

At weekends, with my 'smart' flatmates in their country houses, I and my media friends frequented certain pubs to hear about, and to 'crash', parties. One boring Saturday, Chris Long, a theatrical agent, exclaimed 'There *are* no parties, Donough. So let's give one. You can get the drinks, I'll provide the guests.' One hundred complete strangers arrived, half of them beautiful girls, models and actresses, a very unusual opportunity, to be handled with extreme care. Avoiding the temptation of even dancing too close, I repeated the line 'You are the most attractive girl here, but as the host, I *must* look after everyone. But may I have your phone number?'

Next morning, hung over, I wandered around the flat to find the scraps of precious hidden paper.

When Patrick finally created his own studio, he started with one aristocratic assistant, Lady Elizabeth Ramsay, the daughter of the Earl of Dalhousie who ran it in a brilliantly efficient way. Patrick's next choice was Viscount Encombe. Johnny Encombe was willing but could be rather more amateur.

Patrick was delighted when he got his first Royal assignment – that of photographing the Duke of Kent and his family. He went down to the Duke of Kent's house and arranged the family and the lights to his satisfaction. Finally, he turned to Encombe who had been plucking at his sleeve for some time and asked for his camera. Johnny whispered in agony, 'I've been trying to tell you for the last quarter of an hour that I left all the film in London.'

Thinking quickly, Patrick told the Duke that he had to 'go and get a different lens from his car' and then drove at 100 mph into the nearest village in his Aston Martin. He found the only shop just closing. Patrick shouted through the window to the little old lady, 'Please sell me that film'.

To the regret of the small boys in Belgravia, announcing the return to modelling of Miss Jennifer Wontner

PICTURES BY THE EARL OF LICHFIELD

OPPORTUNITY KNOCKS

Chris Long

ROYAL ASSIGNMENTS, UNREAL ASSISTANTS

Liz Ramsay, Johnny Encombe & Patrick

LICHFIELD

Patrick and Pedro

She refused, pedantically saying that she was closed. Patrick, desperate at the thought of the impatient Duke, lost his temper, 'If you don't sell me the film, I shall back my car right through your window'.

The woman plainly did not believe him, so Patrick leaped into his car and began to reverse towards the shop. Suddenly rattled, she opened up and sold him all the films she could give him. Sadly this resourcefulness did not have a happy ending, because her film was so old that none of the pictures came out well enough and he had to do the whole shoot again.

Patrick had now learned the lesson of recruiting practical and down-to-earth assistants and the one who has now been with him for many years is called Pedro. Patrick tells the wonderful story of Pedro in the pub just before Christmas being asked what he is doing on Christmas Day.

'I'm meeting the Queen' he replied.

His friends all laughed at him, 'Straight up. Patrick and I are going to photograph the Royal family on Christmas Day', which was, of course, true. The routine is that the family come out of church, go to their ordained chairs and sit down. Patrick clicks away and then the Queen comes over and thanks him and Pedro for 'so kindly giving up their Christmas Day'. (This leaves aside the money being made!)

In the pub that night, his friends eagerly asked Pedro if he had actually met Her Majesty.

'Of course I did', said Pedro proudly.

'Well, did she speak to you?'

'Of course she did.'

'What did she say?'

'She said, 'Well Pedro, I sure hope I didn't f..k up your Christmas'.'

PATRICK'S PRIVACY

Whatever people may say about Patrick Lichfield, he has certainly done a whole lot of things in his life and he certainly tells some very good stories about them. One of the best concerns a nude Unipart calendar shoot where he had to take a whole lot of nubile girls off into a rather uncomfortable desert location.

One of these beauties was complaining loudly that she did not want to share with one of the other girls because of the lack of privacy. When Patrick tried to argue with her, she retorted that

LICHFIELD

as a 'Lord, rich and educated at a public school,' he had probably never had to put up with a lack of privacy.

'Rubbish!' said Patrick. 'At Harrow we had no privacy at all. For instance, we had no doors on the lavatories'.

There was a long silence while her lovely face wrinkled in puzzlement. 'Well 'ow did you get in 'em?'

PAINTING THE CHAMPIONS

While Patrick worked in the studio and darkroom, my weekend and evening career as a motor racing artist (the poor man's Michael Turner) continued to expand. Various motoring magazines sent me to races I wanted to attend, armed with press passes. I did oil paintings for Stirling Moss and Tony Rolt and I know that my rendition of Jo Bonnier's win at the Targa Florio hangs in the Porsche offices in Stuttgart. Chris Barber, better known to me as a jazz man, asked me to paint him racing his Lotus Elite.

Stirling Moss was undoubtedly the most accomplished racing driver of his age, although he never became World Champion. He was also extremely versatile, equally at home in Formula One or sports cars, in which his most legendary win was the Mille Miglia for Mercedes in 1956. His navigator, Denis Jenkinson, had

147

450S Maserati

O'BRIEN

written every detail of the terrifying thousand miles on Italian open roads on a huge roll of what looked like lavatory paper. The win was not to be repeated the next year, in the awesome Maserati 450S, which he once described as 'wonderful if you wanted to go very fast, but if you put the brakes on hard three times, all you got was a funny smell!'

It is amazing that years after his retirement following his Goodwood crash in 1963, Stirling remained the symbol of motor racing. My advertising agency used him for our brake-lining commercial for the asbestos industry in 1977. And police to this day are still saying to offending motorists, 'Who do you think you are? Stirling Moss?'

At a dinner I attended in 1998, Stirling commented on the attitudes and ruthless behaviour of modern drivers compared with those of the sixties. Money must be an influence. At the height of his career, he was the highest paid driver in motor racing, but in real terms he earned the same in a year as Michael Schumacher does in just two days.

My artistic highlight was Shell's commission for the official painting to celebrate Graham Hill's World Championship in 1962. I elected to paint the Italian Grand Prix, with Hill in his BRM characteristically saluting Phil Hill in his Ferrari when Phil let him through to win (pay attention, Schumacher). This painting was presented to Graham by John Davies, head of Shell and with Sir Alfred Owen of BRM looking on (left).

GRIMSDALE

Stirling, blackened by 1,000 miles of oil and brake dust

Shell got their money's worth by using the painting for books.

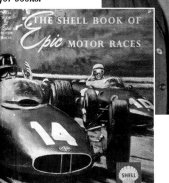

THE SHELL BOOK OF *Epic* MOTOR RACES

PETER ROBERTS

O'BRIEN

The only sadness was that when excitedly I rang my old mentor, George Lane, to tell him of the commission and therefore my recognition as an artist. His wife said, 'Oh dear, didn't you know? George died on Monday.'

When we were visiting Dublin, Brian Alexander and I decided to go to a sports car race near Dunboyne. It was not particularly exciting except that it produced the best loudspeaker announcement at any race I have attended:

'Now Ladies and Gentlemen, I can tell you that there have been no casualities but Lotus number fifty-three has just gone through the window of Brady's Public House!'

THE GIRL WITH MANY NAMES

The extensive publicity from the Graham Hill painting also netted me two girlfriends. The trouble was they were the same girl! I was rung one afternoon by a girl who said she was Susan A* and she worked for *SHE* magazine who were doing a series on young men who had made a commercial success out of a hobby. Could she meet me that evening please? I agreed, choosing a pub just near the flat in Wilton Place.

The young lady turned out to be a very attractive blonde of about 23, and we sat for a couple of hours drinking while I told her my story. She then suggested that she really should 'come up and see these paintings'. I took her up to the flat where-upon, as they say, one thing led to another.

Within a few days, several peculiar things emerged. She revealed the sad fact that she was suffering from a terminal disease and had little time, therefore, to enjoy herself. She also claimed to be an heiress, and was naturally enough going to leave all her money to those whom she liked and had made her last few months happier.

More confusing was the fact that she claimed that she had another name, Lady B*. By now I was becoming bemused and exhausted as I did my kindly duty and I did not question the curious fact that she had these two completely diverse names.

Finally, I decided I needed a break and drove Patrick Lichfield's Mini Cooper in one long drive (before the Autoroutes) down to S'Agaro in Spain to stay with the Ensesas, whose fortunes had been so helped by the publicity of Selwyn Lloyd's holidays in their hotel, La Gavina.

Only two days into my break, I was rung by Brian Alexander who said: 'Your mad girlfriend wants to give you a Ferrari. (Owning a Ferrari was the one thing I had always aspired to.) She knows you're too honourable to accept, and so she is going to give one to Patrick and one to me, and Patrick says you're not to turn her down or we won't get ours!'

This conversation was carried out on the crackly Spanish telephone lines of 30 years ago, so I wasn't entirely sure whether this was meant to be a joke or not.

---

* *Name withheld for legal reasons*

Brian briskly carried on, asking my preferences for colours, back axle ratios and other details, concluding with, 'By the way, she knows you're poor, so she has taken out a £1,000 account at the Blue Star Garage in the King's Road'.

250 GT Ferrari

The excitement of all this, of course, ruined my holiday. For days, I paced up and down the swimming pool waiting for a further explanatory call or for any news about this bounteous automotive gift.

Finally, I could bear it no longer and apologising to Carmona Ensesa for leaving early, I leapt in the Mini Cooper and howled through the mountains to arrive at Beaulieu in the South of France where my friends were sprawled around a pool. Shaking Brian Alexander awake I demanded to know what had happened to our cars. He was vague and negative, claiming that the girl had probably given up on the idea. In any case, she had wandered off with his brother, Shane, to whom she was intending to donate a house by the Thames!

When I got back to London all had come to nothing and I realised that the weird young lady had developed one of the cleverest ways of making sure she had lots of enthusiastic lovers all the time. Of course, she needed an awful lot of nerve and a macabre frame of mind to carry it off. Indeed, I think she was called 'The Poisoned Dart' by London society.

But that is not the end of the story. Ten years later one of my public relations clients said to me at lunch, 'Does the name Baroness C sound strange to you?' Even as he said it a tiny alarm bell began sounding at the back of my mind. He lived in a house in Fulham with two girls and had dropped in late at night to find that they had a very attractive thirty-ish blonde friend chatting to them. He went up to bed, and was stupefied to be awoken by this young lady sliding naked in between the sheets beside him.

'Before you go on', I interrupted 'Did she have anything wrong with her physically?'

'Yes, as a matter of fact she did. Very sad. She was suffering from cancer of the back.'

Very strange people you met in London in those days.

LARKEN'S SAILING JAUNT

Jasper Larken, an ex-army friend, rang me out of the blue and asked me if I wanted to go sailing. I replied that I would, a little reluctantly, as I had never been sailing in my life and I did not know how experienced my friend was.

He turned up with a girl called Louise Laurence and we drove down to the Hamble. On the way the radio was interrupted to announce that the weather was going to be really dangerous in The Solent and that very high winds and squalls would appear quite unexpectedly. I nervously pointed the weather report out to Jasper who appeared to take it in and said that we would merely have breakfast on the boat and do some chores.

We pottered about on *Lynette*, which he shared with Grenadier friends, Algy Cluff and John Pascoe. Then Jasper insisted we ought to go for a little sail as the weather was so pleasant, with which we had to agree. We sailed out into the Solent and everything seemed to be going quite well, however I was taking no chances and was keeping a 'weather eye' open. I think my eyes generally were somewhat better than Jasper's because I pointed out to him that the whole horizon had become a very dark grey.

Right to left, Jasper Larken, Brian Alexander and Algy Cluff

'Nonsense', he said, 'it's blue'.

'If it's so jolly blue', I pointed out, 'why has it just blotted out all the oil refineries?'

Jasper squinted in their direction and started to move rather fast. He took down the sail at the front of the boat (which I later discovered was called a jib) and started the little motor. About five seconds later we were hit with an extraordinary wind and the whole boat keeled over, lashed with horizontal rain. Jasper then instructed me to go forward and take down the mainsail. I found myself clinging terrified to the mast while he tried to tell me which rope to untie.

'No, no the thicker one. No, not that one. The one which is slightly lighter in colour.'

Eventually I managed to track down the right rope and somehow got the sail down. Invisible to us in the squall, two boats had already sunk.

We managed to limp into Cowes Roads, whereupon Louise, who had also never been sailing before and wasn't much enjoying it, announced that she was going to 'stay in that nice, big, safe-looking hotel over there'.

We had moored by the simple expedient of tying up to two other yachts by three lines, one at the front, one in the middle and one at the back. In the morning Louise was ferried back to our yacht and Jasper reassured us by saying that he was going to put up no sail but that at six in the morning we would simply motor back across to the Hamble. 'Nothing could go wrong and there was nothing to worry about.'

He then cast off for'ard, I cast off midships, he cast off aft and the line that he had cast off for'ard fell back into the water, went under the boat and wrapped itself firmly round the propeller. The engine wheezed into silence. Off we drifted in the five knot tide running in Cowes Roads. Time and again we tried to pick up buoys and we approached the rocks at a frightening pace.

Suddenly a magnificent palace of a 1930's yacht, a cathedral of polished teak and brass, appeared and by a seeming miracle, Jasper was able to leap aboard it. Unfortunately, his line was so short that the prow of our boat started to take huge chunks out of this wonderful old yacht. Great pieces of polished wood were sailing into the air when an elderly man in a boater and blazer came storming out with his teaspoon still in his hand and breakfast napkin around his neck.

'MY GOD. YOU STOVE ME IN. GET OFF MY BOAT, YOU YOUNG HOOLIGAN', he ranted while Jasper, with twelve tons of boat dragging on his hands, was forced slowly down the rail with our prow taking its regular bites out of the side of the palace. 'Its like this, Sir …' Desperately still trying to explain the circumstances, Jasper was finally lying back on the stern flagstaff when it snapped and he was forced to let go.

Louise and I were now drifting towards the rocks in a boat that neither of us had the slightest idea how to control. Faintly, across the water, came Jasper's advice like, 'Find the anchor' or, even more ridiculously, 'Put up the mainsail'. 'You're joking', came my reply.

As we approached the rocks, I turned to Louise and said, 'Get out all the mattresses and cushions.'

Puzzled, she said, 'This is no time for a kit inspection' and I patiently explained that I was going to try to protect the boat when it hit the rocks.

Luckily, out of nowhere came a little Harbourmaster's pinnace, which threw us a line and dragged us clear. We went home ignominiously on the ferry to fill out the insurance forms.

While I have scarcely ever gone sailing again, I have certainly been connected with it. My first wife's brother, Martin Read, came second in the 'Round Britain' race in a trimaran called *Three Cheers*. He only failed to beat Robin Knox-Johnson because Mike McMullen, his partner, fell off the stern. By almost a miracle of seamanship, Martin turned the boat, which was travelling at about 30 knots, and rescued him in time. (I was told this by Robin Knox-Johnson who admitted he only won the race because of the delay caused to *Three Cheers* by the incident.)

Three Cheers and the charming Mike McMullen had a tragic

end. A couple of years later Mike's new wife was polishing the hull prior to the Single-Handed Trans-Atlantic race when she dropped the electric polisher into a puddle, reached down and electrocuted herself.

A distraught Mike elected to go on with the race and was lost at sea. One can only speculate as to how and why it happened.

After about eighteen months working for him at Rank Screen Services, Martin Stevens was generous enough to tip me off about a new division which was forming to handle Rank's existing interest in motorway service areas and what they hoped was going to be a hotel chain. As a result I joined what was known as the Top Rank Motor Inns and Motorway Services Division. The Top Rank name had been inherited from their bingo halls and I was always rather worried about the implied superiority, a worry that was confirmed when a suggestion card from one of my service stations said 'If this is Top Rank Service, Christ knows what Bottom Rank Service is.' To begin with we were only three people, and I ended up doing an enormous amount of work. Not only was responsible for the petrol side of the division, I was also the Marketing Manager for the growing number of hotels we built and almost single-handedly had to control all the openings, the print and corporate identity for each hotel, the advertising, PR and so on. I remember once working through 22 weekends in a row.

I liked my Managing Director John Hastings very much, although he did get beaten down by John Davis's Rank Organisation eventually. He had the highly efficient habit of working in the back of his chauffeur-driven car to and from his home in Reading. Thus you did not attempt to get a paper on to his desk, but to his briefcase. His carefully thought out, dictated response would always reach you by ten the next day.

One great story he told was during the war when his aircraft carrier paused for two weeks in Simonstown, South Africa on its way to the Far East. He and all the other Fleet Air Arm pilots were billeted with generous South African families. One of his friends announced before going ashore, 'You're not going to believe this but I've been allocated to a smashing young widow.'

The two weeks passed and the ship waited to sail. No sign of the lucky pilot. Eventually a jeep was sent for him to the lonely farmhouse, shortly to be followed by an ambulance. What had happened was that the very randy widow had very nearly screwed him to death, literally. He was delivered to the ship and, in front of 2,000 delighted and applauding shipmates, his naked and doubled-up form was carried up the gangplank under a blanket.

TOP RANK SERVICE?

It took three weeks at sea for him to recover. You can have too much of a good thing.

I was looked after by a simply splendid secretary, Joan Royce, who was at least 15 years older than me. A widow, she had joined us from the publisher Lord Iliffe and had the appearance of a rather classy nanny with miniature brooches on her pie-frill blouses.

Under strain, her acting as a buffer with the outside world was immensely valuable. For instance, a space salesman would ring and Joan would say 'It's Mr Robertson from *Catering Times*'.

I would snarl, 'Joan, get that stinking bastard off the line.'

This would be translated as, 'Mr Robertson, I know Mr O'Brien is just *longing to talk* to you, but he is *as busy as a bee* at this moment and will have to call you back'. Everybody congratulated me on the incredibly friendly office I ran.

Looking back on it, I realised that Rank were once again stumbling into things and we ended up with a rag bag of hotels from city centre business hotels to quite smart resort establishments like the Hotel Romazzino on the Costa Esmeralda in Sardinia. There was not really enough thought put in to it and long term, the enterprise was going to have a very patchy progress.

THE RANK RACING CAR, A CORPORATE LESSON

One of my more radical suggestions in The Rank Organisation led to an early lesson in corporate power politics.

There is little doubt that the Chairman, John Davis (J.D.), was a powerful, forceful and frightening man. Each Division attended a monthly Management Board Meeting with John Davis and his central staff. These were awe-inspiring affairs and I twice witnessed grown men leaving them weeping. There was a huge horseshoe-shaped table at 38 South Street in London's Mayfair. Davis sat at the head of it, flanked by his Managing Director, Graham Dowson. All his staff sat down one side and we sat down the other.

It was the closest thing I have known to descriptions of attending meetings with Hitler's inner court. One often felt like generals from the Eastern Front bearing bad news and facing a row of Keitels, Himmlers and Bormanns.

The Motor Inns Division was in its honeymoon period, having only been operational for about a year. I suppose Davis must have found about my knowledge of the motor racing scene through my painting and journalism. Anyway, one of his characteristic, very short, and worrying notes appeared on my desk saying 'Report within a few days how Top Rank Motor Inns could benefit from some form of involvement with motor racing. J.D.'

Only a few weeks earlier, I had covered the 24-hour race at Le Mans for a magazine. A new Lola which had struggled to reach the circuit in time (driven from England with trade plates!) lasted till the Sunday morning, behind a phalanx of all-conquering Ferraris. I thought it showed enough promise to be our candidate.

Within one week I had convinced Lola that they should be sponsored by Rank, I had persuaded Graham Hill to drive the car, Stirling Moss to manage it, BP to be the supporting oil company and Ferguson (through Tony Rolt) to provide a four-wheel drive version.

'Ah' I thought. 'Let's be careful before submitting this type of idea to the board.' I went to see Graham Dowson, a much more relaxed, cheerful and friendly kettle of fish than the Chairman.

His exact words were 'My dear boy, this is one of the finest and most imaginative things ever put forward to The Rank Organisation. I will fully support you at the board meeting'.

The proposal was included in the papers, which went in a week before the board meeting.

Nervous as one always was (and I was easily the youngest person in the room), I had good reason to suppose that the scheme would either be supported or at least I would get full marks for such an idea. Imagine my devastation when the Chairman turned to Graham Dowson and said, 'I don't think much of this motor racing idea. What do you think, Graham?'

Without batting an eyelid Dowson said, 'I agree with you, Chairman.' Then, inexplicably, he added the gratuitous damning remark, 'And I told young O'Brien not to bring it forward'.

All eyes in the room turned coldly towards me. Even my friends and supporters must have thought 'What a lunatic! He actually goes to see Graham Dowson, who turns it down and then he still persists with his ridiculous idea'.

Knowing what I do now, I should have got up and probably hit Davis and Dowson with a convenient chair and would have been given about three years salary tax-free. As it was, I sat paralysed, red-faced with eyes downcast.

My article, while acknowledging Ferrari's present superiority, pointed to the new cars that were beginning to compete - including the Lola, bottom right

The Lola, as it first appeared at Le Mans

155

The 7-litre Ford GT40, winning the 1967 Le Mans with Dan Gurney and A.J. Foyt

The really sad part of this story is that my instincts about that car were absolutely right. It was Ford who stepped in, and took over the car as a ready-made prototype for the Ford GT40 which won Le Mans four times in a row and gave Ford immeasurable world-wide publicity for many years.

Years later I asked Graham Dowson why he said it. He didn't appear to know – or even remember.

Graham, whom I continued to like a lot, later did exactly the same to Bill Andrewes, who followed me back into Rank, forcing him to put up the rates at a hotel which made it hopelessly un-competitive. When John Davis questioned this, he said, 'I told Andrewes not to put the rates up when he asked me'.

Graham was completely unashamed about this and explained to Bill (as if to a child), 'When John Davis says black is white, as far as I am concerned, black is white. I have to keep my job'.

THE CHAIRMAN

John Davis was well known for summarily dismissing loyal Rank Organisation staff including, sometimes, his own public relations people.

There was to be a small press conference at 38 South Street and Davis came down half an hour before, stared at the chairs that filled the room and said, 'I don't think we need chairs. It will only be a short press conference. Get rid of them'.

At this short notice, the PRO and his two secretaries had no choice but to take their coats off and remove and stack the chairs. A quarter of an hour later, Davis came down, stared round the room and said, 'It looks a bit empty. Put back the chairs'.

Gritting his teeth, the PRO led his staff in laying out all the chairs again.

Two minutes before the press conference was due to start, Davis entered the room again, looked around and said, 'I think I was right the first time. Get rid of the chairs'.

The executive finally snapped and retorted, 'As I see it, you are the f...ing Chairman, why don't you move the f...ing chairs?'

He was dismissed on the spot but with sufficient money to start his own PR consultancy.

However scary John Davis was, he must be given his due. J Arthur Rank took his inheritance from his father 'Holy Joe' Rank the miller and tried to make religious films. (As one film reviewer put it, 'The mills of Rank grind slowly, but they grind

Sir John Davis

out the same old corn'.) When the cinema chains turned these down, he bought the chains, Odeon and Gaumont. The war, where cinemas were warm and companionable, brought temporary success, but it was Davis who helped J Arthur to diversify, especially in a mutually excellent deal supplying his network of worldwide offices to the American inventors of a new innovation called Xerox.

Peter Lendrum – an urbane, efficient and unruffled ex-Household Cavalry officer – worked for 17 'traumatic years' as PRO to John Davis. He points out that behind the often brutal behaviour were acts of personal kindness, but always behind the scenes (almost as if J.D. wished never to reveal any weakness).

After the Wall Street analysts' meetings concerning the biggest take-over of British companies ever tried, (Watney's), Davis quietly asked Peter to fix up for his secretary, Pauline, the most wonderful week of theatres, sightseeing and dinners in New York. A month later she died of cancer.

However a constant and obvious result of his more normal treatment of colleagues was that people were so scared that nobody dared to tell him the truth, a fatal flaw he shared with many tyrants.

Years later, I made a BBC documentary on Rank's 50th anniversary called *The Golden Gong*. It was all about Lord Rank. The current Board of Rank not only refused permission for us to interview Davis in retirement but insisted that none of the stars who we had persuaded to appear would mention him. Not Michael Caine (our presenter), not Joan Collins, not David Lean, John Mills, Richard Attenborough and Stewart Grainger.

They made us edit out any reference to him. Only Norman Wisdom managed to slip in his name. Davis had become a non-person, which he did not deserve. The board was now headed by Sir Patrick Meaney – sort of appropriate.

James Robertson Justice disapproves of a flirting Leslie Phillips.

In 1965, one of the hotels we were planning to build was The Coylumbridge at Aviemore, where skiing in the Highlands was getting going. I began to go up to Aviemore quite often on the sleeper train. In the dining car one night, I ended up chatting to James Robertson Justice,

MAGNUS MAGNUSSON'S HIGHLAND FLING

the bearded actor, famous as the gruff consultant in the 'Doctor' film series. He was actually quite intimidating to meet in the flesh. We walked back to his sleeping compartment, which was next to mine and I happened to look inside as he opened the door. There on the rail of the top bunk was the splendid sight of two hooded peregrine falcons, swaying with the rhythm of the train. Having told the actor of our plans for Coylumbridge, he turned to say goodnight but added the disapproving note, 'Thank God, you'll not be coming to Sutherland, at least!'

In fact, the Coylumbridge Hotel gave me a spectacular public relations coup – one which might even had rivalled those of my father. Our 'highland fling' had run into a serious problem. The owners of the small guesthouses saw this large hotel investment as a threat to their livelihood, and contrived to get the liquor license application turned down, a real disaster.

But there was to be an Appeal in the little local courthouse at Kingussie. I decided to call the newspaper which would most worry about the blocking of vital investment in the Highlands, *The Scotsman*. I was put through to a bright young feature writer called Magnus Magnusson, now better known of course for *Mastermind*. After a three-hour telephone conversation to Edinburgh, I was certain that we had a really effective ally.

Three days before the court case was due to be held his half-page article appeared headlined THE MOMENT OF TRUTH FOR SPEYSIDE. Not only was *The Scotsman* article absolutely spot-on, fingering the selfish interests of the locals, but it had the even more important effect of alerting the other media.

At what should have been a quiet local affair, the magistrates and witnesses had to fight their way through a great throng of journalists, photographers and television cameramen with glaring lights and humming generator vans. Being, quite literally, in the international spotlight, they simply did not dare to turn down unfairly the licence a second time. The hotel was built and the rest of the Aviemore resort took off.

A few months later, a similar incident occurred in Kinsale in Ireland, for which my Managing Director kept congratulating me, although I could claim no credit whatsoever. Similar shenanigans through the Cork County Council had stopped the building of the hotel at our Angling Centre at Kinsale, then a small village, rather run down.

A huge demonstration took place, led by the Catholic priests and a local Monsignor no less, carrying placards with such slogans as 'Who will feed the children, if Rank's don't start?'

This protest again led to the collapse of opposition to our plans 'Brilliant work again, Donough'. I gave up protesting that it really wasn't me and just nodded sagely every time the

Magnus Magnusson

Managing Director told the story of how I had cleverly organised the 'Bishop's protest'.

> At our Angling Centre in Kinsale, clients were allowed to have cooked any of the fish they had caught.
>
> After spending all day in a boat above the wreck of the *Lusitania,* an American walked in and pulled out one miserable small fish.
>
> Furious, he snarled 'That goddamn fish cost me a thousand dollars'.
>
> The cook replied helpfully, 'Well, sorr, thanks be to Christ you didn't catch two of them'.

ESTABLISHMENT CLUB

One evening, my father insisted I join a party going to the Establishment Club in Greek Street, Soho. I soon discovered why.

A few days before, a friend of his had insisted on taking him to this club which was really an extension of the brilliant Cambridge Footlights, 'Beyond the Fringe' scene, and was run by Nick Luard and featured budding talents like David Frost, John Bird, Peter Cook and Dudley Moore.

In one of the sketches, two actors representing Prime Minister Harold Wilson and George Brown appeared, the latter insisting that the Labour Party had to improve its image and announcing that he had approached 'the leading political PR man in the country, Toby O'Brien'. My father was amazed to see himself played by an actor who entered drinking brandy from a decanter, and who then proceeded to give sound PR advice to the political duo.

'Have you not noticed,' he said, 'that most promotional messages are centred round sex?'

'Harold Wilson' said suspiciously, 'No, Mr O'Brien. I can't say I have'.

'Well,' 'Toby O'Brien' said, 'Consider, for instance, POLO, THE MINT WITH THE HOLE or UNZIP A BANANA.'

'George Brown' appeared to grasp this only too quickly. 'I see what you mean,' he said. 'You mean we could have slogans like UNZIP A LABOUR CANDIDATE.'

'Er, not quite,' said 'Toby'.

'Well, perhaps THE LABOUR PARTY, WITH POLICIES WITH HOLES IN THE MIDDLE'.

'No, you haven't got it at all,' said 'Toby'. 'I think it would be best if I showed you a commercial I have made, just as an example'.

A black and white film flickered on. A beautiful girl in a bikini was running through the sand dunes pursued by an attractive young man – a bit like cigarette advertising of that period. The girl flung herself on her back, panting, and stared up into the young man's eyes. The music rose sensually to a crescendo and a sincere male voice intoned 'SUDDENLY, I REALISE LABOUR IS GOING TO GET IN'.

Immediately after the show, my father went up and bought a drink for the actor impersonating him, and then revealed his identity. He was extremely shaken to be introduced to the real Toby. But it had a beneficial effect. My father took parties of friends down there nearly every night and the actor impersonated him better and better.

WHISTLING WHITTAKER

In 1964, Roger Whittaker came into our lives. He met my sister Natalie, who was the secretary at his recording manager's office at Philips (Fontana), and married her only weeks later.

He had just obtained a degree in Biochemistry and Zoology at the University of Wales and was trying out his singing talent, 'perhaps just to get it out of his system'. He had been playing the guitar and singing since his teenage years in Kenya. Indeed, he had began to annoy members of the future independent Kenyan Government with his rendition in the Equator club in Nairobi of 'Uhuru' ('freedom' in Swahili):

> Uhuru, Uhuru.
> This is what we are going to do.
> No more work and no more tax
> We'll live in the sun and just relax.

This song expanded to reflect world wide topical events. The American U2 spy plane had just been shot down and Gary Powers, the pilot, put on trial in Moscow.

> When Powers asked for Uhuru,
> Khruschev said, 'Up U2!'

Roger worked his way through the British club circuit, had a show on Ulster Television and suddenly hit the big time almost by mistake at a music festival in Brussels. He sang, *If I Were a Rich Man* which won the Press Prize (Roger didn't even know there were any prizes) and then went on to be number one in France. He also performed *Mexican Whistler* for the first time.

This song with its amazing whistling became number one all over the world and was recorded in just ten minutes, all he could manage as he had stayed up drinking with my father and had a ferocious hangover!

In spite of this, Roger was on the point of quitting the music business to teach zoology in New Zealand when, quite suddenly, his breakthrough occurred with *Durham Town* which itself had a controversial history. My friends pointed out the geographical error of singing about the River Tyne, because Durham is on the Weir! Roger still counters that he knew that. The point of the song was troop ships were leaving and the Weir was too small, so he needed the Tyne. In the meantime, the error had become something of a national joke and helped publicise the song.

Roger's successful and worldwide career of 30 years was in the future. Another amusing and talented friend was just getting started, Rolf Harris, who was fascinated by Roger's African rhythms. The two used to swap advice and try out techniques. One evening in Roger's Chelsea flat, Rolf's Australian didgeridoo caused multiple complaints from other tenants 'about the plumbing'. At another equally hilarious dinner, we all helped Rolf to create a bizarre huffing background to a song about a dog and a boyfriend which Rolf celebrates below.

Natalie & Roger's wedding

Rolf Harris in his famous role as Jake the Peg with the extra leg, alongside one of his drawings

161

CARS IN CANADA

Natalie and Roger Whittaker went on holiday with me once in Portugal and there we met another Roger, one of the most fanatical car collectors you could meet.

Roger Lucas was, like his father, a prominent jewellery designer in Montreal. But cars probably interested him more than carats. An attractive but fierce looking French-Canadian, he was not a man to be crossed. He told me of a woman in a car park dumping her heavy make-up bag on the pristine paint-work of his Corvette and how, without a word, he hurled the offending article out on to the freeway where a truck ran over it.

Roger had found a D-type Jaguar left wrecked down in South America after some sports car race. He brought it back to Montreal and was lovingly restoring it. It ended up with eighteen coats of paint! He discovered that there was one other D-type owner in Montreal and halfway through his restoration project, Roger dropped in on him. The man looked up from the engine of a car and said, 'You're Lucas, aren't you? I've never heard of a man with such patience. Do you want a drive in my car?'

They removed the aluminium panel which revealed the so-called passenger seat (just there for the sports car race regulations), put on goggles, fired up the engine and headed out of the garage.

Montreal had a 25mph speed limit, which his new friend proceeded to exceed by 50mph. Then the road to the airport opened up and the 3-litre engine began to howl as he took it up to about 140mph, roughly 80mph above the limit. Approaching the airport, Roger noticed a car pulling over and

the passengers running away from it. His shouted enquiry got a bellowed response, 'Yes, that happens quite often when I come down this road. They see these bright quartz-halogen lights, they hear this racket and they see something going this fast and they probably figure it's a plane landing on the road by mistake!'

Eventually Roger's own D-type was restored and he told us the story of 'the last friendly policeman in Montreal.'

Roger Lucas' D-type Jaguar, 18 coats of paint.

When at last driving his gleaming pride and joy, he was pulled over by a patrolman who walked over from his police car with his notebook, 'I'm afraid, sir, that your exhaust contravenes Montreal city noise limits,' he said in a loud voice. Then he leaned forward and whispered, 'Actually, this is the most magnificent car I've ever seen,

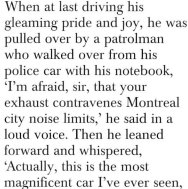

and the noise it makes is just lovely. I've got the Sergeant in my car so I'm going to have to pretend to book you. Do me a favour, let's pretend I need to hear that noise again. Just start up the engine please'.

Roger turned on the fuel pump which ticked away and the three Weber carburettors filled with fuel. He turned over the engine and it would not start. The starter ground on while the policeman stood, unfortunately, just where the two exhaust pipes curled out sideways.

Suddenly the engine fired and a 4 foot sheet of flame burnt off the patrolman's trousers. The Court ordered Roger to pay the fine for the noise infringement and for a $40 pair of police-man's trousers. So that was the last friendly policeman in Montreal!

RANK OUTSIDERS

One night their Chairman, John Davis, invited Martin Stevens and Ed Chilton to a private dinner at Rank's South Street headquarters. He was obviously probing these senior Rank executives for some purpose.

'Stevens, what, do you think is wrong with Rank Bush-Murphy?'

'They are not selling enough televisions' replied Martin.

'Huh, what do you think, Chilton?'

'I consider there has been a shortfall of consumer off-take.' (Meaning, of course, exactly the same thing!)

'You see, Stevens. There's a proper marketing professional speaking' smirked Davis, instantly promoting Ed Chilton to Managing Director of Rank Bush-Murphy!

The Rank Organisation had, as I have implied, the habit of arbitrarily mistreating and losing its best people. So many of us went on to be successful after leaving the Organisation (often fuelled by the generous payments necessary to keep us quiet) that we formed a club, the 'Rank Outsiders'. We would meet every six months in private rooms in restaurants like Rules. Eventually we even invited John Davis, for whom we had a grudging admiration.

My demise from Rank was fairly typical of the Organisation's style. I missed one of our management board meetings through illness, but I was tipped off by Martin that John Davis had started weighing in to my Managing Director, for whom the honeymoon period was definitely now over. It was no longer 'John' and 'John' but 'Hastings' and 'Mr Chairman'. John Hastings had presented the plans for the next year and Davis remarked that he thought 'it was all rubbish except for the marketing plan and the trouble is that O'Brien is too young to understand it'. The now beaten-down Hastings, instead of admitting that I had written it all, said, 'Yes, Mr Chairman I suppose you are right'.

I was therefore pretty well prepared when John Hastings, weeks later, called me in to his office and said that the Chairman thought I was too inexperienced to be the Marketing Manager. He had found someone else to become my boss, but I should carry on being the PRO and I could keep my company Ford and my drinks cabinet. I replied that I had effectively held down several jobs, I hated their Ford so much I had bought myself a Lotus Elite and if I wanted to have a drink in my office I would have one. They really were not the key things I was working for. I resigned.

The man who was to replace me never turned up. It transpired that he was a drunk who went off to America to find his estranged wife and never returned. It took several people to replace me and about ten times my salary. Ridiculous, typical wasteful Rank Organisation behaviour of the sixties!

With my less than mega pay-off, I went to join my father's PR business for a period of mixed success.

It was national news when John Davis finally turned on his faithful henchman, Graham Dowson.

'SUN: 20 SEPTEMBER 1975

RANK. CHIEF HAS NOW FIRED OVER SEVENTY EXECUTIVES

FRANKLIN

" TRY TO SQUEEZE IN DOWSON OVER THE MANTELSHELF ...."

By now, in spite of the best efforts of Harold Wilson's government, Britain really had become a centre of change. Pop groups like The Rolling Stones and the Beatles were world famous (the Beatles had even been awarded MBE's), Mary Quant, Biba and Carnaby Street were household names and the roads were full of Minis and Mokes. Mini skirts had become short enough to be classified as children's clothes and therefore tax free – for a while.

Behaviour was changing quickly. My sister Natalie saw a friend one Sunday morning walking along the King's Road in a fur coat.

'How was the party last night?'

The girl opened the fur coat to reveal that she was totally naked underneath. 'Judge for yourself', she smiled.

Looking back, you begin to realise quite what a watershed the sixties were, not least with sex. At the beginning of the decade protective mothers of debutantes catalogued eligible escorts in a secret document called The List. About the worst thing you could have against your name was 'NSIT' – 'Not Safe In Taxis', as if snatching a kiss was the most dangerous thing in the world. Later in the Swinging Sixties, not attempting to sleep with a girl on your first meeting might arouse suspicions and could even get you labelled by the girls as gay.

Michael Beby, a tall, thin, balding, working class and not brilliantly attractive friend of ours, used to while away tedious afternoons by approaching strange girls outside Harrods with an unrivalled directness. 'I'll screw you for nothing'. He claimed three out of ten turned him down. Even allowing for 'the Bebe's' exaggeration, it was an almost frightening success rate.

The relaxation of attitudes coupled with the sudden and wide adoption of the pill, meant the girls could take on a real predatory role for the first time. It sticks in my mind that one lovely girl, on our second date, announced 'It might as well be you', meaning she had selected me to end her virginity. I found this thoroughly unnerving, first because of the cool act of choice and second, the sobering thought that I had not actually to my knowledge taken out a virgin before!

I asked an old friend the other day what he most recalled

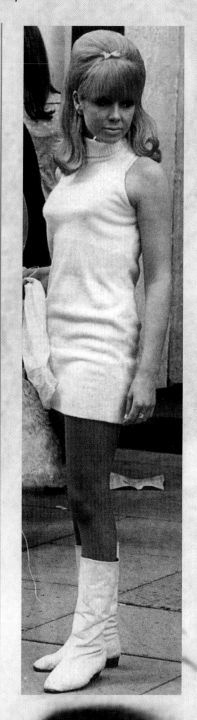

about the sixties. He replied that it was that 'if you had the desire, nerve or stamina for it, you could make love to several people a day'.

Whatever the faults of later generations, from drugs to internet addiction, you cannot accuse them of our casual and routine sexual irresponsibility.

'SIBYLLA'S', DEFINITIVE DISCO

All in all London life had become more colourful, faster moving and great fun. So it was with great pleasure that I joined a new adventure. In 1965, some of my friends decided to create the definitive discotheque in London. Up until then there had only been two stylish establishments to replace the fading, upper class nightclub. These were Mark Birley's 'Annabel's', still going strong all these years later, and the first genuine lively sixties-style discotheque, the 'Ad Lib', in Leicester Square.

One night at the 'Ad Lib', Terry Howard turned to his friend, Beatle George Harrison, and said, 'You know, we are spending too much money in this club. Why don't we start our own?'

Located in Swallow Street, Piccadilly, 'Sibylla's' was named after a beautiful Marshall Field heiress, Sibylla Edmondstone, one of Terry's girlfriends. I say 'one of' because David Sheffield, the manager, reminds me that Terry often had the nerve to go down to the club with other girls because he was confident that the shortness of Sibylla's eyesight and the loyalty of his staff would ensure that he was undetected! Designed by David Mlinaric the club was really stylish and had a major advantage. Our friend Dermot Butler, who had road-managed the folk group Peter, Paul and Mary, had cleverly designed the sound system to be extremely loud when you were on the dance floor and much quieter, three feet away, where you were sitting down, because the speakers were pointed vertically downwards and carefully controlled.

The sound system was installed by a company called Three D Sound (which Dermot had persuaded me to join as the third D). Whilst the system itself worked beautifully, we had yet to cure the problem of the amplifiers which overheated after about three hours when the sound would become rather woolly.

So it was with great trepidation that we approached the opening. It is one thing telling someone else that the Beatles 'always sound a bit fluffy round the edges' but it is quite another thing to tell them to their faces! Because the Beatles and the Rolling Stones were to come to the opening party and George Harrison was indeed now one of the owners.

Anthony Haden-Guest, who was writing a feature for *Queen* magazine (now *Harpers & Queen*) dropped in some weeks before and asked who was coming to the opening party. Terry casually gave him the draft list that was lying on the table, forgetting that this was a working list and included cryptic notes about the people invited and, what is more, a reserve list of 'less important people' to be invited only if any of the first 200 could not turn up.

Unfortunately, the whole list was typeset word for word and reproduced in *Queen*, which caused sensational offence to the reserve list!

Kevin McDonald, Terry Howard, Bruce Higham: partners in Sibylla's

SIBYLLA'S DRAFT
OPENING PARTY GUEST LIST

Tara Browne & Nicky
Gerard Campbell & Theodora ●
Frank Phillips & Partner
Roger Shine & Partner
Martin Myers & Ingrid Hepner
George Harrison ● & Patti ●
John Lennon & Cyn
Ringo & Maureen
Paul Macartney
Mick Jagger & Chrissie
Brian Jones ● & Anita
Keith Richard & Partner
Eric Swayne & Partner
Terry Donovan ● & Valerie
Jonathan Abbot & Maggi
David Bailey ●
Chester Jones & Sandy Moss
Johnny Gaydon & Clare Bewicke
Rudi Russell & Partner
Peregrine Eliot & Jacquetta ●
Michael Rainey & Jane Ormsby-Gore
Julian & Victoria Ormsby-Gore
Don Bessant & Julie Christie
Ian Ross & Bunty Lampson
Trevor Dawson ● & Partner
Nick Head & Sue Locke ●
David Enthoven & Partner
David Olivestone & Partner
Vic Singh & Jane Lumb
Johnny Gilbert & Partner
Alexander Plunkett-Green ● & Mary Quant ●

David Mlinaric ● & Elizabeth Hayes
Alan Lorenz & Partner
Bobby Lorenz & Partner
Bon Freeman & Partner
David Anthony & Celia Hammond
Mark Palmer & Lucy Hill
David Heimann & Wife
William Pigott-Brown & Partner
Terry Howard ● & Partner
Kevin MacDonald ● & Partner
Roland Wells ●, Ingrid Boulting●
Donough O'Brien ● & Partner
Nigel Dempster ● & Partner
Dermot Butler ● & Partner
Chris Long ● & Partner
Jean-Claude & Belinda Volpeliere
Bruce Higham ● & Kitty Gordon Hersy
David Tree ● & Annegret
John d Green ● & Partner
John Fenton & Partner
Charles Cyzer & Partner
Jacqui Bissett ● & Partner
Lord Ednam & Partner
Bluey Mavroleon & Partner
Lord Shelbourne & Partner
Lance Percival & Partner
Mary Bee ● & Partner
Robert Wace & Partner
Mike Margous & Anita Harris
Brendan Phillips & Partner
Gordon Waller & Partner
Trish Locke

Jessica Kitson ● & Partner
Rory Davis ● & Partner
Digby Bridges ● & Partner
Su Cornwallis ●
Linda Keith
Clive Atkins & Partner
John Simeone & Partner
Michael Caine ● (thru. Johnny Gilbert)
Nick Gormanston
Lucy Stockwell
Michael D'Abo & Maggie London
Caroline Percy
Edina Ronay ●
Sue Murray
John Barry & Wife
Tony Harris & Penelope
Danny Volpeliere
Danny Levin
Morag McEwan
Alan Freeman
Joanna Lumley ● & Partner
Sue Lloyd ● & Partner
Andrew Oldham
Mim Scala ● & Partner
Leslie Caron
Cathy McGowan
Annabella Macartney ●
Nigel Mallinson
Clive Atkins
Gabriella Licudi ● & guest
Anthony Haden-Guest ●
Charlotte Rampling ● & Partner

Reserve List

● Feature in this book

The possible failure of my sound system made me drink rather more than I would have done at the opening, which was a splendid event. It was a true manifestation of the social amalgam that the sixties came to represent – lords and ladies hobnobbing with the Rolling Stones and the Beatles.

One missed opportunity was when the actress Charlotte Rampling, according to my friends, suddenly declared her love for me. I drunkenly paid no attention to this, staring over her shoulder at a man in a cloak and muttering, 'Batman has got into the club.'

In my office the next day, Kevin McDonald, one of the partners and a brilliant advertising copywriter, kept saying morosely that he felt 'unhappy and guilty that he had created a place in which people drank, danced, laughed and enjoyed themselves', which I thought the whole exercise was about. I put this talk down to our hangovers and it didn't seem to be a very significant remark at the time. I was wrong.

Charlotte Rampling was fourteen when I first met her with her older sister, Sarah, and she was but one of the young people I met who later became well known in entertainment. Joanna Lumley, a beautiful, lively and impoverished model, appeared on the scene. Jacqui Bisset plainly never fancied me but seemed to like me and we became very good platonic friends, seeing each other about once a week. Fiona Lewis, her flatmate, however, did fancy me and admitted hunting me down at a party like some innocent prey.

Edina Ronay (daughter of Egon Ronay of gastronomic guide fame) was also quite a good friend for a period. I remember dropping in on her at her father's flat in Kensington and her saying, 'Do you mind if we carry on rehearsing?' as she introduced me to a young man called Michael Caine.

Michael Caine

Below, Fiona Lewis, star of 'Inner Space'
Below right, Jacqueline Bisset, good friend and companion

'Sibylla's' was a real success and was to remain one of the centres of sixties nightlife for the next three years, with David Sheffield as its owner/manager. 'One of the amazing things about the place was the loyalty of the staff', remembers David. 'We had 45 and not one of them ever left, in marked contrast to most restaurants and nightclubs.'

Equally amazing was how little the club was bothered by crime, organized or not. One reason was Laurie O'Leary, who acted as doorman. Live performers were booked through a legitimate agency owned by the notorious Kray brothers and Laurie was their representative. When protection gangs, like the Richardsons, came down to look over the place, one glance at Laurie convinced them that the Krays had 'got there first'. There were a couple of incidents involving young East End thugs who did not recognize Laurie, but a bit of head-butting and taking away of guns seemed to solve the problem.

David Sheffield

LICHFIELD

David Mlinaric, the club's brilliant designer

With the London club booming our friends decided that Sibylla's could have a similar success overseas, starting with the Bahamas and New York.

My friend the wine merchant Steven Spurrier had supplied the drink in London and then put quite a lot of money into these foreign dreams – and is still wondering, with reasonable good nature, where the money went. At the end of the sixties he moved to Paris, where he bought a small wine shop which soon achieved a huge reputation. He started France's first private wine school and many other ventures. In 1988 he was made the 'Wine Personality of the Year' for his services to French wine. This was in spite of the shock created by his famous 1976 International Wine Tasting which had two Californian wines beating the finest from Burgundy and Bordeaux.

BAHAMAS BEATLEMANIA

Sélection Steven Spurrier

'Union' Jack Hayward

Steven financed the first trip to the Bahamas to see if we could create a club there. Terry, Kevin, Bruce Higham and I were met at Grand Bahamas Island by Jack Hayward, one of the leading lights on the island, where he was known as 'Union Jack' because of his enthusiasm for all things British.

Because of George Harrison's shareholding in 'Sibylla's London', and because we had longer hair than the average American (which at the time was very short indeed), people in the Bahamas thought we actually were the Beatles, in spite of the fact that at least two of us were fair haired. It began when we were driving in a cab and the beaming driver said, 'I know's you's travellin' incognito, but I know you are the Beatles. You were just in a film and one of you had a ring.'

'Sure', we said pointing to Kevin, 'Ringo.'

'Yes, Ringo', he exclaimed, 'Yes, I recognise you now.'

We stopped at the Freeport Holiday Inn and watched him rush back down the line of cabs shouting, 'I just had the Beatles in my cab!'

A day later Terry Howard was wandering to the beach with his towel and bathing suit when a big fat American woman came up to him and growled, 'You're one of the Beatles, ain't you.'

He said, 'Well, actually, no.'

She started to shout, 'Tell my little daughter you're one of the Beatles.'

'Well, I'm not.'

'You big fink!' she shouted and stormed off down the passage.

Actually, this was not the first time Terry had been mistaken for a Beatle. He had previously been on holiday with George Harrison, again in the Caribbean, and lots of little children had come up and said, staring from one to the other, 'Can we have the Beatle's autograph?'

'Sure', said George Harrison pointing at Terry. It's rather sad to think that lots of little children went off with 'Terry Howard' written in their books, who months later found that they could not get a terribly good price for such a signature.

Invested with the glamour of the Beatles, we had a very good time in the Bahamas. However, I shared a room with Kevin who continued to suffer from almost inexplicable mood swings. 'Sibylla's' Bahamas never transpired but Bruce Higham did go on to create a nightclub called 'The House of Lords'. This was quite successful but owed rather too much money for too long to the Mafia, and a few years later he only got off the island by the skin of his teeth.

George Harrison

POOR KEVIN

Suddenly, something terrible overshadowed the Sibylla's dream.

We were holding a planning meeting in the studios about our projected 'Sibylla's' in New York. Someone remarked that they hadn't seen Kevin for a while and that his Volkswagen was parked with a ticket out in the Fulham Road, and it was going to get towed away.

The next day I had a call from our boutique-owning friend, Sue Locke. She was distraught. Kevin had committed suicide by throwing himself from the fifteen-storey apartment block the other side of Fulham Road and she had had to go and identify the body.

Kevin's funeral was one of the most dreadful occasions of my life. I had to drive there from Kevin's agency, Lintas, after picking up Derek Haas, the well-known art director, whose wife had killed herself exactly one year before. So the mood was already very sombre indeed.

When I got out of the car, the sudden visual effect was shattering. Funerals tend to be full of older people's relations or at least there is a mixture of ages. But across the car park was a silent mass of attractive young friends, all between twenty and thirty, 'black mini skirts' as it were. This visual underlining of a wasted life cut off in its prime reduced me immediately to tears, from which I suffered uncontrollably throughout the funeral.

Young 'swinging London' bereaved is an image I shall never forget. I might well have been even more depressed had I known that several of our friends on that sad morning would themselves have tragic deaths. No less than three more committed suicide, Trevor Dawson and Chris Radmall, who were 'Sibylla's' shareholders, and Peter Mallock, the club's lawyer. What is more, Charlotte Rampling's sister Sarah and Sibylla herself were later carried off by rare medical conditions.

RUPERT

'Rupert', a restaurant in Park Walk, Kensington, was another rather maverick enterprise owned by Terry Howard, David Sheffield and our architect friend, Digby Bridges.

Like 'Sibylla's' it became a major haunt of the sixties glitterati. Once, John Lennon called to book a table but was told it was fully booked. When he then revealed his name, a table became suddenly available. 'Forget it, man. I don't like your politics!' growled the Beatle. But he still came often.

At the opening the place was totally full, in fact booming.

David Sheffield sidled up to Terry and murmured, 'Have you noticed anything?'

'Well, Lennon's here, Michael Caine, Joanna Lumley…'

'No! Nobody's eating. There's been a knife fight between the chefs and the police have sealed off the kitchen!'

Eventually, the crisis was settled and some food began to reach the starving customers.

Terry claims that, like 'Sibylla's', 'Rupert' never really made any money, but it was great fun.

RISING STARS

Many of our friends at the beginning of their careers were then unknown. At about this time, my friend Mike Bowling was at his insurance brokerage one lunch-time when he was told that two young men had arrived – a solicitor and his client – asking about mortgages.

Andrew Lloyd Webber

LICHFIELD

He went down and showed them into a conference room and asked them how large a mortgage they were looking for. They said 'about £100,000', which was then a huge sum. He suddenly paid more attention, although at that time the name Tim Rice meant nothing to him. The rest of the meeting continued with Peter Cook and Monty Python imitations.

Tim and Andrew Lloyd Webber became good friends of Mike's and he acted as an 'angel' helping to raise money for their early shows like *Joseph and the Amazing Technicolor Dream Coat* and *Evita*.

At Mike's wedding Tim Rice helped to belt out the music with Paul Jones and the Blues Band.

PARTY PLANNER

LICHFIELD

In 1960, Lady Elizabeth Anson, Patrick Lichfield's sister, attempted to manage all the details of her own 'coming-out' party. She became so tired and upset that she saw a niche. So with Jessica Scott-Ellis, Lord Howard de Walden's daughter and £25, she started Party Planners. It was so successful that she has never looked back. While being the Queen's cousin may have been useful, it is Liz's organisational skills that has enabled her to run literally hundreds of parties, from huge events for 1,200 people down to intimate gatherings, and for royalty to media stars like Mick Jagger.

I introduced Liz to Dermot Butler in 1966 and our 3D Sound mobile discotheque, with its superb equipment, became the 'Party Planners Discotheque,' which provided the music for, among others, The Queen Mother's 70th birthday, Prince

Philip's 50th and for parties for Princess Margaret, Prince Charles and Princess Anne. (We should have asked for a disco Royal Warrant.)

I only helped with the discos occasionally as I would have preferred to be a guest, especially after Dermot and I in our Ford Transit drove along completely empty roads towards Winkfield Lodge for Susan Alexander's 'coming out,' thus being the only people I know not to watch England winning the 1966 World Cup.

GOSSIP'S GOSSIP

Another long and successful career was just taking off at this time.

In 1963, Nigel Dempster had decided that a lifetime at Lloyds was not for him and he moved to journalism joining the William Hickey column of the Daily Express. This was exactly the same time as I fixed up Patrick Lichfield's photographic retainer there and the two became partners in the arrangement.

Soon Nigel was off to America for the *Daily Mail*, for whom he returned to create his famous Diary in 1973, now the leading source of quality gossip in Britain. His unrivalled social connections have enabled him to write successful books with a special insight into genuine royalty as with *HRH The Princess Margaret –A life unfulfilled,* and 'money royalty' as with *Heiress: The Story of Christina Onassis.*

Nigel has no fear of controversy, as his law suits and 'Grovel' column in Private Eye attest. His book *Dempster's People* pulls few punches with his enemies, and indeed his friends, like Lichfield, Jonathan Aitken and Brian Alexander are subjected to robust and honest criticism. In a way, I'm quite glad I have never been famous enough for his eagle eye to have focussed upon me.

Some people get an early boost. One of Mike Bowling's insurance clients was Lord Portman. Just after he inherited the title, Mike asked, 'Well, Eddie, what came with it?'

'A hundred acres', he replied.

'Well, that's not much. You've already got thousands of acres all over Britain.'

PORTMAN INHERITANCE

'Ah yes', said Portman, 'But these acres are all around Marble Arch!'

MECHANICAL SAM

I was at a party when I passed a very pretty blonde girl and I heard her say '… and the bolt sheared off close to the head.' Now, pretty blondes don't normally talk in such mechanically precise terms, so fetching myself another drink I found myself chatting her up. Sam really was mechanically knowledgeable and claimed that, taught by a previous boyfriend, she could strip and re-assemble a Vincent Black Shadow motorbike.

She confessed that Sam was not her real name. Her first name was Christine and her surname, which she invited me to guess was 'like a screw'. My jaw dropped as my mind raced. 'Good God. Not that surely?' I thought. 'No, it's Grubb. You know, like a grubscrew.' Mechanically minded to the last.

Anyway, the re-named 'Samantha A. Metcalf' and I ended up living in Wilton Mews with two ridiculous Bassett hounds for about a year. Among their many misdemeanours, the Bassetts' most spectacular one was outside Safeway on the King's Road. We heard a huge commotion and emerged to find that Kipper and Bella had joined forces to rip the steel 'dog hitching rail' out of the concrete and were running up and down the King's Road, taking people off at the knees like Boadicea's chariot.

A sadder incident occurred when we visited my sister Natalie and Roger Whittaker in the country. While Natalie was out shopping, their beloved bulldog, Barney, suddenly took a shine to Bella. He chased her round and round the garden, ejaculating furiously, and dropped down dead.

My sister Geraldine's new boyfriend, Roger Linn, tried to give Barney the mouth-to-mouth 'kiss of life'. Even for a Royal Marine officer, that showed true grit!

Sam's mechanical knowledge also helped out one day with Sibylla Edmondstone whose Lotus Elan had caught fire in the garage where it was being serviced. The garage people, who were plainly pretty crooked, were trying to claim it was not their fault.

Sam agreed to go with Sibylla to argue with them. The garage mechanics seeing a blonde girl with a mini skirt and long boots accompanying the dark haired Sibylla plainly said to themselves 'This is going to be a pushover, Sibylla has brought another dolly bird to see us'. The garage people tried to explain the fire by a series of automotive jargon phrases until Sam said something like, 'Look F-off, you know perfectly well the float chamber on the Weber DCOE 40 is at the other end,' – a quick saving of £1,000.

Soon afterwards in 1967, an acquaintance of mine asked me to become involved in one of the commercial cock-ups which have punctuated my life.

His American-inspired idea was to create a large club of people called the British Air Travellers Club. With the subscriptions, we would buy a second-hand aeroplane, a Bristol Britannia, and go off on holidays in it, rather like an aerial timeshare.

The promotion of this scheme actually went rather professionally, but on the very day of our press launch two elderly aircraft crashed, one in Blackpool. So instead of 1,000 members we achieved precisely four. The scheme slid into the oblivion it probably deserved, luckily without serious loss.

For me, the only upside of this brief venture was meeting the Chairman, Admiral Sir Charles Evans. 'Crash' Evans, as he had been known in the Fleet Air Arm, told me a strange story of when he was commanding *HMS Eagle* off Korea. During a brief refit in a Japanese port, the Australian commander asked him if he would like anything at all done. He replied that he would like his shower, next to the battle bunk on the bridge, to be tiled.

The next day he found a Japanese workman busily grouting and tiling. Evans politely said, 'Good morning'.

'Good morning, Captain,' said the workman in fluent English.

Rather startled, Evans said, 'Are you enjoying yourself?'

'Yes, it's good to be back on a carrier.'

'So, you were in the Imperial Navy then?' asked Evans.

'Sure, I was Captain of a carrier. By the way, may I give you some advice about safer ammunition storage for your anti-aircraft guns?'

Recovering quickly from his surprise, Evans ordered his Flag Officer, Air and Flag Officer, Ships, with notebooks, to meet him in the Ward Room. 'What are you doing for lunch?' he asked the workman still bent over his grouting.

With his staff furiously scribbling down valuable advice during lunch, he then invited the erstwhile foe to come on a tour when they sailed. Sadly, General MacArthur found out about this and put a stop to this 'fraternising with the former enemy'. 'Crash' Evans sadly never saw the rather over-qualified workman after he had finished the last tile.

Would, one wonders, a former British Naval Captain quietly work away at such a menial task - or be any good at it?

THE TRAVELS (TRAVAILS) OF SIR CHARLES

HMS Eagle

THE BIRDS OF BRITAIN

Above, Ed Sullivan with John Green and Art Director David Tree

Below, left to right, Mary Bee, Vicky Mills and Jacquetta Lampson

Opposite, Patti Boyd, married to Beatle George Harrison, was the cover girl.

In 1966, Roland Wells and Terry Howard collaborated with the very successful advertising photographer John d. Green to produce a splendid and rather unusual coffee-table book with the, now extremely politically incorrect, title of *The Birds of Britain.* In a series of dramatic black and white photographs he extolled the new generation of very attractive and adventurous British girls of the sixties.

The book took two years to produce because John was very busy as were many of the girls, who were therefore shot at weekends and in the evenings. As most drank quite a lot of wine during the sessions, the result was several photographs that the girls later slightly regretted. Shirley Ann Field at one time claimed rather unconvincingly that her photograph had ruined her career.

Several people tried to get the book banned, especially when the *Daily Express* decided to serialise the photographs. Lord Hillingdon, the banker father of Victoria Mills (of Glyn Mills fame), was particularly incensed at the apparently bare-breasted picture of her playing cards and vowed to not only ban the book but also to stop its serialisation by ringing Robin Esser of the *Express.* He didn't seem to have much influence because the next day the series started and, guess what, Vicky Mills was the first to appear.

After the London launch at 'Sibylla's', John took eight of the girls on a tour of American cities like Detroit, Boston, Albuquerque, Las Vegas and New York, where the highlight was a national television slot on the Ed Sullivan show.

The book was a great success, selling 55,000 copies world-wide and is now a collectors' item, because John refused to allow it ever to be reprinted. So I am very grateful that he has allowed me to reprint some of the 'birds'. The ones you see on these pages are the ones I knew personally.

Clockwise, from top, fashion guru Mary Quant O.B.E., actress Juliette Harmer, the irrepressible Cilla Black, actress Edina Ronay (daughter of Egon Ronay), and model Annabella McArtney

ALL PHOTOGRAPHS JOHN d. GREEN

Clockwise from top left, Rory Davis, Lady Mary Gaye Curzon, daughter of racing driver Earl Howe, and appropriately covered in engine oil, actress Sue Lloyd (Ipcress File, the Saint, Crossroads) and actress Charlotte Rampling (The Damned, The Night Porter, Great Expectations).

179

*Clockwise, from top left, Ingrid Boulting,
Jacqui Rufus-Isaacs (daughter of the
Marquess of Reading), Su Cornwallis,
Diana Macleod (daughter of Tory
Minister, Iain) and Venetia Cuninghame*

With the money that John made from *The Birds of Britain*, he created a night-club on a boat moored in the middle of the River Thames near Cadogan Pier. This was the Sloop John D, because of his name John d. Green. The Beach Boys flew over to a special opening because of their hit song The Sloop John B. He recalls:

'The horrifying thing about the catering industry is how many people steal from you. The Sloop was full every night but within months the club had lost sixty-five grand rather mysteriously, which was an enormous amount of money in those days.'

So John then hired a catering manager whom he made a partner. But the money was still leaking out of the ship which was in danger of sinking. He realised that his partner was also stealing from him. So he said that this was totally ridiculous and 'Why didn't his partner at least give him half of what he was stealing so long as it was never from customers'. From then on the cash poured in and John's whole apartment became stuffed with £5 notes!

One of the features of the Sloop was that you had to get out to it on 25 foot power cruisers which were piloted by Thames Watermen on the insistence of the Port of London Authority. John had provided immaculate uniforms for these men – white trousers, blue blazers and white polo-necked sweaters. However, he could not ever stop them wearing an old piece of rope around the outside of their jackets, which they had done for centuries to keep out the cold and which slightly spoiled the appearance he was trying to achieve.

These men were typical rough and ready watermen. One night one of the members of the pop group, Hot Chocolate, turned up and was informed that regrettably the club was private.

'But I'm a member of Hot Chocolate,' said the star.

'I don't care if you own a whole f..ing sweet shop, mate, the Sloop is still a private club.'

'Out' Crowd, (back row from left), Tom Maschler, David Benedictus, Nicholas Tomalin, (middle row), Cathy McGowan, Jonathan Aitken, Tom Hustler, (front row), Christopher Gibbs, Lady Mary-Gaye Curzon

By 1967, the Sixties had reached their hedonistic heights, with Britain leading the way in fashion, music and sex. This page shows the 'in' and 'out' crowd as defined by Jocelyn Stevens and photographed by Patrick Lichfield. Recently I found a copy of Jonathan Aitken's book *The Young Meteors* and, knowing I was featured in it, eagerly looked for what he had written about me, perhaps predicting a brilliant future. I was very disappointed that all he had on me was my own prissy prediction that "a lot of us who have grown up through the sexy sixties will take a much stricter line with our kids". Very funny. The main reason people have stopped hopping into bed is AIDS.

But Jonathan's book provides an excellent contemporary insight into that era. In fashion, it is hard to overstate the influence of Mary Quant who said to him:

'Middle age has been abolished by the new fashions. Provided you are prepared to take trouble about it, you just suddenly get old somewhere between 65 and 80, and until then you can stay looking young. We have perpetuated youth.'

Mary is now 65 herself and she does look young. Hers is also the one of the few names to have endured. Top Gear, Count Down, Mr Fish, Hung on You, Sue Locke, Annacat, John Stephen and Granny Takes a Trip are all long-distant memories.

182

LICHFIELD

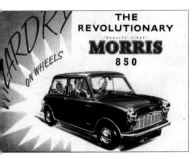

WIZARDRY ON WHEELS

THE REVOLUTIONARY MORRIS 850

The extraordinarily successful Biba tried to make a comeback years later but the moment had passed.

Britain's photographers became household names led by Snowdon and the working-class 'Terrible Trio' of Donovan, Bailey and Duffy.

As did the models; Twiggy, Jean Shrimpton, Jill Kennington, Verushka and Donyale Luna (the first black model) graced the covers of magazines all over the world.

And miracle of miracles, even the food was getting better! *Alvaro* kept going, but my friend and neighbour, Nick Clarke, is sadly gone (page 210) as are cheaper places like *Grumbles* (first called *Get Stuffed* until someone pointed out that a mother hearing her daughter say: 'I'm going to get stuffed tonight' might cause a problem.)

Finally, Britain had learned to build machines that people wanted to buy,

'In' Crowd, (clockwise from top) Peter Cook, Tom Courtenay, Twiggy, Lucy Fleming, Miranda Chiu, Michael Fish, Joe Orton, Susannah York

Graham Hill and Colin Chapman with his brilliant Lotus 49

notably the Mini (and the Mini-moke) and of course, the E-type Jaguar – a sex-symbol in itself. A roll-call of British Formula One World Champions had followed Mike Hawthorn – Graham Hill, Jim Clark, John Surtees, Jackie Stewart – with designers such as Colin Chapman of Lotus creating a motor racing technology lead we have never lost.

LICHFIELD

DAVID NIVEN'S METHOD

Across King's Road from our house in Wellington Square was *Alexanders,* the restaurant started by Mary Quant's husband, Alexander Plunket-Greene beneath their boutique, *Bazaar.*

There Toby and I often used to bump into his old Stowe friend David Niven, one of the world's best-loved actors. One night he recounted a typically silly Niven experience.

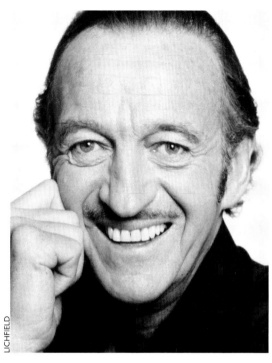

As a young officer, Niven was on a lonely hillside during a TEWT (Tactical Exercise without Troops). He had stashed a couple of bottles of beer down a rabbit hole and was dozing in the hot afternoon sun. Suddenly, he scrambled to his feet as the General's party approached. The General said, 'Well, Mr …?'

'Niven, Sir.'

'Suppose, Mr Niven, you were to attack that hill over there. Which method would you use?'

Niven hadn't the slightest idea, so he blurted out 'The Middle Method, Sir.'

The General was bemused. He had never heard of The Middle Method but was also somewhat unsure of himself, lest this 'Method' be some new, bang-up-to-the-minute product of the Staff College. He probed further.

'Why would you use the Middle Method, Mr Niven?'

Niven blustered on. 'Well it would be, er, shorter than The Outer Method, sir, and, er, at the same time more, shall we say, more flexible than The Inner Method.'

David Niven, archetypal 'Officer and Gentleman'

The General, becoming impatient, turned to his staff. 'What is this Middle Method?' he asked.

One of them dryly said, 'I rather think it's a product of Mr Niven's fertile imagination.'

The General, perhaps reluctantly, ordered, 'Place that young officer under arrest.'

UNBRIDLED POWER

My Rank company Ford had been so boring that I foolishly bought a really dangerous car from a friend at a cocktail party. It was a rather battered Lotus Elite. This early brainchild of Colin Chapman was brilliant but conceptually beyond the manufacturing abilities of Lotus at that time. It had no real backbone or chassis, relying instead on a futuristic monocoque sandwich of fibreglass and aluminium.

Lotus Elite, beautiful but fragile

After a few weeks of things always going wrong I took it down to Len, my mechanic in Chiswick. He at once pointed out that one front wheel was two inches further forward than the other due to a crash, and secondly that 'it was just a heap of bloody oil-soaked

Ryvita.' Eventually he convinced me that it was really too dangerous to drive and should be broken up for its parts.

I went along with this but we kept the recently rebuilt Coventry Climax engine which we then dropped into a very light Lotus Seven, thus replacing 30 brake horsepower with 85, in a car that weighed about 600 lbs. A modern Kawasaki rider would have been perfectly satisfied with the resulting shattering acceleration – 0-60 mph in under five seconds.

On one of its first outings, I took a new girlfriend, Jessica Kitson, to the cinema on a Sunday afternoon. I picked her up in Marble Arch from her mother, who was Paul Getty's interior designer. Jessica stared gingerly down at the tiny aluminium projectile I was asking her to share.

As we proceeded down Park Lane, we came up behind a bus. Suddenly the car howled forward with a will of its own. I managed to slam on the brakes and switch off the ignition. I started the car up again – it was perfectly normal. Jessica was petrified.

Coming into Hyde Park Corner, the same terrifying surge occurred. Again, I managed to reach the ignition key in time. Down Knightsbridge there came a third demonic blast of power. I pulled the car over and pulled off the bonnet and my inspection revealed what had happened.

Lotus 7

The throttle linkage came across from the driver's side and rested against the passenger's thin flexible aluminium scuttle. Jessica had the longest legs of anyone who had been in that car before. In her nervousness, she had firmly pressed against the scuttle, willing the brakes to go on, thus slamming open the throttle herself and unleashing, unwittingly, the full power of the car.

Thank God that this incident took place in broad daylight and in good weather, otherwise these words might not have been written.

When we found that the Lotus could 'out-drag' his Cobra (0–60 in 4.2 seconds!), Brian Alexander and I decided to use it in club racing with Brian doing the driving.

We used to test it round the nice country roads near Winkfield Row where the Alexanders lived. I remember the Field Marshal suddenly noticing the distant howl of the Coventry Climax engine and complaining about 'young hooligans spoiling the countryside with the noisy cars'. I did not dare tell him that he was referring to his son.

Winkfield Lodge was a charming house and the Alexanders the kind of excellent hosts that you would have expected. It was only when you examined the house carefully that you began to notice the many landscape paintings signed 'Alexander'.

'Alex' really was an excellent painter, much better that other famous amateur, Winston Churchill. He was undoubtedly influenced by his life-long artist friend, Edward Seago. Once when walking together in London, a lady rushed up to 'Alex', stopped him and

Alex painting on Leave', Seago, Winkfield, April 1944

gushed for minutes about how much she had wanted to meet him. Rejoining Seago, 'Alex' typically remarked 'I don't quite know who she thought I was.'

When he died his paintings were unfortunately priced so low by the gallery that by the time I turned up to buy one they had all been snapped up. Luckily his son Shane has several, so you can get a flavour of 'Alex's' art from some we have photo-graphed. Several of them date from when he was Governor General of Canada.

Silver Valley, British Columbia, 1950

Quebec, 1951

Cintra, Portugal, 1950

Ottawa, 1949

UNSUCCESSFUL SOLICITING

Rupert Deen

The Lotus never did make it to the racetrack. Brian's enthusiasm waned. It may have had something to do with the fact that its fierce ability to accelerate was not matched by a similar ability to decelerate, owing to its feeble little Triumph Herald drum brakes. So being neither a racing car nor a sensible road car, it had to go.

I decided on something a little safer and more comfortable and bought a rare silver Lancia Flaminia with coachwork by Zagato from a raffish Lloyds underwriter and 'man about town' called Rupert Deen. I decided to have it resprayed white in a slightly disreputable paint shop in Brixton.

The price of this paint job seemed to be mounting to the point where confrontation was necessary and I asked Joynson Hicks, to provide me with a solicitor. Ian Gow turned up, even at that time slightly plump and prematurely balding. We went down

187

on the tube to try, with much noisy argument, to take the car away but at the height of the row the burly man in the paint shop slowly closed the gate behind us, thus ensuring that the car was going nowhere. After much bluster, we finally paid them off in full.

Ian Gow went on to become one of Margaret Thatcher's favourite Ministers and a supporter over Northern Ireland. For this, as in the case of several of her friends, he was sadly rewarded with assassination by the IRA.

THE BEST KNOWN CAR IN HERTFORDSHIRE

Reflecting on cars, the most extraordinary must be that of Patricia Barnet's grandmother. Soon after I had started to go out with Patricia she invited me for the weekend at her parent's lovely house near St Albans. Her father Cedric was a senior partner at the august stockbrokers, Cazenove's, and her mother was a slightly eccentric Russian. However, it was the grandmother who was the most eccentric of the lot.

Patricia tried to warn me that her grandmother, Lady Barnet, was a superb gambler and bridge player and drove a 6.3 litre Chrysler-powered Bristol.

As she was over eighty, I had not quite believed this until I heard the rumble of a classic American V8 out in the drive, and a little old lady came bustling in. I am not sure if she was actually wearing one of those green eyeshades that American gamblers used to wear, but in my mind's eye she did.

Her strange behaviour had driven Cedric and the Hertfordshire Police to despair. She drove down the middle of all roads to equalize the tyre wear. She never indicated when turning into her drive. And when ticked off by the police retorted, 'Silly boy, everyone knows where I live'. One day, she roared up Cedric's drive in the Bristol, which was now painted in two colours. But it was not as you would normally paint a two-tone car, it was black on one side and duck-egg blue on the other, with the dividing line running straight up the middle of the bonnet, over the top and down over the boot.

Cedric asked her with horror what she had done to the car, and she explained, 'Well, Cedric dear, I am getting into so much trouble with the police that I thought if they saw me doing something naughty going one way they would say, 'Ah, a black Bristol.' And coming back, a few minutes later, they would say, 'Ah, a blue Bristol, it's not the same car'.'

She seemed to have totally ignored the fact that she had created the most distinctive Bristol in the world, which would soon be the talk of the county, let alone the police stations of Hertfordshire. Cedric grasped the opportunity and took away the Bristol and gave her a nice, safe Morris 1100 and a chauffeur.

CASENOVE'S KNUCKLE-RAP

Cedric Barnett, as a partner of Casenove's in the 1960's, belonged to a City of London whose tone and atmosphere are now long gone. Someone told me the other day a punishment that the Stock Exchange once imposed upon Cazenove's for some minor infringement of the rules. They merely called a short meeting in London on 12th August demanding that all the Cazenove's partners attend.

The act of denying a grouse-shooting fraternity the ability to be on the moors on the 'Glorious Twelfth' was subtle or cruel enough for anyone.

TIPPING THE DRIVER

Let's return to Toby, by now generally regarded as the 'Grand Old Man of Public Relations.' With quite a reputation for representing countries in a political sense, my father was approached by some of the emerging countries in Africa.

But, having suffered all his working life from the slow payment by some of his overseas clients, namely Spain and Saudi Arabia, Toby at last thought he had learned his lesson and sent off a bill to the Government of Ghana in advance.

He flew into Accra for his first familiarisation visit. He stepped down from the VC10 onto a VIP's red carpet and for a whole week he was driven about in a large black Mercedes with a chauffeur and an enthusiastic and jolly Ghanaian Minister of Protocol.

He stayed up late every night and therefore used the car and chauffeur about sixteen hours a day. So, when they finally drove back to the airport my father thought it would be only fair to give the chauffeur a little tip.

Mindful that local customs should be adhered to, as the car approached the step to the plane he leaned over to the Minister of Protocol, whilst reaching for his wallet, and whispered, 'Do you think £5 would be in order?'

The Minister of Protocol beamed, snatched the note and said, 'Perfectly in order. Thank you very much Toby.' My father had to scramble around to find another £5 for the chauffeur!

His efforts to get paid came to nothing. When he discovered that the first three months' invoice had not been paid, he visited Dr Kofi Busia, the Prime Minister, who was being treated in the London Clinic, to complain.

'Don't worry, Toby. I will send a signal this afternoon,' said the no-doubt sincere Dr Busia. Unfortunately, unbeknownst to him, that very afternoon he was being deposed by a Colonel in his absence. The money never came.

BANKS AND BANKERS, TASTY OR NOT?

Relationships with bank managers can be very important. There is no doubt that managers and banks vary. In my experience, when you really need them, they often let you down.

In 1966, I published a letter in the *Daily Telegraph* when there was evidence that the banks were turning rough on their customers. I pointed out that bank robbers like Bonnie and Clyde and Pretty Boy Floyd only became unpopular when they stopped shooting bank employees and starting hitting bystanders.

In a similar vein, Toby returned from a trip to the Congo, when working for Union Minière, the Belgian mining company, and in an article in the *Daily Telegraph*, reported that local tribesmen had eaten their bank manager. He commented that, 'Judging by my own bank manager, he would have been a boiler rather than a roaster.'

Cyril Randolph, his bank manager at Childs, then sent him a witty cable:

> SURELY BOILERS ARE TOUGH
> AS CHILDREN ARE ROUGH
> BUT ROOSTERS ARE TENDER
> LIKE CHILDS BANK THE LENDER

My father responded:

> YOUR WIRE WAS MOST CHARMING
> AND VERY DISARMING.
> BUT WOULD YOU HAVE SAID IT
> IF I WEREN'T IN CREDIT?

Sadly, jocular telegrams between bank managers and clients are long gone (in fact, bank managers themselves are going).

IF YOU FROWN, TURN IT DOWN

There are occasions when it is simply not worth taking on a public relations assignment, whatever the money. In the case of a shipping line the first part of the project went well. The maiden voyage of their newest liner from Europe to New York was broadly a success. Toby had managed to fill the ship with socially important people and top journalists. However, one incident gave a hint of potential trouble to come. The ship had passed the Statue of Liberty, the guests were gathered to admire the view of Manhattan and the dresses for the ball that evening were on hangers on deck so as not to get crumpled. Suddenly there was a shower-burst and the guests ran for cover. So did all the members of the crew, leaving the ball gowns hanging on their trolleys in the middle of the deck and, of course being ruined by the rain. Toby turned to Leo and said 'God I'd hate to be on one of these ships if they got into trouble'.

There was one mistake that could have been serious.

At Boston, my stepmother, Leo, and Roger and Griselda Keyes rashly went ashore to do some last minute shopping, their taxi-driver lost his way, so that they just missed the ship. The Boston Daily Globe headline could not avoid a pun:

——BOSTON DAILY GLOBE——
PEER LEFT ON PIER
Boards Tug to Overhaul Liner

But the best account came from the Boston Post:

It continued:

'Officials on the dock rushed Lord and Lady Keyes with their friend, Mrs. Leonora O'Brien of London, over to Joseph Connolly, Superintendent of Piers for the Port of Boston Commission'.

'If anyone can help you, it's the superintendent of Piers'.

'Superintendent of peers!' said his lordship, 'Such a really extraordinary service' 'Not peers! Piers!' someone volunteered 'Quays'.

'Ah, superintendent of Keyes!' said Lord Keyes, even more impressed.

The rest of the voyage passed off without further incident and for a couple of years Toby forgot about the shipping line until one evening he was watching the Nine O'Clock News on television. There was another passenger ship from the line on fire, not far from New York and certainly close enough for the television camera crews to be able to film in great detail the crew abandoning ship in the boats and largely leaving the passengers to their fate.

The telephone rang and his friend the Chairman of the line said 'Toby, I wonder if you would like to handle our public relations again?'

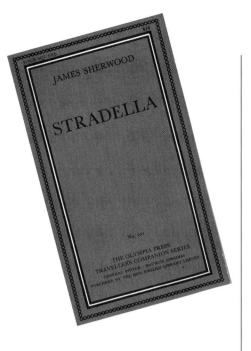

'Bugger off, old chap,' said my father 'I've got a television set!'

There were a couple of other assignments where Toby paid less attention than he should to the type of client he was taking on. One of his staff brought in a new client called Olympia Press, headed by Maurice Girodias. Indeed, the client had been with them for several months before Toby realised something which practically any visitor to France could have told him. Olympia Press, while the original publishers of Henry Miller and other distinguished writers, was now the leading producer of French pornography books ('Her ripe young body pressed against her over-tight clothing as if searching to be free!'). Once he had discovered this rather embarrassing fact Toby terminated the contract but not without some difficult correspondence with both the client and the media.

The second assignment was International Life Insurance, the UK arm of Bernie Cornfeld's Investors Overseas Services. IOS was a gigantic mutual fund complex, which at its peak turned super salesmen into millionaires almost overnight. During those years, one was continuously being approached by quite good friends who then revealed that they were IOS salesmen. Cornfeld had recruited all sorts of names to make IOS more respectable, including Ambassador Roosevelt, Count Bernadotte and in the UK subsidiary, Anthony Montague-Browne, my father's old friend who had helped him with Churchill, de Mille and the 'Ten Commandments'.

Toby started working for IOS but was always bemused and distrustful about the whole operation referring to 'Corny Bernfeld and his friends'.

He was right to be suspicious. As the excellent book *Do you Sincerely Want to be Rich?* explains:

> By the end of the 1960s, IOS had $2.5 billion of other people's money to manage. Bernie Cornfeld had made £100 million personally with a hundred of his associates millionaires as well.
>
> Cornfeld was the most talked-about financier in Europe and IOS was asserting the right to sit at the golden table of the world's most respectable financial institutions.
>
> The only trouble was that IOS was not a respectable financial institution.
>
> It was an international swindle.

In the event IOS went away. It collapsed in one of the greatest financial fiascos of the 1960's but luckily without damaging Toby's reputation.

I was able to avoid the trap of taking on a 'no-win' situation when I was asked to meet an American potential client at the Great Eastern Hotel. Entering the suite I was confronted by the bizarre sight of an elderly American cowboy, complete with Stetson, with an equally old and scrawny wife dressed identically. There was also a worried looking young man who, it transpired, was from another public relations company.

The American turned to me and explained that he ran an attraction in Texas with a cowboy and Western theme and that he intended to open a similar one here in the UK. So far, so good. He then said, 'The main purposes of public relations is to make me famous. So the next time I come in from Heathrow airport, I expect crowds to be lining the route!'

I did not even bother to try and explain the futility of such an objective or even to reveal that it was quite difficult even to get the Mall lined with anybody when the Queen escorted really important foreign Heads of State.

I asked the young man who he was. When he officially revealed that he was from another PR consultancy, I quickly announced, apparently reluctantly, to the American that 'Institute of Public Relations rules did not permit me to cut across the briefing of another member consultant' and that I therefore had to withdraw. The poor young man was waving desperately, his face a picture of panic, but I politely insisted and left the ridiculous meeting. I am not sure I did not actually break into a run in the corridor.

It is bad enough having clients that are very difficult. You should certainly avoid clients that are actually mad!

My stepmother, Leo, used to make a superb, heavy, sweet liqueur wine out of the elderflowers that grew all around our house in Braughing.

One Sunday, Cyril Ray, the prominent wine writer from *The Times* came to lunch and my father, mischievous as always, produced a dusty bottle of wine claiming that it had been in his cellars for some years, and the label had fallen off. Could his friend enlighten him as to what it might be?

Cyril sniffed and tasted it and finally declared, 'Chateau d'Yquem, but I could not put my finger on the year.'

After several minutes of praise, Toby revealed that the wine was actually created from the weeds around the paddock. I'm sorry to say that Cyril scarcely spoke to him again.

I suppose the old-fashioned Gentlemen's Club is something of an anachronism now. Rising costs and falling membership have forced many to amalgamate, and shockingly, even to let the ladies in! But many prosper still. I have belonged to three clubs, but I still count it a privilege.

WINE
WHINE

GENTLEMEN'S CLUBS,
AN ENGLISHMAN'S
CURIOSITY

193

The first is Pratts, owned by the Duke of Devonshire, a funny little basement off St James's 'full of incredible fish and impossible stories,' or perhaps it was the other way round.

The other club which I use often for lunch is Buck's, started by Captain Herbert Buckmaster who with a group of friends in the murderous trenches of the First World War, resolved to form a club if any of them survived. Three brothers were founder members; two won Victoria Crosses and the third a DSO and Bar, and a DSC (he was known as the coward of the family). It is small and charming and, curiously enough, about a quarter of its members are Americans.

I was told that shortly before he died, Harold Macmillan was being helped down the stairs by Joe, the barman, and remarked that he had known the club when it was a private house and he had gone to parties there.

Joe said 'Ah, Sir. That must have been before the First World War, because the club was formed in 1919.'

'Of course, it was before the First War!' snorted Macmillan. 'When on earth do you think I was going to parties?' tottering out into Clifford Street.

Above, Buck's
Right, Harold Macmillan at 90
Below, Boodle's

One of the other 'characters' of Buck's was John Loder. In 1915, he was the young officer who accepted Padraic Pearse's surrender after the Dublin Easter Rising. Pearse was so impressed by John's kindness that he handed him his cap badge and other mementoes 'in case he was executed' – which he was.

John became a heart-throb actor in the thirties and was married many times, one bride being Hedi Lamarr. Years later, when some Buck's members consulted him about Grace Kelly, he paused and asked, 'Was she one of the ones I married?'

Clubs and eccentricity certainly seem to mix. One old boy at the turn of the century came staggering out of Boodles' (my other club) and hailed a horse-drawn Hansom cab. After a long silence and delay, the cabbie lifted the little hatch to communicate with his passenger.

'Where to, M'lord?'

'Don't be so bloody inquisitive!' was the unhelpful retort.

Hansom cab,
by Robert Bevan

(That is a bit like the story of the well-wined gentleman who ordered a first-class return ticket. When the clerk said: 'Where to?' he replied 'Here, of course, you fool!')

A rather eccentric peer only came up to White's from the country every few months. The doorman pointed out that the lavatories had all been carefully re-tiled. Later the doorman asked him what he thought of this refurbishment.

'Very nice, very smart. But it certainly makes your cock look shabby.'

In the bar of White's is a cartoon that refers to an incident when an irate member once tried to kick the Labour Minister, Aneurin Bevan, down the steps of the club. The cartoon shows one Bishop restraining another from kicking an Archbishop down the stairs of the Athenaeum Club with the line 'Have a care, Fontwater, this isn't White's, you know'.

Indeed, the Athenaeum is famous for its ecclesiastical connections. My father once lunched there and when he wanted to leave, he found his nice umbrella had been taken.

A month later the doorman rang him and said 'Hello, Mr O'Brien. We've found your umbrella. One of the Bishops, I'm afraid. My Lord of Truro had it'.

Members of the Athenaeum could be classed as sensitive souls. Once the club was giving exchange hospitality to the 'Rag' (the Army and Navy Club), whose members I have always found to be a most kindly collection of retired warriors and mariners. Said a Bishop to an eminent retired civil servant 'Hear those fellows from across the way are coming here next week.'

The other sighed and said 'Yes. A pity. Those *brutal, brutal* faces.'

When the Guards Club was still in Brook Street, they were given hospitality by their neighbour up the street, the Saville – a club which, while not as bohemian as the Savage, nevertheless tended to be a bit BBC and 'booksy'. One young Guards officer was discussing their former hosts with a friend. 'Delightful people, quite delightful,' he said. 'But tell me. Why do they make their own trousers?'

Such clubs can have extra pitfalls. Imagine the position of a young officer on his first visit to the Guards Club, who was asked his name by a silver-haired General. When he responded, the General snorted with some satisfaction. 'Pleasured your mother before the war.' What kind of response was possible? 'Oh. Jolly good, Sir.'

White's

Satire does not always travel well. It is especially worrying when the audience does not even know that it is being presented with satire at all. In 1965, the height of the Rhodesian UDI crisis, my father received a letter from an old friend living in Zambia, enclosing a cutting from the main newspaper *The Times of Zambia* which had quoted a piece direct from *The Daily Telegraph.* The paper plainly thought that it was tapping the attitudes of the British by quoting verbatim from such an opinion-forming British newspaper.

The trouble was they had decided to quote from that bizarrely

WIND OF CHANGE FOR RHODESIA

satirical column called *Way of the World* by Peter Simple. This is what it revealed:

> The whole of Great Britain is now behind the idea of a military solution to the Rhodesian crisis. Last week half a million people gathered in the working class district of Sloane Square in order to sign a petition demanding that the Government act. When the police were sent in to break up the rally, they revolted against their aristocratic officers and joined the petitioners.
>
> The Government is now really worried about the wave of industrial unrest sweeping the country because of Rhodesia. Of particular strategic importance is the strike which is paralysing the vital atomic submarine base of Bournemouth.

It takes only an instant for one's imagination to leap ahead and envisage how many more press cuttings could be lifted from the columns of 'Peter Simple.' What other African, or indeed perhaps Russian, readers would puzzle at the brandy swigging antics of J. Bonington-Jagworth or marvel at the goings-on in the Hampstead home of those prominent left-wing thinkers the Dutt-Paukers. The mind boggles at the thought of how much international trouble, or at least confusion, could be caused.

It was exactly at this time that my father received a secret invitation to meet Rhodesia's Foreign Minister, PK van der Byl, in Geneva. PK had been sent by Ian Smith to ask my father, as the leading political public relations man in England, to take on the cause of Rhodesia and to try to use propaganda to alter British public opinion.

Toby had to point out that as Ian Smith had broken away and declared his Unilateral Declaration of Independence, it would be not only potentially damaging to his career but also perhaps treasonable. While the penalties might not be the same as in William Smith O'Brien's day, the risk was simply not worth it and he had to gracefully decline.

Years later I met PK living in South Africa. Tall, rather strange looking, and obviously extremely handsome in his youth, he lived in a rather anachronistic Dutch house with his German wife, who was many years his junior.

He was an interesting man but one became a little disturbed by the stories of how many people he had to execute when he was Minister for Justice.

POISON DWARFS

After one of our press conferences, I went out to lunch with Richard Kershaw, later to be a well-known television presenter. He described how he had served during National Service as an officer in an anti-aircraft regiment in Germany. They operated two types of gun: the heavy 3.7 inch and lighter 40 mm Bofors gun. The former were served by the bigger men and the latter by little Cornishmen or Glaswegians who, with drink inside them, came too close to the newspapers' famous description of 'poison dwarfs'.

One night, in 1950 as Picquet Officer, he was summoned to the Guardroom and was confronted with a memorable sight. There were two huge and immaculate German policemen holding up at arm's length an appalling, dirty, squirming, shouting, drink-sodden figure.

As it was only five years after the war, they were both certainly former Wehrmacht soldiers. Etched on his mind was the wonderful look of puzzlement as they dumped the little drunken apparition on to the desk like a rag doll.

Quite obviously, going through their minds was, 'How on *earth* did we lose the War to people like this?'

Martin Stevens rang me one day to say that he was anxious to help a young officer leaving the Household Cavalry called Anthony Nares to get a job in civilian life.

'As a matter of fact,' I said, 'we are looking for a trainee account executive, why don't you send him to see my father.' Anthony turned up and I briefed him as much as I could. He was a charming, intelligent, lively young man who spoke fluent Spanish having lived in South America. I took him up to see my father who as usual offered him a large drink and then left them alone.

At about 3 o'clock, Anthony had tried to call me to tell me how the interview had gone. Unfortunately, the elderly lady on the switchboard put him through to the wrong Mr O'Brien (my father and I also had almost identical telephone voices).

'Well, I saw the old fart,' said Anthony, who had been fed several large drinks by my father and then had gone out to lunch.

'Really,' said Toby, never one to pass up a practical joke. 'So, how do you think you got on with him?'

'Well, I think I managed to con the old chap that I knew something about public relations and I might be half useful to him.'

'Is that so,' said my father and spun out the conversation for several minutes. Finally he inquired, 'What about the money?'

'Well, I think he looked a bit of a mean old bastard about the money.'

'I AM THAT MEAN OLD BASTARD,' shouted Toby, 'but you've still got the job. I'll see you Monday morning.'

I think that was the first time I coined the phrase, 'Naughty Nares.' Anthony turned out to be a very good friend and a very successful one.

LICHFIELD

Debutantes were getting prettier, Lady Charlotte Curzon

TELEPHONE BLUES

Anthony Nares

197

30 years on and capturing the Sixties nicely, Liz wrote this poem for the

Many of the changes during the Sixties, including fashion, began as mostly an urban, and especially a London thing. One newspaper photographed conventionally dressed young people arriving from Croydon or Southend, slipping into the Sloane Square lavatories to change, then strolling up and down the King's Road dressed outrageously until evening when they changed back into 'civilian clothes' to face their parents in the suburbs!

At exactly this time, parental disapproval of Sixties fashions nearly ruined my future wife's advertising career. With long blonde hair and miniskirt, Liz was about to set off from the country for her most important interview with, no less, the Creative Director of the advertising agency for Peter Robinson and Top Shop. Imagine her distress when firmly told by her mother, 'You can't possibly go to an interview looking like that.'

A teenager of the mid-60's, with no money, no transport and a very minimal wardrobe, had little choice but to succumb to parental guidelines. So off she went decked in her mother's long skirt, 'sensible' flat shoes, thick stockings and a tweed golf

---

Buck's v Boodle's 30th Anniversary Shoot – 2nd July 1998

'REMEMBER'

Remember the Sixties, what you used to wear?
Your ultra-slim waistline, the length of your hair?
The flower-patterned kippers and trouser leg flair?
They say if you do, you simply weren't there!

Some of you, sadly, were just born too late
To enjoy all the fun of the year '68
But others, unless your memory is rotten
Had it so good, you can't have forgotten!

Remember the birds? What more could one want
Than a mini from Biba or Courrèges or Quant!
Remember the birds of the other sort too,
Not the ones in the Kings Road, the species that flew...

Can you guess at the cost of the average rate
For a great day out shooting in the year '68?
A whole day of pheasants for thirty one pounds
And your pint just three shillings in subsequent rounds!

And remember the cost of buying a gun ?
At just fifteen hundred to choose was quite fun.
These days, you'd need rather more cash in hand
The same gun could cost a cool thirty grand

Remember, as well as fabulous minis
The fact that it cost you just 44 guineas
To be a member of Boodles or Bucks for a year
Rather more pricey these days, I fear!

Remember being paid in pounds, shillings and pence
And meals for a fiver and laughable rents?
And nights at Sibylla's and Spots One and Two,
And days when the Beatles' "Hey Jude" was new?

Remember the Twist, Locomotion and Shake
And paying around ten and six for a steak?

Remember when Wilson governed our fate
And the exorbitant rise in the income tax rate?

And do you remember – lots of us will
Ah, blessed relief – the birth of the Pill!

Remember five bob a gallon at Chelsea's Blue Star
And the way you could park at a restaurant or bar
In your E type or Mini or new MGB
With a girl just like Twigs or Penelope Tree
Or spruce yourself up and join the young cruisers
Who flocked round the bar at the chic Aretusa's?

Remember, as well as fashionable bars
That in late '68 there were 5 million cars
And not twenty million like there are today
In long queues of traffic blocking your way.

In '68, too, trains still ran by steam
For some we could mention, a visual dream.
And what was the normal salary then?
Just £12 a week was the average for men
Compared with three hundred and fifty today
Yet it still left you plenty of money to play!

And cast your mind further, across the Atlantic
With riots and scenes and the world going frantic
When, in the US, in the year sixty eight
Two great leviathans met with their fate
Bobby Kennedy killed, then Luther King shot
And civil obedience going to rot
With Vietnam fears and the dread Tet offensive
And President Johnson upon the defensive.

Going back now to Buck's and Boodle's and Britain,
History was also being re-written.

Buckmaster died in the year '66
At which point old Boodle's got up to new tricks
Luckily, Buckmaster never did see
His Buck's team defeated so horribly
Let us thank God for the fact that he died
Before Boodle's superior '68 side!

And let's thank *The Field* for all their support
And 30 years helping our fabulous sport
We may be much balder and wiser and fatter
Well, some of us are, but what does it matter?
The 90's are still a great deal of fun
For those still proficient at pointing a gun!

So please raise your glasses on this special night
As long as you're shooting, the world's still alright!

Liz O'Brien

jacket. In spite of her appearance, the interview went splendidly and she got the job.

However, the Creative Director had a parting shot, 'Tell me, do you always dress like that?' Having mumbled something to the effect that she *could* dress more in tune with a Sixties ad agency, Liz went to join her mother at the Ceylon Tea Centre in Haymarket, delighted to be able to announce her success. Her mother felt vindicated. 'There,' she said, 'didn't I tell you? Good clothes always pay.'

CHAPTER 13 SPANISH ESCAPE

At the height of the sixties, I left town and found myself on a golf course. Sotogrande sits on one of the world's historic crossroads, facing the shimmering mountains of North Africa from whence Tariq landed his first 600 horses at nearby Guadaranque (River of the mares), the start of centuries of Arabic domination of Southern Spain.

The narrow straits of Gibraltar, the 'pillars of Hercules', have always controlled access to the Mediterranean. A strong, cold Atlantic current flows in, replacing evaporation of the warm and shallow Mediterranean. It slowed old sailing ships to a crawl. The pirate galleys from Tarifa rowed out to the helpless merchantmen and menacingly demanded a tribute – which we call a 'tariff'.

As a resort, Sotogrande is now famous and is one of the smartest places in Europe to own a holiday home. Spanish politicians and international millionaires look out from their houses at the beautiful golf courses and polo field. Its inland course, Valderrama, is often home to the Spanish Open.

In 1968, it was very different, with the first golf course just built and only 12 houses on its 4,000 acres. The Carretera Nacional was a narrow, potholed road, twisting and frightening, but you could still out-race your own call to Marbella, so primitive was the telephone system.

I had been handling their public relations for a couple of years when, quite casually, Joe McMicking, the American owner, asked me to go and live there. He wanted to increase the number of British residents because 'the British were the only people who knew how to behave on a golf course'. His ambition had been somewhat thwarted by the quarrel between Spain and Britain over Gibraltar and the closing of the border.

Quite suddenly, I decided to take him at his word.

STEVEN TAYLOR

Whether it was the mounting problems of the British Air Travellers Club, my relationship with girlfriend Sam or the bassett hounds (which took about nine months to become house-trained) or some mounting debts resulting in my father's irritation, for whatever reason, I piled everything into the Zagato Lancia that I had bought from Rupert Deen and set off all the way down to this Southern tip of Spain.

Sotogrande was the creation of Joe McMicking and the Zobels, the family he had married into, the most powerful in the Philippines. One night on the terrace at the front of the Golf Club, we strolled up and down whilst Joe told me of his life, which was both very successful and very lucky. Just before the war, he had married Mercedes Zobel and he had also had one very lucky hobby. He used to give flying lessons and one of his pupils was no less than Douglas MacArthur, Commanding General of all U.S. and Philippine forces. When Japan struck the Philippines, the Americans were forced to retire first to Bataan and then on to the island 'Rock of Corregidor', the McMicking couple being amongst them. President Roosevelt eventually ordered MacArthur to escape and allowed him to take a number of staff officers and their families in three PT boats. Joe was sufficiently 'top of mind' to be included. After the surrender of the Rock, many of the Zobels were wiped out by the Japanese and neither of the McMickings might have survived the 'Death March', which killed so many prisoners.

General Douglas MacArthur

As it was, Joe McMicking joined MacArthur's staff throughout the island-hopping campaign in the Pacific and took part in the liberation of the Philippines. After the War, he went on to make a great commercial success of Makati, a new commercial centre outside Manila and a residential area with golf courses and polo fields that you now see mirrored at Sotogrande.

He was also extraordinarily lucky in another commercial venture. Apparently during the war Dr Goebbels was very anxious that it might become obvious to the German people that Hitler was hardly ever in Germany, but holed up in his bunker complex in Rastenberg directing the Eastern Front.

Goebbels wished his Führer to record some 'home-front' speeches, but the wire recorder of the day was inadequate technically, revealing that the speech was not live when transmitted over the radio. German engineers created the magnetic tape recorder for the specific purpose of overcoming this problem.

One of these crude devices in a wooden box was later captured by a young American officer who took it back to California to try to develop magnetic tape commercially. McMicking bought the company when it only had 20 employees. It was called AMPEX and he later sold his shares for $250 million.

Brian Jones

To achieve our objectives of increasing land sales, especially to the British, I persuaded the Sotogrande management to let me recruit two English secretaries. Susan and Angelica were a great success and became good friends.

To my surprise, working at Sotogrande was very tiring. We worked Northern European hours, 8.30 am to 6.00 pm, with an hour for lunch. But we had to 'play' Spanish hours. Apart from Dominic Elwes from down the road at El Cuarton, our main friend was Clara Larios, daughter of Paz Lerma (the Duchess of Lerma), and her handsome, former Civil War fighter-pilot husband, Jaime Larios, whose eye for the ladies was legendary.

Clara, who never got out of bed until noon, would call and arrange to meet at, say, ten to go into Marbella. She was always late, so our evenings often went on until four in the morning. Angelica, Susan and I were often on our knees with fatigue the next day. To counter this, I used to trick Clara into turning up on time by telling her events started 2 hours earlier than they did.

We gave a number of rather good parties at my little house. The bath was filled with Sangria, which cost only £5, and all the wealthy Sotogrande residents turned up, partly because things were a bit stuffy and boring in those days and my raffish guests created a welcome break. Mim Scala turned up from Marbella, with Brian Jones of the Rolling Stones, who I had last seen at the 'Sibylla's' opening. He now looked rather sad and introspective. A few months later he was found floating in his swimming pool, dead of an asthma attack.

Another visiting friend from Madrid was Pedro Gamero, the heir to a huge shipbuilding firm in Barcelona, whose sister was to marry Clara Larios's brother. With the road to Marbella now one long and ever changing construction project, it became obvious that my Lancia's suspension was not going to make it. Patrick Lichfield kindly solved the problem by selling me his Mini Moke very cheaply. Angelica and I went back to London to collect it and having driven from Bilbao, resolved to break the journey in Madrid, where Pedro Gamero delightedly arranged a special evening for us. This began, bizarrely, with a visit to a huge model slot-racing (Scalextric) bar, which was then one of the social centres of Madrid. 'I think the Duque's car will beat the GTO of the Marques this time.'

We then joined a party of the smartest and richest young people in Spain, i.e. young Señor 'Sugar of Spain' and Señorita 'Spanish Steel'. After 400 miles in a Moke, we were looking forward to a meal of taste and style to match the company. Not a bit of it. Pedro had decided that a 'muy tipico' café specialising in beans would intrigue us. Finally to Madrid's most fashionable disco. Angelica was a very pretty blonde with a short crop hair-cut. In the disco one of the young men asked me quietly how long Angelica had been my 'novia' (fiancée). 'No, no. She's just my secretary.' I assured him. A tenth of a second pause. 'Angelica, would you like to dance?' I spent the rest of the evening placating furious dark-eyed beauties, who now thought I had imported a thoroughly disruptive element.

Next day we headed south in our little low vehicle with its flapping canvas sidescreens which gave little reassurance as we slowly crossed the high pass in the mountains above Malaga, watched balefully from the snowy verge by two very large wolves.

Angelica Morgan-Ellis

EXCITABLE SCOTS: GALLACHER AND CONNERY

My boss in Sotogrande asked me to put up in my spare room a very nice young golfer who had recently turned professional and wanted a few weeks practice in the sun of Spain to smarten up his game. Bernard Gallacher, who had never been out of Scotland before, arrived and began to practise either on the main golf course or on the driving range. There I came across him one evening looking somewhat down in the mouth.

He said, 'You know, I haven't improved at all. I'm not hitting the ball any further than I did in Bathgate.'

I stared down the golf ball-littered driving range at big signs with 50, 100, 150 written on them and an idea came to me. 'You realise that those signs represent metres,' I said.

He stared at me wide-eyed, 'Well, what's a metre?'

Having reassured him that it was an ancient form of measurement, moreover ten per cent longer than the yards he was used to, he cheered up immensely.

Sean Connery, a keen golfer, often came down the coast, delighted to find a fellow Scot to play with. Talking of playing, we bullied young Bernard into a *Vogue* fashion shoot, riding shirtless and clutching a gorgeous model. He got so excited they had to suddenly stop the shoot! Bernard went on to become one of Britain's best golfers and Britain's Ryder Cup Captain. We see a delighted Bernard (right) with his trophy.

AN O'CONNOR TO AN O'BRIEN

I had another guest in Sotogrande, Ulick O'Connor, a well-known author who had already written an extremely good book about the Irish literary renaissance and Oliver St John Gogarty. He stayed in my little house to write his biography of Brendan Behan, my secretaries helping him with the typing.

When I read the book, I suppose the bit that I liked most was Brendan Behan's own description of the IRA's incompetent blowing up of Lord Gough's equestrian statue in Phoenix Park, a poem that Behan then desperately tried to disown, lest his IRA colleagues retaliate. As an example of cynical Dublin humour, it is worth quoting in full:

> Neath the horse's prick, a dynamite stick
> Some Gallant Hero did place.
> For the cause of our land, with a light in his hand
> Bravely the foe he did face.
> Then without showing fear, he kept himself clear
> Excepting to blow up the pair.
> But he nearly went crackers, all he got was the knackers
> And made the poor stallion a mare.
> This is the way our heroes today
> Are challenging England's might.
> With a stab in the back and a midnight attack
> On a horse that can't even shite.

Ulick, who could be very amusing but also very difficult, sent me a signed copy of his book with the inscription 'With thanks from an O'Connor to an O'Brien and F. the begrudgers', a reference to the notorious Irish habit of knocking any other Irishman who is doing well.

SHERRY BEATS THE GUARDS

GRIMSDALE

As they had in Manila, Joe McMicking and the Zobels were very keen to start polo at Sotogrande. They went as far as to hire General Claude Pert, who ran the Household Brigade Polo Club at Windsor, to come out in the winter to set up the polo field and the stables and to train the ponies.

Claude Pert thought it would be a good idea to try out the polo by inviting his Household Brigade team to play against the closest Spanish team, which was that of Jerez.

The British team was captained by Ronnie Ferguson, later, of course, to achieve wider fame as the father of 'Fergie', Sarah, Duchess of York. On the eve of the Polo match there was a major party attended by all concerned including the Jerez team, which was led by José Ignacio Domecq with his brothers and sons, all working in the family sherry firm.

At about three in the morning in the disco, someone

suggested to Ronnie that perhaps they should go to bed in preparation for the match in the morning. Ferguson replied something to the hazy effect of: 'If these damned Spaniards can drink all night, so can I'. He was forgetting that his Jerez competitors had sherry running in their veins all their lives and were impervious to drink.

The next day Jerez beat the British nine goals to nil. Ronnie and his friends could scarcely see their ponies, let alone the ball.

One of my self-appointed tasks at Sotogrande was to make it better- known among younger people in Britain. So I devised a series of trips for who I thought were my smart young friends. I also fixed with my opposite number at the Marbella Club, Count Rudi Schönburg, to bring over a similar group to meet us. As the club was owned by Prince Alfonso Hohenlohe, these were mostly rich young Germans. They came over to us for a 'tienta', a trial bull fight with small bulls. Next day we went over to them for a swimming party and then lunch and a flamenco display in the hills, to which we travelled on mules.

During the flamenco party, one of the girl dancers was foolish enough to drag Anthony Hayden-Guest to his feet to dance with her. We had seen 'the Hateful Beast', as we affectionately called him, dance before. So we were ready for the grotesque Quasimodo-like gyrations, the 'wounded crow', that he suddenly performed. Squatting on the grass my group fell over laughing as if hit by machine gun fire.

I turned to look at the Germans who were staring with horrified disapproval. They were plainly thinking 'these English have brought their crippled friend and now are laughing at him'. The 'Hateful Beast' thought he had done very well and when he realised he was the subject of ridicule became ever more drunk on the Sangria. On the way back down the hill he slowly fell head-first off his mule and was concussed. Anthony Nares ran back to help him and Hayden-Guest woke up for long enough to punch him on the jaw before lapsing back into unconsciousness.

Anthony was forced to recuperate from his concussion for a week at my house and there regaled me with many amusing stories, including his attempted coverage two years before of the May Day Parade in Moscow.

With a girlfriend and an Australian journalist, he had set off for

MARBELLA MIS-UNDERSTANDINGS

Anthony Hayden-Guest

Red Square on the Metro but, at that time, all the station names were written only in Russian. They overshot by three stops, emerging into the forming-up area for the parade. The NKVD marshals, thoroughly confused by their press badges but seeing they were foreign, ordered them, protesting feebly, into the North Vietnamese contingent. The band struck up, past the saluting podium they marched and all over the world friends watching the parade on the television news thought: 'Christ! What on earth is Anthony up to now?' (Anthony has gone on to be a successful writer in New York. However, I insist that his real claim to fame is that his sister-in-law was the sexiest Peeress in the House of Lords, Jamie Lee Curtis.)

Another trip had been designed to coincide with what we thought was another smart event which is the Interclub Polo Championships of Spain. Lichfield's pal Jon Bradshaw, the American writer, took one look at the beautiful blonde wife of the Captain of one of the teams and said 'I'm going to have her before the end of this trip.' We scoffed.

He actually succeeded, but at an unexpected risk. He saw her go into the sea off the beach not twenty yards from where her husband was playing on the Polo field (admittedly shielded by a bamboo fence). Jon took off his clothes, plunged into the water and duly seduced her.

Afterwards, she put on her bikini and strolled ashore. Jon, who had no bathing suit, planned to follow at a decent interval, but suddenly a group of little children and their nannies came to play on the beach. For forty-five minutes he stayed in the water, which is quite cold so close to the Atlantic. His friends had some difficulty later saving him from hypothermia.

LICHFIELD

The outrageous Jon Bradshaw

ANNIE LAMBTON AND 'THE ROWER'

One of our biggest allies in promoting Sotogrande was Annie Lambton who was the 'agony aunt' of *Woman's Journal*. She was pretty, elegant and very worldly.

On a fashion photographic trip we were organising at Sotogrande, I was with Annie and Liz Ramsay, Patrick Lichfield's right hand helper.

I got talking to a tall, powerfully built young man called Josh Jensen, who had been given his trip to Sotogrande as a reward for being part of the winning Oxford crew at that year's Boat Race.

He stated that he really fancied one of the girls I was with. I began extolling Liz Ramsay's virtues when he said, 'No, no, the other one with the red hair'. I explained tactfully that Annie, at about forty-four, was exactly twice his age but he insisted on pressing his suit.

Back in London she turned him down on the grounds that

Josh Jensen, the rower.

'The Rower' was really much too young for her. When she refused to answer his calls, he reverted to more unconventional methods to re-establish the relationship.

He wrote to her in the regular mailbag of *Woman's Journal* on the lines of 'I have recently met and fallen in love with an older woman, etc., etc. What do you advise me to do?' This sufficiently softened her heart that they eventually ended up living very happily together for several years.

Eventually, Josh went to France where he learnt all about vineyards. He then returned to California and currently produces Calera, one of the most prestigious red wines to come out of the United States.

Half way through my stint in Spain, two new personalities entered my life. The first, a gift from the departing hotel manager, was Nicholas, a loveable, typically mad, Red Setter. Rather snobbish, he barked at servants and the golf caddies and particularly terrorised my maid and her mother. They used to call by phone from my house, 'El perro, el terrible perro!' and I found them being circled as by Indians round a wagon train.

The second was Clare, a friend of my sister who I met at a dance on my last night on a trip to London. So taken was I by her that I turned up hours later on her doorstep at 7.00 am on the way to Heathrow and made her promise to come to Sotogrande. She did, we became engaged and were married on my return to London.

As more people arrived, Sotogrande was becoming much more fun, so it was a bit of a surprise that it suddenly ended.

NEW INFLUENCES

CHAPTER **14** BACK TO THE MAINSTREAM

Being told you must leave a delightful place and a pleasant job is not often seen as a step forward. After a year and a half working at Sotogrande, Joe McMicking advised me to get back to London 'into the mainstream of life' – advice I will always bless him for. I enthusiastically wrote to nearly a hundred companies looking for a job and received a cruel lack of response. So I returned to Britain in a state of some anxiety, engaged to be married to Clare, with all my worldly goods packed into my Lancia Flaminia, including the mad Red Setter which had to be left miserably in a quarantine cage on the boat from Bilbao, and rather less than £100 of savings.

After slogging around a few unsuccessful interviews, I was becoming extremely depressed and a friend of mine to cheer me up invited me to go to 'Sibylla's' for what proved to be the last time.

My depression was further increased when, driving away from 'Sibylla's' and running over a kerb in Piccadilly, I burst both right-hand tyres. The next morning my remaining liquid capital of £70 was halved when I had to pay for two new tyres, but as luck would have it, four hours later I was offered a job at the London office of Hill & Knowlton, then the world's largest public relations firm, by my father's old friend and former British Council colleague, Colin Mann.

Colin was a delightful, if raffish, character. Indeed my father once had to fire him for being absent from the office every afternoon during a two-month period. Knowing that he had been with some lady during the afternoons, my father concluded with the dry words, 'And by the way, Colin. If there is any f...ing to be done on my time, I am perfectly capable of doing it myself!'

A few years later, Colin was complaining that he had got involved with a lady rather too eagerly. Toby responded 'Well, I'm sorry, Colin, but you really went into that one with your flies open'.

Colin was quite capable of a witty crack himself. At a dance he saw a gorgeous girl in a flimsy summer frock, through the revealing folds of which, however, could be seen some slightly inferior underwear pinned together with odd bits of elastic. Colin remarked, 'What a pity to spoil the slip for a ha'porth of bra'.

During the Hill & Knowlton days, Colin took his team to a night-club in Geneva, which featured a exotic striptease by a girl with a leopard. The leopard was trained to snarl and appear to strike out with its paw, whereupon the girl let another piece of clothing tantalisingly fall to the floor. Colin

Colin Mann

thought this was thoroughly splendid. He decided that he and his party should remain for the second show.

When the leopard and girl appeared again, Colin in his champagne-fuelled enthusiasm took his red carnation from his buttonhole and threw it onto the stage. The leopard, bored with his normal routine, spied the carnation and started to play with it like a kitten, tossing it into the air and chasing it round the stage, totally ignoring the young lady who had to strip off all by herself ignominiously in the corner, while the audience roared with laughter at the unscripted performance.

The management was not at all unhappy to see Colin's party leave.

The first colleague I was introduced to was Anthony Masterton-Smith. Intense but very funny, he became one of my firmest friends and was best man at my wedding. We went out to the pub at lunchtime and he revealed that he was choosing a company car but that Colin had said:

'Don't tell the new chap Donough or he'll want one, too'.

So, while poring through the Citroen brochures, we resolved to call it the 'Moulton', a curious new bicycle.

In the event, Anthony's brand new GTS lasted exactly five minutes. The '3 day week' caused by the Miners' Strike meant that electricity was cut both for the car park lifts and traffic lights.

Anthony, driving round the Swiss Centre looking for somewhere to park was hit by a Mini Cooper going about 80 mph. His new car was towed back to Milton Keynes backwards, presenting the distributor with a wrecked car with no miles at all on the clock.

Anthony Masterton-Smith

PARTY PROBLEMS

Anthony told me two stories of disastrous debutante parties. The first was in Norfolk, when a young friend of his joined a house party to attend some ball in a castle up the road. He returned from the ball and went somewhat drunkenly to bed. At about 4.00 in the morning he was desperate to relieve himself of the results of an evening of champagne but he simply could not remember in the dark, unfamiliar house where the bathroom was. However, he searched under the bed and found an old fashioned chamber pot which did the trick.

The next morning he was embarrassed about the maid finding the full chamber pot and decided to dispose of its contents. He opened the window and looked down at a huge hedge and decided it would be safe to toss the contents of the pot into it. Unfortunately, the handle detached itself and the full chamber pot flew in a beautiful high arc over the hedge. There was a tremendous crash of breaking glass. Thinking that he might have hit an old greenhouse, he strolled down into the hall where he found the butler.

'Where is everybody?' he asked.

'Oh, they are all in the conservatory having their breakfast.' replied the butler, pointing in the direction that the errant potty had targeted. Anthony's friend ran to his room, packed, scrambled into his car and drove away.

Anthony's own story had a similar embarrassment level. Invited to a ball on the Isle of Wight, he was met at the ferry by the daughter of the house to which he had been allocated. She took him back and introduced him to her rather grand parents and then suggested they go for a drive around the island. Anthony exclaimed that her car was 'exactly like the one he used to have' and asked if he could drive. He promptly put it into reverse by mistake and drove straight back over the croquet lawn and the superbly planted flower beds. They drove off in embarrassed silence knowing that two pairs of belligerent parental eyes were following them. Anthony just managed to avoid making any more mistakes in the house. He put on his dinner jacket in the stifling heat and left his window open to make sure his room was cool when he returned.

At the ball, his dancing became extremely enthusiastic, with an exaggerated imitation of Mick Jagger flinging his clasped hands to left and right, unfortunately, catching a huge platter of passing strawberries and cream which splattered over 15 guests. After most of the dinner jackets and ball gowns had been wiped clean, Anthony was told politely that perhaps it was time for him to go back to his house party.

As they arrived back, in the moonlight Anthony remarked that 'something sparkly was lying in the drive'. This, they discovered, was the shattered remains of a priceless, antique mirror which had hung on Anthony's wall, around which his curtain had, in a sudden breeze, wrapped itself, scooping it out of the window.

When he descended to breakfast the next day his hosts, with tight lips, told him that the next ferry sailed at 10.15. It was normal for guests to stay for lunch but Anthony got their drift and left.

WHAT'S IN A NAME?

One of my Italian colleagues at Hill & Knowlton was Giancarlo Bertelli, who had a charming wife called Chanda. It was only later that I discovered that she was the daughter of Bill Lear, the American

inventor, aviator and creator of the Lear Jet. Almost unbelievably, he had named her Chanda. One imagines that Chanda Lear was only too delighted to become a Bertelli.

Norman Parkinson

When Anthony Masterton-Smith became engaged, he and his future wife, Caroline, decided that it would be good idea to get her uncle over from Tobago to take the wedding photographs. He was, after all the celebrated photographer Norman Parkinson.

Caroline sent him a cable saying that 'YOU ARE INVITED TO THE WEDDING OF THE YEAR. AM MARRYING THE CLOCK MAN,' in reference to Royal Weddings and to Anthony's hobby of rebuilding old clocks.

Unfortunately, the Tobago post office translated this into the rather more dramatic:

'YOU ARE INVITED TO THE WEEDING OF THE YEAR. AM MARRYING THE COCKMAN'.

Norman Parkinson obliged anyway.

HE DOTH PROTEST TOO MUCH

At a party in 1968, I met Corin Redgrave, son of Michael Redgrave and sister of Vanessa. I think they are a superlative thespian family but they should stick to acting. Corin and Vanessa were major activists against the Vietnam war. On March 17th there was a huge rally in Trafalgar Square which was addressed by Vanessa and then moved illegally to Grosvenor Square in front of the American Embassy, where things got very unpleasant, a full-scale riot.

At the party, Corin was proudly discussing this. Pretending not to know who he was, I innocently put forward my theory that Grosvenor Square was a highway and that it was illegal for pedestrians to step off the pavement unless at a zebra crossing, so every single person in the square that night should be arrested for jay walking. He simply did not know how to handle this unusual line of argument and just spluttered with fury.

Incidentally, I find very few people have really thought through the question of the later siege of Greenham Common. This American base was surrounded for years by rather squalid camps of women and children and it became a major nuisance for the unfortunate people who lived in the area.

I have often asked 'Why Greenham Common?' Most people will say, 'Well, it's atomic weapons, isn't it?' I then point out that there are probably 20 bases, British and American, whose prime purpose is to deliver atomic weapons, many of them equally conveniently placed for people to carry out sieges if they wished.

The answer is that Greenham Common was the first home of the 'cruise missile'. The Russians had spent enormous amounts of money on anti-ballistic systems to destroy rockets and on air defence systems to shoot down conventional bombers. The

Tomahawk cruise missile

cruise missile, as we now all know, has the extraordinary ability to fly extremely low, hugging the ground using the kind of technology that only the Americans can handle and delivering its payload, whether conventional or nuclear, to within yards of its intended target. As such, the cruise missile was for the Russians an extremely unwelcome addition to the arms race and, indeed, probably played a role in making them run out of money while trying to match the Americans.

I cannot believe that most of the women who surrounded Greenham Common could have told you the technical significance of the weapon about which they were protesting so vigorously. If so, it does not take a tremendous leap of imagination to guess who might have financed the siege.

Incidentally, the Americans had developed another

weapon of extreme inconvenience and discomfort for the Russians. This was the Cobalt Bomb. Its advantage over other nuclear weapons it that it is capable of killing the crews of armoured vehicles. As Russia's strategy for invading the West would have been entirely based on the use of thousands of tanks, you can well see why, with mysterious spontaneity, all sorts of riots against the cobalt bomb sprang up across Europe.

During my two years in away Spain, our old flat in Wilton Place had finally been bulldozed to become the Berkeley Hotel and my flatmates had gone from strength to strength. Patrick Lichfield had his own studio in Aubrey Walk and Brian Alexander had followed me into Rank. He also had a beautiful girlfriend, Joanna Lumley, who first saw him on a modelling assignment at Rank's Albufeira hotel, when to her irritation he had totally ignored her.

Joanna, now the star of *Absolutely Fabulous*, has an almost identical background to me, with a grandfather in remote parts of India as a District Officer, speaking many dialects, and a father also born there, later a Gurkha officer.

She, too, remembers being poor in the company of richer young people. She shared a flat with four other girls and, unable to afford a fridge, had to leave the milk on the windowsill. They had one shared frock between them to go to smart parties. On her first, terrified, visit with Brian to Shugborough, she mused to Liz Anson 'What a funny world, with me in a box of a flat and you with this huge stately home'. Liz merely responded, 'What's *really* bad is that we now only have part of it.' On that visit Patrick drove up on his motorbike and nearly died of cold. (I rode big bikes too, but never for long distances in Winter.)

With many of our friends, she 'crashed' bottle parties, where the hosts were *really* expecting us, having spread the word in the pubs and leaving the door on the latch (the technique was to send in our prettiest girls first with our bottles. If we didn't like the party, we snatched up our bottles and our girls and left!)

Gradually her modelling progressed from mere fashion catalogues to working with Duffy, Donovan, Bailey and, of course, Patrick. The year I returned from Spain came her breakthrough in the Bond film *On Her Majesty's Secret Service*. She drove to the studios in a magnificent 1949 Rolls-Royce Silver Wraith, sold to her by a neighbour. Its front-opening doors could fly open, with great danger to cyclists. *The Breaking of Bumbo* followed, curiously about a Guards officer who goes to jazz clubs and has

ABSOLUTELY FABULOUS

LICHFIELD

Joanna Lumley and her Rolls-Royce

213

'unsuitable' girlfriends. It was never shown in Britain because Lew Grade disapproved of the anarchy of Joanna and John Bird attacking a statue of Churchill.

Since then she has never looked back, a second Bond film, two *Pink Panthers*, *The New Avengers* and, of course, *Absolutely Fabulous*. More remarkable is that she has also edited a column in *The Times* and has written four books. *Stare Back and Smile* (her life), *Forces Sweetheart* (with the Imperial War Museum), *Girl Friday* (surviving on a desert island, only possible with the guidance of ex-SAS and Irish Guards RSM Paddy Shields) and *In the Kingdom of the Thunder Dragon* (a serious account of her grandfather, Col. Leslie Weir's adventures in Kashmir).

'Easily the most frightening thing in my life', she admits, 'was addressing the Royal Geographical Society after I had been proposed by Lord Shackleton'. She follows her father's advice 'Always present a moving target', moving quickly between each of her talents. A beautiful, talented, versatile and really nice person, Joanna was, and is, a pleasure to know.

COUNCIL HOUSES

After Clare and I had struggled to finance our little house in Fulham, we were fairly broke. To earn more money, Clare decided to renounce being a secretary and join 'Take A Guide', which employed college graduates to guide foreign visitors round London and Southern England. You had to provide your own car in good, clean condition.

One bonus was that it was very interesting going round with Clare when she was practising for her final exams and I learned an awful lot about London. However, our car was a bit of a problem. It was a hot rod Triumph 2000 with three Weber carburettors, a lowered suspension and a noisy racing exhaust, which scraped on the ground if the car was heavily loaded.

Clare went to pick up her first guests from the Dorchester who turned out to be two very large American ladies. 'I am sure one of you would like to sit in the front.' she tried nervously.

'No, Clara (they never *could* get Clare O'Brien), we're just fine both of us here in the back.' The car slumped down on to its suspension and growled off towards Maidenhead, occasionally grinding down on to its exhaust system.

The plan had been for Clare to take the two visitors to Maidenhead's boat dock and then meet them again at Windsor. They discovered the boat at Maidenhead was not running. The season had not started. However, the boatman said he could make an exception for the ladies as he had a group of 200 mentally defective people who were being given a treat. They could join the party.

'Wa'al Clara, I think we'll take a rain check on the loonies. Let's drive there.'

Unfortunately Clare had never before been in Maidenhead and certainly didn't know the way to Windsor. She went into a garage hissing at the attendant not to wave his arms around or point and asked him the way. He told her the wrong way. She started wandering around a huge municipal housing estate, desperately looking for the exit and the road to Windsor.

She improvised, 'I brought you here to show you British housing policy. These are council houses and they are subsidised by the Government so they only cost $14 a week.'

'Hey, Clara that's really interesting. Isn't that neat, Bertha?' This distracted them for long enough, in their musings over housing policies in Britain, for Clare to find the road to Windsor. There, believe it or not, her passengers were rather disappointed that it was not another council estate but that they had to make do with the grandeur of Windsor Castle. They drove all the way back to London 'looking out for council houses' and when she got back to the Dorchester she was rewarded with a $20 tip. 'It was because of all those council houses, Clara. They were really interesting.'

She had some clients who were even more eccentric than that during her six month stint, including a kleptomaniac who stole everything in sight with Clare busily putting everything back again. But, all in all, it was quite a rewarding job.

It had a bit of a downside in my social standing with my neighbours. One of them finally overcame his embarrassment, and came round and said 'Look Donough, I know you like cars, but I think making your wife wash your car every morning at seven is going just a little bit too far'

PILLOW BITES

My father coined the family phrase 'pillow bites' – awful things you do on the spur of the moment, and years later wake up in the middle of the night and bite your pillow in remorse.

I suffered badly from one of these incidents, thanks to a colleague's foolish chattiness. Annie Lambton had invited the General Manager of Royal Air Maroc to lunch in her beautiful apartment above Prunier's restaurant. The purpose was to help get us the airline's public relations account, which, after an hour, we had succeeded in achieving. 'Yes,' said the very nice Arab, 'I think I like you all. I will give you the account.'

Annie was making the coffee and I was clearing the plates when I heard my colleague ask, 'Mohammed, how long have you lived here in London?' Our new client replied, 'It must be three years now.'

'It's amazing how you haven't lost your tan.'

I dropped the plates. It is the only account I have ever retained for only 30 seconds.

CHAPTER 15 IMAGE WORLD

It would seem churlish to regard working for the world's leading public relations company as a stop-gap, but while it was fun working with Colin Mann and Anthony, I was not professionally happy at Hill & Knowlton, mostly because of my rather boring clients. So it was with excitement that I received an approach from Martin Stevens, this time to re-join him at a design consultancy called Lippincott & Margulies, an American firm which had virtually invented the concept of 'corporate identity'.

Some of the identities created by Lippincott & Margulies, many still in use 30 years later

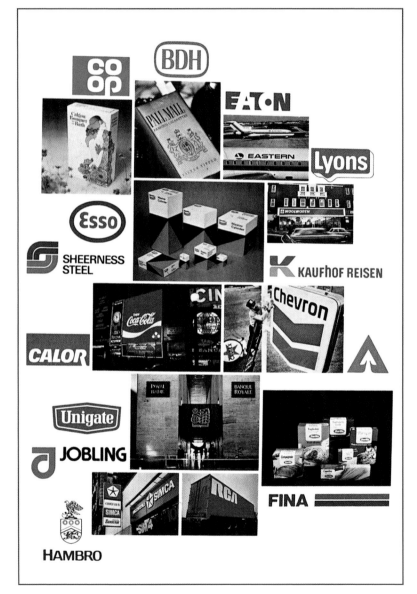

I went to several interviews, obviously secretly, but his American colleagues had yet to make up their minds. The Hill and Knowlton European conference was coming up at Vevey, Switzerland and I was embarrassed that H&K were about to spend a couple of thousand pounds on me to attend, when I had the intention of leaving. There was not much I could do about it, so I resolved to try and perform as inconspicuously as possible. In the event, everybody else made such terrible speeches that, when I warmed to my subject, 'hotel marketing and promotion', I was easily the best. Bill Durbin, the American President came up to me and said, 'You have a long career ahead of you with H&K, my boy.'

Of course, as soon as the weekend was over, I received the confirmation that my job with L&M had come through. I must say that Colin Mann and the H&K people were very nice about it.

A nice surprise and another welcome addition to our team was Anthony Nares, for whom I had fixed his first civilian job working for my father.

216

Within weeks of us joining, Anthony turned up in unusually scruffy clothing and explained that his flat had been burgled. He was sharing his flat with a Canadian* friend of ours who had also worked for my father. Anthony explained that he had been burgled and had lost all his clothes and the Canadian had lost his mother's jewellery. The trouble was that Anthony's insurance had lapsed, so while the Canadian would be fully reimbursed, Anthony had suffered quite a blow.

Years later when the Canadian had left the country, Anthony was called on by the head of the anti-terrorist squad and asked if he could verify a statement made by the brother of one of the most wanted IRA terrorists.

> *We used to go drinking in a pub with this Canadian fellow, who one day revealed he was very short of money trying to keep up with the rather smart set he was involved with. He suggested that we should burgle his flat, keeping the proceeds and he would claim the money on his mother's jewellery. One Saturday night we turned up. The Canadian was there and said that we were one week early but, 'never mind, let's get on with it and I will help you load the stuff.'*

> *We drank so much from their drinks cabinet that I got really pissed and stupidly left my Irish Guard's identity card in my jacket which eventually helped me to get caught.*

I am not going to reveal the name of the Canadian, because he is alive and kicking across the Atlantic. But he knows who he is and all my friends know who he is, several of whom got burgled later in the same way. Whichever way you look at it, to be accepted by a very nice group of people and then to repay them by robbing them blind is shabby to say the least.

One of the more interesting projects that I handled at L&M was Rolls-Royce Motors. We were conducting what we call a 'communications audit' to find out the attitude of owners and distributors to the company and its cars.

Having been brought up on the myth that Rolls-Royce cars seldom went wrong and if they did they were taken away in a grey van and no bill was submitted, I was amazed at the ferocity of the angry views of their distributors.

One of them said to me, 'They are so bloody arrogant up in Crewe that if there's something wrong with a gearbox, they ring back and say 'well, it was all right on the rig, so it must be your fault down there'.'

___

* Name withheld for legal reasons

ROLLS-ROYCE:
DENTED IMAGE

I had to present all this and more to the board of Rolls-Royce who sat there stony faced so you could have heard a pin drop. Suddenly my projector jammed. While I was struggling with it the Production Director, who was, after all, being the most criticised, leaned forward and laconically muttered 'It was all right on the rig'. The whole room collapsed into laughter and from then on they were willing to listen to the criticism much more openly.

Sir John Plastow, the Chairman, said over lunch the immortal words, 'I'm really shocked to find out how badly we're perceived. We give our distributors lunch once a month and they never say a word.'

Some of the senior executives we met at that time appeared simply not to want to know what their customers thought. At a meeting with the Chairman of Woolworth we had suggested retaining the colour red in their identity. He began to disagree with this and we asked why did we not research it and conduct colour acceptance tests with the public. He stared at us and said 'Ask the public? What the hell have the public got to do with this? This is a board decision!'

On another occasion we were presenting to the Chief Executive of Lloyds-BOLSA (Bank of London and South America). We began to explain why we had created the recommended identity. He put up his hand and announced, '*You* do not create. *I* do not create.' And, pointing upwards, he said, 'Only the Lord God creates'. He was an enthusiastic Christian Scientist and, as long as we kept the word 'create' out of the rest of the presentation, we were able to persuade him to accept our recommendations.

Rather less uptight was the Finance Director of Aer Lingus. 'In the old days you'd have dealt with pilots, men with clear, blue eyes and firm, dry handshakes. Now you have to deal with accountants like me.'

ULSTER BLANK

One presentation that did not go well was in Northern Ireland. Martin Stevens and Barry Lillis, an older and even less mechanically-minded colleague, decided to go off to Belfast to try to sell companies there the concept of corporate identity. They were evidently having some difficulty with the slide projector because they kept ringing us from the Europa (the world's most bombed hotel) to ask our advice. The deadline for their first potential client was getting closer so they rang for the Assistant Manager of the hotel to help them. A man appeared in the door of their room and they quickly had him on the floor struggling to get the plug working under the table.

After a few minutes, Martin looked at his watch and said to the sweating man 'I do wish you could hurry up, the man from the Ulster Bank will be here in a moment'. A muffled voice said 'I *am* the man from the Ulster Bank'. As you can imagine, they got no work from this potential client.

THE ROCKY ROAD TO FULHAM

Martin Stevens continued to be the same brilliant mentor that he had been at Rank. I was able to repay him for his kindness in a decisive way, although only just. Martin had never ceased in his desire to become a Member of Parliament. He had slaved away in Dulwich for many years and was now looking for another constituency.

I had moved into Fulham, where there had been a major political shift in spite of the Labour Party's best efforts to stop the 'gentrification' of the area. The danger for them was natural young Tory voters arriving from Chelsea and Kensington. The Labour Party had tried to bulldoze the area immediately to the west of Stamford Bridge football ground to create a barrier by

building council blocks between the King's Road and Fulham Road (an old Labour gerrymandering trick started by Herbert Morrison). But a protest movement had arisen which had fought to re-build and improve the houses in what is called the Moore Park Estate, rather than knocking them down. When the council elections came up a whole lot of my young friends put their names forward as a joke. They were amazed and shocked to find themselves voted in, controlling the Council and with the unexpected duties of Borough Councillors.

This changing constituency was the one that Martin set his sights on and I was a Conservative Ward Chairman. One evening, having arrived exhausted from the office, I was called by Peter Fane, my Constituency Chairman, who said, 'You must get your people to the Town Hall on time, because it is the voting for the new candidate and if you are a moment late your votes will be disallowed'.

Frantically, I called my fellow committee members, who included Ernie Ibbott, a stoker at Fulham power station, and told them to get to the Town Hall and 'however good anybody else was, to vote for the little fat one called Stevens'. Martin won the nomination by just one vote and went on to be one of the best constituency MPs in the Conservative Party.

Martin and Mrs Thatcher and a dog who seems to have voted him in.

WEEKEND LOVE-IN – LICHFIELD, BAILEY & STERN

There have been times when Patrick Lichfield has plainly regarded me as the 'friend of last resort' in a social occasion which might be fraught with difficulties. Thus I was once quite suddenly invited up to Shugborough for a weekend which was likely to be a photographer's love-in in that Patrick's friend David Bailey and the acclaimed American photographer Burt Stern were arriving with girlfriends.

David Bailey

David Bailey arrived with the model Penelope Tree who was the daughter of Ronnie and Marietta Tree. Burt Stern turned up with a extraordinary girl with whom he got into a furious sulk because she refused to sleep with him.

He need not have been so offended because the reason became apparent a few hours later when she made a very firm pass at Clare, my wife.

MOHAMMED ALI, 'BOXER CHAPPY'

One morning Martin Stevens called me from the House of Commons and asked cryptically, 'Have you ever heard of Mohammed Ali?'

'Yes Martin. In fact, a survey voted him the most famous man in the whole world last month.'

Martin paused, 'A sort of boxer chappy?'

'Yes Martin, you could call him 'a sort of boxer chappy', like a World Champion Boxer Chappy.'

'Quite so, I have to take him to lunch at the House of Commons with another MP and some young boxers from Brixton. Would you help me get through this occasion?'

Three days later I turned up at the House of Commons. We entered the Visitors' Dining Room, and I sat on Ali's right for two hours.

He was absolutely charming but already showing some signs of the slowing of speech and other symptoms of the Parkinson's Disease that has now driven him from public life, except for his brief, rather sad appearance at the Atlanta Olympics.

All through the meal people started coming up to him for his autograph – visitors, Members of Parliament, Ministers, Secretaries of State. He signed away, smiling and agreeable, as we chatted. I was the only person *not* to ask for his autograph within miles. I was just too uptight and embarrassed.

Eventually, the word had plainly spread to the staff and the chef arrived for his autograph. Then the inevitable happened. 'Mad Maureen', my jazz club dancing partner and House of Commons waitress, bounced through the swinging door from the kitchens. She strode up to Ali, slapped him on the back so hard that he fell forward into his pudding and said, 'Hello, Ali. I'm sure glad you're a friend of Duns.' Thus was the most famous man in the world suddenly lucky that he was a friend of mine!

Houses of Parliament

THE SUPERNORMAL

While I happen to believe in ghosts and UFO's, the supernatural or supernormal has only twice entered my life.

Mike and Joy Bowling invited me to dinner to meet a prominent clairvoyant, indeed one used by Scotland Yard from time to time. Halfway through dinner, he said to me, 'I think you are going to be quite successful, nothing really spectacular but quite successful. You are going to be offered a job involving crossing the ocean in the next few weeks which you may not take. But in any case I see a big letter W above your head.'

Dinner parties being what they are, I forgot the entire conversation for weeks until a friend of mine, who was a head-hunter called John Withers rang me and offered me a job with a container company. They would 'need to fly me to San Francisco for a three week induction course'. In fact, I turned the job down because a few weeks after that I was talking to my friend Roland Wells and we decided to take over an advertising agency called Felden Advertising and make it into Wells O'Brien.

And years later Sampson/Tyrrell, the design company in which I was a shareholder, was taken over by Martin Sorrell's WPP group. It may all be a coincidence of course, but it really does appear that the letter W has had some major effect on my life, at least in a commercial sense.

Sometimes, the supernatural can have an actively beneficial effect. In 1979, I knew a pilot called Dave, who flew 707s for British Airways. He had learned to fly in South Africa and had a curious heart condition which showed up strangely on the ECG machine although he was more than perfectly healthy (indeed he had been an athletics champion).

One day his sister went to visit a medium, an elderly woman, in Clapham, who half way though the session suddenly revealed 'Someone close to you wears a blue uniform, but he will soon not be wearing it, because of medical problems'.

Very concerned, she revealed this to her mother who castigated her for believing in the supernatural and resolved to visit the same woman under an assumed name to see if she said anything similar. With slightly different wording, this is exactly what happened. Somewhat embarrassed, the mother and sister then worked up the courage to reveal all this to Dave, whose attitude was 'Stuff and nonsense, silly superstitious women'.

However, a few weeks later, Dave himself was at a party at which there was a ouija-board. The session had already reduced one girl to tears because it had revealed that her fiancé had just died and the ouija board claimed to be the spirit of a Turkish man killed at the end of the last century in a hunting accident. It then went on to say that Dave was going to lose his job for medical reasons.

Dave went back and checked on his loss of employment insurance policy (with the Guardian Royal Exchange, I recall), and as a precaution, he started to pay twice the premium. Three months later he went for a routine medical. The British Airways medical team pointed out his heart condition, but he said, 'You have my file and know all about it'. But the file had gone missing, and Dave was made, to his fury, redundant. He claimed on his insurance and got the equivalent of about six times his normal salary tax-free, buying, incidentally, a large house in Fulham with the proceeds and, with the balance, going to South Africa to pick up his original medical files.

Once he returned, British Airways, although convinced, now had a surplus of pilots so there was no job any more with them. However, they kindly let him use their 707 simulator to get a job with Freddie Laker who was just starting up. He's back with British Airways now, in perfect health – and wealth.

And before we leave the supernatural and planes, my sister, Nathalie, got a premonition and begged Toby and Leo not to fly from Rome. Leo left her jewellery behind and they luckily missed the Comet flight which crashed (setting back, incidentally, Britain's civil aviation leadership over the Americans for ever).

The last time I tried to help the Conservative Party in any significant way is an Irish story. Paul Dwyer, a young prospective Tory candidate, had correctly assessed that the hundreds of thousands of Irish people living in England tended instinctively to vote Labour, in spite of the fact that they would vote Fianna Fáil or Fine Gael at home. Quite a minor shift in their voting pattern in the UK would dramatically alter the results in no less than eleven marginal constituencies. (Harold Wilson won by four seats in 1963 in three in 1974). So together with various Irish councillors and local politicians in London, Manchester and Liverpool we formed the Irish-Conservative Association.

We went to see the current Tory Party Chairman who was enthusiastic and allocated a young man ' who knew about Ireland' to look after the project. After inexplicable delays, we had a meeting with him. He suddenly said, 'Of course, I'm a Unionist at heart. I don't actually like the Irish'.

It was this bone-headed attitude rather than a vague threat from the I.R.A. that made Paul and I feel we had better things to do. A real wasted opportunity.

For years my father reviewed books for *The Illustrated London News.* I think he got eight guineas a week for this quite onerous task. Nevertheless he loved doing it and he did tend to get masses of books, some of which I still have. One of them was called *Send a Gunboat.* I had always been under the impression that 'gunboat' was a euphemism for any kind of naval vessel and I was fascinated to discover that a gunboat was a special class of tiny boat mounted with one small gun. Queen Victoria's navy had employed these as one of the cheapest methods ever devised for creating and holding down an Empire.

I was talking to someone at a cocktail party some time later who seemed to know something about the Royal Navy and I said to him, 'Well, as you're interested, you should read this excellent book called *Send a Gunboat.*'

'Yes,' said Antony Preston, 'I wrote it.' Thank goodness I had said it was an excellent book. Antony has gone on to be one of our leading military historians.

One of the enduring legacies of my father's stint at Conservative Central Office was a dining club he created called the Burke Club. This was designed to strengthen the relationship between the Conservative Party and potentially positive journalists and their newspapers, typically *The Daily Telegraph, The Yorkshire Post* and so on. My father forced through my election to this club on the basis that he had founded it. I had no right to be there as I was neither a Member of Parliament nor a prominent journalist or newspaper editor.

It has, however, been extremely interesting and helpful for me to be a member. For instance, when I was handling Northern Ireland's publicity both my Secretary of State, Tom King, and my Minister, Rhodes Boyson, were already on Christian name terms with me. Nigel Lawson, for instance, was elected a member of the Burke as a journalist rather than as a Minister.

Soon after returning from Sotogrande I attended the Burke Club and the subject of Gibraltar came up. Faced by the possible de-colonisation of Gibraltar, Spain had closed the border and 'dago-bashing' became the evening's sport.

However, I had studied the situation at first hand in Gibraltar and was able to point out some home truths. The Treaty of Utrecht by which Britain was ceded the Rock had a number of clauses which had been flouted. There were, for instance, to be no Arabs and Jews among the population – certainly a clause which has not been met. There was to be no population on the Rock other than those who served the garrison. This had been exceeded long ago.

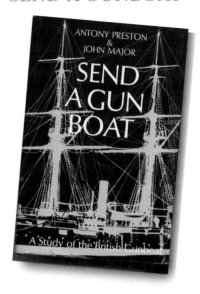

SEND A GUNBOAT

GIBRALTAR INSIGHT

In Spain, the border closure was popular.

Above all, no smuggling should be allowed that might damage the economy of Spain. In the 1960's smuggling had flowered in Gibraltar as one of the great new industries. For instance, the year that nearby Tangier's smuggling trade was closed down, Gibraltar's apparent consumption of cigarettes jumped from five million to 85 million! There were dozens of suspiciously fast boats in Gibraltar harbour, one of which was powered by a jet engine! Fishermen at night came quite close to the beach of Sotogrande and would throw a dog overboard which would paddle ashore towing thousands of cigarettes in waterproof plastic bags. When it got to the shore those waiting for it released the dog, which loped off into the night and through the Gibraltar border.

One Spanish dockyard worker who used to go across the border to Gibraltar at La Linea became richer and richer. On his retirement the Mayor of La Linea asked him how he had done it, in spite of the searches of him and his bicycle for diamonds, drugs or whatever.

Actually, it was easy. He was smuggling bicycles. He went out on the Gibraltar ferry with just the bicycle basket. At the end of his stint in the British dockyard, he walked up the hill to the Raleigh bicycle dealer and picked up a black bicycle, which had already been covered with dust by the conniving shop-keeper. He then came back every night through the border past the customs night shift, making approximately £20 on each identical new bike every day for about 8 years.

All this I revealed to the members of the Burke Club, pointing out that Spain was almost completely in the right. I was turned on savagely by all sorts of Tory backwoodsmen. Suddenly, Selwyn Lloyd, who was the visiting speaker, intervened on my behalf and admitted that, as Foreign Secretary, he had also only just realised the implications of the other key clause of the Treaty of Utrecht, which was that if Gibraltar was ever to change status, it must first be offered to Spain. The Foreign Office had blithely proceeded with its latest retreat from Empire and it was the plan to give Gibraltar *independence* that the Spanish were objecting to. They didn't mind the British retaining Gibraltar but they sure as hell were not going to have the 'Rock Scorpions', as they called them, taking over and expanding their economically threatening smuggling activities.

CUNEO, ECCENTRIC PAINTER

One of the reasons I became quite good at painting machines, was a little book I picked up at school called *How to Draw Tanks* by Terence Cuneo, soon to become one of the best regarded illustrators in Britain.

Once you've mastered the perspective of drawing the wheels and tracks of tanks , racing cars, to which I was to graduate, are quite easy. I never thought I would meet the great man, but several years later I did in the company of Mike Bowling, whose godfather Cuneo was.

Terry was something of an eccentric, painting little mice into every painting he ever did. He drove a splendid vintage Delahay, with a solemn green parrot perched on his shoulder, who had mastered two phrases: 'Bugger off' and 'You are all doomed'.

He had a legendary love of horses and in the Esher and Hampton Court riding fraternity he and his horse *Shadow* became a serious talking point because Terry wore a complete cowboy outfit and *Shadow* boasted a Western saddle.

But his best eccentricity concerned his wife Kate's dinner parties. Every few weeks she used to give extremely smart black tie parties for twenty or thirty people. This was not Terry's idea of a good time and the beautiful long table with silver gleaming and candles lighting the scene was something he actually hated.

When it was time for the ladies to leave for the drawing room, Terry would signal this in a rather unusual way. Not the discreet cough and glance at his wife for him. He would take down a flint-lock blunderbuss from the wall, charge it with wads of paper torn from *The Times* and black powder, and then discharge it from the end of the table blowing out all the candles. This had the electrifying result of sending the ladies running wailing from the room, and even some of the men. The tablecloth often caught fire. And his wife could be heard stridently above the chaos, 'Terry you've ruined my party and you know damned well that that tablecloth belonged to my mother'. She was wrong, of course. The blunderbuss *made* the parties and peopled talked of them for weeks after. Indeed, the men left at the table usually took in turns to relight the candles, recharge the gun and have a go themselves.

For those of us chaps who have to protect their curious habits like model railways, we probably all need a Terence Cuneo to put things into perspective with our wives.

TED HEATH – PARTY POOPER

While I met a great number of Ministers and backbenchers through my father's political connections, I was not exactly on intimate terms with many Prime Ministers. Anthony Eden I met once as a child although my father knew him well enough. Harold Macmillan and Sir Alec Douglas-Home I only met later in retirement at our club, Bucks. Maggie Thatcher I met when she was a guest at Burke Club evenings in the Commons and when entertaining her as we shall see during the 'Blue Revue'. So my only direct contact with a Prime Minister was with Ted Heath and this proved to be a somewhat frosty encounter.

Every November my father gave his legendary 'no strings'

CUMMINS

George Brown and Toby, political enemies but personal friends

parties which had no PR strings attached. Most of the Tory Cabinet, several members of the Labour Shadow Cabinet, dozens of MPs and all the important newspaper editors and other media commentators all pitched up. In fact, so well known were these yearly events that advertisements for the *Economist* Diary once used a typical diary page of an anonymous important person in their advertisement and in among the other VIP events was the cryptic note, 'Toby's No Strings,' which of course could only be interpreted by those in the know – 250 or so.

They were usually great fun and punctuated by the odd incident such as when George Brown, Labour's Foreign Secretary, already – as the papers dubbed him –'rather tired and emotional', fell through a glass table.

In 1973, Ted Heath, as Prime Minister, was due to arrive and Toby deputed me to go and wait on the steps of 2 Old Burlington Street to greet him. Beside me was a policeman and as the Prime Minister's car drew up and Ted Heath emerged, he remarked, 'Glad to see I've got some security.'

The policeman foolishly interrupted saying, 'Oh no, Prime Minister, I'm not here to protect you, I'm here to look after Colonel Giles' (Norrie Giles was my father's brother-in-law, a Parachute Regiment colonel and this was not too long after Bloody Sunday in Londonderry).

The Prime Minister was plainly furious and stormed up the stairs and into the party with a face like thunder. It took a long time to stop my father saying to me 'I give you one simple job to do and all you can do in a couple of seconds is annoy the Prime Minister'. The whole *amour propre* incident was an interesting echo to the story of Iain Macleod's pique in Spain.

The last time I saw Ted was on a plane to Brussels. I re-introduced myself as 'Toby's son' and he enigmatically responded, 'Yes. The first person to give me political credit – and the last.' Then without another word, he worked on his papers in a curious way, passing them, when signed, backwards over his head to his assistant behind. Most of us would sit *with* our staff.

Ronnie and Honor Waring would have to be described as a remarkable, even redoubtable, couple.

How many of us can claim to have rescued our mothers *personally* from a concentration camp, killing her guards? For that matter, how many couples do we know who, dining quietly at a restaurant, have been attacked by terrorists and each had to shoot one, she with her .32 Special and he with a Colt .45?

This incident in Luanda occurred as a result of President Salazar of Portugal turning to Ronnie for advice because of his war record and a little book he wrote on the Mau Mau in Kenya. In spite of Ronnie's repeated warnings, an inexperienced Portuguese Army now faced full-scale revolt in its African colonies of Angola and Mozambique. There was nothing half-hearted about this war, either.

As Ronnie wrote in his book *The Owl and the Pussycat*:

> On the following day, on another patrol, we ran into another ambush. This time a terrorist came rushing out of the elephant grass, and with a machete he chopped the head of a Portuguese soldier clean off. The soldier was standing next to me, and he had started firing his sub-machine gun as soon as he saw the terrorist running at him. I could actually see the 9mm bullets hitting the terrorist as he came on, but they seemed to have no effect on him whatever. He rushed across the track and into the elephant grass on the far side. I took a snap shot at him as he vanished. When the action was over, we searched the area and found the man with nineteen 9mm bullets in him; he had been so high on bhang (unrefined hashish) that he had not felt a thing.

For nineteen years Ronnie, later the Duke of Valderano, was an instructor at the Institute for Advanced Military Studies outside Lisbon, and it was in April 1974 that a very amusing but significant incident took place.

It all started in Chelsea. One of my friends from Stowe that I kept up with was Robin Behar. His father had sold a chain of shops to Tesco and Robin eventually became the property director of that supermarket group. He was also an excellent mimic. One night he rang to ask me to join him and a group in 'Nikita's', which was a Russian restaurant owned by my friend and neighbour, Old Etonian Nick Clarke of 'Nick's Diner' fame.

The purpose was 'to entertain a Soviet Marshal at the request of the Foreign Office'. I turned up and there was no sign of Behar, but in the corner there was a pin-striped Foreign Office type with a burly, middle-aged Russian officer in heavily-medalled uniform pontificating in a deep Russian accent. In the half light it took me several minutes to realise that this *was* Robin Behar, with grey hair, brilliantly made up to look 20 years older and acting perfectly. Certainly, Nick Clarke was

PORTUGUESE BLUFF

Ronnie Waring, after more normal game

227

Marshal Rakov, alias Robin Behar

hanging on to his every word. He had previously been called by Richard Syme (the Foreign office type) to reserve Nick's private room. 'Clarke? Mr Nick Clarke? Rathbone at the Foreign Office here. Now look here, are you discreet? We've got a very important guest we want to entertain without him being stared at. A Russian guest, which is why I am calling you.'

After half an hour of listening to Soviet military exploits, I was getting hungry and beginning to get bored and I finally spoilt it all by saying 'Come off it Robin, can't we have dinner now?'

At first, Nick Clarke, who actually knew Robin but had failed to recognise him, was stupefied that I could insult our guest but the evening ended in a bout of amusing vodka drinking with Robin refusing to drop his Russian accent.

The story did not end here, because this was just a rehearsal for an event in Portugal. Robin was due to go to the wedding of another school friend, Marcus Waring, Ronnie's son. Invited to the wedding dinner were the top Portuguese Generals, plus the military attachés from 'friendly' Embassies. Dress was 'white tie or uniform', hence the whole idea and the dress rehearsal at Nikita's. Standing at the top of the receiving line, Ronnie suddenly said to his son, 'Good Grief, a Russian officer has gate-crashed my party'.

Sure enough, 'Marshal Rakov' of the Soviet Union was announced, followed by an 'American General', actually Alexander Zafiropoulo, another Old Stoic.

Marcus Waring whispered to his father, 'Look more carefully, it's Robin in disguise'.

Staring at first in disbelief, Ronnie then decided to have some fun out of the situation. 'Ah,' he said, 'It's brilliant. Let's see who we'll introduce him to.'

But Robin had already introduced himself to Colonel Juan Alvarez, the silver-haired Spanish military attaché, an officer with little sense of humour but with the Order of San Fernando, equivalent to our Victoria Cross. Robin's opening gambit was to ask if he could have the Colonel's chair as he was suffering from an old back wound. Replying to Alvarez's enquiry as to how this had happened, he said it was on manoeuvres in 1952 and he had been accidentally shot by one of his own men.

'What happened to him?' asked Alvarez.

'He shoot me in back, I shoot him in front!' said Robin bellowing with hearty Russian laughter.

228

There was a moment's pause. 'I rather wish the Spanish army was like that.' said Alvarez wistfully. They then got into a long, deep conversation about the Russian Front and the brilliant performance of the Spanish Blue Division, which had fought with great heroism on the side of the Germans. (Franco's clever token effort to avoid any further involvement with Hitler.)

After a while, Ronnie Waring noticed with horror that the joke had gone too far and, highly embarrassed, decided to disengage his 'Russian' from the trusting Alvarez. After Robin had made himself scarce, he then tried to break the news to the Spaniard that this was an impostor.

'My dear Juan,' he stuttered, 'I have to confess. That was *not* a Russian officer'.

'¡Ridiculo!' the Colonel replied, 'I've been talking to him for nearly forty minutes. Of course, he's a Russian officer'.

'No he isn't'.

'Well, who is he?'

'A school friend of Marcus's', blurted out the embarrassed Ronnie. The Spaniard was so angry at this apparent insult to his intelligence that he stalked off in a huff, refusing to believe a word of it.

There was a real bonus from this charming if rather schoolboy prank.

Just ten days after that reception, the Portuguese revolution came, and normally Ronnie would have been one of the first victims to have been picked up, being so much part of the Salazar Establishment. In fact the revolt was led by one of his own students at the Institute, who had joined his course on the 'destabilisation of governments!; But many senior army officers behind the revolution were also at that reception and had seen for themselves a Soviet officer, apparently on intimate terms with the Waring family.

Ronnie often wondered afterwards whether this hadn't made some of them think that he too was connected with the revolution, that the presence of the Russian had been something to do with its planning, and had made the newly-installed authorities hesitate to pick him up during the first sweeps of the old regime.

Thus a joke that started in Chelsea helped his family, with an extra few days' grace, to make good their escape by a pre-planned route overland with most of their belongings.

CHANGE OF PACE

In the days before car bombs in Lebanon and London, and widespread international terrorism, the American Embassy used to have a splendid little cinema and lecture hall and ran a regular programme of films. One month they were running some *cinema verité* films, shot with hand-held cameras – very much like a newsflash or documentary. They had advertised, one evening, a film on Al Unser, who was one of the great American Indianapolis-500 racing drivers and I decided to drop in.

When we sat down the audience appeared to be strangely mixed. There were a lot of young men in jackets with Ferrari and Porsche written on them with extremely attractive blonde girlfriends, some of them similarly covered in badges. Then again there seemed to be a lot of silver-haired old ladies.

A middle-aged woman appeared on the stage and announced that she was very pleased to see "such an unusual turn-out for a lecture with epidiascope slides on the prominent 18th century American botanist and naturalist John Bartram". There was a stunned silence and three quarters of the room scrambled to their feet and left. The poor lady would have had no way of knowing that the programme had been misprinted and was appalled that merely her opening words were capable of emptying the hall. I was so sorry for her and the lecturer that I stayed put and listened for two hours to a subject in which I was obviously not incredibly interested. Somehow I just couldn't bear to leave with the rest.

Speaking about botany reminds me of another story. Lionel de Rothschild of the banking family was a distinguished botanist, and was renowned for his work on gardens. While he was on a foreign trip, the City Association of Allotment Owners and Gardeners wrote to him on the off-chance that he could come and speak to them about gardening. His secretary, by mistake, answered in the affirmative and when he returned she said, 'Of course I will cancel that for you, Mr. Rothschild. I am sorry I made the mistake.'

'Nonsense,' he said, 'If I promised to go and talk to them, I will go and talk to them.' So he prepared with great care a presentation and turned up at a hall with thirty or forty allotment owners and gardeners.

Halfway through his presentation he came out with the immortal observation that 'no garden, however small, should contain less than two acres of rough woodland.'

PLANT TALK

The Botanist.

PLANT TALK

John Bartram 1699–1777, and the famous 'Lost Franklinia' he discovered, now extinct in the wild.

230

Saudi Arabia was one of my father's longest standing public relations accounts.

Roger Linn (the stalwart ex-Marine who had tried to give Roger Whittaker's bulldog the kiss of life) and I were once asked to look after four senior young Saudis who were destined for great things as Ministers. We devised a programme for showing them around London, including a visit to the Metal Exchange. I well remember the day, because Christopher Moorsom burst into my office and said, 'Somebody has shot our client'.

Indeed, trusting King Feisal had been assassinated in his throne room by a relation. I had to get this message, very urgently, to our group of Saudis. I rang the Chairman of the London Metal Exchange who walked down the steps and informed them that their King had been killed. Roger then accompanied them in the Chairman's Rolls-Royce, in stunned silence, back to the Embassy, and respectfully sat outside while they went into the Ambassador's inner sanctum. Sounds died away and after about an hour Roger became somewhat anxious and hungry, as it was now about 3 o'clock. He asked the secretary what was happening inside and she brightly informed them that the group had gone out to lunch!

He later became very good friends with them, visiting Saudi Arabia as a guest. During this visit one of his hosts, soon to be a senior government Minister, said two things quite casually to Roger. Firstly, that during the 1973 Israeli Arab war '*there had been no battle on the Golan Heights, it was a piece of Israeli and Western propaganda*'.

It took Roger a long time to persuade his friend that the Syrians and Israelis had lost nearly 1,000 tanks on the Golan Heights. While he eventually conceded that there had been some kind of battle on the Heights, he then offered his second stupifying theory. '*You know, the Israeli pilots do not wish to fly. They are chained to their planes*'. Once again Roger had to point out, respectfully but firmly, that Israeli fighter pilots, as the cream of their armed forces, were regarded as so much more valuable than their planes that they were told to eject as soon as they thought a missile had really locked on.

ARABIAN FLIGHTS OF FANTASY

LICHFIELD

King Feisal

A King Feisal audience photographed by Patrick Lichfield, sadly showing the lack of security.

Israeli Air Force ace, Col. Giora Epstein (17 victories). No doubt about to be handcuffed to his plane!

The extraordinary part of the story is that a very nice, intelligent and Western-educated future Minister could seriously trot out to a military professional this kind of bizarre self-delusion, unworthy of a Bedouin just out of the desert.

My friend, Avi Rosental, now head of the Israeli Hotel Association was fighting in the fierce battle of the Golan Heights. Eventually the Israelis prevailed and they found themselves looking down at Damascus. Their commander told them to halt, but if they had a peep out of the Syrians they should continue their advance right into the city.

In fact, the fighting petered away and for several months he endured the shelling on the Heights. One night, after a period of rising tension, the troops in the front line suddenly saw all the lights of Damascus go out. Radios crackled, Headquarters were immediately alerted, tanks went to full readiness and Mirages and Phantoms roared into the air. The troops stared through their infra-red sights to see if a Syrian attack was coming. Equally suddenly all the lights of Damascus came back on as the city power company mended the fuse.

Toby helped the political image of Saudi Arabia for thirteen years, through thick and thin (the Yemeni War to the devastating BBC exposé, *Death of a Princess*). Being hopelessly uncommercial, he never increased his fees (remember 1973 and 1974 had 25% inflation). The Saudi Information Ministry was also routinely slow in paying. After my father's death they owed us months of fees and expenses. An international lawyer had told me about the State Immunity Act of 1978, brought in by Harold Wilson's Government to protect a Polish shipbuilding deal. This said that, even if a contract was written for foreign jurisdiction, if it could be proved the foreigners were not going to give you a fair shake, it could be referred back to the High Court in London.

I resolved to evoke this Act by attempting to send my stepmother Leo, as the widow, to Jeddah to argue our case. I was counting on the Saudis not letting her on the plane as a single woman, and I would have then won the case and distrained all their Government (and Royal Family) assets in the UK, no doubt with the drama of locking up Saudia airliners at Heathrow as well.

A white-faced young man from the Foreign Office arrived and begged me not to do it. The Saudis had little enough comprehension as to why our Government could not just bar the TV screening of *Death of a Princess*, let alone having their money frozen, distrained for such a trivial sum as £45,000. A huge British Aerospace defence deal might be scuppered. Firmly, I advised him to see the Lee Marvin film *Point Blank* and he would then understand my principles.

Sadly, my planned dramatic gesture never occurred. The Saudi Ministry just happened to pay up two days later.

S ome years ago, working in New York, I sat in a cafe and I found this rather neat definition of advertising on a packet of sugar:

'He who has a thing to sell and goes and whispers in a well is not so apt to get the dollars as he who climbs a tree and hollers'.

My advertising experience was triggered in 1972 by Roland Wells who had become Managing Director of a small advertising agency, Felden, whose main claim to fame was that it had broken away from Colman, Prentis & Varley with the image-building account for Britain's nationalised gas industry. Roland had been part of the CPV team that had created the slogan 'High Speed Gas'. I offered to join him to help him to turn it around from a very tenuous position.

We then bought Felden from an old rogue whom *Campaign* magazine once described as 'Xerxes Duckpond, the wiliest breakaway of them all', and two very nice old colleagues who were usually so drunk by 11.30 in the morning as to be incoherent. We had borrowed £40,000 to buy the agency, a huge, risky commitment. First we had to make the gas account secure. We managed to sell the Board of the Gas Council, soon to be British Gas, our proposed campaign, 'Gas Promises', which included a poster campaign pointing out the good value of gas, especially in an era of high inflation. One poster showed a magnificent roast (the price of beef had just risen to £1 per pound) with the slogan: 'You can't do much about the price of beef, but you can cook it with gas. Gas promises better value'. A similar one had a house with: 'You can't help being gazumped, but you can heat your house with gas'.

Naturally there was a long period between the approval of the posters, their production and the actual posting of them all over Britain. In the meantime Ted Heath's Government was being engulfed in a sea of troubles, not least soaring prices, rampant gazumping and inflation that had now risen to 24%.

It never occurred to us that this had anything to do with gas advertising, but the bosses of nationalised industries were sensitive souls. So when the Chairman of British Gas was being chauffeured through South London one September morning and he spotted one of his new posters for the first time, he immediately thought, 'Oh my God! They'll think I'm attacking the Government for mishandling the economy. Bang goes the knighthood and maybe my job!'

In what he later privately admitted was an over-hasty reaction, he ordered that the hundreds of posters be covered up immediately. A journalist on the *Sun* newspaper was driving home late

We launched the identity of British Gas the same day Britain entered the Common Market, February 1972

HOW GAS IS HELPING BRITAIN TO SAVE

Natural gas from the North Sea is helping Britain to save – to the tune of over £1,000 million last year* on the balance of payments. But for nearly ten years now natural gas has been saving us huge amounts of precious foreign exchange by reducing our dependence on imported oil, and this crucial contribution to the country's economic health will continue for a very long time to come.

Even after North Sea oil begins to come ashore in large quantities, gas will continue to help our balance of payments–for the less oil we use, the more we can export.

Natural gas is a vital resource for Britain–and fortunately an abundant one. Provided that the country continues to follow sensible depletion policies and takes the necessary steps to recover and exploit offshore resources, Britain will continue to benefit from natural gas well into the 21st century.

*The Treasury/European Weapons Report (July 1976 conveyed a saving of £1,060 million for the year)

SAVE IT

BRITISH GAS

GAS–DOING A GREAT JOB FOR BRITAIN.

CREATIVE STEPS

that night when he saw a man with a ladder, bucket and paste in the act of putting up a brown paper poster. Seeing that there was a brand new gas poster already on the hoarding, he sensed a story.

Three days later I was sitting in my bath listening to the radio describing 'what the papers say'. To my horror I heard: 'Today *The Sun* leads with British Gas being forced by Government pressure to cover up its posters all over the country at great public expense, under the headline 'HIGH SPEED GAG FOR GAS MEN'.'

We were convinced that we were about to lose the account through no fault of our own but, when the dust had cleared, our clients admitted that it was more their fault than ours and we kept the account for many years.

Soon after setting up Wells O'Brien, we were joined by one of my old friends, Jorge Potier. I first met Jorge in 1945 with Tim ffytche when they allowed me to join the gang of little boys who frequented Cadogan Gardens. Jorge was the only son of the Chargé d'Affairs at the Portuguese Embassy which at that time overlooked Sloane Street.

He had been to Westminster School where, as a small Portuguese boy, he could have expected to be bullied. He thought up the rather good idea of hiring a huge Canadian friend called Kerry as a minder. By paying him sixpence a week, this ensured that anybody threatening Jorge just got hit.

Intelligent and funny, Jorge had a chameleon-like personality, so it was often difficult to keep up with the latest persona that he decided to adopt.

At 15, my father dubbed him 'Man About Town Potier' because he started wearing frock coats, a monocle and carrying a silver-topped cane. However, this phase did not last long. A little while later, he emerged in beatnik guise with a beard, black leather gloves and jeans, calling everyone 'Man'. Scarcely had we got used to that character than he was dressed in tweeds, living in an ivy-clad rectory and quite the country gentleman. During this phase, his wife used to meet him off the commuter train, on which he travelled first class, with a ready-mixed dry martini for him to enjoy during the drive home.

Jorge had started his working life as an engineering apprentice, then switched to go into banking. He wasn't really suited to either, so he decided to try to break into advertising. He wrote to all the big agencies and was lucky enough to gain an interview at what was then called the London Press Exchange. The interview was with the Creative Director, Hugh Bergel – a vintage car enthusiast. In fact, he and his son used to race a Bugatti in vintage car races and he kept a model of it on his desk. Noticing this, Jorge said, 'Ah! Type 35B, 2.2 litres, super-charged, with alloy wheels, I see.' They talked about motor racing for 40 minutes, then about advertising for 5 minutes. Needless to say, Jorge was offered a job as a copywriter and that was the start of successful career on the creative side of advertising.

Jorge, who has never claimed to be athletic, suddenly rang one day from Padstow to say he had caught the world's largest Porbeagle Shark. This feat was in the Guinness Book of Records for 20 years.

Jorge Potier attended the Film Festival at Cork and was greeted one morning by a classic Irish interchange. The bright girl behind reception said, 'Would you like a news-paper, Mr Potier?'

'Yes, I would.'

'Would you like yesterday's or today's?'

'Today's, please.'

'Well, that doesn't arrive 'til tomorrow.'

Roland Wells also got into the creative side of advertising by unconventional means.

He had started in the Civil Service. When asked what he did, he used to say, 'I'm an EO, in the EIB at the ECGD.' Which, being translated, meant that he was an Executive Officer in the Economic Intelligence Branch of the Exports Credits Guarantee Department. Fed up with a life of acronyms and the 'dead men's shoes' promotion policy of the civil service, he decided that he would like to try the more fast-moving world of advertising. After sending off several dozen letters and attending numerous interviews, he was taken on as a trainee at an agency called Napper, Stinton & Woolley, where he soon progressed to the rank of Account Executive.

Having decided that being a 'suit' was not for him either, and having always been interested in writing, he decided to become a copywriter. That was easier said than done, and although he managed to get plenty of interviews, he was each time advised that he would need to get some experience before they could consider offering him a job. Very discouraged by this, he said to the last interviewer, 'How do I get the experi-ence if no-one will give me start?' The reply took him aback. 'Your best bet is to lie.'

Roland shared a flat with Terry Howard, already a successful copywriter, who agreed. 'Quite right. I've been doing a lot of

HOW TO BLUFF
YOUR WAY INTO
ADVERTISING

freelance recently, so why don't you use some of my samples? As a matter of fact, Lintas (his then employers) are looking for writers at the moment and because it's freelance they won't recognise the work.' So Roland wrote to Terry's boss, the Creative Director of Lintas, and was subsequently summoned to an interview.

Ushered into his presence, he spread Terry's work on the table and the Creative Director became enthusiastic. 'This is just the kind of work we like and we need more writers at the moment, so you're on. Now, whose group shall I put you in? I think Terry Howard would be the right man.'

Roland's heart skipped a beat, as he hadn't even mentioned to Terry that he was coming into the agency that day. The Creative Director rang Terry, who came in and coolly said, 'Hi, good to meet you', as to a complete stranger. 'How do you do, Mr Howard,' Roland replied politely.

Having been introduced to the new recruit, Terry then looked down at his own work and said, 'Hey, this is really great.'

'Well, I'm glad you say that Terry, because I'm thinking of putting him in your group.'

'Glad to have you aboard, Wells.'

'Thank you very much, Mr Howard.'

So Roland got a job working with Terry, using Terry's own work! In the pub at lunchtime Roland suddenly remembered something. 'Christ!' he said, 'I've put our address on the application form, so they'll know we're in cahoots.'

'Don't worry about it,' Terry reassured him, 'They'll never notice, and anyway, I'll think of something.'

He did think of something. Some days later he mentioned casually to the Creative Director that 'the new guy Wells has quarrelled with his landlady and as we seem to get on well, I've invited him to share our flat in Pimlico.'

Thus are successful careers started.

We were quite a small agency, about 10 people. One day our young Account Executive, Colin Prescot, announced he wanted to leave to see if he could turn his hobby, ballooning, into a commercial venture. The Hot Air Balloon Company, with its dramatic balloons in shapes such as Coke bottles, is a world leader. Moreover, Colin in 1999 set the record for the longest flight of any aircraft in the earth's atmosphere. So our tiny little advertising agency actively spawned two world record holders which must be a record in itself.

Colin's balloon

During our agency's many years working for the gas industry, there was one amusing incident, which shows that all presentations must be carefully tailored to the audience. Tony Vinegrad, the Head of Public Relations, took the leading British energy journalist from *The Times* up to Theddlethorpe, one of the gas industry's sophisticated research stations. He had asked the scientists to put on an informative presentation. They had nothing to hand and were too busy to create a special one, so the boffins decided to show a presentation that they had prepared a couple of weeks before for the Energy Minister to demonstrate that much more investment was required to ensure the safety of the ageing gas distribution system.

Tony sat with mounting horror watching the opening sequence, which was a film showing what happened when a 24 inch pipeline at a pressure of two thousand pounds per square inch ruptured. The camera lovingly recorded a whole hillside erupting, with chunks of metal weighing half a ton sailing 400 yards through the air. The next presenter turned to the rest of the distribution system, announcing there were 'ten thousand ruptures in the medium pressure system annually'.

Suddenly, from the back, someone said, 'No, that's not right'. Tony heaved a sigh of relief. Obviously, someone at last had seen sense, realising what dangerous information they were handing the journalist.

'It's more like fifteen thousand'. said the helpful scientist!

This disaster went on all morning and as they flew back to London, Tony could only beg the journalist, in the event successfully, not to print a word of what he had heard, supported by the threat that British Gas would never, ever advertise in *The Times* if he did!

CHOOSE YOUR AUDIENCE

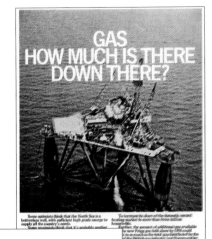

Cheeky advertising for gas at the time of the OPEC oil embargo

HOTEL SAHARA

Hotel people tend to be nice and one of our nicer clients was Inter-Continental Hotels. We had done the advertising for the launch of their Park Lane property and had then gone on to look after them in Europe and the Middle East.

One day the Marketing Director asked us to organise seminars on the importance of the customer. One group consisted of Sales Managers from their hotels in the Middle East, most of whom were Pakistani or Arab.

We realised they would not be very interested in how an advertising agency worked but, nevertheless, we were lumbered with them every afternoon for a week. We decided to hire the excellent training films from John Cleese's training company 'Video Arts'. So, every afternoon, we ended the session with a film called 'The Customer is Always Right' or whatever, followed by a discussion or role-playing.

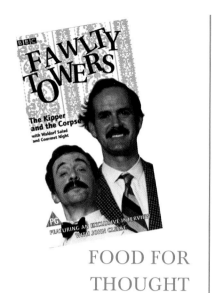

FOOD FOR THOUGHT

For Roger Linn and me, the temptation was too great. On the last day, I stood up and announced, 'We are now going to see the last of Mr Cleese's films. This one specifically focuses on our industry, hotels.' The hotel men got out their notebooks.

I slid the Fawlty Towers 'Gourmet Night' video into the player. For about ten minutes we were able to keep straight faces while our guests earnestly took notes, trying to make sense of Basil Fawlty, Sybil, Manuel, the drunken chef and so on. Eventually, Roger slid slowly under the table, bursting with laughter. At last they knew they were allowed to laugh themselves. I would say it was one of the golden moments of my commercial life – and our guests said it was the best course they had ever been on.

Mary Gunther, my client at the Inter-Continental Hotel on Park Lane, asked me to help her with a group of journalists and travel agents visiting their hotels in the United Arab Emirates and Oman. Flying out on Gulf Air to Dubai, I got talking to my neighbour, a young man who was, curiously enough, reading a model railway magazine. David Johnson revealed that he was actually a British Airways pilot, so I asked him what he was doing with our group.

He revealed that he had a special relationship with Inter-Continental Hotels. He was a friend of the Food and Beverage Manager in Dubai and a few months before he had asked him where he was getting his food supplies. His friend replied that it was very difficult because the quality of his suppliers in Cyprus and Athens was inadequate.

So, he asked, 'Would you buy from me if I supplied your food?'

'Don't be silly, you're an airline pilot, not a food man.' he retorted.

'Yes. But would you just give me a chance?'

His friend agreed rather reluctantly. David returned to negotiate with all kinds of suppliers in Smithfield market and elsewhere, including a Scottish lobster farm and even the Brooklyn Lobster Tank Company (I remember this because I went to Brooklyn with him one Sunday morning). He installed a telex in his little house and telexed for his first order. This came through from the hotel; 500 fillet steaks, 700 sirloins, 100 lobsters and so on. He immediately telexed the orders to the suppliers and the products arrived at a central point to be packed into a Gulf Air container.

The Inter-Continental Dubai was delighted with the quality and signed him on. After two months, he asked if he could deal with other Inter-Continental hotels in the region and after a couple more months he asked if they would mind if he dealt with the Sheratons and Hiltons as well.

Our advertising for Inter-Continental in the Middle East

Within 6 months his little company, Cobellon Foods, was supplying 16 hotels in the Gulf and he was the biggest freight customer for Gulf Air. With two telexes now, his Italian wife was busy processing the orders.

I forgot about all this for years until one evening when I had flown back from Belfast and a voice called out to me in the terminal. It was David in the uniform of a British Airways Captain. I waited until his co-pilot was out of earshot, in case I might get him into trouble, and asked him how his little food company was getting along.

'Oh, I sold it to Tiny Rowland's Lonrho for £10 million.'

The last time I saw David, he owned the biggest house in Haslemere, Surrey. A pillar of local society, he was Chairman of the local Conservative Association. This is one of the best examples of *part-time* enterprise that I can think of.

THE HOME FOR BATTERED HUSBANDS

My love life has tended to consist of long periods of faithful and happy relationships with rather hectic intervals between them. I am not proud of it but two of my three marriages have collapsed with no discernible fault on either side. Clare and I split up in September 1974, with desperate sadness not least because of the effect on my son Murrough.

What I did not know was that Clare was saying to her best friend, Liz Cowley 'I'm not really suited to Donough but if there is one person who is, it's you. You should marry him one day'. As, we shall see, fifteen years later she duly did.

My house in Clonmel Road was suddenly empty and cheerless and I for the first year shared it with three girls thanks to my carefully worded and heart-tugging ad. HELP ME TO MAKE A FULHAM HOUSE INTO A HOME. John Cleese used to come to supper and we discussed military history very seriously. Like many comedians, it was hard to get him to smile.

Clare and Murrough

When two of the girls moved on, my friend Mike Bowling moved in together with me with one of his pals, John Dyson. As they had both suffered very rough divorces we now call the house 'The home for battered husbands'.

WRONG TARGET

On my second visit to New York to visit Inter-Continental Hotels, Christopher Moorsom advised me to look up an old friend, Charles Childs, who was a publicity executive with Union Carbide and, as I was to discover later, something of a general entrepreneur. He was also black.

He was living with and later married an English girl, Gay, who was editor of *Working Woman*. Up till then I had never had a black friend, so I was intrigued to be shown New York by Charles. He picked me up from the Gorham Hotel on 55th

Charles with President Jimmy Carter

Street and asked me if I'd like a drink in a bar around the corner. It was one of those smart bars in New York which are a little careful who they let in.

The bouncer at the door approached us as we entered and said, 'I'm afraid you can't come in'. I was mortified. Through my mind flashed the horrific embarrassment for Charles of this obvious, blatant display of racial prejudice. I had supposed that at least in New York all *that* was over. I flinched at Charles's humiliation at not even being allowed to give his new British friend a drink.

You can imagine my double mortification when the bouncer continued, 'Mr Childs, your friend is not dressed smartly enough!'

THE GAY DISCOTHEQUE

One August Sunday afternoon in Greenwich Village, I met up with a very nice English artist, his American wife and another couple. They invited me out of the steamy heat of Manhattan to New Jersey. We had a very pleasant afternoon by a pool. I met his wife's parents, and two Wall Street brokers also joined us for a swim.

As evening drew on they asked if I would like to come to a Manhattan discotheque before going back to my hotel. Unattached, the thought of meeting girls was not so awful and I agreed. We emerged from the Lincoln Tunnel and drove down to an extremely rough broken-down warehouse district on the lower West Side. Just before we arrived at the club, my friend's wife said, 'By the way, Donough, this place has got a little bit of a 'gay base'. I hope you don't mind that.'

I reassured her that a 'little of that' did not bother me too much ('Many of my best friends etc'). We drew up outside a huge converted warehouse. On the pavement were literally hundreds of men. In those days, British gays tended to be rather effete, artistic and gentle people. Here was a contrast. Milling around on the pavement were huge men, stripped to the waist with chains around their waists, their bodies clearly capable of immense feats of physical strength.

As we left the safety of the car, my confidence in the protective ability of my group was suddenly diminished by our two stock-brokers suddenly holding hands and announcing 'what fun it was to dance together'. So we entered the club with me clinging as closely as possible to our two women.

In the hugely loud, strobe-lit warehouse, I was appalled to discover that this 'bit of a gay base' meant that there were 500 men dancing together and a total of five women – and we had just brought in two of them!

Without so much as having a drink, my whole group abandoned me to dance to the first number. Suddenly I was left up against the wall looking, in the strobe lighting, long-haired, blond, available and tasty. Usually if you enter a gay bar by mistake, it becomes quickly obvious that you are straight and *not* interested. With the incredible noise, this was not obvious and I quickly learned to say 'No thank you, sir,' very politely to a series of huge men who came up to say 'Let's go baby' and who became irritated and then aggressive when I turned them down. After all, what was I there for?.

It took me only minutes of this agony to decide to leave. I fought my way out of the club and through the throng at the door, many of whom made interesting suggestions as to how I should spend my next few minutes in New York.

By lucky chance, a lonely cab rescued me from this new ordeal. Some days later, I drove past the club with Charles Childs, my new friend. All he could say was, 'Christ! Not **that** place!'

FUN FURS

One friend from home trying his luck in America was Willie Feilding, the cousin of Rollo Feilding, now the Earl of Denbigh. Willie was a marvellous painter and had a specialist peculiarity, painting dragons. One of his more dramatic ideas was to paint on the inside of a lavatory door a dragon apparently bursting in. I once had to carry one of these rather bizarre doors with him for about 20 blocks down Fifth Avenue to deliver to some rich couple's brownstone and it certainly attracted a number of curious and suspicious stares.

Willie was going out with Wendy, one of the Vanderbilts, descended from the family that controlled the New York Central railroad. We discussed how she could trade on her family name (much as Gloria Vanderbilt later did with jeans). We worked out that one of the coming fashion items was the so-called 'fun furs' and these could be produced from Chinese rabbit and the best place to finish off the garments was in London. So I did a deal with a furrier called Frank Cooney, and he ran up an excellent collection of furs, which were going to be the 'Wendy Vanderbilt Fun Furs Collection'.

Unfortunately, such was our basic lack of knowledge of the fashion scene in New York that we scheduled our sales trip at exactly the time that every fur buyer was down in Miami on vacation. Another 'Commercial Cock-up.'

LICHFIELD

Willie Feilding

A very English friend of mine suddenly said 'The Irish are rather strange'. He had booked a rental car for a holiday in Cork and was advised by Hertz in London to take an Opel or, if unavailable, a Volkswagen.

When he arrived late at Cork Airport, the Hertz girls had gone home and a little old man was manning the desk.

'I think you have an Opel for me.'

'No, sorr.'

'Then it's a Volkswagen?'

'No, sorr.'

He pointed through the window at a solitary, boring little Hillman Avenger.

'No, no. I don't think you understand. I've paid extra money for an Opel or a Volkswagen.'

'That's right, sorr. 'Tis for those who order an Opel or a Volkswagen, for whom we keep the Hillman Avenger!'

ASBESTOS SAVIOUR

There have been a number of promotional successes of which I have been proud. One would be my work for Northern Ireland's economic development, another the help I have been able to give the hospitality industry over the smoking issue in hotels and restaurants and the third would be helping to save the British Asbestos industry from a premature demise.

At Wells O'Brien for some time we had run, under Anthony Masterton-Smith, the Asbestos Information Committee, quite a low-key affair dealing with the medical problems caused by the use of asbestos. The fibres from asbestos, when inhaled for long enough, cause two very distressing diseases, asbestosis and mesothelioma. Most of the deaths that were occurring in Britain (about 100 a year) were caused by asbestos workers not wearing their masks correctly during the blackout years of the war, so that 25 years later the diseases sadly emerged.

Quite unexpectedly, one week all hell broke loose. On the Monday, the Ombudsman brutally tore into the negligence of the Factory Inspectorate over the lax practices at the asbestos factory at Hebden Bridge. On the Tuesday, blue asbestos started falling out of ceilings in council blocks in the East End. On the Wednesday an asbestosis widow called Nancy Tait launched a

242

book called *Asbestos Kills* with the backing of 30 members of Parliament led by Max Madden, MP for Sowerby, which embraces Hebden Bridge. (Max, curiously enough, had been one of our clients at British Gas a few years before.)

On the Friday we confronted a tense meeting of the whole asbestos industry with, pasted on a huge board, the glaring headlines that were now on the front page of every national and provincial newspaper. We presented our plans for redressing the situation, which basically had not changed. Media and public attitudes had just become completely hysterical.

One fool of a man from one of the client companies suddenly looked up and said, 'I don't think we need to do anything other than sue that woman Tait. She is exaggerating and I am sure we would win.'

There was an appalled, pregnant silence. Suddenly my partner Jorge Potier came out with one of his immortal quips, 'I can see the headline now:

'ASBESTOS BARONS RUIN CANCER WIDOW.'

Everybody stared at their blotters with extreme embarrassment and the asbestos industry then let us get on with our jobs.

In the event we succeeded in saving the industry by reducing the hysteria, putting everything in perspective and explaining how important the material was. Later on, however, massive asbestos claims in America not only brought down the asbestos industry but helped to wreck the Lloyds insurance market and ruined the lives of many Lloyds 'names'. Safe substitutes have now been developed.

A leaflet to brief the trade unions

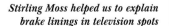

Stirling Moss helped us to explain brake linings in television spots

GENERAL'S DAUGHTER

Pippa Janes came into my life in 1978, daughter of Major General Mervyn Janes. Extremely mild-mannered and very tall, he had been Director of the Royal Artillery. I once had to deal with his former Brigade Commander over a charity matter and Mervyn filled me in, 'Biggest bluffer in the Army. We'd be sitting in Germany with all our self-propelled guns in bits all over the workshop floor and the Divisional Commander would ring to check our status. 'Ready to move at a moment's notice, Sir'.'

Pippa and I later married and our son Edmond has inherited Mervyn's height, towering over me.

'UNIDENTIFIED FLYING OBJECT'

Michael Pitel, my friend who tried to rent the Irish Opel (page 240) told me how in 1952 he was flying his RAF Vampire 30,000 feet above Kent. Suddenly a huge light filled his windscreen and he desperately dived, avoiding something which roared past above him at enormous speed. Buffeted by the turbulence, he and his wingman landed shaken (and shaking) to report. Their controllers confirmed that their radar screens had plotted something big which had traversed England from Dover to Cardiff in just four minutes, about 4,500 miles an hour.

As the Vampires, together with all contemporary jet fighters, could manage under 600 mph, they all had no difficulty filing another 'Unidentified Flying Object' report.

ANTHROPOMORPHY

Barry Skrine was an Art Director friend at Benson's Advertising who told me of his adventures with Baron Beck, who made a fortune from Molyslip, a lubricant additive for car engines. Beck was a real, extraordinary eccentric. He had a menagerie of pets that he called by their generic names. Thus 'Dog', 'Cat', 'Canary', 'Mongoose' and so on.

'Bear' did not last very long because, when he grew bigger, he suddenly attacked the Baron who had to stand on the kitchen table and shoot poor 'Bear' with a rifle.

Baroness Beck once asked Barry Skrine to accompany her to the bedroom, whereupon she opened up the front of her dress and said, 'I don't believe you have met 'Rat''. Faced by a little furry head with whiskers emerging from her bosom, Barry beat a hasty retreat.

Any public relations exercise is at risk of something going wrong. We had been asked by the sherry industry to support an exhibition that they were planning at Reed House, in Piccadilly. We expanded this into a whole month of activities, which we called 'Sherry Month October'. The opening ceremony was to start with a parade down Piccadilly of horse-drawn carriages containing Jerez leaders such as José Ignacio Domecq, to be greeted by the Duke of Wellington, because he had extensive interests in Jerez.

We had also hit on the idea of creating an escort of beautiful young debutantes to ride in the parade, side-saddle, dressed in those splendid frilly dresses that they wear in Seville and Jerez at Feria time.

We had hired the girls' horses from the riding school behind St George's Hospital (now the Lanesborough Hotel) and had taken the precaution of meeting with the police with the express purpose of ensuring that our parade did not encounter the Household Cavalry in the middle of Hyde Park Corner. Indeed, a case of whisky had changed hands to ensure the smooth management of traffic.

In the event, of course, our fears were realised. The two equestrian groups *did* meet and the horse at the back of our column reared and dumped one of our poor Spanish girls ignominiously on to the road. She staggered to her feet and watched helplessly as her colleagues trotted into the distance.

Suddenly a motorcycle messenger skidded to a halt. 'I think you've lost your friends luv, ain't you. Hop on'.

The girl jumped on the back of his motorbike, which then roared at about 100 miles per hour up Piccadilly to the head of the column. It drew alongside the elegant carriage containing a startled José Ignacio Domecq. 'You lost one of your girls, mate,' said the messenger and helped her into the carriage.

The resulting television and press pictures of the Duke of Wellington greeting his Spanish guests was somewhat marred by the shaken girl puffing desperately at a cigarette to calm her shattered nerves. I am sure the bike ride was much more frightening than falling off the horse.

CAIRO CAPERS

All in all, Egypt is rather a nice place and Egyptians are fun people. This did not make it any less intimidating for me the first time I arrived there, especially when a little man babbled at me, grabbed my passport and disappeared into the crowd. I hoped he really *was* my official guide and not a man in the passport-selling business.

British American Tobacco asked our agency to go to Cairo to help their Du Maurier cigarette brand. Simply arriving could be traumatic. Once you had gone through the passport routine you then drove in from the airport in a black Misr state taxi. One night our apparently mad driver took his vehicle up to 100 miles an hour and kept it there. I asked gently, 'Could you slow down please?' Then I insisted, 'Please slow down,' and finally I resorted to reaching round his neck and starting to strangle him saying, 'I really would slow down'. After this drastic action, he did.

You may think that 'over-booking' is a new phenomenon. Not at all. I think the Egyptians invented it. We had a special man, especially paid to go and make sure that our bookings at the Nile Sheraton were always in order. But, late one night we arrived and the receptionist smilingly told us, 'I am sorry, Sir. President Sadat *himself* has booked 40 rooms for some distinguished VIP guests and I am afraid I am going to have to send you back to the Sheraton Heliopolis next to the airport.'

We rang our Public Relations lady in Cairo, Amina Fahmy, who turned up and asked for the Assistant Manager. He was all charm and smiles and apologised for this unexpected development. Over the coffee he had offered us, Amina was equally charming and said, 'Of course, my clients are happy to go back to Heliopolis. But if I may ask you, could you please get your secretary to type out a letter stating that President Sadat has *personally* reserved these rooms, so that I can have it officially in writing?'

There was just a fractional pause before the Assistant Manager turned to me and said, 'Your usual suite, Mr O'Brien?'

Ten minutes later, we saw 40 rather miserable American tourists being loaded on to a bus going back to Heliopolis.

We created a rather eccentric project called 'The Du Maurier Center'. It was destined to fund such soft sponsorships as a short story competition in the daily *Al Ahram* and the re-signposting of Cairo's Zoo (negotiating in bad Spanish with a Cairo sign manufacturer was one of the stranger things I have had to do). We also sponsored a pigeon shoot, which is like clay shooting but with live

Cairo Zoo sign system, all designed in Covent Garden.

I watch with Amina Fahmy the rather strange competition we have created.

pigeons. The few that were missed as they left their baskets, trustingly circled back to their loft to be used again. This 'sporting event' was aided by Hassan Marei, President Sadat's very nice son-in-law. As Mrs Sadat was Egypt's leading anti-smoking crusader, this may have caused some family problems.

At the end of about five days of Cairo business negotiations, you suddenly wished to leave. One morning, Amina's car came to take us to the airport. Normally, when a chauffeur comes to collect you, you don't often ask, 'Have you got enough petrol?' You sort of assume he has. Wrong. In the middle of a teeming suburb, we sputtered to a halt and our driver disappeared into the crowd, which milled around our hot little car. He eventually returned with a huge fruit tin with petrol slopping all over his clothes. We reached the airport very late and fought our way through the shouting crowds and arrived at our VC10 to be offered champagne by the smiling hostess.

There used to be an excellent Foote, Cone and Belding commercial for British Airways featuring a man eating sheep's eyes at an Arabic business dinner, then bumping across a desert in an ancient cab and finally reaching the safety and calm of a British Airways VC10. I still think that was the best commercial ever for British Airways. Every trip to Cairo reinforced that belief.

One of our clients at BAT was Alan Searle, and he told us a story about his somewhat eccentric father, a Professor well known for his leading edge inventions.

BOFFIN WAVES

One day Professor Searle invited some very top brass from the armed forces down to his house in the country. Staff cars disgorged a bevy of Air Marshals, Generals and Admirals. After coffee in his drawing room, they were invited to climb the stairs and then up into his attic, which was filled with a huge model railway. The distinguished officers started looking at their watches saying, 'Look, Professor we really are rather busy and while we all like model railways, we do have jobs to get back to'.

'No, no. Please bear with me'. He then put on an old motor cycle crash helmet with wires trailing down under the railway layout. He looked at his guests and said, 'I am now going to move the freight train out of that siding.' Sure enough the train slowly moved out of the siding. 'I am now going to get that passenger train to leave the station.' The passenger train left the station.

The officers were amazed, as he was plainly not using his hands in any way. It transpired that he had rigged the inside of the helmet with sensors able to pick up the Alpha Waves emitted by the brain through the skull, capable of being translated into commands.

The house was put under an immediate security blanket, because what Professor Searle had managed to achieve was the harnessing of thought processes to execute commands. Especially in air combat, the saving of fractions of seconds to enable a pilot to arm and fire a missile by thought process alone might be invaluable – the difference between life and death.

I never discovered whether Professor Searle's invention was actually incorporated into modern combat systems. I think I was mostly intrigued by the thought of a fighter pilot landing his jet and thinking to himself 'Blast that bloody Squadron Leader' and two Sidewinder missiles immediately leaving his plane to smash into the Officers Mess.

DESERT SKYJACK

Thinking of Arabia reminds me of the horrific experience of Roland Wells' brother-in-law from his first marriage. Trevor Cooper was a BOAC pilot. He was unfortunate to be involved in the sky-jacking of four aircraft to Dawson Field, the lonely desert airstrip in Jordan in the terrorist attempt to get Leila Khaled released.

While he was adjusting some equipment on the stranded VC10 the terrorists became convinced that Trevor was trying to signal. He was bundled into a jeep, taken half a mile away and forced to dig his own grave. Threatened again and again with execution, his captors eventually gave up and drove him back to the plane.

A day later they blew up all four planes with spectacular pictures, which went all over the world. For years Trevor was affected and suffered from appalling dreams. Hardly surprising.

FISHY BUSINESS

Anthony Masterton-Smith was a fanatical fisherman, and fishing is the biggest participant sport in the world and certainly in Britain where there are said to be six million anglers.

Anthony thought up the idea of an International Angling Fair to be held at the National Exhibition Centre outside Birmingham. Unfortunately, 1976 had one of the hottest and driest summers in Britain's history. The rivers and canals dried up, and the local authorities were so worried about the build up of algae and weeds that they poured chemicals into the few waterways that did have any water, thus killing off most of the fish. The result was an angling fraternity that had seen its sport virtually killed off with the fish and any potential sponsors were suddenly very much on the defensive. My PR company had paid a deposit of £30,000 to the National Exhibition Centre which was non-refundable. We had to cancel the fair, and this sad non-event joins the roll-call of my 'Commercial Cock-ups'.

From the age of about 20, my younger sister Geraldine started to suffer from inexplicable and persistent mental problems, which were to affect her all her life. (Once you get involved, you realise that one in eight people and one in five families are affected by mental conditions). After years of turmoil for her and everyone who cared for her in London, she married a kind and patient Norwegian, Rolf, and moved to Bergen and had a beautiful daughter, Astri.

We used to visit them in Bergen, which must be one of the most unsuitable places on earth to live if you get easily depressed. Its mountains ensure it has an extra ration of snow or sleet in winter and rain in summer. On these visits, however, I was always cheered up by one of its landmarks, a large timber house on the harbour with a tourism plaque commemorating a moment in its history.

Many years ago, a rich merchant had, in old age, became increasingly annoyed by his huge family plainly waiting for him to die so they could grab his fortune. So he secretly sawed half way through all the wooden joists of his house and then instructed that, in order to inherit, the whole family must attend the reading of his will after his death. When about 150 of them had crowded in, the house duly collapsed, killing many of them. I am sorry for the lawyer – or maybe I'm not!

Someone told me that on Mondays there was jazz with Max Collie playing at the Six Bells pub in Chelsea. As I walked in, there was Maureen, my jiving partner of the fifties, and amazingly we were just as good at it as ever.

Maureen revealed that the 100 Club was still operating and so the next week off we went to return to the world that I thought had long passed.

The very first jazz records I ever had back at Stowe were Ken Colyer's 'Going Home' and 'Back to the Delta'. Ken, a merchant seaman, had spent years getting to New Orleans and ended up producing the best disciplined traditional jazz band in Britain with

BERGEN'S BEST

Geraldine

BACK TO THE DELTA

Max Collie

249

musicians later to overshadow him, Chris Barber, Monty Sunshine and Lonnie Donegan.

Ever since I have been going down to the 100 Club with 'Mad' Maureen, one real regret persists. Once a week my hero Ken (whose brother Bill 'Bilko' Colyer is a good friend) would come off the stand and have a drink at the bar.

Every week I thought 'I'm going to buy him a drink and tell him how he fired my enthusiasm'. Every week for some reason I held back. And one day he wasn't there, fighting terminal cancer abroad.

So I never had a drink with my jazz hero.

HERE THEY COME TED, IT'S THEM CAKEWALKIN' BABIES FROM HOME...

Ken Colyer

IRISH LIFE

Irish Life Assurance is one of the biggest financial institutions in Ireland and a pillar of the financial community. One year we were handling a major press conference at the 'Inn on the Park' in London for financial journalists and insurance brokers. I happened to tell Bob Willis, the Chairman, what I thought was quite an amusing Irish joke just before he got up to make his speech. This was drawing to a close when he said, 'At the conclusion of my speech we will be serving you with drinks and lunch. And talking of service, I would just like to share with you something amusing that Donough O'Brien has just told me.' I nearly died because I knew what was coming.

'There was an old widow living in the West of Ireland and she had a cow, but no bull to service it so that she could have a calf. 'Don't worry Mary,' said her neighbour, 'You just call the Department of Agriculture and they will send somebody down to do something called artificial insemination.'

A smart young man duly arrived from Limerick in a car and

with a brief case. The widow took him down to the barn and pointed at the cow.

'There's Daisy, all ready for you. There's soap and a bowl of hot water for you to wash your hands. And there's a nail on the back of the door for you to hang your trousers.'

After the laughter had died down, 300 faces turned to stare at me, clearly feeling that this was a rather strange story to tell the head of Ireland's leading financial institution at such a prestigious occasion.

Trying to be an advertising 'suit'

BLUE REVUE

Just before the 1975 Conservative Party conference I was rung up by Zara Tait, the most glamorous of my Hammersmith political colleagues. 'We need you for the *Blue Revue*'. This was the travelling fund-raising cabaret that she and Sally Neubert, wife of the Tory MP for Romford, Michael Neubert, had created in 1967 to 'cheer up the Party after the 1966 defeat'. Zara brushed aside my complete lack of acting or singing talent. 'You'll be fine, it's easy'. So I found myself with this zany gang trying to rehearse in a Blackpool boarding house with paper-thin walls.

In fact, my nervous debut was something of a success. One of the more embarrassing parts of the show was when I was brought on stage on a trolley as a piece of furniture, a 'magnificent tallboy', dressed only in bathing trunks. (In the auction, Reggie Maudling's wife bought me). This moment was shared with millions, as it was chosen by BBC television as the lead-in to the conference.

The most popular sketch was when I was a naive canvasser, with Elisabeth Whittaker acting all the people I visit.

Christine Boyes (pianist), me, Elisabeth Whittaker and Sally Neubert

Zara (left) and Sally blew Maggie Thatcher off the front pages

Entry-phone voice, 'What is it?'
Canvasser, 'We're having an election.' Pause, 'Don't be **disgusting**!'

'Miss, eh, Report?' Rapport, cherie, Rapport'. 'I'm canvassing on behalf of John Smith'. 'Cherie, John **always** has our support. He likes **all** ze girls. He **comes** on Mondays, zat's why we call it ze Monday Club! Why don't **you** come in and meet ze girls. You look like a big, strong boy'. (We changed the Member's name for each constituency we visited.)

It was great fun and I stayed with them for two years until work pressure (or better actors?) caused my replacement.

DAILY EXPRESS

Wednesday October 8 1975　　Weather: Sunny spells　　Price 6p

Out of the blue! Saucy girls come to the aid of the party

Express Staff Reporter

BEYOND the fringe of the Tory conference in Blackpool this week the body politic is helping to boost the party's ailing finances.

Mrs. Neubert with a true-blue lollipop

Baby batterer walks free

Margaret Thatcher loved the show which not only lifted the mood of the conferences but raised money for the constituencies that clamoured for it. The team never missed a show either with illness, or even, twice, bereavement. Michael Neubert points out, 'It really was quite testing to create a new show in 8 weeks, which was good enough for a Prime Minister – and with amateur talent.' In 1987, after twenty hilarious years, Sally and Zara packed it in, to the immense regret of a grateful Tory party.

PIONEERING PEER

'Bubbles' Hesketh and his winner, James Hunt

James, World Champion, 1976

In 1974, Wells O'Brien moved to 43 Conduit Street, sharing a building with David Hicks, the interior designer. This was at the behest of an old Irish Guards friend of mine, Billy Guinness, who introduced us to Lord Hesketh, who was involved in the business in some mysterious way.

Alexander Hesketh had decided to use his own money to create Hesketh Racing, a brave attempt to become a force in Grand Prix racing. His driver was the dashing and talented but rather inexperienced James Hunt, at the time known as 'Hunt the Shunt', for obvious reasons, but later to become World Champion.

We had fun creating a cuddly bear symbol for Hesketh Racing which then became a very useful merchandising tool, appearing on everything from T-shirts to bumper stickers. We later made a joint attempt to sell it as an advertising property to Firestone, who at the time were suppliers of tyres to several motor racing teams. We hoped to get a large account out of it and Alexander hoped to get sponsorship for his team. Unfortunately, on the day of our presentation to the main board, we opened our morning newspapers to read the news: "Firestone pulls out of Grand Prix racing". We went ahead with the presentation, but only because it was too late to pull out. I think that was one of the real low points of my advertising career.

Alexander's mother, the Dowager Lady Hesketh, was a splendid woman with a black eye patch which gave her a faintly piratical air. She was full of amusing anecdotes, and I remember her telling me that when Alexander was living in the United States, he got the butler to ring him from England to give him a wake-up call. When I said that that was a bit of an extravagance, she laughed and said, 'No, Alexander never actually picks up the phone, so we never had to pay.'

My father gradually deteriorated after his heart attack and died, sadly, but peacefully on 9th January 1979.

Apart from sadness, my immediate emotion was a sudden hatred of the Transport and General Workers Union. They were carrying out a tanker drivers' strike at the time, which meant all the garages were short of fuel and had to ration it. I was leaving for the theatre when Leo came on the line to tell me of Toby's death. I did not have enough fuel in my car to get down to his death bed and had to waste precious minutes borrowing cans of petrol from my partners. This was a very personal experience of the 'Winter of Discontent' which Jim Callaghan ignored to his peril. 'What crisis?' he foolishly remarked, and gave Margaret Thatcher her chance to change Britain for ever.

While the trade union movement played a valiant and vital role early on, having lived through its dominance I have never much liked its excesses. Advertising suffered from the ACTT's bullying in TV commercials production and the artwork feud between the NGA and NATSOPA. Anybody with memories of the 60's and 70's until Margaret Thatcher broke the power of the unions will recall the kind of misery they could impose on others. But I will always remember that particular union for that particular incident.

Toby's funeral started very sadly but later became something of an Irish wake. The change of mood was helped by a letter I had received that very morning from the manager of his bank where he had been for 30 years, which I read out to the mourners:

James Callaghan, 'What crisis?'

> I am sorry to read in *The Telegraph* this morning of the death of your father. I had always appreciated his skill in the field of Public Relations, but I was very intrigued by the Obituary; he must have been a very interesting father for you.
>
> Unfortunately, as you know, he died indebted to us to the extent (on today's balance) of £13,455.56. We shall be calling on the estate for repayment of the indebtedness.

Norman Collins officiated at his Memorial Service at which 700 people attended. Anthony Montague-Browne sent this charming and heartfelt tribute to *The Times*:

'He never failed to sharpen a dull dog

Nor help a lame one over a stile.'

ascination with the success and dynamics of American business had been fuelled by my years at Hill & Knowlton and Lippincott & Margulies. At Wells O'Brien we also attracted a variety of American clients, including Intercontinental Hotels, Hershey chocolate, musical instrument makers like Gibson Guitars, Moog synthesisers and Lowrey electronic organs, and Union Carbide Agricultural Chemicals.

It was at a Union Carbide meeting in Jacksonville, Florida that I thought up the Euro Center concept. Chatting to seven of the executives of their Atlanta advertising agency, it transpired that only three of them had ever been abroad.

Checks with the State Department revealed that only 1.48% of US citizens had valid passports (compared with 28% in Britain). Of course, Americans have every kind of tourism in their country plus they do not need passports to go to Canada, Mexico, and the Caribbean. Nevertheless, it meant that only a tiny number of business people had overseas experience. While markets in the US are huge, American business was having to export much more vigorously. So I devised a linked network of smaller PR, advertising and design firms to help what we called the 'new exporter'.

THE NEW EXPORTER

I needed an office in New York and, above all, a partner. Someone told me that a young man called Chris Spring had been looking for a job there. I tracked him down to the Frankfurt offices of Compton Advertising where he was running the British Leyland car account for Germany. We met in London, liked each other and he agreed to go to New York.

SPRING IN THE BANK

New York City was rather a poor place for a single woman and thus a rather good place for a single man. Available women out-numbered heterosexual men by about four to one. This could lead to some desperation on the part of the girls and an abrupt directness. In the month after he arrived in Manhattan, Chris, who was attractive and amusing, was standing in line in our bank talking to a colleague. A girl in front of him suddenly spun round and asked, 'Are you British?'

'Yes', said Chris.

A few seconds later she spun round again and said, 'Are you here on vacation or do you live here?'

'I live and work here', said Chris.

She faced her front again. Only a few seconds later, she spun and said, 'Are you married?'

'No I'm not.' said Chris.

'So what are you doing tonight?' the girl said.

Having escaped the bank queue, Chris found that he could not even retreat to the office safely. A rather attractive girl had sold him a new photo-copier and had supervised its installation. Chris looked up and she was hanging around his doorway, leaning against the wall. 'Hi,' he said, 'Everything OK?'

Chris Spring and I at the Euro Center launch

'Well yes, but Chris I would have thought I'd made it pretty obvious how I felt about you, so I just wondered why you hadn't asked me out yet.' As you can imagine, Chris never came back from New York.

THE PROBLEMS OF LANGUAGE

One of the early revelations was quite how poor Americans are at speaking foreign languages. A country built on a hundred nationalities had deliberately turned its back on their languages over the decades so its citizens would become 'more American'. Faced by linguistic problems one client even said, 'Why can't the Belgians just speak Belgian?'

One executive from the advertising agency William Esty, with whom we were working on MasterCard Travellers Cheques, seriously thought all foreign bank clerks spoke enough English to understand the complex instructions for cashing cheques. After a heated argument, I said, 'Look, if I gave you two contractual letters, one in Flemish and one in Portuguese, gave you a minute to study them and asked you to sign, would you?' Reluctantly conceding, he agreed to let us translate the MasterCard material into the 22 languages required.

But it is not just the Americans that find foreign languages a burden. Europeans can be just as bad. If you go to Seville in Southern Spain, you can still see the tobacco factory on which Bizet based his opera 'Carmen'. Every time I hear the word 'Carmen', I smile because of this bizarre translation which *Playboy* reprinted in 1970:

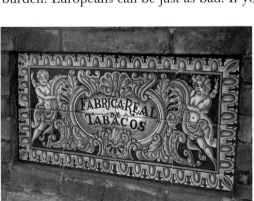

The old Royal tobacco factory, Seville

For opera lovers and opera haters alike, we reprint herewith the 'English' synopsis of Carmen, as it appeared in the program for a recent performance in Genoa, Italy. Doubters should leave the auditorium; we have seen it with our own eyes.

Act 1.   Carmen is a cigar-makeress from a Tobago factory who loves with Don Jose of the mounting guard. Carmen takes, a flower from her corsets and lances it to Don Jose (Duet: 'Talk me of my mother'). There is a noise inside the tabago factory and the revolting cigar-makeresses burst into the stage. Carmen is arrested and Don Jose is ordered to mounting guard her but Carmen subduces him and he lets her escape.

Act 2.   The Tavern. Carmen, Frasquito, Mercedes, Zuniga, Morales,. Carmen's aria ('The sistrums are tinkling'). Enter Escamillio, a balls-fighter. Enter two smuglers (Duet: 'We have in mind a business') but Carmen refuses to penetrate because Don Jose has liberated her from prison. He just now arrives (Aria: 'Slop, here who comes!') but hear are the bugles singing his retreat. Don Jose will leave and draws his sword. Called by Carmen shrieks the two smuglers interfere with her but Don Jose is bound to dessert, he will follow into them (final chorus: 'Opening sky wandering life').

Act 3.   A roky landscape, the smuglers shelter. Carmen sees her death in cards and Don Jose makes a date with Carmen for the next balls fight.

Act 4.   A place in Seville. Procession of balls-fighters, the roaring of the balls is heard in the arena. Escamillio enters(aria and chorus: 'Toreador, toreador, All hail the balls of a Toreador'). Enter Don Jose (Aria: 'I do not threaten, I besooch you') but Carmen repels him wants to join with Escamillio now chaired by the crowd. Don Jose stabbs her (Aria: 'Oh rupture, rupture, you may arrest me, I did kill her') he sings 'Oh my beautiful Carmen, my subductive Carmen'.

How can such oddities occur – amusing as they are? Why do organisations rely on translation by non-English people, plainly working from dictionaries?

The Japanese used to be hilarious in their instruction manuals for cars and motorbikes but now do them very well, so that it is usually difficult to recall the real gems.

However, I discovered a real linguistic treasure-trove in a collection of old Japanese model tank kits, which suit the scale of my model railway. My son Edmond and I have even bought kits we do not need, just to read these wonderful explanations and instructions.

First a look at their attempts at historical perspective:

'Crazy Hitler got his administrative power, their efforts had been already reached to the goal line of its production.'

'Adolf Hitler who trusted too force of the invincible armoured division, took aim at U.S.S.R, the communistic country, which had the vast territory.'

'Although it was obvious that the Soviet Russia had the newest tanks, the military force was enigmatic at all, so to attack.'

Then they extol the uses of the famous 88 mm gun:

'This 88mm gun showed its tremendous power toward the sky and also on the ground too. It crushed British tanks before they reached to their shooting range, by taking the best possible advantage of its long gun barrel, paralleled to the ground, where was no obstacle there at sight.'

Other vehicles seem to have achieved almost human attributes:

'The transport truck thought much of its mobility, so that it could move at any place battle fields, was decided that the half truck was suitable for the porpose.'

'The scene of this 8 ton truck marching, with many soldiers ridden, looks like to show off the overwhelming power of the German mechanized Corps at that time.'

'The body had the shell refusing slope in big incline to improve the shell proofness.'

We know the Japanese have difficulty pronouncing their r's – but writing them, surely not?

'Why don't you make DIOLAMA and take its picture?'

In the tourism industry the list of silly and absolutely genuine translations is endless.

'Leave your values in reception.'

'You are invited to take advantage of the chambermaid.'

'Visitors are expected to complain at the office between the hours of 9 and 11 a.m. daily.'

'The flattening of underwear with pleasure is the job of the chambermaid.'

'Our wines leave you nothing to hope for.'

'Teeth extracted by the latest methodists.'

'Ladies, leave your clothes here and spend the afternoon having a good time.'

'It is expressly forbidden to be run over by the sports trains.'

'All snow must be left at the station of depart: sports-passengers must not melt in the cars.'

After visiting Monet's garden at Giverney, Liz and I paused at a little town nearby. The tourist brochure raved on, giving real personality to inanimate objects:

'The river appears to have lost itself and is wandering aimlessly through the valley.'

and an unintended human dimension.

'The town is full of charming crooks and nannies.'

Foreigners should be forgiven for making mistakes with the convoluted spelling and pronunciation of English. Someone years ago in NATO produced a tongue-twisting test (below). Try reading it out fast. Most English people can't get further than three verses before stumbling. Pity the foreigner. After trying, a Frenchman said he'd prefer six months hard labour than reading six lines aloud!

English Is Tough Stuff

Dearest creature in creation,
Study English pronunciation.
I will teach you in my verse
Sounds like corpse, corps, hearse, and worse.
I will keep you, Suzy, busy
Make your head with heat grow dizzy.
Tear in eye, your dress will tear.
So shall I! Oh hear my prayer.

Just compare heart, beard, and heard,
Dies and diet, lord and word,
Sword and sward, retain and Britain.
 (Mind the latter, how it's written.)
Now I surely will not plague you
With such words as plaque and ague.
But be careful how you speak:
Say break and steak, but bleak and streak;
Cloven, oven, how and low,
Script, receipt, show, poem, and toe.

Hear me say, devoid of trickery,
Daughter, laughter, and Terpsichore,
Typhoid, measles, topsails, aisles,
Exiles, similes, and reviles,
Scholar, vicar, and cigar,
Solar, mica, war and far,
One, anemone, Balmoral,
Kitchen, lichen, laundry, laurel,
Gertrude, German, wind and mind,
Scene, Melpomene, mankind.

Billet does not rhyme with ballet,
Bouquet, wallet, mallet, chalet.
Blood and flood are not like food,
Nor is mould like should and would.
Viscous, viscount, load and broad,
Toward, to forward, to reward.
And your pronunciation's OK
When you correctly say croquet,
Rounded, wounded, grieve and sieve,
Friend and fiend, alive and live,
Ivy, privy, famous, clamour,
And enamour rhyme with hammer,
River, rival, tomb, bomb, comb,
Doll and roll and some and home.

(etc, for 2 pages!)

Pronunciation - think of Psyche!
Is a paling stout and spikey?
Won't it make you lose your wits.
Writing groats and saying grits?
It's a dark abyss or tunnel,
Strewn with stones, stowed, solace, gunwale,
Islington and Isle of Wight,
Housewife, verdict and indict.

Finally, which rhymes with enough –
Though, through, plough or dough, or cough?
Hiccough has the sound of cup.
My advice is to give up!!!

Gotham is a village near Nottingham in England. When King John sought to visit the place in 1210 on a Royal Progress with a view to creating a hunting lodge, the villagers realised they would be financially burdened by this 'honour'. So, when the King's advance party arrived to inspect the village, everyone acted as if they were mad and the King's plans were changed to avoid 'infection', making Gotham the epitome of madness. But those they had duped were, perhaps, even more stupid.

'We ween there are more fools pass through Gotham than remain in it.'

The English nursery rhyme goes:

> 'Three wise men of Gotham
> Went to sea in a bowl
> If the bowl had been stronger
> My story'd be longer!'

This early tax evasion success brings us to the American connection. By 1800 New York City had achieved its own level of madness as far as its detractors were concerned and the name of Gotham was given to the city by Washington Irving in his book *Salmagundi* in 1807.

Moreover, the original English village achieved brief notoriety in 1992 because both US Presidential contenders, George Bush and Bill Clinton, could claim ancestry to Gotham.

Nowadays, 'Gotham City' is enshrined in the Batman comic strips as the archetypal, out of control, metropolis.

Modern New York City is still an incredible and marvellous place, for all its hassle, crime and tensions. Canyons of huge buildings bursting with people and money.

So, one of the more exciting projects to come out of our Euro Center venture was to promote the city. Three bodies, the New York Chamber of Commerce and Industry, the New York City Partnership and the State of New York had combined to create an industrial development campaign called 'Make it in New York City'. Most of their efforts had hitherto been devoted to preventing *existing* manufacturers from leaving the city and they had paid little attention to attracting overseas companies. My colleague David McDonough had dropped in on them at exactly the right time and we managed to land the assignment for Britain, Germany and Japan.

New York had participated in an exhibition in Zurich called 'Invest in America's Cities'. What struck

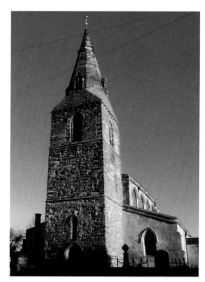

Gotham Church

us is that they all looked the same. Same smiling Mayor saying he was business-friendly, same low costs, same friendly black and white workers.

We realised we had to differentiate New York from its competitors and what really mattered was the spending power within a day's delivery time. So we coined the phrase: MAKE IT WHERE THE MARKET IS.

David Rockefeller at No 10 Downing Street

John Lindsay (right) and Walter Heithaus, in a Chester pub, showing solidarity with the British in the Falklands War

It was decided to take investment missions to Britain and Germany led by David Rockefeller, Chairman of the New York City Partnership and of Chase Manhattan Bank. He was supported by some major players from the city like Larry Tisch and also the former Mayor, John Lindsay.

The first mission was quite a success except for a marked lack of co-ordination between the speakers. David Rockefeller, in particular, did not accept our draft for his keynote speech at lunchtime. After the opening ceremony, we had spirited him away from the main conference for a meeting with Mrs Thatcher (quite an achievement as it was the first day of the Falklands War). So, when he announced that he thought his audience 'would be surprised that there were half a million manufacturing jobs in New York City in 20,000 enterprises', his audience really wasn't that surprised because four speakers had already laboriously mentioned this fact!

John Lindsay, by contrast, was a much more subtle operator. He was to lead the mission after London and his speeches in Chester, Frankfurt and Düsseldorf were tailored and personalised to the audiences he addressed. As a result, he was a great success and very popular both with those audiences and with the other members of the mission. In fact he was probably too nice, especially when he was Mayor of the city. One of our group said that as Mayor he had been hopeless at negotiating. The Police Federation once came in to demand a pay hike. He actually gave them more than they were asking for.

As he once confided in me, 'I discovered that being Mayor of New York was a bit like being a bitch on heat. If you stand still you get screwed, and if you move you get bitten in the ass!'

The missions were so successful that we repeated them a year later, this time under Lindsay's exclusive leadership. There were two interesting incidents. The first was in Frankfurt. We had devised a multi-media slide show whereby Lindsay had described the life, both commercial and personal, of someone living and working in the five boroughs of New York. We had simulated him driving from home in Staten Island into Manhattan and then out to his plant in Queens and so on.

At the end of all the American speakers we had a couple of German accountants to describe the tax situation. They had no audio-visual aids and they both spoke for twenty-five minutes instead of the ten minutes that had been allocated to them. I was sitting behind the curtain with the projectors in despair, assuming the audience would be bored rigid. I sneaked a look through the curtains and found the German audience scribbling notes, happy as anything. My suspicions that different audiences wanted different things were confirmed when we sent out a questionnaire about the speakers and speeches. The most telling remark was that 'Mayor Lindsay was very charming and amusing, *aber nicht seriös.*

An advertisement I wrote to attract people to the New York presentations

Another more bizarre incident occurred in London. Our executive leader General Joe Healey had suddenly left the team because of a family illness and we were now under the control of a very pushy girl of about twenty-six. We were due to inaugurate the Inter-Continental Hotel's video conferencing facilities between London and New York as part of our presen-tations, with Mayor Koch in New York conducting a debate with John Lindsay in London. We thought it a good idea to have some of our potential investors ask questions of the Mayor's group in New York and we chose four. My secretary whispered, 'Number three is rather small.'

At first I did not understand until the gentleman came up to me. He was indeed very small, in fact a dwarf of about 3 foot 5 ins. 'I *did* tell them I was a bit short', he grinned. Nevertheless, he was a serious potential investor, so I set about building a ramp so that he could get up on to the stage. We then realised that he would disappear from the camera's view behind the lectern (rather like our Queen once did in America) so I explained the problem to our lady client, who said impatiently in an extremely loud voice: **'Lose the dwarf, Donough'**.

Hoping no one had heard, I got into a furious whispering argument with her and finally persuaded her to lean over to address our small investor when he was on camera. We got away with it, but it was one of those dodgy moments.

Our efforts got about 200 foreign companies interested in investing in New York City. Naturally that was the moment when Ed Koch decided to close the department down and withdraw the funding. It's one of a series of incidents in my commercial life when just as everything is going really well, the client shoots himself carefully and accurately in the foot.

CHOCOLATE TOWN

The ultimate company town must be Hershey, Pennsylvania. Main street is Chocolate Avenue and the social centre, the Cocoa Inn. When US troops gave the kids of Europe Hershey bars in World War II, it was a symbol of a bountiful America.

Over-sweet, over-weight and over here

For Hershey Foods, we ran a series of meetings for the financial community of which one of the triumphs was getting Claridges to serve a three course meal in exactly 35 minutes (*that* was the largest tip I ever gave to a head waiter).

We sent a questionnaire to the people who attended and I was amused to read: 'We liked the President, Bill Dearden. We liked the presentations and we liked the company. But the chocolate they gave us as a gift, I could not eat. Neither could my girlfriend and, amazingly, neither could her dog.'

Another lesson of how tastes vary either side of the Atlantic.

THE SHADOW OF BHOPAL

We used to visit Union Carbide's headquarters in Park Avenue to discuss our agricultural chemical advertising and design work in Europe. We were also asked to show our work which helped to save the British asbestos industry to their corporate affairs team. In passing, I pointed out that Union Carbide, even with sales of $9 billion, was a virtually unknown company, especially abroad, although it had strong brands such as Ever Ready batteries. I asked them why they did not do more to build up the prestige and image values of the overall company. They insisted that the brands spoke for themselves and there was no need to promote the company at all.

'Ah, but what would happen if, say, you ever suffered a bad accident? You could have an explosion like the one that destroyed the ICI chemical plant at Flixborough in 1974 and killed many people. But ICI's corporate image was so strong that it was not affected by the disaster'. The Union Carbide people scoffed at my ideas and I dropped the subject.

A year later, in December 1984, a disgruntled employee sabotaged the chemical plant partly owned by Union Carbide at Bhopal in India, killing 2,500 and injuring hundreds of thousands. In spite of the fact that it was a minority

262

shareholding, that no Americans had been allowed to work at the plant for years and that Union Carbide had repeatedly told the local community not to let any inhabitants near the plant, the company's name was blackened forever. If it had built a strong image as a responsible company, it might have been given the benefit of the doubt. In the event, Union Carbide's lack of corporate image has meant that the world will always associate the name with a terrible disaster which was not its fault. It is now a shadow of its former self.

In 1641 a Spanish ship, the *Concepción*, loaded with two year's vital output from the mines of Mexico of silver to pay the Spanish army, struck a coral reef off Hispaniola, in what is now the Dominican Republic.

In 1978 a fanatical marine treasure hunter from Pennsylvania called Burt Webber realized his life-long dream and managed to find the wreck and brought 60,000 coins to the surface. His company then hired Chris Spring in New York and me in London to realise the maximum value for them. I slogged round the coin departments of Christie's, Spinks, Sotheby's and so on and it soon appeared that only a few were really valuable and the crude pieces-of-eight 'cob' coins were only worth a fraction of what Webber thought they were. This was unfortunate, especially as he then decided not to pay our fees.

But he had forgotten that he had provided us with a box of 1,500 of these coins to show around London and we had prudently deposited these in our bank in Covent Garden (quite a heavy box by the way). We got paid.

There was an interesting episode while visiting this client. Chris and I arrived at Chicago's O'Hare airport and got into a Checker cab to go downtown to the Loop. Our driver turned out to be an Iranian new to the freedoms of the United States. This was at the time of the hostage crisis when fifty-two Americans had been captured in its Embassy in Teheran and America's trees, lamp-posts and houses were festooned with symbolic yellow ribbons, while President Carter figured out how to get his countrymen out.

Our driver ranted on about how the 'great Satan' was the evil one and that the Ayatollah Khomeini was absolutely right. This went on for half an hour and when we got to the Loop and I paid him off, I said, 'Look, we are British. Perhaps we don't care quite as much about those poor hostages. But if you will take my advice, I should stop talking like that or some good citizen of Chicago will shoot you straight in the back of the head.'

He looked puzzled, muttered to himself and drove away. I wonder how long he lasted.

TREASURE TROVE

Sunken Treasure

The sea holds many treasures, but gives up few. It has given up one of its most fabulous, the sunken treasure from the Spanish galleon Concepción wrecked in 1641. The treasure coins, set in Tiffany jewelry, are now available at Tiffany. Prices range from $250. to $10,000.

TIFFANY & CO.

NEW YORK FIFTH AVENUE & 57TH STREET · ZIP: 10002 · TEL: (212) 755-8000

Red Smith

THE NEW YORK TIMES, FRIDAY, NOVEMBER 9, 1979

The Lost Treasure of the Concepción

It was noon on Nov. 25, 1978, when Burt Webber's magnetometer whined — a signal that the sensor had detected metal of some kind

of buried treasure. Inevitably, this lends excitement to "The Lost Treasure of the Concepción," a documentary film to be shown on CBS-TV

salvage license from the Dominican Republic and recruited a crew — Bob Coffey of Pennsylvania, divemaster and second in command, Harry Wel-

Phips's ship, the Henry, in the Kew Archive in Maidstone, England Webber and Haskins were in Ma stone within 48 hours.

Burt Webber searches the coral with his Magnetometer.

The Treasure of Silver Shoals

Science

Galleon sunk in 1641 is found

A^t a teen-ager in rural Pennsylvania, far from the sea, Burt Webber had visions of finding long-lost treasure in sunken ships. First he took up scuba diving; later he embarked on a long trail of treasureless sea hunts, barely supporting his growing family as a peripatetic encyclopedia salesman and brickworker. But last November Webber's ship finally came in. Blessed by coincidence and new technology, the 36-year-old adventurer located the site of a 17th century Spanish galleon, the Concepción, some 80 miles north

uary 1977. He was be tium of bankers and a divers, cartographers, electronics technicians was equipped with sop instruments in additio of maps made from ac This was not, as Webb tain Kidd operation. Inst ly academic, based on entific technology." We strike a sort of treasure however. In a contract icans, he promised the ge fifty split of any treasure fil Five months and 11 later, Webber conceded though he knew he had p right over the Concepcio his principal tool, an onbo

Webber and colleague with Chinese cup

263

Charles Childs became fascinated with the European sport of long distance bicycle racing. Inexorably we were drawn into his idea of running the equivalent of the Tour de France in America. Because the Americans were yet to become as good as they are now at this sport, it was decided that it should be an amateur race running from Montreal to Miami. There were gaps, of course, but nevertheless, it was a total distance of 1,300 miles with stages ending in major cities like New York, Boston, Washington and Miami. As we were ourselves complete amateurs at running bicycle races, I decided to co-opt Phil Liggett, who ran the Milk Race in Britain, to join our planning team. It was a vast and ambitious project involving months of negotiations with city officials, state and federal legislators, police forces and the highway patrol (we had difficulties enough just explaining that a bicycle racing downhill could exceed the 55mph speed limit in America).

We were working with a marketing company, and the account manager Rob Ingraham told me a funny story about their sponsorship efforts for the previous year's Lake Placid Winter Olympics.

He was called by the Montclair Canadian bottled water company who asked what the price was for the sponsorship for the water category.

'$50,000' responded Rob.

'Hey, you've got a lot of balls asking that kind of money.'

'So. You've got a lot of balls bottling water.' replied Rob.

Eventually, we obtained our main sponsor and briefly the race become the 'Planters Peanuts Transamerican Bicycle Race'. However, we had foolishly allowed ourselves to accept $600,000 instead of the million we had specified. We had broken the cardinal rule that your main sponsor must cover the total cost of the race – about a million dollars.

Our financial backer for our American company, a rich Saudi Arabian called Omar decided to intervene in our negotiations and flew to New York. We had a planning session and then he invited us to dine with him at the Waldorf Towers. As we walked down Fifth Avenue, he suddenly announced that he was going to invite a girl to dinner who was 'a friend of his sister and who lived here in New York'. We entered his suite and an absolutely gorgeous dark-haired girl of about 20 was introduced to us.

Sitting at dinner, one of my American colleagues turned to her and said, 'Well Daphne, how long have you been living here in the City?'

She stared at him and responded in a strong cockney accent, 'Nar, I don't live 'ere. I came over wiv Omar this afternoon on Concorde, did'n I?'

Omar shared with other of my Arabic friends the curious habit of telling 'untruths' which are going to be found out only minutes later.

In the end the problems of the bike race became insuperable and Planters Peanuts, who were part of Standard Brands refused to pay the next instalment cheque. Not only were we forced to close our little planning office in New York, but we resolved to sue them for three million dollars.

What we did not realise was that Standard Brands was about to merge with Nabisco as was described in *Barbarians at the Gate.* The last thing they wanted was a major public row with a sport which was growing very rapidly in the United States. (Greg Lemond was to win the Olympics some years later.) So in fact they paid us off quite generously and far from the venture being the commercial disaster we all actually made a small profit.

However, a sad outcome for all. It would have been much more fun to have created a major sporting event in the United States, and one which would have eventually made a great deal of money.

Some time after the demise of the Transamerican Bicycle Race, Chris Spring hopped into a cab on Fifth Avenue. Without turning round, the burly black driver said, 'Where to, Chris?' It was our friend and erstwhile partner, Charles Childs. In Britain, if you suddenly saw a former senior corporate public relations executive driving a cab, you might assume he had fallen on hard times. Not in New York. Charles was now the *owner* of six cabs. He did not normally drive them, but happened to be delivering a new one. He could not resist picking Chris up.

In New York, cabs only cost about $10,000. But 'medallions', the traded 'Right to Operate disks' then cost $60,000 each (now an amazing $240.000).

Where had Charles got the money? It was another typical New York story.

NEW YORK STYLE

Walking past a bookshop, he had noticed an excellent book *The Cotton Club.* This was about the famous Harlem night-spot, where the staff and musicians were black, the girl dancers were beautiful 'high yellas' or octaroons (one eighth black) and the audiences were exclusively white. Duke Ellington and Cab

Calloway had been made famous by the Cotton Club, and in turn had enhanced its prestige as the 1930's 'place to go' in New York.

Charles took the book, created a screenplay, sold it for $350,000 and it was turned into the Richard Gere film. So Charles got his money, his little fleet of cabs and drivers and has made lots of money ever since. He's now graduated to limousines. Typical New York.

OUT ON A LIMB

One of the most important projects that Chris Spring and I undertook were the communications aspects of a British insurance company's take-over of a company outside Washington. We knew from research that we had to reassure both the policy holders and the sales force that this British company with a strange name was going to look after their interests.

The Marketing Director of the American company was a very amusing and eccentric character whom we will call Jim. Jim was a ladies' man, in spite of being happily married to a very nice woman. One of his stratagems for getting off with girls was to associate himself with younger men (he was about fifty-five) whose presence would enhance his chances. This involved us in unexpected and therefore terrifying lapses from the truth. For example, he would call me and ask me to meet him in a smart bar attached to a Sixth Avenue hotel and a singles pick-up joint. Thinking he needed to discuss an urgent point of strategy, or review some copy I would scurry down and find Jim surrounded by three quite attractive 'thirty-something' girls.

'Ah, here's Donough O'Brien. Now, as I've told you girls, he is the leading glamour photographer in the UK.'

For the next few minutes I panicked, pretending to be a photographer and a possible source of photographic assignments (I cannot remember whether the scant knowledge picked up helping Patrick Lichfield did me any good during this conversation). Chris Spring was presented with an even more demanding alter-ego when Jim similarly introduced him as 'the Rolling Stones' manager'. 'Oh, how is Mick?' twittered one of the naive girls clustering around them.

This sort of thing led to one of the more amusing incidents during our insurance assignment.

We had to reassure the sales force about the strength and solidity of the British company. It was decided to run a sales conference for about two hundred people in Nashville, at the Opryland Hotel, a sprawling conference hotel out of town and quite close to the new 'Grand Old Opry' the world-renowned Country and Western concert hall.

Jim and Chris Spring went down to Nashville to make the arrangements. I had not believed Chris when he accurately described every single member of the hotel staff, including the cleaning ladies, to be beautiful, blonde and twenty-four. Chris went off somewhere leaving Jim chatting up the lady Maitre d' of the hotel's best restaurant, the Chateaubriand. The following morning Jim, obviously appallingly hung-over and dog tired, slumped without explanation into the taxi, remaining silent all the way to Nashville's small airport.

As they were checking in, the tannoy boomed, 'Paging Mr X, please pick up your nearest red courtesy phone.' Jim picked up the telephone and a female voice said, 'Jim, it's Mary-Lou. Why did you leave without me?'

Frantically searching his hung-over memory, he said, 'How do you mean honey?'

'Good Grief, darlin', don't you remember?' she said, 'After what we did last night, you promised me that part in Hollywood, you being a film producer an' all.'

Jim desperately made excuses about having to leave early to 'meet with Preminger' or someone, and they got out of town. However, he had a problem. They were due back in Nashville for the conference in a month and this time accompanied by wives. I was the only one privy to this background when we arrived at Nashville. We had a brief planning meeting as to how to handle the Chief Executive of the British company and we decided 'to run through the slide presentations and go to dinner and then take the British boss to dinner at the Chateaubriand'.

Jim suddenly blurted out, '**No, the coffee shop.** I really would advise the coffee shop. The food is much better.' Everyone stared at him as if he'd gone mad, with Chris and I desperately trying not to laugh. 'The coffee shop is much better,' he persisted, 'I've tried them both.'

His American boss said, 'Jim, don't be silly. It's got to be the Chateaubriand for our British owner. What do you think you're saying?'

Jim, frantic, then said, 'Oh, okay. I'll go reserve it then.' And he almost ran down the corridor to the restaurant and burst in. Luckily, his 'girlfriend' was not on duty that night and he said to the girls there, 'Please tell Mary-Lou that Jim will do anything - but please don't recognise me.'

Very kindly, she didn't. He got away with it once again.

PLANE IN THE POTOMAC

Mind you, Jim was doubly lucky ever to have met us. When we first started working with an American company we arrived to conduct an interview programme to see what the company's attitude was to their new British masters.

Jim and a sales manager called Tony grumbled to us that they could have been on the flight to Florida that afternoon, 'instead of hanging around talking to a couple of Brits.' That afternoon snow starting falling quite heavily and our hosts said that Maryland was about the worst state in the Union at clearing snow, and so everybody would have to go home postponing things until the morning.

We trudged back to our motel through the deep snow and, when we got to our rooms, Chris Spring ran in and said, 'Turn on the television, there's something terrible happening'.

The Air Florida plane which Jim and Tony had been booked on had lumbered into the air with its wings still covered in snow. Slowly losing height it hit a bridge across the Potomac River, killing several people stuck in cars in a traffic jam, and had then plunged through the ice. We watched the frantic attempts of a Parks Police helicopter and civilian helpers trying to rescue the four or five survivors who has escaped from the tail protruding through the ice.

The next evening Chris and I had to fly off down that same runway at Washington National Airport. The whole concourse was strewn with newspapers showing pictures of the crash. It was a very tense and silent take-off, especially as the de-icing trucks had come back three times to ensure our safety.

Our plane awaiting de-icing

ROCK ISLAND AND OTHER LINES

People who visit my model railway at home, and notice that it is all 1950's America, often ask me why I am interested in the railroads of the United States. The answer is that in Europe the railways were superimposed on an established society, on existing cities and villages. The main change of their coming was mostly confined to the total collapse of the stage coach system in every country in Europe (look how many coaching inns remain in Britain or Relais de la Poste in France).

By contrast, the railroads helped to build America. They were pivotal in the creation of half of America's cities and industries. They superimposed a standard time system on the continent, created the mail order industry and they gave birth to a language. So if you feel you've been *side tracked*, you are getting *steamed up* and might *blow your stack*, try some *Rock'n roll* (a nasty swaying motion of articulated steam engines of 1915).

Most people know the story of the railroads forging Westwards propelled by land grants, and sometimes by appalling financial skulduggery. But few Americans know the story of one of the key political changes created by the railroads.

In 1855 the dominant transport system in the US was provided by the two great rivers flowing South, the Mississippi and the Missouri. Steam boats ruled these waters, with the steamboat towns as key economic centres, especially for the Southern states.

It became absolutely apparent to the South that if railroads were able to go from East to West it was going to undermine one of the financial strengths of the South in the favour of the North. St Louis, Memphis and New Orleans would lose out to New York and Chicago forever.

Mississippi Senator and Secretary of War, Jefferson Davis, encouraged the steamboat men to try to ban the 'bridging of navigable rivers'.

The Chicago and Rock Island Railroad was the first to reach the Mississippi and they decided to build a bridge at Rock Island, now better known for the song.

Unfortunately, Rock Island was right opposite the archetypal steam boat town of Davenport, Iowa. The steamboat men resorted to dirty tricks. They loaded a ship called the *Effie Afton* with inflammable materials, set fire to it and floated it towards the bridge. In the event it did no serious damage, but the Mayor of Davenport was quick to demand that it was obviously dangerous to navigation and that his side of the bridge should be taken down.

First train to reach the Mississippi

The Chicago and Rock Island people hired their usual trouble-shooting lawyer, Abraham Lincoln, who fought the case all the way to the Supreme Court and won. Important men in the East noticed him and backed his political career.

Not only did this mean that the railroads went West and that the North became ever more dominant, but it is also an interesting thought that Abraham Lincoln would not have become famous except for this case and that he ended up fighting a Civil War against Jefferson Davis for the same economic reasons for which he had fought the Rock Island Bridge Case.

I chose to model the Great Northern Railway, which is one of the only transcontinental railways never to have received Government money, and was the dream child of James Jerome Hill. High in the middle of the Cascades Mountains I recently visited Skykomish, a little railroad town which looks almost exactly as it did at the turn of the century.

I stayed in a funny wooden inn that is unchanged since it was

Abraham Lincoln, at the time of the Rock Island Bridge Case, 1857

Last vestige of Rocky the Goat, the symbol of the Great Northern Railway

built in 1920. Every half an hour the diesels of huge freight trains would rumble in the mist through the town, East to Chicago or West to Seattle.

Just a little way along the line is a town which *has* changed. Indeed, it had to. In 1960 Leavenworth lost its railroad 'Division Point' status. This meant the loss of a whole lot of jobs connected with the workshops and organisation of the railroad. The little town was facing ruin.

They called in the University of Washington as consultants, who after four months came back and gave them their studied recommendations.

'You have to go Bavarian.'

The City Council must no doubt have been stupefied, with many of the people saying, 'But we were fighting those guys only a few years ago'. However, they were persuaded that the downtown area should look exactly like something in the Alps, and so it does. It is effectively a theme town. You get out of your car and you begin to hear the yodelling and Germanic music from the main square. People are all dressed in dirndls or leather shorts like a bizarre but realistic parody of Switzerland, Austria or Southern Germany.

Even the Safeway supermarket signs are in gothic lettering, as is the Chevron gas station. As far as I could see, the only person with a sense of humour about this was the owner of a sausage shop who had a sign saying: 'The Best of the Würst'. But Leavenworth, Washington, is booming and I recommend a visit if only out of curiosity.

Leavenworth's only humourist

My model railway tries to reflect all this, and it has the same kind of buildings that you would find in the Cascades. When he was sixteen, my son Murrough pointed out in a model car shop some splendid little figures of naked women lying on beds. 'You could build a brothel, Daddy.' he suggested brightly and pruriently. As luck would have it, I was building a model of a hotel that week and I duly made of the top of the establishment into a house of ill repute.

A few months later I was taking my son out from his school with his mother, Clare. During lunch I announced in this rather smart restaurant and in rather too loud a voice, 'I've built the brothel'. The restaurant went very quiet.

'We've got enough girls now,' I continued merrily. The restaurant fell completely silent. The other guests presumably had come to the conclusion that I was sucking my son into an evil family business like Big Jim Colisimo recruiting Johnny Torrio.

So when I finally said, 'So, all we need is enough customers,' it really was too late to turn round and say, 'It's alright, they are only one and a half inches tall.'

CENTRAL CASTING

The Citicorp Building

Chris Spring had a tenant in our offices in Rockefeller Plaza, a young Englishman called Rory Taggert. Rory was running a hotel guide 'A-Z' and had his finger on the pulse of what was going on in the business internationally. Rather behind with the rent, he was a bit pressed financially. He was not the only one because it became apparent that Pan American Airways was getting into serious financial trouble, and the only thing they could sell in order to raise cash was likely to be the Intercontinental Hotel Group, our client.

Rory had been a salesman with the British hotel group, Grand Metropolitan, and brilliantly got himself into the position of being able to negotiate a deal with them. The potential commission from the *purchaser* was 1% of $564 million, ie $5.6 million. The trouble was he knew he was much too close to the purchasing group, Grand Met, who thinking of him of just as one of their former employees might have been tempted to say, 'Here's $200,000 Rory, don't spend it all at once.'

So, on the morning of the penultimate meeting with Pan Am, his former colleagues said, 'Where are we meeting them, Rory?'

'Oh, in the Citicorp building.'

'Why on earth are we meeting them there?'

'Ah, I forgot to tell you, Citicorp are my partners in this deal.'

I am told that Rory effectively gave away a third of the commission, nearly $2 million to Citicorp, for the use of a conference room twice and the presence of couple of serious-looking Citicorp executives, nodding a lot, taking notes and pouring the coffee. But the big brother impression worked.

It was nearly at the end of the New York City project that I was invited to address a body called the Northern Ireland Economic Council. Here was a group plainly desperate to see Northern Ireland's 'other' story. I told them that the job had to be done methodically and professionally because the image problem was probably as bad as it could get.

A nice senior Government official, Ken Bloomfield, snuffling with a terrible cold, listened.

Belfast in 1983 presented a grim first impression. First there was that bunker-like check-point just outside the airport with armed soldiers and police examining every vehicle. Then the sight of all the police stations covered in armour plate, buttressed with sandbags and festooned with netting to foil grenades and missiles. In the city, patrols cruised the streets, either in armoured personnel carriers, the so-called 'pigs' (the same vehicles I had commanded back in Germany) or special armoured Land Rovers, with soldiers pointing their weapons in every direction.

Then add foot patrols, flak-jacketed soldiers and police moving carefully down the streets among the shoppers. Whole areas of the city centre were cordoned off, with checkpoints to monitor briefcases and shopping bags. It reminded me rather of a battered version of

Liverpool, an industrial city with none of the Georgian elegance of Dublin and, moreover, a city under siege, with nightly bombings and shootings.

This, then, was the capital of the Province we were to be asked to sell to the world as a successful, modern-thinking export-orientated industrial centre – which, as it turned out, it was!

How had Northern Ireland got to such a parlous state in image terms? I wonder how many times I have been asked, particularly by Americans, how a 'religious war' could still be taking so many lives (about 2,500 at that stage).

A little history will help to explain Northern Ireland's situation, with the help of some modern and sinister words, 'racial' and 'ethnic'.

> ***'The Irish never forget.***
> ***The English never remember.'***

It did start with religion. Ireland had embraced the Catholic religion with fervour and when Henry VIII broke with Rome (for very non-religious reasons connected with wanting a new wife!) the Irish did not like it. For some time Ireland became a natural springboard from which France and Spain could return Britain 'to the fold'. In reaction, Henry VIII, and then Queens Mary and Elizabeth all tried the process of 'planting' Protestant settlers in Ireland.

It was in Ulster that the most determined but unsuccessful

resistance to this process occurred, first under Hugh O'Neill, second Earl of Tyrone. In 1607, the 'Flight of the Earls' removed many of the Irish leaders to the continent and their lands were confiscated and given to loyal Protestants. Meanwhile an unofficial migration of Scots to Ulster had begun to alter the balance between native Irish Catholics and Protestant settlers. The English Civil War continued the process, with Cromwell defeating the Irish Catholic supporters of Charles I and rewarding his Protestant soldiers with their lands.

The final blow to the Ulster Irish was their defeat in 1690 by William of Orange at the Battle of the Boyne. Thereafter *Penal Laws* excluded the Irish from property and power. The scene was now set. The Irish, a majority in the rest of Ireland, were in Ulster discriminated against by the Protestant majority, themselves fearful of losing their privileges, especially within a potential United Ireland.

Thus in 1914, when England at last decided to give Ireland Home Rule, it was the Ulster Protestants who threatened to resist it by force:

> *'Not an inch.'*
>
> *'No surrender.'*
>
> *'Ulster will fight and Ulster will be right.'*

It was a strange alliance between a blue collar industrial population and fanatical Anglo-Irish gentlemen like Sir Edward Carson, which then illegally landed thousands of rifles from Germany to fight the British and so stay British (exactly the position of the *pieds noirs* in Algeria in 1953). Only the outbreak of World War One stopped the Easter Rising happening in Belfast and not in Dublin.

The seeds of today's Northern Ireland problem were finally planted by Ireland's war of liberation and the compromise Treaty, which allowed Ulster's six counties to remain part of the United Kingdom. Eamon de Valera's supporters fought a civil war to protest the Treaty, a bitter war which killed more Irishmen than the British ever did.

I am sure that the well-meaning English between the two world wars thought that the Irish would sort out their differences. Sadly not. The Protestant majority frankly stitched up the rules to preserve their position. NO CATHOLICS NEED APPLY was a familiar notice on the gates of Ulster's factories and mills. What is more, only in Northern Ireland were you *only* given a vote in local government elections if you were a property freeholder or leaseholder (i.e. most likely to be Protestant).

In Northern Ireland *local* government was the key because it determined jobs and housing. So Londonderry, 80% Catholic, always had a Protestant Council because the Catholics had been stuffed into the Bogside, like a ghetto, and the Protestants parcelled out into wards in the rest of the city. In Newry, 90% Catholic, the only Catholics given jobs in the town hall were eight lavatory cleaners!

In a province with 22% unemployment and poor housing, such discrimination was truly racial and housing policy close to being ethnically discriminating.

That is why I was so surprised and shocked by the freedom marches, led by Bernadette Devlin in 1968 and the violent police and paramilitary reactions. Nothing in my years in the Irish Guards, with its complete 'equal opportunity' policy had prepared me for the revelations from Northern Ireland. I am sure I was not alone in my ignorance. Certainly my father, who had been, after all, the closest real Irishman to advise the Conservative and Unionist Party, was amazed and embarrassed by the Unionist games, when I spelled them out for him.

By the time I got involved, the image of Northern Ireland had been dealt further blows by the self-imposed deaths of Bobby Sands and the other IRA hunger strikers in 1981 and the DeLorean car fiasco in 1982.

John DeLorean, a previously successful if rather flashy General Motors executive, had persuaded a desperate British Government to pour millions into his car factory. (In Dublin, the IDA had wisely turned him down).

My Northern Ireland clients were always wary of him. One senior official remarked to me, 'We were really nettled travelling at the back of the New York plane, while that bastard travelled up front, first class, on our money!' Nor did their affection for him increase when they realised he had never spent one night in Belfast, always scuttling back to London on the evening plane. 'An American guttersnipe' growled someone. In any case, his car became overpriced with mechanical problems. Asked for advice, the Lotus Chief Engineer drove the prototype down a runway test track for 400 yards, stopped and returned on foot, saying it was too dangerous to even drive back!

So, things were at a low ebb when Ken Bloomfield asked me to pitch for the new Industrial Development Board for Northern Ireland's promotional account. I nearly never made it. I was so tired working night after night on the pitch that I fell asleep on the motorway near Luton in the middle of the day and took half the car's side off on the central Armco.

One of the key points which made the IDB choose my team was my insistence that they should find out what the business world *really* thought of Northern Ireland. I brought in my friend Bob Worcester of Market and Opinion Research International and we worked together on a research project in the US, Britain and Germany. The results were shattering to our clients in Northern Ireland, if less so to Bob and me.

MORI revealed that all the positive factors they counted on – productivity, strong work ethic, low costs – were discounted by the perceived dangers of violence and political instability. Moreover, the fact that a visit might convince one foreign executive to consider locating a plant in Northern Ireland was being undermined by something I later called:

THE BARRIER <u>WITHIN</u> THE COMPANY

People said, 'Recommend Northern Ireland? Before or after picking up my last pay cheque?' or, 'My colleagues would think I had gone mad to suggest such a thing!'

The IDB decided, with some courage, to go public on these attitudes, to try to banish complacency for ever. At the news conference, Bob Worcester put it bluntly. 'These are the image gaps you've hired Donough to try to bridge.'

We initiated a complex, interlocking campaign using all the appropriate marketing tools. Nine videos in five languages helped to address the 'barrier within the company' being suitable for colleagues and even wives who might be anxious about living in Northern Ireland. (It is a little-known fact that many British soldiers actually *volunteered* for more Northern Ireland tours. Why? Because they wanted their children to stay in the excellent schools there, so superior to those in the rest of the UK.)

Our advertising, after much research, featured the headline: 'Views of Northern Ireland rarely seen in the media'. This carefully avoided accusing the reader of being ignorant or cowardly, and blamed the media for partial exaggeration. Our pay-off line 'Northern Ireland. Judge us on the Facts' was voted the most effective in *Business Week* in the US.

Our brochures, designed by Sampson Tyrrell, focused on the excellent performance of Northern Ireland's industry with productivity and, above all, educational standards which could be the envy of the world. We advertised our videos with the line: 'Watch some good news about Northern Ireland on T.V.' Colin Anderson's then tiny Belfast agency created a campaign to ask the local community to participate, including splendid TV

276

commercials: 'Come on, Northern Ireland, come on.' However, I knew that all this was not enough. We had to go to meet our audiences, to show that the Province was not entirely peopled by psychopaths and gunmen. So we needed missions abroad.

I decided on a radical step, to copy the New York City Partnership and create a similar vehicle for Northern Ireland. The Northern Ireland Partnership was designed to contain all the main companies in the Province, plus academics, the media, professions and even the arts, with the Opera House and the Ulster Orchestra.

Before launching the idea I visited John Kenny in his role as PRO of the Ulster bank. I had first met John as the legendary Recruiting Sergeant for the Irish Guards in Belfast. He was an extraordinary, powerful, witty man who was on first-name terms with members of the cabinets of both the Republic and Northern Ireland and, we think, had been the only man then to be able to go into Ireland in a British Army uniform.

'What do you need from us?' John asked at the lunch he fixed with Ulster Bank's Chairman, Victor Chambers. 'When we launch the Partnership, please be the first to show support.'

Sure enough, a month later, 300 of Northern Ireland's leading personalities sat in the Europa Hotel. Right on cue, when Partnership Chairman, Sir Desmond Lorimer, ended by asking for questions or comments, there was the muffled gasp of a banker jabbed by a pencil, followed by, 'We at the Ulster Bank feel that this is the finest initiative offered for many years.'

And so it was that under the name of the Partnership our missions went to the USA, Holland, Belgium and even the UK (the largest existing investing country). It worked. Headlines said: 'Protestant, Catholic telling Belfast's other story'. What is more, Chambers of Commerce in the cities we visited commented, 'If you had just been another development agency, we could not have welcomed you in the same way.'

One of the secrets of success was keeping the presentations really short. I rehearsed my volunteer speakers, academics, business people and accountants down to 3–5 minutes each, so the whole presentation could be squeezed in after lunch while the coffee was served. One was Ed Haughey, who had moved from his native Ireland to set up Norbrook, a wonderfully successful veterinary pharmaceutical company in Newry. He seemed to be taking seven

The Queen Mother laughing with James Galway, the flautist (left) at an Ulster Orchestra concert, backed by the Partnership

Secretary of State for Northern Ireland James Prior asking audiences to 'judge us on the facts'

minutes for a four-minute speech. I later realised that he was slightly dyslexic. But Ed worked all night to learn his speech by heart. He was down to four minutes by the time we stood up in the Plaza Hotel in New York and three minutes by the time we reached Los Angeles. Ed is now one of the richest and most respected figures either side of the border and an Irish Senator.

It was gratifying after all this to see this from Jock Elliot, Chairman of Ogilvy & Mather, written to the Duke of Albercorn.

> *'Dear James,*
>
> *Your presentation was absolutely first rate, professionally prepared, executed and convincing – as was your printed material. I've never seen a better presentation than yours.'*

I was willing to put so much extra effort into this project because it was so gratifying and intriguing for me (who would be regarded either as an Englishman or from Southern Ireland) to be helping the North in this way. I regarded it as a real mission. Anything I could do to create an improved economy which discouraged Irishmen killing each other was worthwhile.

While we were able to present a place in which sectarian violence had vastly reduced since the really dark days of the early 1970's, it was sadly always there. In Toronto, I had to slip a note to the Partnership mission leader saying that a bomb had gone off at Queen's University (most of the Mission members had children studying at Queen's).

Memories of the IDB

Glass from the Chairman's Office Bombed 1986

A year later a truck bomb across Chichester Street reduced the IDB's offices to a shambles. My Partnership computer was blown right through two walls like a cannonball with horrible glass-gouged striations along all the partitions (luckily the 300 employees had been given 5 minutes warning to evacuate, otherwise the carnage would have been terrible).

So now we were reduced to only one office, the Chairman's, to present in. Sure enough, the IRA then blew up the Law Courts next door and I have this chunk of glass mounted in a frame with 'Memories of the IDB. Chairman's office, bombed 1986'.

Sometimes it got really close and personal. Denise Gourley, for whose IDB Food Group I had created a special video, later had both legs blown off by a bomb under her car parked outside her suburban house. How a really nice woman whose only job was to create food

manufacturing jobs could be judged a legitimate target I cannot fathom.

But there were lighter moments too. The people of Northern Ireland have the same love of 'craic' as those in the South. It was also fun to be working with my friend David McDonough again, who, for all his humour, looked and sounded a great deal more English than I did. One evening he was in the Europa Hotel and decided to go to have a drink in the discotheque on the top floor. He fell into a bizarre conversation with a young and rabidly Paisleyite Protestant who spoke in the strongest of West Belfast accents but was very happy to discuss politics with David, providing he was fed double Black Bush whiskeys. He went on and on about how Mrs Thatcher should 'be much tougher with the Nationalists' and David asked him how she should address them. Downing another of David's doubles, he responded:

'She should turn to the Nationalists and say, 'Stop it, you focking stop it, or I'll hurt yous, I'll hurt yous bad.''

For weeks the thought of Margaret Thatcher talking in such an accent kept us laughing. When we would go to the IDB offices, David would say, 'Stop it' and would emerge from the lift to meet our clients trying to stop our almost uncontrollable and childish giggles.

Less amusing was the sad fact that my second marriage broke up, partly because of my overwork and excessive travelling. For whatever reason, it left me very upset and depressed that, for a second time, a small child was left with an apparently inexplicable family break-up. In the long run, my son Edmond has weathered the storm and has become a very clever, articulate and amusing young man.

For several years my first wife Clare had been living with a charming man called Michael Stevens, whom my son Murrough adored. Eventually Clare and Michael broke up. He was fairly devastated. I was in the same state after the collapse of my second marriage and we used to see quite a lot of each other.

One day, he invited me to lunch to meet his neighbour, a former model friend of his and he wondered who to bring in order to make up the party. 'I'll bring Liz Cowley,' he said, 'but we'll have to have her little daughter as well'. Thus did my present wife and step-daughter enter my life. After the lunch in an Italian restaurant we repaired to Michael's house. I made a cursory date with the ex-model but then circled back and took Liz home. Two days later was our first date and we have been together ever since.

After about a week, Liz had to take me to a boring Ted Bates business dinner which was hosted by two rather tedious

For years the threat of IRA bombs on mainland Britain was a constant security worry. My brother, Officer Cadet Lucius O'Brien, forgot this for a moment when, going on a week-end leave, he carelessly left a holdall sitting in the car-park at the Royal Military Academy, Sandhurst.

The guests at that day's Passing Out Parade, including Princess Margaret, were not amused to be locked in for hours while the Bomb Squad investigated. Not surprising, too, that on his return, innocently asking the Guard Sergeant if 'anyone had handed in his camera bag', Lucius was promptly locked up.

NEW HORIZONS

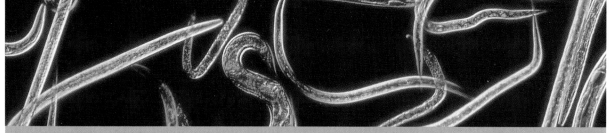

NEMAT ODE

'Aha!' he cried 'The nematode!'
And launched off into explanation
Another fine (he thought) oration
If not, precisely, conversation.
It didn't matter, this was fun
And if it wasn't really done
To blast right on, and quite ignore
The fact that nematodes could bore.
His ally was, well quite as bad
And just as loud, and even had
The same technique of quickly topping
Every story. Worse, not stopping
To listen to what others said
Interrupting them instead.
(If not with facts on nematodes
Still breaking dinner party codes

On letting others have their say
Ah reader! That would be the day!)
A conversational disease
To chatter with such selfish ease?
Well, if the host was not delighted
Her fault, of course. They'd been invited.
And if they weren't asked round again
To spare her friends from going insane
They'd only laugh, this tactless pair
And say 'We can't go anywhere'.
A perfect match, the world might say
'They'll talk themselves to death one day
Poor fools, they're simply quite unable
To grace a proper dinner table.
And someday sure, they'll get their due
Stuck nightly with a meal for two'.

lesbians in the media department. I became so desperate that I decided to use my knowledge of agricultural chemicals to tell them about nematodes – only discovered in 1865 when microscopes got powerful enough. They destroy 10% of the world's crops. Liz was so embarrassed at the way I hogged the conversation that she wrote an excellent poem of apology (above).

The Cowley family is a formidable one and was headed by the patriarchal General Sir John Cowley. At one stage, the media called him the 'Rebel General'. This was because he questioned the Conservative Government's (and particular Duncan Sandys') reliance on total nuclear response to any attack by the Russians. I have read his far-sighted and fully approved speech to the Royal United Services Institute, the press cuttings and, particularly interestingly, the correspondence with other Generals including Montgomery after this silly row broke.

John Cowley had the distinction of acting extremely bravely in the Quetta earthquake before the war where he was given the Albert Medal for his courage in rescuing many Indian patients, some of them lepers, from a hospital building.

Scrap H-bomb says the 'rebel' general

By Our Political Correspondent
A SECRET revolt of leading generals against ment's defence into

MINISTER SLAPS DOWN BRASS HAT

Row over 'suicide' bomb speech

Defence Minister Mr. Harold Watkinson in the Commons today and assurance that future

War Office 'revolt' is foiled

I vetted Cowley speech—Soames

His H-bomb criticism

ABOUT-TURN FOR DEFENCE PLANS

FAR-REACHING pla to rebuild Britai dwindling forces defend the cou against conventi attack are urgently worked

they publicly revealed their wish for a number of new aircraft which Mr. Sandys was at that time resisting.

TIGHTER GAG ON SERVICE CHIEFS

MR. HAROLD WAT-KINSON, the new Defence Minister, will

By ANGUS MACPHERSON

'Lieutenant Cowley and his party were the first to start relief work at the Civil Hospital where the walls of all the wards had collapsed bringing down the roofs intact on the inmates on whom the debris of the walls had already fallen. At first the men were too few in numbers to tear off the roofs, so they raised them up for short periods whilst Lieutenant Cowley crawled under them and dragged out survivors from their beds. The survivors were pre-earthquake hospital patients and mostly quite helpless. Lieutenant Cowley lifted many men in his arms regardless of the warning that they were suffering from all manner of diseases. Had it not been for the work of this officer and the excellent example shown by him to his men, far fewer men would have been saved alive.' (*London Gazette 19th November 1935*).

General Sir John Cowley

The Albert Medal then became the George Cross and John became the Chairman of the George Cross and Victoria Cross Association. Every year there is a tea party at Buckingham Palace and Liz was the last of his children to be allowed to attend – with startling results.

The Queen greeted John and his wife Sybil, moved along, and had just got into her first sentence with Liz, 'Have you ever been to Buckingham Palace, my dear?' Then an amazingly loud whisper came from Liz's mother, **'John, did you see her hair piece? You can't see the join at all. You remember, I wore one like that in Malaya. But it always went frizzy in the heat'**. Her Majesty was whisked down the line so fast that Liz never got a word out.

John with the Queen on her visit to Wellington College, having just asked a fair-haired boy his ambitions. 'Formula One World Champion'. 'Foolish boy', said the General to James Hunt (page 250).

John could be a little unscrupulous in his dealings with others. He took great pride in describing sharing a cake in the nursery with his own brother, who was to become a canon. John took most of the cake leaving a little slice for his brother, who normally mild-mannered, was forced to protest.

'Well, which slice would *you* have taken?' said John.

'The smaller one, of course.'

'OK. You got what you wanted,' chuckled John, tucking in.

He was so competitive that a little mild cheating was not beyond the pale, which sometimes went wrong. When partnering Sybil at bridge he once patted his chest, indicating that she should lead with hearts. He was furious when she failed to bid and not mollified by her explanation. 'I thought you meant 'left tit' so I left it.'

In later life he became a bit eccentric. Walking into his club, an old member said, 'Phillip?' John replied, 'David?' When they both shook their heads, John commented 'Must have been two other men'.

He had a bizarre and cutting wit. He once said to a lady fellow guest, 'I know your name. Can't remember your face'. But then he was half Irish.

In his 80's John's short-term memory started going. He would ask Liz several times of me, 'Who is that man in the garden?' when we had already been at his house for two days. He sent off for the Dale Carnegie 'How to Improve your Memory' book (send no money now). After about four months a young man turned up at the door and said, 'Sir John Cowley? I believe you have a copy of our book'.

'Never heard of it!' said John closing the door. It has always struck me that that particular book might well have had a lot of unwanted returns.

One of our most successful trips together was when Liz and I were given some discounted tickets for the Orient Express from Venice back to London. While it was very romantic, Liz had plainly not adjusted to my interest in trains and wrote this – literally on the back of an envelope.

EARLY TRAINING

'You're sure? The Orient Express?
Of course I'll come!' A hasty 'Yes!'
Well, not all chaps would ask her this
Such holidays one couldn't miss.

She saw it all, the great Express
The style, the chic, the evening dress
The twenties look, cuisine, champagne!
The chance might never come again.

Poor lady, how was she to know
Just why the fellow chose to go?
That his real motives could be less
Than those to do with tenderness?
That this was but a planned progression
From model trains, his true obsession?
And so it was they climbed abroad
And what was this? His spirits soared!
She gazed at him, he gazed at gauges,
Recording all the dates and ages
Before they'd even left the station
She'd kissed goodbye to all flirtation.

'What brass! What logos!' he exclaimed
She hung her head, a mite ashamed
Preferring scenes of alps and lakes
To metre widths and discs and brakes.

'The badges! Photograph me here!'
He ordered her with merry cheer
'This Pullman! Oh what fascias! Steering!
Just look at how the train's adhering.
The walnut inlays! Ventilation!
The layout of this railway station!'

If all this ranting went right past her
Surprise! The trip was no disaster
Trains may have been his greatest passion
She, runner up, still got her ration
When tired out by his manic glee
With every technicality.

And if it really wasn't tennis
To bring her all the way from Venice
Expounding on the wondrous train
She doesn't mind seeing him again....

Revenge! She'll just bang on for hours
With things he doesn't know, like flowers,
And anyway, who'd spoil this marriage
Twixt him and bits of railway carriage?

Such marriages are made by God
If mortals sometimes think them odd

At the age of sixteen Liz found herself in one of the most eccentric households you could imagine. Madame Whettnall and her husband lived in a rambling house in the village of Barbizon near Fontainebleu, South of Paris. She was there to teach the four children English. While the husband was one of the last people genuinely to die of absinthe poisoning, Madame Whettnall, formerly a famous concert pianist, was even more extraordinary. She permanently had a pigeon called Coco perched on top of her head!

There was a bath in the house but it was entirely full of books by Hugo, Racine, Voltaire and Molière, so the children were sent off to bathe in the River Seine on their bicycles once a week.

They were returning from one of these expeditions, Liz and her four small charges, all with wet hair and on battered old bicycles. A large American car drew up. To their amazement, because they had never seen such a thing before, the electric window silently slid down and an American lady said with an excruciating French accent, 'Say honey, qui est la route pour Fonton Blue?"

Liz took charge and in perfect English replied, 'You continue down this road about another 500 metres, turn sharp right and then bear left, go straight on for about another kilometre and you pick up the main road signposted to Fontainebleu.'

The American lady stared at her in wonderment and said, 'Gee, thanks honey'. As she began to pull away Liz heard her say quite distinctly, 'Well, you can say what you like about the French, but this baccalauréat *really* works.'

I am sure that the lady is still going around Wisconsin or wherever explaining that even the most poor and ragged peasants in France speak perfect English, thanks to their excellent educational system.

After the break up of her first marriage, and before she met me, Liz had a relationship with a young man called Jerry. This went on for about six months and finally she financed him to go off and start a new life in South Africa. Although she knew he had not exactly been a model of faithfulness, she was sad to see him go and decided to cheer herself up by having some work done on the house.

An elderly builder arrived the same morning that she had seen Jerry off and cheerfully set to work doing the tiling in the kitchen. Liz was typing away in the drawing room when a woman called and asked to speak to Jerry. Irritated that this might be one of her boyfriend's other relationships, she curtly informed the lady that she couldn't speak to Jerry and that she wasn't going to be able to in the future because he had gone to South Africa on a one-way ticket.

'Are you sure?' said the woman.

'Of course I'm sure. I bought the ticket myself. In fact I've just come back from the airport', said Liz, ringing off.

Some time later she went in to the kitchen to inspect progress and said to the builder 'Ah, Mr Lennox, would you like a cup of tea?'

'Yes please dear, that would be very nice, but you can call me Jerry'.

With mounting horror, Liz asked, 'Does your wife ever ring you at work?'

'Certainly, she always rings me at about 11 o'clock'

'Well, I think you better ring her back' said Liz, 'because I've just told her that you've gone to South Africa'.

The poor builder stared at her aghast and did not pause to ring but left the house in his car immediately. He did not return for three days and recounted to Liz how he burst into his home to find his wife being consoled by the neighbours. It never pays to jump to conclusions.

CLEAR AND PRESENT DANGER

The Institute of Directors, Pall Mall

Our Northern Ireland Partnership Mission to London reinforced a valuable lesson – never take anything for granted. At our many planning meetings I often brought up the question of security. Invariably I was told to stop worrying. 'The Secretary of State's security people deal with all that.'

I had deliberately chosen the Institute of Directors building in Pall Mall as being more, I imagined, secure than a hotel. Wrong. The night before I asked the security man about his preparations for the morning. He looked non-plussed. 'You know, Northern Ireland, Secretary of State, Minister, 12 Members of Parliament, the cream of the Province's business leaders, 300 guests?'

'Never heard about it, sir.'

'How many other entrances to this place are not guarded?' 'Six, sir'. 'Please get the local police station on the line.' To my horror, they had no knowledge whatever of this sensitive event, were extremely grateful for the call and agreed to have police present the next day.

As it happened, two Sinn Fein supporters got in by pretending to be potential investors and leaped up after lunch and shouted at Jim Prior before being ushered out. Was I paranoid? No. Six weeks later the IRA bomb in Brighton nearly succeeded in wiping out Margaret Thatcher and her Cabinet.

When we took a Northern Ireland Partnership mission to Belgium, Tom King was Secretary of State for Northern Ireland, someone I had known for many years from the Burke Club in the House of Commons.

I'm not altogether sure that my Civil Service clients particularly liked it, but it gave me some pleasure when he stepped out of the lift at the Sheraton, Brussels and said, 'Oh, hello, Donough. I'm glad you're in charge of all this. Do you know the Ambassador, Peter Petrie?'

Peter said, 'Yes, we all used to play in the street together.' He was the son of my father's friend and neighbour, the historian Sir Charles Petrie, and fancied my sister Natalie a lot.

The mission was nearly marred by a strange incident. While we were a respectably large party of about 350 people, unbeknownst to us, the Sheraton was trying to feed a delegation of 6,000 Chinese in a ballroom below us. This meant that our food took an extraordinary length of time to arrive, although the wine did not.

Amongst us was a BBC journalist who was also a minor Protestant politician. Half way through the question and answer session, Tom King committed something of a blunder, saying, 'I'm sure Garret Fitzgerald and the Irish government probably now realise that there will not be a united Ireland in the foreseeable future'. The Belgian guests nodded amiably, not realising the significance of the remark. But our unfriendly journalist was recording the whole proceedings and slipped away to Belgian Radio with his tape. By 3 o'clock it was on both Ulster BBC and Irish radio.

That evening we were at the splendid Chateau de la Hulpe entertaining the most important businessmen and women in Belgium. Urgent telephone calls started coming in from Luxembourg. The recording had caused a furore in Ireland. Garret Fitzgerald had been handed a transcript as he was sitting across a table from Margaret Thatcher at a European Prime Ministers' meeting. He must have said something like, 'What on earth has your boy gone and said, Margaret?'

The calls started arriving at the chateau, first to Tom's Private Secretary and finally, very insistently, for him, with the Prime Minister herself on the line. There was only one telephone in this chateau, which happened to be in the kitchen, and I will always retain a picture of Tom King sitting on a wine crate, apologising to his strident Prime Minister over the hubbub of waiters and chefs all around him. It must have been one of the more inconvenient places for anyone to receive a Prime Ministerial tick-off.

Tom King before his summons to the kitchen

Hyster fork lift trucks, one of Northern Ireland's many success stories

Just as our programme was going really well, relationships started to go downhill. The original IDB promotional team was split up (my closest friend there, Ian McMurtry, now looks after the North of England), Saxon Tate, from the sugar family, went back to England and a new Chief Executive arrived to replace him from a strictly Civil Service background. His first memo to the staff banned anyone from using his Christian name. A great start.

It became perfectly obvious that the new regime wanted to hire 'the biggest PR firm in the world' regardless of what my Euro Center team had achieved. When it was announced that there was to be a pitch, I refused to participate except to do a special presentation. I addressed the Committee, nearly all of whom were unfamiliar faces and had played no part in our successful four years. I said I was there just to give them advice, which included:

Don't hire anyone who:

- ❏ Does not care about Northern Ireland and Ireland
- ❏ Presents with a team that you then never see again
- ❏ Says all their offices abroad are equally good

and so on. The Committee were also amazed to hear about the success of the past few years and said, 'We didn't realise you did all that'.

'Then why are you on this Committee?', I just could not help retorting.

As you can guess, they *did* hire the largest PR firm in the world who proceeded to treat the IDB just as I had predicted, at four times our fees.

At the handover in London, the young girl Account Executive admitted, 'We are charging them a fortune already, and I'm the only one on it. If I worked day and night I could not justify a quarter of the fees'.

In New York, her counterpart said to Chris Spring, 'My God, you don't do all this work personally do you? I'm going to get one of the new kids to do it'.

I was resigned to severing my links with this demanding challenge. You sometimes need to move on in life. As I said at the time, 'You can tell when you are travelling to a place too often. You get upset when someone has taken your favourite parking spot at Heathrow Terminal One.'

However, I was then told something extra after the handover which really shocked and infuriated me. Someone within the new PR firm told me that the European Chief Executive, who had led the IDB pitch, had instructed his teams to go slow, to discuss the contract for weeks but to do no real work, all this while racking up the massive monthly fees. The reason was that this executive wished to deliver the most profitable account in the worldwide firm, to help him get the top job in New York. He was on his way to succeeding.

Talking with my remaining friends at the IDB confirmed that something strange was going on. After all, most of the hard work had been done, the videos, the brochures and leaflets, even the scripts and slides for missions had all been handed over. There was no reason for the new advisors not to hit the ground running. I said to my former client Brian Musgrave, during a social evening in London, 'Do you ever feel you might have a communications DeLorean on your hands?' He grimaced ruefully.

Later something spectacular and rather dreadful occurred. The radio announced 'International PR Chief X has been found dead in a London hotel. Murder is suspected'. It transpired that the PR man had been having an affair with the wife of a former colleague who came to remonstrate and ended up stabbing him.

The PR firm immediately started working in their normal professional way. But it was all a rather sad and even sordid end to one of the most gratifying and worthwhile challenges I have ever faced.

Signs of progress in the media

CHAPTER 19 DESIGNER LABEL

As the Industrial Development Board for Northern Ireland's project was winding down, 'Sam' Sampson, one of the two partners in the little design company that I had helped to create said 'Why don't you stop being an uncle figure and join us as a working director? As long as you promise not the throw telephones around.' This must have referred to some incident in the past where a telephone conversation with a client had ended so disastrously that I actually smashed the instrument to pieces!

Promising not to destroy our telecommunications equipment, I joined Sam for what was to be a six-year stint. After about five months, Sam told me that an approach had been made to buy us by someone called Martin Sorrell of an improbable sounding company called WPP (Wire & Plastic Products Ltd).

WPP turned out to out to be a vehicle for Martin Sorrell to realise his dream of creating an advertising and communications empire which would be bigger and better than the group of which he had been Financial Director, Saatchi & Saatchi. Sam, Terry Tyrrell and I duly met Martin Sorrell in a restaurant in Covent Garden and he expressed his desire to buy us as one of the stepping stones to greater things on both sides of the Atlantic.

Martin was very intense, although with a lot of charm. He waxed lyrical on how he regarded the future as *not* being in paid advertising (which he thought was slower growing), so he was going to buy design companies, research, business development consultancies and so on.

Thus, we became the sixth company WPP acquired. Martin used the ploy of metaphorically dropping a cheque for the initial £1 million down on the table, a technique he had apparently dreamed up when buying a company in Edinburgh for Saatchi & Saatchi.

Martin continued to acquire companies. One morning we were electrified to hear that he had put in a bid for J Walter Thompson, one of the

Sorrell set for Ogilvy victory

WPP's fight for US advertising giant the **Ogilvy Group** looks set to end in another victory for WPP chief Martin Sorrell.

by Joanne Ha

Today Ogilvy announced that it has entered into discussions with Sorrell following indications that he is willing to raise his terms beyond the $50 a share offered to Ogilvy only last weekend.

Should Sorrell win the day, and there is no real reason to assume otherwise, he will find himself at the head of a group with billings of around $13.5 billion, roughly equal to the Saatchi empire.

Currently the bid is worth around $900 million but Sorrell is expected to end up paying about $53 a share.

The Ogilvy share price has shot up from $18 a share at the beginning of the year to $52 at

Now, despite marke tions of discontent amo stitutions, Samuel Mo WPP's leading banker] that it is confident of fi cash and intends to fu fer with a combinatio and convertible pr shares.

Sorrell is also suppor US by top acquisiti Wasserstein Perella a experts Wertheim Schr

As reported in ye Standard he is said to t reach agreement with t group before its board next Tuesday.

Followers of the ager have been scentical of

Martin Sorrell: likely to pay $53 a shar

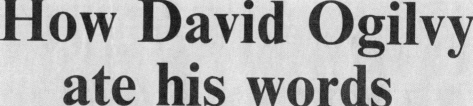

How David Ogilvy ate his words

Roman's) brains out in the next competition," Mr Manning said. Mr Roman said there was less client overlap between Ogilvy and WPP than any other potential new owner.

Even if size was not Mr Sorrell's

US trade magazine, Advertising Age, which suggested that Ogilvy might lose billings of up to $500m – a tenth of its business – if the takeover went ahead.

Mr Edgar Bronfman Jr, Seagram's

JWT, who bridled at his attempts to manage them.

Mr Sorrell says he hopes to use the two agencies' combined strengths to develop WPP's advertising business outside the US and its "non-media most respected names in the advertising world. The trouble was that JWT had allowed itself to be seriously under-valued. For instance, one of things Sorrell discovered was that the Tokyo freehold office property was valued at £20 million, when in fact it was worth £120 million. At one stroke he was able to sell the building, lease back the space, and thus pay for one third of the total acquisition cost just with this one under-valued asset. Our shares in WPP continued to climb from the £5.50 level, when we were purchased, towards £10.

Suddenly we received another bombshell. Martin was attempting to buy Ogilvy & Mather. This acquisition received far more opposition, not least from David Ogilvy, my father's old prep school friend, who described Sorrell as someone who 'had never written an ad in his life'. Miraculously, and no doubt through Martin's charm, a few months later David Ogilvy became our Chairman. His agency had been absorbed into WPP.

However, to complete the Ogilvy purchase, a huge debt had been taken on and the financial community began to get anxious. One night I had frightful food poisoning and my wife and son Edmond had to look after me all night (he lay at the foot of the bed like a faithful dog, which I thought was quite touching). In the morning I had to stay in bed and drifted in and out of conscious-ness. At 10 o'clock the radio's financial news talked about 'shares on the move, WPP down to 288'. As the shares had been at 420 the day before I assumed I had misheard, that 'journalists were getting slack', and went back to sleep. But at 11.00 it was 185. At noon it was 93 pence. I had personally lost half my worth on paper.

I never lost faith in Martin as he negotiated with the banks and institutions and brought the company back. We became socially friendly because he had two sons at Winchester while my eldest son was there (Murrough said with awe, 'Those Sorrell boys already have a reputation for fiendish work'). Martin has now been knighted for his successful efforts.

Loss of Volvo account and advertising downturn spark profits warning and share slide

WPP's share price plunges

By Alice Rawsthorn

WPP GROUP, the world's largest marketing services company, yesterday saw its share price plummet by 98½p on the day to close at 279p after it issued a profits warning.

Mr Martin Sorrell, chief executive, said WPP had been affected by cuts in marketing budgets "across all areas of the business". Cutbacks had been most severe

Volvo, its largest and oldest client. The account loss followed controversy over Volvo's advertisements that some of SMS's advertisements had been misleading. Volvo's had been strengthened before undergoing a test in which trucks were driven over them.

Mr Sorrell said that, even without the loss of the Volvo account, this year's profits would not have

via as well as the US and UK.

He said WPP detected the downturn last month and reviewed its forecasts for the fourth quarter, its busiest time of year. When WPP published interim results in August – a 77 per cent increase in pre-tax profits to £46m on revenue of £826m for the six months to June 30 – Mr Sorrell was confident about

ago – because of investors' concern over heavy debts.

Analysts yesterday downgraded 1990 profit forecasts from around £110m to £90m. Mr Mark Shepherd, advertising analyst at UBS Phillips & Drew in London, described the outlook for WPP next year as "anybody's guess".

Most analysts were more concerned about the impact of the

WPP Group
Share price (pence)
420
400
380
360
340
320
300
280
260
Nov 1990
Source: Datastream

terms of banking agreements.

WPP is the latest in a series of marketing groups to have fallen from grace in the past year. Saatchi & Saatchi, Mr Sorrell's former employer, is desperately trying to restructure its finances. Yellowhammer and the Michael Peters Group, two smaller UK companies, have gone into receivership.

The WPP expanded rapidly in the

Sorrell in bank talks as WPP's shares plummet

Emily Bell

WPP, the world's largest marketing services company, is reeling from the blow dealt to

indicated as much to WPP's bankers last week.

With debts expected to reach £315 million by the end of the

back of last week's corporate news.

The episode marks an abrupt end to Sorrell's honeymoon

WPP saved as investors agree deal

Sorrell secures his future at the top

MARTIN SORRELL, founder of WPP, the world's largest

Rufus Olins

would back the WPP proposals. "[Fidelity] feels that

WPP cautious on fragile upturn

By Roland Rudd

WPP GROUP, the marketing services company, remains cautious about an upturn in its markets in spite of reporting pre-tax profits of £34.1m, up from £1.8m, in the half year to June 30. The result was helped by the absence of last year's £13.5m restructuring charge.

the US and the UK. On the basis of client experience to date, it is possible that a recovery will be delayed for some time".

The group is paying an interim dividend of 0.50p, as it forecast at the time of its rights issue in March. Its first payout since

revenues rose by 16.4 per cent to £699.8m, although more than 10 per cent of that rise was due to the weaker pound.

Revenues in media advertising increased by 7.4 per cent in the first half. J Walter Thompson and Ogilvy & Mather generated

Clinton's tax proposals could affect US companies, which in turn might cut back on their advertising.

Public relation companies continued to lose money. Hill & Knowlton and Ogilvy Adams & Rinehart reported combined

of its £86m rights issue.

The group hopes to reduce borrowings further with the sale of Scali McCabe Sloves, the US agency. That sale is expected to fetch between £40m (£38.8m) and $60m.

In the long-term WPP is con-

WPP back with a divi but cautious on recovery

by Richard Wachman

time. Hill & Knowlton and Ogilvy Adams & Rinehart pitched in with combined

Turnround complete at WPP

By Martin Waller

ALAN WELLER

THE turnround at WPP Group, the world's biggest advertising and marketing combine, is now largely complete, and the group has given an optimistic view of a booming world advertising market.

WPP saw like-for-like revenues grow 8 per cent in the first half of this year, through a mix of new business and extra work from existing customers. This, and improving margins across the group, sent pre-tax profits ahead 34 per cent, to £48.5 million.

Martin Sorrell, chief executive, said that prospects for the second half of 1995 looked good, as did those for 1996, when the industry could look to the benefits of the "crowding out" effect in the US. This refers to the upward pressure on the cost of media advertising caused by a squeeze on supply because 1996 will feature both the Olympic Games in Atlanta and the US presidential election.

However, he cautioned that

I was quite proud that I was now part of the same group that owned J Walter Thompson, a superb agency then, as now. My uncle, Turlough O'Brien (Toby 1), worked at JWT and he told me the nice story of Sergeant Hawkins, the caretaker and general factotum, who in 1939 went off to war.

JWT, 40 Berkeley Square

Naturally enough, many members of JWT did the same, but the older Douglas Saunders, the Managing Director, stayed behind as he had served in World War I.

Soon after demobilisation they were all back at 40 Berkeley Square and Douglas Saunders came down and spotted Hawkins and said, 'Sergeant Hawkins, can you please get this package round to the client right away'.

Hawkins was dressed in a suit instead of his former commissionaire's uniform and said quietly, 'I think 'Mr Hawkins' would be more appropriate, Mr Saunders. If you insist on using ranks, you have to call me Colonel Hawkins, Major Saunders.'

It was true. The commissionaire had been promoted to Colonel, and the Managing Director was still only a Major.

AGENCY PRESENTATIONS

Advertising agencies have to present to be hired in the first place, later showing prospective work to clients. A friend of mine was one of the bright young creative stars of J Walter Thompson. One morning in the lift a colleague said, 'I hope the Rowntree MacIntosh work is finished and looking good.'

'Surely that's next Thursday, not today?' said the horrified copywriter.

'Don't be silly, the clients are all down in the lobby, ready for the meeting.'

The meeting started, and after some time discussing strategy and media policy, all eyes turned to my friend for the creative ideas. He rose to his feet, and then affected a brilliant imitation of falling down in a fit. The men from Rowntree MacIntosh were so concerned and nice, as they fussed about helping to get glasses of water, that they postponed the meeting for a week, luckily not asking to look at what was in the empty portfolio.

This shows that if things are going wrong you should confine yourself to a limited defensive ploy.

This play did not work for a friend of Liz's, a copywriter in New York who was working on a major presentation to get more business out of their client, Hertz. He had been working so hard that he overslept and decided that it would be better to go into work sufficiently late to miss the presentation altogether. Unfortunately, the meeting had been delayed and he met the whole group in reception. 'Where on earth have you been?' demanded his boss.

'I'm really sorry.' he said, and then in sheer panic, for some bizarre reason he continued, 'My wife died in the night.'

Horrified, both the agency people and the client crowded around him with commiserations and advice to go home at once to look after his affairs. He was just able to get to his home in the suburbs before the first bunches of flowers arrived from the agency and the client.

He blurted out to his wife that on no account was she to answer the telephone or appear outside the house. He maintained the charade for three days while the flowers and telegrams piled up, but then cracked and revealed the truth to his colleagues. Whereupon, sad to say, he was fired.

FIRST IMPRESSIONS

A misunderstanding in a presentation can sometimes be turned to good effect. The board of Thomas Cook were coming to a presentation at Ted Bates. Partly because of the importance of travellers cheques, Thomas Cook was now controlled by a consortium of banks.

Liz, as Deputy Creative Director, was asked to lead the presentation but as she tended to dress in either jeans or rather outrageous clothes, was actually given money by the agency to go and 'buy a suitable black suit'.

As the bankers drifted into the presentation room, Liz was the first of the agency people to appear. She entered by another door just where the coffee and biscuits were laid out. 'Good morning' she said. 'Hello dear', said one of the bankers, 'Two coffees with sugar please'. Liz got them their coffee and then tried to explain who she was. 'Another white coffee here, dear, and perhaps some biscuits for Sir Charles'.

Even though her other colleagues had now arrived, it was absolutely plain that she could not shake off the impression that she was part of the catering staff. Eventually, the Chairman of Ted Bates suggested everyone should sit down and, of course, Liz sat down in her appointed place. The bankers stared. Why was the tea lady joining their meeting? Once they had fallen silent, Liz said 'Good morning Gentlemen. Now we've had our tea and coffee, perhaps we can begin the presentation.'

The men stared at their blotters in embarrassment. Probably this is why the agency landed the huge account.

We have all had times when the world seems too conspire against us, and all our plans go wrong. This happened to Liz when she was due to fly to Paris to present to Guy Laroche and his board for the next campaign for their fragrances in Britain.

She drove her car to the agency to pick up the finished artwork but when she went down to the car park, she found she had been blocked by other cars, and frantic efforts to find the owners failed. So she took a taxi back to her Richmond house to collect her suitcase and as soon as the taxi had disappeared, realised that her keys were still on the key ring in her car, back in the West End. She had left an upstairs window open and a workman came past with a ladder. She begged him to help her get into the house. When they were both halfway up the ladder, a police car stopped, thinking it was an attempted daylight burglary. Liz had to get into the house and produce the deeds to stop herself being arrested.

She ordered a cab to get to the airport and was determined to give herself a steadying drink on the way, so she put a mixture of gin and tonic in a thermos. Halfway to the airport the shaken-up thermos exploded. Liz, who had prepared herself immaculately for the meeting, with a new hairdo, perfect clothes and of course Guy Laroche scent, was now covered with a sticky gin and tonic mix. She turned up in Paris very bedraggled and smelling of anything other than Guy Laroche.

Maybe she should have combined this presentation with another one.

Deciding that she should impress a client by sweeping into his car park with an immaculate car, she stopped at a car wash. She sat in the car and the machine went back and forth and back and forth, covering the car with layer after layer of suds. Concerned, she banged on the horn for minutes with no response from the man at the desk. Eventually she was forced to leap out of the car at what she thought was the right time. Wrong. The suds sprayer caught her and she ended just as bedraggled as at the Guy Laroche presentation, but cleaner.

At Ted Bates, sometimes her own colleagues could create difficult situations, as did our friend Leon Lerner who, as the enigmatic Managing Director, was leading a presentation to try and win the Buxted Chicken account.

The presentation to the chicken men was going very badly, and Leon decided he didn't want the account anyway. He suddenly let out a low and very realistic squawk. Everybody turned and stared. He got to his feet and started clucking like a cockerel and then, wagging his arms up and down and squawking to himself, left the meeting for ever. It's very difficult to work out what, as a colleague, you should say to the

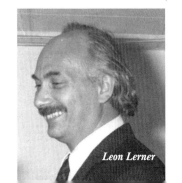

Leon Lerner

potential client when your boss has done something like that.

Another unfortunate incident occurred when a colleague of Liz's was leading the presentation for Zip Firelighters. The Account Director, Warren Goodwin, smoked a pipe and liked to use the ritual of lighting the pipe or tapping out its ashes as punctuation for the presentation. Unfortunately, at the height of the Zip presentation, he tapped out his ashes into his waste paper basket, which promptly caught fire. Warren attempted quietly to put out the fire, hoping the client would not notice, by pressing his foot into the waste paper basket. This failed. His foot got stuck. The meeting descended into farce as Warren had to leap up with a burning waste paper basket on his foot.

There are times when even the names of your team can be unfortunate. Take Liz's colleagues on the Predictor pregnancy testing account: Kevin Fallas, John Thomas, 'Dick' Gilmore and Brian Longfellow. (Her bank manager Robert Sole must be one of the few to be *ordered* never to use his initial.)

SEX: ALL CHANGE

Keeping to this salacious note, Russell Gore-Andrews (with whom I used to run an incredibly bad pheasant shoot) was Vice Chairman of the American advertising agency Leo Burnett's company in London. His very nice and rather demure secretary came in one morning to give in her notice, announcing she was going into business on her own. The result was the Anne Summers sex shops, which became quite a large and successful chain. I know. My office is right above a branch in Charing Cross Road.

Russell looked after a drink account and his client told him that he was going to take some time off. Three months later he called Russell to say he was coming into the agency and added enigmatically, 'Don't be surprised by my appearance'.

Russell's secretary announced his client with some agitation. In walked not the tweedy forty year old man he had expected, but a tweedy forty year old woman.

THE NEW ROSSELLINI

In the early 1980's, Isabella Rossellini, the daughter of Roberto Rossellini and Ingrid Bergman, landed a huge contract with the cosmetics company, Lancôme. Liz was the head copywriter on the account at Ted Bates, Lancôme's advertising agency and had the job of writing Isabella into a television campaign to run worldwide, particularly in the US. It took several months to agree the scripts, not only with the London end of the company, but also with Paris and New York, and it was with some relief that she eventually boarded the plane for the New York filming, to be followed by further work in Puerto Rico.

In the Meridien Hotel in Manhattan, she waited for the film crew and the star. Imagine her horror when the film director

Night-time has never been used so effectively

In make-up, the bump is beginning to show

arrived to inform Liz that he had, that day, discovered that Isabella was 5 months pregnant. So every single script she had written was defunct, since they all involved long shots, revealing the unfortunate bump. The frenzy and phone calls that followed can only be guessed at, with shooting scheduled to begin for the following day, but by working all night Liz managed to turn things around, although she eventually ended up staying in the U.S. for six weeks rather than six days.

A more than irritated Liz

Sweet revenge came in Puerto Rico, when the real culprit for all this agony, Isabella's infuriating agent, was spotted by Liz by the pool, about to lower her ample buttocks on to a resting hornet. A little guilty that she didn't warn her of the impending danger, Liz always enjoys recounting the story of the 'sting in the tail.'

OLD BOY NETWORK

During my five years working full time at Sampson Tyrrell we become one of the most successful design companies in Britain. I played my part directing the revamped corporate identity of my old clients like British Gas and Legal & General. I was also New Business Director and one last family connection proved very useful.

A response from our mailing shot brought me face to face with an elderly PR man at Royal Mail. 'So you're Turlough O'Brien's nephew, are you? One of the kindest men around and taught me everything I know. I'll put you on a 'recommended' list before I retire next week.'

Months later I was summoned at the last minute to a meeting by a frantic Royal Mail director, David Lane, who gave us a tiny but very urgent task. My colleagues pulled out all the stops and we eventually ended up with the gigantic task of implementing the Royal Mail's identity. I approve of merit, but please, give me the 'old boy network' once in a while.

During a Sampson Tyrrell project for the Government of Dubai, Emirates Airlines sent me a car and the driver told me a nice story. The week before he had been assigned to pick up an American VIP, flying in to a Royal Air Force base in the middle of England.

As the drivers waited, out of the clouds suddenly emerged a plane. Not the expected Boeing 707, but the long black shape of the SR71, an enormously fast reconnaissance plane known

as the
Blackbird. With parachutes
popping out behind it to slow it down, the
sinister aircraft stopped and two figures in space suits emerged.

Lockheed SR71 Blackbird

My driver was assigned to the pilot and enquired if breakfast would be needed. 'No, we just ate in Washington', said the pilot.

When asked how long ago that was, he replied 'an hour and twenty nine minutes'.

THE LAST SPY IN BRITAIN

Some time ago I went to a dinner party at which there were two interesting guests. The first was Countess Taxis und Therme. This was the family that was given the rights to run the courier services for the Hapsburg Empire. It is their name which has, of course, been immortalised in the international word 'taxi'.

Of more interest to me was Miles Copeland, who was formerly with the CIA and often appeared on television as an expert on the world's secret services during the 1970's and 1980's.

The conversation did not start very well. I asked him what his children did and he said that his son played drums with 'The Police'. Not being much of a pop music fan, I asked, 'Metropolitan or City?' It took me some time to persuade him that I was not being disingenuous and really was just ignorant about his musician son Stewart. (Miles, had been a keen a jazz trumpeter, and was the only white musician in Erskine Hawkins's band at the Cotton Club.) Over dinner he told me the wonderful story of the last German spy in Britain.

Miles Copeland

'When we arrived in the UK after Pearl Harbour, we were determined to take our counter-espionage duties seriously. But the Brits told us that they had captured all the German spies and there was 'no need for our services and could we please not interfere'. To keep us distracted and happy, they kept inviting us on picnics with pretty Wren officers. However, we discovered that there really was one last German spy operating in Britain and determined that one Saturday we were going to capture him. So we went down to the armoury to collect smaller side-arms which were less conspicuous than our heavy Browning automatics, but the armourer seemed to be out (probably on another goddamn picnic) so we strapped on our huge guns and went down to the motor pool.

All the cars were out (no doubt on some god-damned picnic!). So we went out into the street and hailed a cab. We arrived at this house near Baker Street and told the cabby to keep his engine running as we prepared to suprise the German spy.

Now you know how in films the doors burst in easily when you shoulder them? Well, this one didn't and damned near broke my shoulder. We found the German actually on the radio and my friend escorted him downstairs at gun-point while I carried the radio. Radios are little tiny things now, this was a great big heavy thing. When we got in the street, the cab driver was a bit shaken. 'I sure 'ope you young fellas know what you're doin', he muttered, but we bundled the spy into the back of the cab and drove back to our building near the Embassy.

The cab driver became even more worried when we clumsily waved our huge guns around under his nose whilst fumbling for some change to pay him. Anyway, in spite of the Brits' opposition, we had captured the last German spy in Britain.'

DIXIE STRAND

LBJ, Lyndon Baines Johnson, was a United States President who people are only just beginning to appreciate. Over-shadowed by the glamour of the Kennedys, it was, nevertheless, Johnson who pushed through most of the great reforms, particularly in the area of race relations.

My admiration for Sam Johnson, his nephew, has to be rather more muted. Sam, a charming, drawling Texan, came into our lives not once, but twice. The first time was when an architect friend, who I knew from the Hundred Club, revealed that Sam wanted to buy it. He had elaborate plans for refurbishing it and for making it even more of a top jazz venue.

The owners, Roger and Pat Horton, were willing to sell, and Sam Johnson asked for our help in creating a group of additional investors. Max Collie, then one of the best known band leaders on the jazz scene, was even prepared to mortgage his Winnebago mobile home to raise his share of the money.

Eventually the day for the completion of the deal arrived, and everybody waited for Sam who did not turn up. Instead, his wife

Sam Johnson and the girls from Oklahoma

arrived in tears saying, 'The money is on its way, it will all be alright'. But, of course, it was not alright and the deal fell through.

In early 1983, Sam resurfaced. This time he was intent on starting a new club altogether at 75 The Strand, near Covent Garden. Once again, and I can't imagine why, I agreed to collect a band of investors.

The 'Dixie Strand Jazz Café' was quite an ambitious project, not only being a jazz club but a restaurant. Sam brought in special ovens from Texas to cook the authentic barbecued ribs and even imported hickory wood to give the grills the right smoky taste. He also brought over from Oklahoma City a number of extremely pretty waitresses, which seemed to us to be rather a good idea.

I was deputed to handle the advertising and public relations, which was quite successful, and at the opening we had lots of luminaries and excellent media comment.

Leading jazz bands, including Max Collie, Kenny Ball, Ken Colyer and George Melly, were all booked in the first few weeks. Basically the place was still under-financed and it takes time for a club to become well known especially as the Hundred Club was still there and thriving.

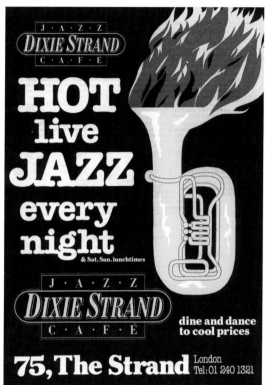

So, the financial storm clouds gathered and Sam suddenly announced that he was going back to Oklahoma and Texas to raise more money, perhaps from his aunt, Ladybird Johnson (yes she *is* called Ladybird). Sam left on the Wednesday. On Saturday night the pretty girls from Oklahoma emptied the till, switched off the lights, locked up the club and took the Sunday morning Delta flight back to Oklahoma City. So, I was left behind to explain to the investors where their money had gone.

Days later, I obtained the key for the club. It was just like exploring the *Marie Celeste*. Everything was exactly as it had been on that Saturday night with rows of bottles, unwashed glasses and, more seriously, a foot thick pile of bills on the doorstep. Sam never returned, never explained and certainly never apologised to me or anyone else. He had, moreover, done an amazing lease deal with Trust House Forte which meant that they as landlords could not get control of the space for years.

Five years later I was walking along the Strand one night and looked up. Suddenly an electrical fault briefly illuminated the sign above the old club's door. It was a ghostly reminder not to be bitten more than once.

I have a colleague in Ireland called Bart O'Brien (no close relation). We were handling a project in the West of Ireland, and Bart recalled that twenty-eight years before he had worked as a young travelling salesman for Guinness and how he had to virtually bribe the shops with trinkets to take the product at all. As we drove through the little town of Ennistymon, Bart spied a small establishment with the words *Blake* written above the door.

Mrs. Blake (left) and a giggling friend

'My goodness, I wonder if Mrs Blake is still alive and if she would possibly remember me?'

We entered the dark little shop and there was a little old lady. Bart said, 'Hello Mrs Blake, do you remember me?'

'Hello Bart,' she says, 'Now do you have any of those tea towels or trays for us?'

Twenty eight years had gone by, Bart now had white hair and she was greeting him as if he had missed maybe a couple of monthly visits!

DAVID IN SCOTLAND

The strange adventures of my in-laws deserve recognition. My brother-in-law, David Cowley, seemed to have some bad luck with his girlfriends in Scotland. First there was the occasion when his very grand hostess sat him down in front of a huge fireplace at her Scottish castle and announced 'You must understand that there *are* only two families in Ayrshire.' (He did not wonder aloud if the Burns family, with its poet son Robbie, was the other.)

Then there was the time that he arrived late for a cocktail party before dinner and was curtly told to 'Pick up a tray of glasses and hand them round' by his host, who plainly thought he was a hired Italian waiter. When dinner was served and David sat down in his appointed place half way down the table, the old gentleman glared at him for several minutes until somebody put him straight.

The worst occasion was when he had driven in his Mini all the way from London. When the butler unpacked his suitcase he remarked that he did not appear to have his dinner jacket which would be necessary on Saturday night. David admitted to the butler that he had forgotten to bring it.

The next day, on the pretext of visiting local castles, he drove all the way down to London, picked up his dinner jacket and drove all the way back, a round trip of about 600 miles. He was just in time to proudly descend the stairs in his dinner jacket to find that everybody was dressed in suits, the kindly butler having tipped off the rest of the party that 'Mr Cowley had forgotten his dinner jacket.' Why he did not just drive to the nearest town and hire one, of course, has never been related.

THE TWO-LIPPED DOOR SNAIL

David and his wife Nikki had a nice house near Kew Bridge on the quite narrow road which was designated the South Circular Road. They wanted to build a garage between their house and the railway embankment on a patch of scrubby wasteland about five yards wide.

When they applied for planning permission, they ran into a bizarre objection. Their application was refused on the grounds that the minute piece of scruffy bushes and grass was the home of the 'Two-Lipped Door Snail'.

They countered this by demanding that gastropod experts (see page 71) come and inspect the land. This they duly did and could find no trace of the rare creature, so David asked if he could re-submit his application.

'No,' was the response, 'even though the Two-Lipped Door Snail is not there, it *could* come and live there.'

David could not help blurting, 'How the hell is it going to arrive – by the District Line?'

While these strange arguments were going on, it was announced that the South Circular Road in front of David and Nikki's home was going to be enlarged into a major thoroughfare as part of a set of plans for improving the roads of West London. This would have disastrously lowered the value of their house, so we suggested that if the snail was formerly so jolly rare (which it is, *Balea biplicata* is nearly extinct), its possible presence could now be used to stop the widening of the road. This legal ploy was never put to the test because all the road improvements were shelved and Nikki and David moved to the country.

I pass their old house at least once a week and I can never forget the possible presence of the subversive snail.

BORING FELLOW

Another reason I always remember their house is one of the more embarrassing incidents that could ever happen to anyone. David came home from work and could not find Nikki anywhere. His disquiet increased when he discovered the telephone swinging off the hook. He searched the house and then went out into the garden and found Nikki hiding in the garden shed, crying and muttering to herself – a bit like the little girl in *Jaws 2*, who has seen her friend eaten by the shark.

It transpired that Nikki had been telephoned by a man who said, 'Is the old man there?' Nikki only knew one person who referred to David that way. So she made a fatally wrong assumption as to the identity of the caller, and asked, 'Who on earth would you recommend we have to dinner with that frightful bore John and his wife?'

A few seconds of silence. 'It's that frightful bore John speaking,' said the caller who happened to be David's boss. There could be no back-tracking from such a situation and Nikki was right to go and hide in the shed, because David's boss referred to the fact that he was 'that bore' for months afterwards. Eventually David had to change jobs.

DRUGS HAUL

I don't think many people would dispute that Britain's hard-pressed police force is not quite what it used to be.

My sister-in-law Susan – then married to a Brigadier – had rented their flat to some somewhat dubious characters. The tenancy ended, Sue rang her tenants to say that she wanted to come and look in on the flat and got a rather evasive answer, so she just decided to drop in. She let herself in with her own keys and took a quick look at the place which seemed reasonably in order and then sat on the bed watching television before going out for a drink with a friend. Her hand brushed along the bed and touched a plastic bag. She looked under the mattress and there were two large rubbish bags. When she pulled them out she found they were full of plastic parcels with white powder in them. She suspected the worst and pulled both bags out from under the bed as her friend, who was a Doctor, turned up. They agreed that these should be delivered to the local police station and Sue asked her friend to help carry them because they were too heavy for her.

My sister-in-law Susan

They went to the police station and dumped them on the desk, the Police Sergeant took all sorts of notes and promised to send round someone the next day to investigate what was obviously part of a drug gang. Having changed all the locks and somewhat fearful, Sue had to stay at home all next day and indeed the day after that. After 48 hours, she rang up to say she wanted to go back to the country and ask why the police had not turned up.

The voice from the police station said, 'I'm sorry Madam, but we don't have any record of this incident, may I ask if you obtained a receipt for these alleged goods?' Susan spluttered that of course she had not demanded a receipt, she thought she was simply reporting criminal activity, not delivering lost property. It became apparent that as far as the police were concerned, she had never visited them and the drugs had simply disappeared.

Her husband, Robin Rhoderick-Jones, was on a course with some senior people from the Metropolitan Police a few weeks later who simply shrugged and said that the drugs would have been used as a 'drop' (plant) or sold back on to the street immediately to the immense enrichment of several policemen.

Why did she not report this?

The frightening thing is that Susan did not feel it wise to issue any kind of further complaint.

There is a very smart girls' school in Connecticut where my second sister-in-law, Sally Jane, completed the last year of her education.

When Sally-Jane arrived for the 1963 fall semester, the school was still giggling about the Summer Ball.

One of the teachers had rung the local military academy. 'Would you please like to send us thirty cadets for our Summer Ball? You know, suitable for our young ladies. Perhaps no Jewish cadets, if you know what I mean.'

'I quite understand,' said Captain Cohen, with a smile as he put down the phone.

On the night of the Ball the welcoming committee, all dressed in white gowns, greeted the bus, from which stepped, immaculate in their dress uniforms, thirty tall, beaming, handsome and very black cadets!

There are times when you have no opportunity to explain. Liz and I had sold our houses and bought one together but as part of the deal, I had inherited not one but two cats. One of these I hated and, typical of cats, it loved me. Every morning 'Buttons' would sneak into our bedroom and leap up on me.

Some American business guests, basically strangers, had arrived late and retired early to the guest room next to our bedroom. They did not even know we had any cats. So their opinions of our marriage must have been greatly influenced by my shouts through the wall. 'GET OFF ME, YOU BITCH, GET OFF MY CHEST, YOU DISGUSTING CREATURE, FOR GOD'S SAKE, STOP SLOBBERING ON ME!'

By the time we got up, our guests had packed and quietly departed, never to be in touch again.

After the 'earn-out period' with WPP and about 25 years in the graphic design business, I decided not to sign on for another period and so I left my friends at Sampson Tyrrell to go back to international marketing. Something very interesting came along.

WRONG CALL

Sally Jane (left) gets her exam results

CAT NAP

CONTRACT ENDS

The film business has always been an interest of mine and in 1991 I decided to help an old friend, Barry Palin, a distant cousin of Michael Palin, build up his production company.

Known for his unperturbed *sang-froid* when facing the vicissitudes of film production, he was once faced with a stuntman who suddenly refused point-blank to jump into a studio tank filled with inky black water whilst dressed as a spider – as a result of some phobia. Barry donned the costume and jumped in himself, admitting later to me that he stayed underwater for far longer than the shot required, just in order to impress the crew.

Ironically enough, having produced many films and videos for the tobacco industry, a highlight of his career was a BAFTA award for a Chekhov piece starring Edward Fox, entitled *The Harmfulness of Tobacco*.

An introduction to one of his clients opened up a huge new task. Mary Pottorff, a forceful executive at Philip Morris, asked me how we could 'reach an accommodation between smokers and non-smokers in hotels and restaurants'. Little did I know what I was letting myself in for. Together, in cooperation with the International Hotel & Restaurant Association, we created the *Courtesy of Choice* programme. This complex alliance between the hospitality, ventilation and tobacco industries is now successfully operating in over 50 countries, nearly 10,000 establishments and in material in 28 languages. If I thought myself well travelled before, I had another thing coming as I criss-cross the globe to Asia, Latin America, Africa and Europe. It has been fascinating, not just the job but the involvement with the politics and social issues of so many countries – not least those who have recently emerged from Communism.

FALKLANDS ADVICE

One of the first people I worked with was a genial and huge American, Dan, who introduced our *Courtesy of Choice* programme to Chile and Costa Rica. He spoke fluent Spanish and had lived in Argentina for many years.

He was drafted into the American army during the Vietnam War, where he was a Signals Officer. After Vietnam, he moved back to Argentina, where he lived with his wife who was from Chile. On 1st April 1982, there was a knocking on the door. There was a captain in the Argentine army who said, 'The Military Junta wish to see you immediately'.

In Argentina, when military cars came for you, it was wise to pay some attention. He was driven to the Casa Rosada, the famous pink parliament building and was ushered in to a room full of officers, and General Galtieri and other members of the Junta. There was one other foreigner in the room, an Israeli called Mr Cohen who imported fruit. It transpired that these two were the only people in the whole of Argentina, population 32 million, who had any combat experience.

A senior officer turned to my friend and said, 'Señores, tomorrow we attack the Malvinas. What do you think of that?'

Not knowing if the Argentinians celebrated April Fool's Day, Dan responded, 'If you attack with two thousand little children waving flowers or maybe 2,000 penguins, I think you will be alright. But if you attack with real troops, I think that Señora Thatcher will attack back.'

The officer stared coldly at him and exclaimed, 'Ridiculo!' Even though Mr Cohen agreed with Dan, they were ushered from the room while the High Command continued with their ill-fated plans.

Throughout the Falklands War, every few days a staff car collected Dan, another collected Mr Cohen and drove them to the Casa Rosada, and the military command asked their advice as if they were the ultimate in strategic planners. On one occasion they said to Dan, 'Now, where do you think the British will attack?'

He said, 'I don't know, I am just a public relations man, as I have been trying to tell you. But,' he said, 'looking at this map, I am sure they will not attack near Port Stanley, because I should think the water is too rough. They will probably go somewhere more protected like this place ... San Carlos.'

'Ridiculo!' once again. As before, the two were bundled into staff cars and driven back home. Next day, the British, of course, went ashore at San Carlos.

This bizarre pattern continued throughout the Falklands War. I later recounted this to Sir John Nott, the British Defence Secretary, who was suitably amazed to think that the only strategic advice to counter the might of his Task Force was the very tentative opinions of an Israeli fruit importer and an American PR man!

There is a footnote to this. Dan, having seen how appallingly the Americans had treated their Vietnam veterans, suspected that the Argentinians would be even worse after a failed war against the British. So, he took several weekends off to visit the hospitals and resettlement centres in the South of the country to try and help the young Argentine troops who were shell-shocked from their experience, yet were now ignored by their own people.

Captured young Argentinian troops

VINCENT BRAMLEY

Israel is another country with which I have become familiar, and whose problems I have been able to observe. While I have great sympathy with the Palestinians, you also have to admire the way the Israelis have built their country. But the tensions are there all the time. There is constant trouble with neighbouring countries, there is terrorism and people openly carry guns stuffed into the back of their trousers.

In 1995 the International Hotel Association held its Congress in Tel Aviv, 600 of us attended the opening ceremony which started with one of the most brilliant musical events I have ever seen, with Israeli dancers and singers performing the songs of nearly every country attending the Congress.

On that first evening Yitzak Rabin, the Prime Minister addressed us, because tourism is vital to the country's economy. While he spoke, I noticed young men with dark suits, microphones and earphones, who were obviously his security people. But there had been no real security check when we entered the hall and Rabin came and sat behind me less than eight feet away. I could have been carrying a gun.

The next day, Shimon Peres, the former Prime Minister and now a Cabinet Minister in the coalition came to address us at lunch. As we entered the hall there *was* security, but it consisted of two seventeen-year-old girl private soldiers from the Israeli army, who casually looked through handbags and briefcases and then asked, 'Do you have a gun?'

I turned to our clients who were hosting the lunch and said, 'If that is Israeli security, it certainly is not what I thought it was'. (One's expectations of their security had been tempered by the extraordinary and boring procedures you have to go through when flying with El Al). Again, if I had smuggled in a gun, I could have shot Peres easily from under our VIP table.

The next night we were at a ball. As it ended Penina Ben David, my main contact at the Israeli Hotels Association, blurted out, 'We've got to go home. Our Prime Minister has just been shot'. The music stopped, and 600 delegates walked morosely down the sea front and locked themselves in their rooms to watch CNN. The awful truth emerged that an Israeli fanatic, assumed to be a chauffeur, had been able to kill Rabin because of the dreadfully lax level of security.

I had to stay in Israel so I watched Rabin's very moving funeral on television attended by President Clinton and world leaders with particularly poignant speeches by Palestinian leader Yasser Arafat and King Hussain of Jordan. At the end of the ceremony, instead of the two minutes silence that we have on Armistice Day in Britain, a two minute sounding of the sirens started, the same sirens that a couple of years before had been announcing incoming Scud missiles from Iraq.

Yitzak Rabin

I went out on to the hotel balcony and was astounded to see that the motorway along the sea front was full of cars that had stopped, the doors open and everyone standing to attention. People were standing to attention in the swimming pool and across the length of the beach were also hundreds of immobile figures. It was a really eerie sight.

The aftermath of Rabin's assassination underlined the fact that Israel is a tiny place and, a bit like Ireland, everyone knows everyone else. Most relationships have also been cemented in hard service in the army or in the turmoil of Israeli politics. Dan Litani, my public relations friend in Tel Aviv had helped with Rabin's first political campaign. Dan was also a childhood friend of the Netanyahu family, who would produce two famous brothers. While not close to 'Bibi', Benjamin, the ex-Prime Minister, he shared an apartment with Jonathan, commander of the brilliant raid on Entebbe, who died heroically rescuing the Israeli hostages in 1976 from their Palestinian hijackers and their Ugandan host, the ridiculous but murderous Idi Amin.

The relationship started when little Danny Litani was given first prize by the matriarch of the family at a children's fancy dress party. When asked why she had not given the prize to a more deserving and pretty little girl, Mrs. Netanyahu replied, 'I didn't know her parents!'

A few years ago something terrible happened to our very good friends, Guy and Frederique Guillemard. Both Guy and Fred have at various stages worked for me, Guy had also been my client when he was general manager of the Dubai World Trade Centre and is godfather to my son, Edmond. We had not heard from them for a while until they suddenly came round to our house for advice. This is the story.

Guy had returned from Dubai after ten years working for Sheik Rashid al Maktoum, the ruler. The generous bonus he got had proved inadequate for launching a business venture, so looking for a way to raise a bit of money or to use something as collateral, Frederique remembered the two 'fancy pink' diamonds, the size of her little finger nail, that her aristocratic great aunt had given her after smuggling them out of Russia just after the 1917 Revolution. (Frederique is a combination of French, Polish, German and Russian.)

On a personal recommendation they took them to the polished diamond division of a very large diamond company. The Director examined the two diamonds for fifteen minutes using the normal instruments, then called in another expert who examined them for a further ten minutes. The Director then stated that, 'This is like finding a Rembrandt in your attic. We estimate that these are worth between $5 and $15 million'.

Rabin's sad funeral, more than a family bereavement

LEGS DIAMOND

World Trade Centre, Dubai

My friends were stupefied, having thought in terms of about £100,000.

The diamond company even gave them a written and signed evaluation of $6 million, subject to a report of a diamond grading laboratory. They also recommended that the diamonds should be sent to New York to have a final purity test because top stones go to the GIA (Gemmological Institute of America). They would then go on to Sotheby's in Geneva. The insurance 'would cost $12,000 a week but it would be worth it'.

The Guillemards had to go back to work in France, so their lawyer arranged for the diamonds to be sent from their bank in a Brinksmat armoured van down to the diamond company for transmission to New York, with several of the company's own large coloured diamonds, theoretically fully insured.

The Guillemards' lawyer rang up after seven days to see if the diamonds were already en route to Sotheby's in Geneva, and what final value had been placed on them. After two or three days when the Director was unavailable, his deputy spoke with the Guillemards lawyer. 'I am sorry' he said, 'but we were a bit worried about these diamonds, so we opened the package and we found they were glass. We also cancelled the insurance policy, *ab initio* because we figured your clients could no longer pay.'

My friends were totally devastated, and have remained so for the past seven years as they struggled with few resources to obtain redress. First it is inconceivable that two experts on diamonds could not notice that the stones were glass when they first examined them. After all, the Director is one of the world's leading experts on top-quality coloured polished diamonds. It is also inconceivable that my friends would have switched the diamonds because they had absolutely no interest in doing so and, indeed, are still recovering.

Financial Times, 16th March 1997

The 12-carat mystery

So you have to draw the conclusion that employees of the eminent diamond company simply took the stones and replaced them with glass replicas which they had had time to do during the theoretical New York validation trip. Incidentally, that division of the diamond company is also the specialist unit that makes imitation diamonds.

Some strange things happen. The Guillemards' lawyer's offices were broken into, and the sole item stolen was the computer on the desk of the partner handling their case. They also noticed that they were the subject of attention of private investigators. As the legal fees mounted to unsustainable levels, the Guillemards felt they could not proceed to court.

They fought this case for seven years. It was featured in a *Financial Times* article called 'The Twelve Carat Mystery'.

Last year the diamond company settled out of court with 'no admission of liability' for a reputed six figure sum.

It proves the old theory that litigation is only for the very brave, and only works for the very rich or the very poor.

Another of my friends got caught up in a similar and completely unexpected nightmare.

Mike Campbell Bowling has always been passionate about racing cars and in the past few years has put all his money into restoring classic sports cars rather than investing in a house as most of the rest of us do. This worked quite well for a while but after the 1987 financial crash, when collectibles suffered even more than property, he was strapped for cash. He had a beautiful dark blue Dino Ferrari and, partly because I had always wanted to own a Ferrari and partly to help him out with cash, I bought a half share in it (sadly at the top of the market.)

For a while we kept this car in a garage in South Kensington, but eventually, even though we could not sell the car for a decent price, Mike successfully sold the garage. Needing a home for the Dino he put it into the fabulous collection at Brocket Hall where it sat, a blue exception among a sea of red Ferraris.

I have never met Charles Brocket, and I don't wish to do so now bearing in mind his subsequent behaviour. But Mike knew him, it cost us nothing to have the car there, and it was not impossible that some Japanese enthusiast might spot the Dino and buy it.

Some time later the press announced that there had been a break-in at Brocket Hall in Hertfordshire and five cars had been stolen. Remembering that our car was still insured for the old price, I jokily asked Mike if the Dino had been among them, and was a little disappointed that it was not.

Soon the story broke that these cars had not been stolen at all and that Lord Brocket stood accused of engineering an insurance fraud. As this event was coupled with the bitter break-up of the Brockets' marriage, I advised Mike to get our car out of the collection and put it somewhere safer. I then lost interest in the Brocket saga.

One evening Mike invited me round for a drink and he and his wife appeared very depressed. It transpired that, in order to

BROCKET'S BLOW TORCH

The Dino with Mike and me

Brocket Hall

Birdcage Maserati at Le Mans

raise insurance money, Brocket had ordered his mechanic and his handyman to cut up five priceless classic cars including a Birdcage Maserati. In my eyes this crime would warrant the death penalty. His wife Isa, now safely back in Latin America, had informed the police of this scam but, for personal reasons, had also mentioned my friends the Bowlings.

At 5.30 one morning, there was a knock on the door at Mike's house in Chelsea. Detectives from Hertfordshire CID took him back to a police station accusing him of being an accomplice to Brocket's fraud. There were some fairly laughable aspects to the interrogation, for instance, 'You were at public school like Lord Brocket, weren't you Mr Bowling?'

'Yes, that is correct,' agreed Mike, 'but as I am twenty years older than Brocket, I would have left Westminster before he was even born, let alone before he went to Eton.'

'Well,' sneered the Sergeant, 'you were an officer in the armed forces like Lord Brocket, weren't you?'

'Correct,' continued Mike patiently, 'but as I have said, I am twenty years older than him, so I would have left the Royal Air Force, again before he was born, let alone before he went into the cavalry.'

'But it is true to say you are an insurance broker, Mr Bowling?'

'Correct,' agreed Mike, 'but I am only licensed to handle life and pensions, so if you are implying that I insure motor cars you will find you are wrong.'

This dim level of interrogation continued for hours and as evening drew on Mike's lawyer said, 'Well, perhaps we could go now and continue tomorrow?'

'No,' snarled the woman police Sergeant, 'Let him spend a night in the cells and see how the other half live.' And so he did. So began a seven-month nightmare. The Crown Prosecution Service and the police had plainly picked on Mike thinking he was a good friend of Brocket's and that Brocket might crack, if only to help his friend. Not only did they not know Brocket very well but, as he was still pleading innocence, he could scarcely say that Mike was not part of his scam.

At several magistrate hearings, the handyman and the mechanic, who had turned Queen's Evidence and admitted their role, kept saying that Mike had nothing to do with the project and his only connection with Brocket Hall was to come up and see how the blue Dino was from time to time.

Eventually, the case reached a proper court and within minutes of the case opening, the judge ordered Mike to leave the dock because there was no shred of evidence against him and he awarded 'all costs' against the CPS.

During this period Mike had lost a lot of money paying for lawyers and barristers. He had to take one of his daughters out of school as she had become ill with worry, and needed nine months of expensive treatment. What is more, during the time he was an 'undischarged felon', his company had been forced by IMRO rules to stop him working on his own with his life and pension clients (people like me), until he was exonerated. This had eroded his earning capacity.

The total refund he received from the Law Society was about £1,000. The horrifying aspect of this story, as *The Daily Telegraph* was later to point out, was that it could happen to any of us and all the innocence in the world would not help us. *Guilty until proved innocent* now seems to be the rule.

Lucky break?

A designer in Gloucestershire once asked Liz to write some leaflets for a do-it-yourself chain, including laying paths and patios. If she had any technical questions, he told her to 'call or visit our handyman called Fred West.'

It's a good thing she did not need help. Fred West was soon to be arrested and charged with murdering 17 women, including his daughter, buried under his patio, no doubt, excellently and professionally laid.

Roger Whittaker and Natalie have certainly lived a full life. Writing 80% of his own material Roger has been a worldwide success. When *Durham Town* took off it persuaded him to abandon academia and throw himself into singing and song writing. Hits have included: *I don't believe in if any more, New World in the morning, Why?* and *What love is.*

Last Farewell was number one in eleven countries, number six in the USA and number two in Britain for eleven weeks. It was recorded later by dozens of artists including the King himself, Elvis Presley.

But it has not all been plain sailing.

ROGER – THE SMOOTH AND THE ROUGH

In the music business it is about as hard for an artist to keep his money as in the film business. As Roger ruefully concedes, 'If you drop out of the charts the receptionist who sent you champagne one week, cannot remember your name the next.' The changes of taste, technology and media demographics (in particular radio airplay for so called 'middle of the road' music) are such that to get his music and recordings to his audience, the long and often arduous concert tours have to continue. Enjoyable but exhausting.

In was during a break from such a tour that Roger received the

most horrific shock of his life – the murder of his father Edward in Kenya. Thieves broke in and beat the old man senseless. When Vi, his 83-year-old wife, returned with the shopping they beat her, tied her up and dumped her in the bath. She resourcefully plunged under water pulling out the plug with her teeth, pretended to be dead for five hours and when the thieves left she managed to roll out of the bath and hit the panic alarm button with her head. Her husband was found rolled up in a carpet, dead. The murderers have never been caught and probably never will be. Vi returned with Natalie and Roger to live in the UK, where she died of old age in 1989.

Natalie's life has not been routine either. Apart from bringing up five children, writing and backing Roger's career, she has been a pilot with both aerobatics and air races under her belt.

Of all their attractive and interesting children, Guy and Jessica have followed the showbiz route. After dancing and singing (sometimes on Roger's shows) Jessica is now a journalist/presenter broadcasting several fashion pieces and travel shows like LWT's *Dream Ticket* and Channel 4's *The Really Dangerous Travel Show*. But it's not surprising that films and music dominate, with several shows for VH1, Sky's Oscar Awards with Barry Norman and interviews with stars like Tom Hanks and Steven Spielberg.

MESSIAH MASSIAH

Roger Whittaker's views on survival in the music business are reflected by our exotic friend Zeeteah Massiah. Born in Barbados and brought up in London, she started singing in her Seventh Day Adventists' Church, and soon became involved with a reggae label, notably with a version of *We've got a good thing going*, courtesy of The Jackson Five. 'I never got paid', laughs Zeeteah, 'I was just thrilled to be singing.'

She has since sung with Michael Jackson, and performances with luminaries such as Tom Jones, Phil Collins, Lisa Stansfield, Lulu, Simply Red, Sting and Julia Fordham have only confirmed Zeeteah's view that 'The best people are incredible, but commenting on the worst would land me in court.' For the record, Zeeteah counts Bob Monkhouse, Tom Jones, Richard O'Brien (writer of the 'Rocky Horror Show' and sadly no relation), Paul Weller and Lisa Stansfield as particularly amazing and rewarding individuals.

Her career has taken her the length of Japan with top star Eikichi Yazawa and touring Poland with Mungo Jerry, where people often came up and touched her, never having seen a black person before.

She has always spoken her mind and it was Zeeteah who marched up to Johnny Hallyday when the show was one and a half hours late and said 'Alright Johnny, we know you're the star, but let's get the show on the road. We and the audience have waited long enough'. She adds, 'The trouble is some top stars are surrounded by 'Yes' people who dare not speak the truth. Who are they kidding? Not the artist'. In this book, Zeeteah certainly didn't dare to 'sing'.

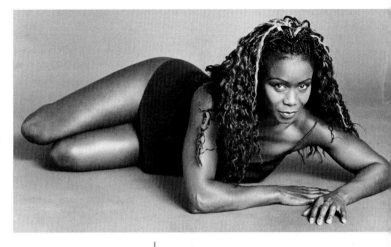

If you have to visit, work or live in Africa, then Zimbabwe used to be probably the best place, mainly for the incredible friendliness of the people. However, economic and political chaos is beginning to affect this beautiful country and we will all have to wait and see.

I first visited the country during the war in Rhodesia, as it then was. We flew in a Viscount from Salisbury to Victoria Falls and it was unnerving that the visible level of military protection escalated at each airport. In Salisbury there were soldiers with automatic rifles, at Kariba it was jeeps with Browning machine-guns and at Victoria Falls it was armoured cars.

Not much has changed since that first breathtaking view of the Falls and the booze cruise on the Zambezi is just the same. The Viscounts have gone and indeed the very Viscount I flew in was shot down by a rocket from Joshua Nkomo's forces, killing the pilot, passengers and no-doubt the pretty and friendly air hostesses that we had chatted up.

Recently my agency has done the tourism and public relations for Zimbabwe, although that has stopped since the country appeared to run out of money. It was one of my visits to Harare that I met Norman Travers. He was introduced by Chris Cox and his girlfriend Julie Garnier, a beautiful French rhinoceros vet who had been involved in projects to revive the rhino population from virtual destruction, due to poachers killing them for their horns. Julie looked after sixty female rhinos in her area in the South of the country, the *Lowveldt*. One of the

TRAVERS OF THE RHINOS

Victoria Falls

Julie with her trackers

methods of testing fertility was to track, in extreme danger, the rhinos through the bush and pick up the faeces for later analysis by the Zoological Society of London computers back in England. On two occasions, I was asked to take a number of sachets of white powder back through Gatwick Airport. Any customs man who had not been convinced by my letter of authorisation from the Zoological Society was immediately convinced by my advice, 'You can taste or sniff it if you like, mate. I wouldn't. It's dried rhino shit'.

Norman's strange herd of rhino orphans, now grown up

Julie also used to visit the rhinos quite close to Harare that were under the care of Norman Travers, an extraordinary man straight out of books like *Sanders of the River*. He had elected to take over the young baby rhinos who had been orphaned after their adult parents were killed for their horns. These little rhinos had been picked up from the bush and nursed to adulthood.

This produced one of the strangest collections of animals living in the strangest of ways. We drove out with Norman to a feeding station on the dirt road. An elephant came wandering out of the bush and then suddenly there were the rhinos, fifteen of them, all now fully grown, happily pottering about in a little herd with their friend the elephant. Accompanying them were three cheerful Zimbabweans, one with a rifle (to shoot at potential poachers) and the other two with sticks with bits of wire with which they tapped the rhinos if they strayed, like maverick cattle.

A group of visiting children came past on a flat-bed trailer and were lifted up on to the elephant while the rhinos continued to munch contentedly. Norman asked Julie to go and look at the rhinos and she wandered in amongst them inspecting them for any medical problems. My friend Chris Cox, however, would have nothing to do with them, having been in the bush with such animals, when keeping an eye open for the nearest tree was the normal best practice.

The rhinos were driven every night like a herd of contented cows back to their protected quarters and then driven out every morning for grazing. Normally rhinos are lone animals in the bush, extremely dangerous to approach, but these had been brought up to behave like cows so that is how they did behave. Incidentally, Norman's territory seemed to be full of curious friendships. Later that day we saw a herd of buffalo, once again led by a lone elephant, whom they appeared to have elected as their unofficial leader.

I hope Norman and his rhinos survive the turmoils.

In the recent crisis, 'paranoia' is often used about Mugabe's regime. My brother Lucius suffered from this when, as one of Zimbabwe's official sugar brokers on a marketing trip, he was about to fly out from Harare. Pulled into a tiny room by a two policemen with sub-machine guns, he was asked why he had not spent more money during his visit.

Stripped completely naked, presumably because he might have been smuggling the sugar farmers' currency out in his underpants, he passed a very frightening and humiliating hour before he was released. How not to treat your friends!

One of the problems of a pervasive media, especially television, is that it makes us all feel we are on the fringe of famous people. There lie the seeds of embarrassing moments caused by mistaken identity.

My sister-in-law Susan got in a long conversation during a country event with someone who she vaguely thought she had met at dinner. Only gradually did she realise she was talking to the Duke of Kent.

Liz, my wife, can be even worse. There was some excuse on the *Highlander*, the yacht owned by the Forbes family, for not immediately recognising Caspar Weinberger, the former United States Secretary of State. She had rather less excuse when she button-holed a man in a restaurant who she was sure she knew as an Account Director at an advertising agency. The conversation went on quite a long time because Liz was asking him about 'his campaigns', so David Steel, leader of the Liberal Party, did not know she had made a mistake, probably thinking she was one of his party supporters and was embarrassed that he could not place her.

Her mind was even less in gear when a friend of hers said they had bought a house 'from the Carrington's', meaning Lord Carrington, Conservative politician and former Foreign Secretary. Liz, then an avid watcher of the glamorous soap opera *Dynasty*, asked 'whether Denver was not rather a long way away to have their main house!'

It can go the other way too. A colleague of mine, Cydney Barker, kindly gave a lift from a party by a man she vaguely recognised. It was only in the pub, where he was giving her a thank-you drink, that the autograph hunters revealed that she was with Steve McQueen.

My wife Liz Cowley's grandfather was the rector of Stinsford, known to readers of Thomas Hardy's novels as 'Mellstock'. The rectory lies just a short walk away from the Lower Bockhampton crofter's cottage where Hardy was born, and for which he retained great affection, frequently walking three miles to visit it from his second home at Max Gate, Dorchester.

The Reverend Hubert Cowley and his wife Ethel were extremely friendly with the Hardys, even though Hardy was an atheist. Ethel was so attached to Florence, Hardy's second wife, that when the latter died, she erected a gravestone in her honour which can still be seen in St. Michael's, Stinsford today. Look out for the inscription 'We did sweet counsel keep' on a little cross tucked just beyond the confines of the churchyard.

My father-in-law, John Cowley, the rector's son, recalled Hardy as an extremely dour and tacit man. He often told us how, as a

MISTAKEN IDENTITY

LICHFIELD

Joan Collins, star of Dynasty and of my documentary, The Golden Gong, daughter of Roger Whittaker's agent, Joe Collins.

HARDY'S HEART

small boy, he used to accompany him on various walks, during which the great man never said a word. John could never understand how he could write prose and poetry of such towering passion.

It was not surprising that John far preferred the more colourful figure of D.H. Lawrence whom he used to see on his occasional visits to Max Gate, or when the two writers ventured over to Stinsford. Liz's grandmother was, conversely, horrified by 'that ghastly man in the Panama hat', and made strenuous efforts to prevent either of her inquisitive sons even catching a glimpse of this depraved author of *Lady Chatterley's Lover* and other 'disgusting' novels.

It was agreed that when Hardy died his ashes should lie in Poet's Corner in Westminster Abbey, while his heart would be buried at Stinsford according to his wishes. As the Mayor put it 'We shall have the best part of Hardy buried with us'. Indeed they did, but not quite in the way that was expected.

What happened then was quite extraordinary, and a long-kept secret in Liz's family, until the story gradually filtered out and eventually exploded into the pages of *The Observer* in December 1995. When Hardy died in January 1928, his heart was surgically removed, wrapped in a tea-towel and placed in a biscuit-tin to await the undertaker.

Unfortunately, a hungry cat managed to negotiate the lid with extremely unfortunate consequences. Upon his arrival, the horrified undertaker found one replete cat and one empty biscuit tin and put two and two together, one and one having already conjoined. With commendably swift action on behalf of the nation, if not the cat, he grabbed the poor animal, wrung its neck, and stuffed it, Hardy's heart and all, back into the tin. It is reputed that he later said, 'Mr 'Ardy wanted is 'eart buried at Stinsford, and buried at Stinsford Mr 'Ardy's 'eart shall be'. And so it was, with the Reverend Henry Cowley and his curate presiding over the service, both of whom were now undoubtedly aware of the disaster.

Hardy was so attached to Stinsford all his life, it is rather comforting to know that when his life ended, his heart did indeed lie here, even if not quite in the way England or he had intended.

A short letter concludes this story. Some years before Hardy's death, the Reverend Cowley had written to ask him if, despite his apparent atheism, he could he count upon him as a parishioner. Hardy's reply had been brief. 'Dear Mr Cowley, Yes, regard me as a parishioner. Certainly, I hope to be still more

Thomas Hardy's Funeral, 1928

Hardy's grandfather, also called Thomas, built the O'Brien vault in Stinsford church. Lady Susan O'Brien, a daughter of the first Earl of Ilchester, disgraced herself by marrying the Irish comedian William O'Brien, a protégé of Garrick. 'Even a footman were preferable,' noted Horace Walpole. They lived a devoted married life for years at Stinsford House, next to the church.

Although she died in 1827, Lady Susan's memory was still warm in Hardy's childhood. 'She kept a splendid house', one of her own workman told him. '– a cellarful of home-brewed strong beer that would almost knock you down: everybody drank as much as he liked. The head gardener was drunk every morning before breakfast. There are no such houses now'. He should come back and visit the O'Brien house in Putney!

one when I am in a supine position one day. Sincerely Yours, Thomas Hardy.' Who could have guessed that he and a furry little cat would lie for eternity as Stinsford parishioners?

Among the artists I am proud to have known was Tom Eckersley, one of the great influences on British graphic art for the past five decades. His successful commercial partnership

with Eric Lombers was broken up when they joined up during the war, with Lombers in the Army and Tom as a cartographer in the Royal Air Force. By 1948, while few knew Tom's name, few could miss his distinctive posters which advised them to avoid accidents, shave with Gillette or fill their cars with Shell. Many of the designers who have worked with me regarded Tom as their spiritual father and many had actually trained under him as Head of Design at the London College of Printing, a post he held for 20 years.

His son, Tony, art-directed this book. Sometimes from the age of 12 Tony took over and replicated Tom's style when he was under pressure. So successful was Tony's ability that his father asked him to move out and move on! Tony duly went into magazine design at *Vogue*, and then advertising. He was pretty miffed when Tom asked to see his work and he showed him some major press campaigns, now using photography, of course. Tom just said 'Yes, but what do you *really* do?'

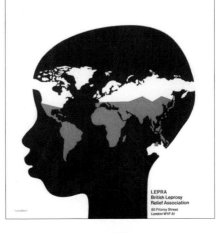

A GOOD IDEA AT THE TIME

It is only recently that I've come to know Sue Lloyd quite well. We'd met often especially in the sixties when she frequented 'Sibylla's' and the 'Establishment Club'. She was easily one of the most startling of the *Birds of Britain* (check out page 179). Her book *It seemed a good idea at the time* gives us a wonderful description of the Birds' fraught tour of the States, especially Middle America's shock at seeing mini-skirts for the first time, 'That's eeemoral, honey.'

Sue has led a dramatic and exotic life, first in modelling, then as an actress – fabulous opposite Michael Caine in *The Ipcress File.*

It was her fame as Barbara Brady in the very successful soap opera Crossroads that gives us two points in common. First at the peak of its success, 18 million viewers, *Crossroads* was inexplicably axed by the station's management. (I have shown how I have always been fired or 'let go' when success has just arrived.) Secondly, the tragic death of her co-star in *Crossroads* and husband, Ronnie Allen, has a nasty echo of my own experience. Ronnie's long-standing private health insurance company refused to pay up, trying to claim that he knew of his cancer when he signed

Sue with Michael Caine in 'The Ipcress File'

up again on returning to the UK from the States. Only when threatened with publicity did they relent. They finally called to say they would pay and Sue said, 'Too late, too late, Ronnie died two hours ago.'

I can absolutely relate to this. Recently, I had a sudden cancer scare which required immediate surgery. As I entered hospital, I learned that my insurance company was refusing to pay-up. 'You knew you had cancer before you took out your company's group policy.' Rubbish, of course. When financial worry is added to the normal anxiety before entering the operating theatre for serious surgery, it's really hard.

In my case, I am going to the Insurance Ombudsman for redress. For Sue and Ronnie there was no such help. Ronnie died and Sue never actually received a penny.

If you rely on the National Health Service you find long waiting lists and, at the same time, stories abound that the private insurance companies are deliberately beginning to question and block claims.

---

* *Insurance company names available on request.*

Catherine Shakespeare Lane has always been an avid collector, starting in the playground. Her difference is that she has been able to turn it into art. She points out 'London is a rich source of otherwise useless rubbish and junk, whether it's along the shoreline of the Thames or the skips and gutters of Soho. It's amazing what you find, can then squirrel away and years later it becomes part of a composition.' She spots photographs, discarded movie film from Soho's production houses, ragged envelopes, even a mouldy slice of bread with a workman's boot print – all weathered and altered by chemical reactions and passing time.

She is not a 'glamorous bag lady' (as somebody put it) but an artist who can make magic of what we discard – a 'modern archaeologist'. She is finalising a photographic exhibition *The Jacket* which features a hundred men over the years all wearing an old leather jacket found in a skip in Chelsea, including a young John Hurt and a Jeffrey Bernard who looks really quite well.

As David Gordon, the Secretary of the Royal Academy comments '*The Jacket* pre-empts Tracey Emin's *Tent*'.

THE ART OF RUBBISH

Soho film fragment (left)
Wooden back of gas cooker (top)
Jigsaw puzzle cutting jig (right)

COUPE

For the past ten years one of my favourite weekends has to be the Coupe des Nations, a clay pigeon shooting contest between British and French clubs. Typically we are Boodle's, Brooks's, the Caledonian, the City of London, Buck's, the Turf and the Garrick and the French include The Jockey Club, Automobile Club de France and so on. The French are a great deal richer than us ('if anything happened to this lot, the Bourse would collapse') and on paper rather grand with nearly everyone a Comte, Viscomte or Baron. But they are incredibly nice and hilarious to be with, as we alternate between superb locations in France or Britain. The two funniest must be Eric Palluat de Besset, and a born entertainer, Remi Danglade, who could quite easily have 'turned professional' as a comic.

As an eccentric Jean de Mouy must stand out. In a desperate attempt to handicap the French when in England, we stipulated only side-by-side shotguns could be used. Jean turned up with an ancient hammer gun. I asked him if he had any more and he replied, '118'. It turned out he is a fanatical collector of everything from rifles to shotguns, cigarette lighters to coffee pots, shoes to books and even buttons and old sewing machines. His wife Marie-Céline says, 'It's not worth opening a suitcase in our Paris apartment, there's so little room. Of course, the chateau is a bit better'.

Remi Danglade

Jean de Mouy

Dick Bilborough   *Ian Menzies*

The golden moment of the Coupe des Nations was when our bus emerged from the clubhouse in the Bois de Boulogne to find that Parisians had parked all over the verges blocking our exit. Dick Bilborough, captain of the Caledonian team said, 'Let's move them', leaping out with his team members *dressed in kilts* and lifting the cars bodily ('tossing the Citroen').

Such was our rapid progress that the bus fell behind and out of sight. I will never forget the startled expressions of the strolling Parisians as a gang of middle-aged men, 'many dressed as women', inexplicably threw cars about.

LOCKERBIE MYSTERY

A friend of mine who comes on these shooting matches against the French clubs told me a very interesting story. On December 23rd 1988, the morning after the Pan Am flight was blown out of the sky above Lockerbie, he arrived at his office in Sloane Street where his company represented Pan Am's in-flight magazine, *Clipper.*

Amongst the routine messages on the answer-machine was a message in Arabic, in which the only words they could understand were 'Lockerbie', 'Pan Am' and 'Air France'. Nobody in the office could understand it. But his boss, fluent in French, thought it sounded like French-accented Arabic. They also played the tape to Air France, for whom they also sold magazine advertising space. They didn't understand the message but they tracked down a Moroccan employee who listened to the tape. He said it was a message from a splinter group of Abu Nidal, claiming responsibility for blowing up Pan Am 103 and saying that they were calling his advertising company because they also intended to attack an 'Air France' plane, who were also a client.

My friend called his boss who then told him to get in touch urgently with the anti-terrorist division at Scotland Yard, who took down some of the details on the telephone and said they would send people round. Two detectives appeared and took

down a full statement. They played the tape, which again no-one understood. After they asked if there was a copy of the tape and were told 'no', it was put in a sealed envelope and taken away by the detectives.

Next day they received a call saying 'there is nothing of significance on the tape, don't waste our time and we advise you in the strongest terms not to mentioned this to anyone'. They did not offer to return the tape.

I am sure that everything has been properly handled, that the evidence on the tape has been looked at carefully, that it may have been a hoax and that both the prosecution and the defence lawyers at the trial of the two Libyan suspects in Holland have been fully informed about it. But it is still an interesting story.

JONATHAN AITKEN

Jonathan Aitken, thirty years on from those happy holidays with Selwyn Lloyd, managed to almost wreck his life at the age of 56. As a Cabinet Minister and Privy Councillor, he was accused by the *Guardian* of having his bill at Mohamed al-Fayed's Ritz Hotel in Paris paid for by an Arab. He sued for libel and lost. He was sent to jail for perjury for several months.

He has long ago 'peacefully accepted' that he had committed perjury and would have to pay for it. However, his fellow prisoners just could not understand that he had done anything wrong. Not only would they themselves expect to commit perjury routinely when pleading 'not guilty' but blurted out 'They'd have to build jails from here to Newcastle for all the coppers who should be banged up for perjury!'.

Jonathan recognises that he had ensured the special enmity of the media by trying to see sue one of their own. 'The media have become a privileged class these days, they seem to have forgotten the old adage about 'people who live in glass houses shouldn't throw stones.' For example, journalists are notorious for being among the world's greatest expense fiddlers, yet look how harsh they are about anyone else's expense reporting transgressions'.

Jonathan is rebuilding his life and is to take a theology degree at Oxford, a genuine interest. But when asked about plans, he ruefully quotes 'What makes God laugh? People who make plans.'

I suppose we all think our children are special and in some cases this is only too true. Take Murrough, my elder son. Not many people would say that he was run of the mill.

At the age of seven he had failed to be accepted by a school called Sussex House in Cadogan Gardens, London. Clare, his mother insisted that he be interviewed by the Headmaster who reluctantly agreed. The interview was going a bit stickily when Murrough leaned forward and said, 'I expect you would like to know about the things that interest me, Sir'.

'Yes, quite right. What does interest you?'

'Dinosaurs.'

'Fine, tell me the name of a few dinosaurs.'

Murrough set off at a gallop through the obvious ones, *Tyrannosaurus rex, Brontosaurus, Iguanadon* and so on. He hammered on down through *Ankylosaurus, Tetradon*. The Headmaster's jaw was beginning to drop when Murrough got into his stride. He rattled right on down to the most obscure chicken-sized dinosaurs that one could possibly imagine and, when he was on about number 85 the Headmaster held up his hand and said, 'OK, OK. What else do you know about?'

Murrough paused and said 'Greek gods.'

'Ah', said the Head, a trained classicist, leaning back more confidently, 'Tell me the names of some Greek gods'.

Murrough repeated the exercise. He started with all the famous ones and rattled straight on down through the semi-obscure to the most unknown chicken-sized Greek gods. The Headmaster raised his hand in defeat and said, 'Don't tell me any more. You have a place'.

This sort of set the pattern of Murrough's education. He passed into Winchester, which most would regard as either the cleverest or second cleverest school in the country. Almost immediately he set the record of being the only boy I know to single handedly to close down a minor sport at a major public school. With his budding acting flair he took the lead part in a strange play called *One Way Pendulum*, which was being directed by Joe Bain (who used to teach me years before at Stowe). At the same time, he had passed immediately into the school fencing team.

The trouble was he kept attending rehearsals for the play without telling the fencing master that he was going to be unable to attend matches. This man appeared to lose it and cancelled fencing for everyone. At Winchester there is a magnificent fencing hall, full of electronic scoring equipment, which remained unused for about five years, thanks to Murrough's casual attitude and the weak-kneed attitude of the Master in charge.

In fact, for such a wonderful school, weak-kneed would be one of the descriptions I would have to apply to Winchester at that time. I turned up at the end of the first term to ask his House Master how he was getting on. 'We're not quite sure. He always forgets to bring his work to class.'

'Well, how did he react the first time you beat him for it?', I asked innocently. His House Master stared at me appalled. I continued, 'Oh, yes, you're not allowed to do that now. So you probably have defaulter parades like we did at Stowe? You know, the ones that make you collapse after about twelve minutes. *That* would sort him out.'

The House Master's only reaction to this was, 'If you want a school like that, Mr O'Brien, I suggest you take your boy away'.

I was proved right, of course. I was very keen that Murrough should make it to Trinity College, Dublin and all his other exam results were on line, but he got a D in French as a direct result of *not turning up to his exam on time.*

He went on to Leicester University where he obtained a first class degree in English but, as an Irishman, I am afraid I do not regard Leicester as the equivalent of Trinity, Dublin.

Murrough remains a learned and charming young man. After University he went to acting school. One of the best results is his imitation of a dinosaur delivering a gin and tonic!

He did this party trick at a huge family occasion and after the clapping and laughter had died down, my mother-in-law turned to Liz and said quietly, 'Are they *all* like this?' presumably meaning my side of the family.

'Yes, just about.'

'My dear, I didn't realise you had so much strength.'

Through various girlfriends, he speaks a smattering of some of the world's most obscure languages and engages you in the most esoteric conversations, usually about the history of the Levant. Dinners have fallen silent when absorbing the news that the Byzantine Emperor Romanus Lecapenus was sired by an Armenian peasant with the equally eyebrow-raising name of 'Theophylact the Unbearable'. Or that the Ambassadors from Turkey visiting 'Vlad the Impaler' to demand tribute refused to remove their turbans for a 'princeling'. Vlad assured them that they need never be exposed to such diplomatic dilemmas again and promptly nailed their turbans to their skulls! The Sultan, far from exploding with rage, exclaimed, 'How can I possible drive a prince from his land who has such style?' Murrough has written a five-hour play called *The City*, which views the Fall of Constantinople from both the Greek and Turkish sides. It is all in *verse.* As I say, some people's children are a bit different and in Murrough's case the claim is justified.

YOUNG WHIPPERSNAPPERS?

Edmond

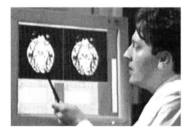

Dominic ffytche looking at brains

Clare in two roles

Currently 19, my younger son Edmond insists I have a pathological distrust of youth i.e. anybody under 50. Not so. I do have difficulty convincing him that a lack of knowledge about a narrow spectrum of pop stars, TV personalities, footballers and professional 'celebs' does not consign me to the subnormal category. My defence is that if you are a) not interested and b) not exposed to the relevant media, you just do not notice people. Thus the genius of the rock group Queen did not register with me until Freddie Mercury was dying of Aids, nor Beckham until he kicked someone, nor Johnny Vaughan until I had to sit in hospital daily with a purple Edmond (penicillin shock) and watch 'The Big Breakfast' on TV.

We seem to be surrounded by young people of extraordinary resourcefulness. I have nieces who have taught in Vietnam and Mozambique and my step-daughter Katy has travelled extensively throughout South East Asia and is currently working in Australia.

Katy

As for my godson, Dominic ffytche, he seemed one day to be grateful for his Christmas £5 note and the next a neuropsychiatrist, specialising in functional Magnetic Resonance Imaging into the brain.

Clare Blackshaw, our slim and pretty video Production Assistant together with another girl are the first women ever to reach the end of Phase 2 training with Britain's crack Parachute Regiment – in her spare time. After two years in the Territorial Army, a very fit Clare, apart from the normal digging, assault courses, patrolling, weapon training and night fighting, had to complete a ten mile TAB (Tactical Advance to Battle) across rugged terrain in two hours loaded down with a heavy Bergen backpack and assault rifle. My own distant memories make me shudder.

But the champion example of such youthful enterprise must be Rupert Wilbraham. An aircraft enthusiast (holding a pilot's licence at 17), he decided at University, aged 21 to find rare aircraft. Through a joint venture with Central TV, the Russian magazine *Ogonyok* put out an appeal and thousands of sightings came in. The Soviet bureaucracy kept saying, 'We don't have any aircraft and, if we did, you can't have them.' But near St Petersburg a forester called Slava helped him to find, under deep snow, an incredibly rare Focke Wulf 190A5. 50 years before, desperately trying to bomb the lifeline to Leningrad across the ice of Lake Lagoda, the fighter-bomber's engine had seized. Crash landed, it had lain intact in the forest ever since.

Rupert outwitted a rival German collector, plus vandals who tried to hold the plane to ransom, and lifted it by helicopter out of the bog. Part of the eventual deal was to provide Soviet veterans with British wheelchairs. Having sold the FW190 to a collector in America, where it is being lovingly restored, Rupert went on to complete a unique 3 1/2 month car expedition from London to New York via Russia, Siberia and Alaska. He's 'settled down' now at 33 to be a banker in Moscow. He flies helicopters nowadays and still has a rock band.

Rupert (left) at the wheelchair handover ceremony. Second from right is Rupert's supporter, General Semilyovich, head of the 'Club of Heroes of the Soviet Union'.

Lieutenant of the Victorian Order. My oldest friend, Timothy ffytche, gets his recognition for a lifetime devoted to helping eyesight, from Indian lepers to our own Royal Family.

BACK TO THE FUTURE

Many of the characters in these pages are no longer with us, some having passed away in the fullness of time but others tragically, far too soon. These include my great mentor, Martin Stevens, and my favourite Anthony's, Masterton-Smith from a heart attack and Nares in an avalanche. They also include my sister Geraldine, whose twenty years of medical and mental problems sadly ended in the little house in which I had set her up in Fulham.

But most of us soldier on. John d. Green and Patrick Lichfield (with Pedro's help) are still taking photographs. Liz Anson plans parties. Joanna Lumley and Charlie Rampling are still acting. Roger Whittaker and his friend Rolf Harris are entertaining. Anthony Hayden-Guest is writing, as is Nigel Dempster, with Britain's most successful gossip column. Brian Alexander runs the paradise island of Mustique, Algy Cluff is as successful in business as ever, Barry Dinan is head hunting and Josh Jensen is producing brilliant wine. My aunt Moira has 6 children, 16 grandchildren and 14 great grandchildren. Aunt Sheila has been an Anglican nun for many years. Of my boyhood friends, Jorge Potier has retired and Timothy ffytche became the Queen's Surgeon Occulist and devotes himself to research into blindness caused by leprosy. Martin Sorrell has just bought Young & Rubicam. Roland Wells and Chris Spring are still in the advertising business and my wife Liz is still copywriting and has taken the ultimate revenge by persuading me to produce plant and botany books with our friend Hugh Synge (page 230).

As for me, I have started a group of historical 'Time Traveller Parks', together with author and film director Robin Hardy, probably best known for his sinister cult film *The Wicker Man*.

When I can pause from my endless air travel, I take pleasure in my fulfilled ambitions of my Ferrari (shared) and my model railway (neglected). I take even more pleasure in that I failed in my ambition to own a jazz club. Best of all, we don't have cats.

It might be tempting to look back on the century covered by this book and to bemoan some of the changes that have occurred. But changes for the worse are usually balanced by changes for the better. I have always felt passionately about change and have even lectured on the dangers of resistance to it.

After thousands of years of glacial pace of change, in the last two centuries the acceleration has been terrific – with people sometimes unable to cope.

Sometimes it was a national attitude problem. As one American said, '**We are prone to confuse change with progress, but the English confuse it with treason.**'

In Britain we seemed to feel that new-fangled ideas might not suit our more traditional ways. A British Parliamentary Committee in 1878 felt that Edison's invention of the electric light was '**Good enough for our transatlantic friends, but unworthy of practical and scientific men.**'

Ford Model T

Readers of *Cosmopolitan* may also smile at the London medical expert who protested at the turn of the century, '**The idea that a woman can actually enjoy sex is a disgusting aspersion on British womanhood.**'

But American so-called experts were no better at predicting the future. Six years before the millionth Ford left the production line a public expert remarked, '**Nothing less than feeble-mindedness, to expect anything to come of the horseless carriage movement**'.

And Simon Newcombe, the American astrologer not long before the Wright brothers' flight at Kitty Hawk, said, '**No possible combination of known industries, machinery or force can be united in a practical machine by which man can fly long distances.**' And another expert's opinion in 1838 was, '**Men might as well project a voyage to the moon as to attempt to employ steam across the stormy North Atlantic.**'

Orville Wright at Kitty Hawk, 1903

And what would our modern hi-tech age make of the Director of the United States Patent Office asking the President in 1899 to let him resign because '**Everything that can be invented has been invented**'?

I have detected some curious laws concerning change. For instance, an innovator in one field can be blind in others. Witness Napoleon turning down in 1805 the American Robert Fulton's offer to use steamboats to tow invasion barges in becalmed conditions in the Channel to overcome Britain's naval dominance. '**What, Sir, you would have my boats fight the wind and waves by lighting bonfires under their decks! pray you, excuse me. I have no time for such nonsense!**'

Napoleon, innovator out of his depth

Another law seems to be that yesterday's innovator can be today's obstructer. Listen to Rutherford, discoverer of the atom in 1933, '**Anyone who looks for a source of power in the transformation of the atom is talking moonshine**' and Admiral Leahy, in 1945 to President Truman. '**That is the biggest fool thing we have ever done. The bomb will never go off and I speak as an expert on explosives.**'

Resistance to technological change can sometimes merely be uncommercial. When Timken in 1930 pointed out that their roller-bearings would vastly improve the performance of American steam engines, all three big locomotive manufacturers turned them down, including the offer to have them fitted free of charge. Timken had to *buy* a top of the line engine to act as a demonstrator. It's rather like buying a Boeing 747 to show off a pump.

But I reserve my wrath for the medical and military professions. Jenner's vaccination against smallpox and Lister's campaign against infection by bacteria were resisted by the establishment for years, resulting in the unnecessary deaths of millions.

Above, Timken's own locomotive "The Four Aces" and left, once roller bearing were accepted they featured in publicity stunts, like pretty girls pulling a 400 ton Niagara.

Hysterical opposition to vaccination

Warfare abounds with catastrophic examples. In my view the most disgraceful was the wooden-headed insistence that men however brave could overcome the dominance of modern shot and shell. Sixty years after the brutal slaughterhouse battles of the American Civil War, let alone more recent examples like Plevna, the Boer War and the Russian-Japanese conflict, generals like Haig, could say, '**The Machine gun is a very overrated weapon**' and even when the answer was provided, the tank, at once reducing casualties a hundred-fold, Haig's ADC remarked, '**The idea that cavalry will be replaced by those iron coaches is absurd. It is little short of treasonous**.'

But attitudes now change fast, along with expectations. My little son Murrough, aged about five in 1978, confided to me while my father listened. '**You know, Daddy, in the olden days, men used to go to the moon in rockets. And they used to wear air tanks on their backs, because, you see, there's no air on the moon, Daddy'.**

For him the Apollo programme was a few years before he was born, roughly equating to Agincourt, the birth of Christ or the dinosaurs. Toby, who had seen so many changes, smiled ruefully.

But we are now accepting change much more rapidly. It took a century for the combine harvester and the typewriter to go from invention to universal acceptance, 34 years for the vacuum cleaner and refrigerator, only eight years for television. The Internet seems to have taken mere months.

Changes nowadays don't take generations, they take weeks or days. They are not local but global. There can be few people in the remotest spots who don't know who Bill Gates is.

So however much we may have enjoyed the past and its drama, characters and eccentricity, we should all follow this advice.

'**If you cling to the past, you wither. If you adjust to the times, you grow with the times. But if you anticipate the future and help shape it, the rewards are the greatest of all**.'

BIBLIOGRAPHY

A

ADAM, Colin Forbes   *Life of Lord Lloyd.* London 1948
ADCOCK, Ian   *Lotus Heritage,* London 1995
AILSBY, Christopher   *Waffen SS.* London 1999

B

BEEVOR, Antony   *Stalingrad.* London 1998
BEVAN, Bobby   *Robert Bevan.* London 1965
BLAU, Tom   *In and out of focus.* London 1983
BOGARDE, Dirk   *Snakes and Ladders.* London 1979
BOLIN, Luis   *Spain the Vital Years.* London 1967
BRAMLEY, Vincent   *Two Sides of Hell.* London 1994
BREDIN, A.E.C.   *History of the Irish Soldier.* Belfast 1987
BROGAN, Colm   *The World of Harold Wilson.* London
BROWN, Dee   *Hear that Lonesome Whistle Blow.* London 1977
BRYSON, Bill   *The Lost Continent.* London 1989
BRYSON, Bill   *Mother Tongue.* London 1990
BUTLER, Rupert   *Illustrated History of the Gestapo.* Wisconsin 1995

C

CHURCHILL, Winston   *The Second World War.* London
CLARK, Alan   *Diaries.* London 1993
COLE, J.A.   *Lord Haw-Haw and William Joyce.* London 1964
COLTRANE, Robbie   *Planes and Automobiles.* London 1997
COOTE, Sir Colin   *Editorial.* London 1965
COLYER, Ken   *When dreams are in the dust.* Kent 1989
COWLEY, General Sir John   *Memoirs* London 1998
CUNEO, Terence   *The Mouse and his Master.* London 1977
CUNEO, Terence   *Tanks and how to draw them.* London 1942

D

DEEDES, W.F.   *Dear Bill.* London 1998
DEIGHTON, Len   *Blitzkrieg.* London 1979
DE MANIO, Jack   *Life Begins Too Early.* London 1970
DENNY, Barbara   *Fulham Past.* London 1997
DEMPSTER, Nigel   *Dempster's People.* London 1978
DOBRON, Larry   *When Advertising Tried Harder.* New York 1984
DUNSANY, Lord   *My Talks with Dean Spanley.* London 1936

E

EARLE, Peter   *The Wreck of the Almiranta.* London 1979
ECKERSLEY, Tom   *His Graphic Work.* London 1994
EVANS, A.G.   *Fanatic Heart.* Western Australia 1997

F

FALK, Quentin   *The Golden Gong.* London 1987
FORD, Roger   *The Grim Reaper, Machine Guns and Machine Gunners.* London 1996
FROST, David with Michael Shea   *The Rich Tide.* London 1986
FULLER, J.F.C.   *Armament and History.* London 1946

G

GILMOUR, David   *Curzon.* London 1995
GOLDHAGEN, Daniel   *Hitler's Willing Executioners.* London 1997
GREEN, John d.   *Birds of Britain.* London 1968

GREHAN, Ida   *Irish Family Histories.* Dublin 1997

H

HALL, Harriet   *Bill & Patience,* Sussex, 2000
HARDY, Thomas   *Collected Poems.* London 1968
HASKINS, Jim   *The Cotton Club.* New York 1977
HASTINGS, Max   *The Korean War.* London 1987
HASSAN, Walter   *Climax in Coventry,* Surrey, 1975
HODGES, David   *Ford GT40, An Anglo American Supercar Classic.* London 1984
HOGG, Ian   *Weapons of the American Civil War,* London 1987
HOLMES, Richard   *War Walks.* London 1996
HOLMES, Richard   *The Western Front,* London 1999
HOWSON, Gerald   *Arms for Spain* London 1998

I

ISHOVEN, Armand van   *Messerschmitt.* London 1975

J

JOHNSON, Paul   *Ireland Land of Troubles.* London 1980
JOHNSON, Paul   *A History of the American People.* London 1997.

K

KIPLING, Rudyard   *History of the Irish Guards in the Great War.* Kent 1997
KOSTOF, Spiro   *America by Design.* New York 1987

L

LAMB, Richard   *Mussolini and the British.* London 1997
LAUBERSTEIN, William J   *The Emerald Whaler.* Victoria, Australia.
LAXTON, Edward   *The Famine Ships, The Irish Exodus to America.* London 1996
LESLIE, Anita   *Cousin Randolph.* London 1985
LICHFIELD, Patrick   *In Retrospect.* London 1988
LICHFIELD, Patrick   *The Most Beautiful Women.* London 1981
LICHFIELD, Patrick   *Not The Whole Truth.* London 1986
LINDSAY, Tom   *Autumn Madness.* London
LONGFORD, Lord   *Abraham Lincoln.* London 1975
LOSSIN, Yigal   *Pillar of Fire – The Rebirth of Israel.* Jerusalem 1983

M

MACARTHUR, General Douglas   *Reminiscences.* London 1964
MACMILLAN, Harold   *War Diaries. The Mediterranean 1943-45.* London 1984
MURRAY, Dr Williamson   *Luftwaffe Strategy for Defeat.* London 1986
MAILER, Norman   *Miami and the Siege of Chicago.* New York 1968
MAJOR, Norma   *Chequers.* London 1996
McELWEE, William   *England's Precedence.* London 1956
MONTAGUE- BROWNE, Anthony   *Long Sunset.* London 1995
MOSLEY, Leonard   *The Reich Marshal.*   London 1974
MORGAN, Ted   *FDR.* London 1986
MURPHY, Emmett   *Great Bordellos of the World.* 1993

O

O'BRIEN, Aubrey   *Cupid and Cartridges.* London 1911
O'BRIEN, The Hon Donough   *History of the O'Briens.* London 1949
O'BRIEN, Donough   *Resistance to Change. Recipe for Disaster.* London 1970
O'BRIEN Hon Grania   *These are my friends and forbears,* Clare, 1991
O'BRIEN, E.D. (Toby)   *Books of the Day. Literary Lounger. Our Motley Notes* (Various)
O'BRIEN, E.D. (Toby)   *Big 3 or Big 2 1/2 ?* London 1945

O'BRIEN, Ivor _Murrough the Burner_, Ireland, Clare 1991
O'CONNOR, Ulick _The Troubles._ London 1975
O'CONNOR, Ulick _Brendan Behan._ London 1970
OGBURD, Charlton _Railroads, The Great American Adventure_ Washington D.C.
OGILVY, David _Ogilvy on Advertising._ London 1993
OGILVY, David _Confessions of an Advertising Man._ London 1993
ONDERWATER, Hans _Gentlemen in Blue, 600 Squadron._ Yorkshire 1996
OWEN, Frank _The Fall of Singapore._ London 1960

P

PAXMAN, Jeremy _The English,_ London 1998
PRESTON, Antony _Send a Gunboat._ London 1967
PRESTON, Antony _Great Warships._ London 1986
PRESTON, Antony _Aircraft Carriers._ Greenwich 1979
PRESTON, Antony _Sea Combat off the Falklands._ London 1982
PRESTON, Paul _Franco._ London 1993

R

RANFURLY, Hermione, Countess _To War with Whitaker._ London 1994
RAW, Charles _Do you Sincerely Want to be Rich?_ London 1971
REES, David _Korea. The Limited War._ London 1964
ROBERTS, Peter _The Shell Book of Epic Motor Races._ London 1964
ROBINSON, Jeffrey _The Risk Takers._ London 1985
RHODES, Anthony _Propaganda._ New York 1976

S

SAMPSON, Anthony _Anatomy of Britain_
SCALA, Mim _Diary of a Teddy Boy._ Dublin 2000
SHIRER, William _The Rise and Fall of the Third Reich_
SHIRER, William _Berlin Diary._ London 1941
SHORT, Ernest _A History of British Army._ London 1953
SIEVEKING, Lance _The Eye of the Beholder._ London 1957
SIMON, Kate _Fifth Avenue. A very social history._ New York 1978
SPELLMOUNT _Irish Guards, The First Hundred Years_ Staplehurst 2000
STANISTREET, Allan _Gainst All Disaster._ Chippenham 1986

T

THATCHER, Margaret _The Downing Street Years._ London 1993
TOFFLER, Alvin _Future Shock._ London 1970
TOFFLER, Alvin _The Third Wave._ London 1980
TOUHILL, Blanche M _William Smith O'Brien and his Irish Companions in Penal Exile._ Missouri 1981

UV

VALDERANO, Duke of (Ronnie) _The Owl and the Pussycat._ London
VERNEY, Peter _The Micks. The Story of the Irish Guards._ London 1970
VELIKOVSKY, Immanuel _Worlds in Collision._ London 1950

W

WHITTAKER, Roger _So far, so good._ London 1986
WILSON, Harold _A Prime Minister on Prime Ministers._ London 1970
WOODMAN-SMITH, Cecil _The Great Hunger._ London 1962
WOOLTON, Earl of. _Memoirs._ London 1959
WYATT, Petronella _Father, dear Father_ London 1999

XYZ

YEAGER, Chuck _Yeager._ London 1986

INDEX

Skrine, Barry 244
Skykomish 269–70
Sloop John D 181
Smart, Major 13–14
Smith, Ian 196
Smylie, Sergeant Dave 129
Sorrell, Sir Martin 221, 288–9
Sotogrande 200–8
Spanish Point 58–9
Spring, Chris 254, 263, 265, 266, 267, 268, 272, 286, 322
Spurrier, Steven 169
Stalin, Joseph 57, 65, 73
Standard Brands 265
State Immunity Act 232
Steel, David 313
Stephan, Brian 93
Stern, Burt 220
Stevens, Jocelyn 182
Stevens, Martin 134, 138–40, 141, 153, 163–4, 197, 216, 218–19, 220, 322
Stevens, Michael 279
Stowe School 14–16, 90–6
Suez 93
swimming 94–5, 96, 98, 100–1
Syme, Richard 228
Synge, Hugh 322

T

Taggert, Rory 272
Tait, Nancy 242–3
Tait, Zara 251
Tate, Saxon 286
Taylor, Elizabeth 84
The Ten Commandments 85
Thatcher, Margaret 93, 225, 252, 253, 260, 285
Thirsk, Tony 25
Thomas Cook 291
Thunder, Corporal Paddy 130
Time Traveller Parks 322
Timken 324
Tisch, Larry 260
tobacco industry 302
Transamerican Bicycle Race 264–5
Transport and General Workers Union 253
Travers, Norman 311, 312
Treaty of Utrecht 223, 224
Tree, Penelope 220
Tryon, Lord 126
Tshombe, Moise 143
Tyrrell, Terry 288

U

Ulster Bank 219, 277
Union Carbide 254, 262–3
Unser, Al 230
Urban VIII, Pope 57
Utley, John 92, 96

V

Valentine, Anthony 125
Valera, Eamonn de 20
Vanderbilt, Wendy 241
Vaughn-Wilkes, 'Sammy' 13
Venn, Lawrence 97
Verney, Peter 112–13, 116
Vestey, Sam 126
Victoria, Queen 15, 112
Video Arts 237–8
Vietnam War 212
Villiers, Nick 144
Vinegrad, Tony 237
Vogüé, Comte Robert-Jean de 98

W

Wallis, Michael 144
War Office Selection Board (WOSB) 109
Waring, Honor 227
Waring, Marcus 228
Waring, Ronnie 227, 228, 229
Webber, Burt 263
Weinberger, Casper 313
Wells O'Brien 221, 233–8, 242–72
Wells, Roland 124, 176, 221, 233, 235–6, 322
West Clare Railway 59–60
West, Fred 309
Whettnall, Madame 283
White's 194–5
Whittaker, Edward 310
Whittaker, Elizabeth 251
Whittaker, Jessica 310
Whittaker, Natalie (née O'Brien) 48, 78, 80, 160, 162, 165, 174, 222, 309
Whittaker, Roger 160–1, 162, 174, 309–10, 322
Whittaker, Vi 310
Wilkins, Sergeant 105, 106–7
Wilson, Harold 17, 139–40
Winchester, Dean of 26–7
Windsor Castle 116, 117–18
Wingate, Orde 11
Wire & Plastic Products Ltd (WPP) 221, 288–9, 301
Withers, John 221
Wontner, Jenny 144
Woolton, Lord 68, 69, 70, 75, 88
Woolworths 218
Worcester, Bob 276
WPP *see* Wire & Plastic Products Ltd
Wynne, Greville 141–2

Y

Young, Katy iv, 322

Z

Zafiropoulo, Alexander 228
Zip Firelighters 293
Zobel family 201, 204